Studies in Phenomenology and
Existential Philosophy

Martin Heidegger

THE BASIC PROBLEMS OF PHENOMENOLOGY

Translation, Introduction, and Lexicon by

Albert Hofstadter

Indiana University Press

BLOOMINGTON

Preparation and publication of this book were aided by grants
from the Programs for Translations and Publications of the
National Endowment for the Humanities, an independent federal agency.

Published in German as *Die Grundprobleme der Phänomenologie*
© 1975 by Vittorio Klostermann

Manufactured in the United States of America

Library of Congress Cataloging in Publication Data
Heidegger, Martin, 1889–1976.
The basic problems of phenomenology.

(Studies in phenomenology and existential philosophy)
Translation of: Die Grundprobleme der Phänomenologie.
1. Phenomenology—Addresses, essays, lectures.
I. Title. II. Series.
B3279.H48G7813   142'.7   80–8379
ISBN 0–253–17686–7   AACR2
     3   4   5   85

Contents

Introduction

PART ONE

Critical Phenomenological Discussion of Some Traditional Theses about Being

PART TWO

The Fundamental Ontological Question
of the Meaning of Being in General

•

The Basic Structures and Basic Ways
of Being

TRANSLATOR'S PREFACE

The Basic Problems of Phenomenology, a translation of *Die Grundprobleme der Phänomenologie,* is the text of a lecture course that Martin Heidegger gave at the University of Marburg in the summer of 1927. Only after almost half a century did Heidegger permit the text of the course to be published. *Die Grundprobleme der Phänomenologie,* edited by Friedrich-Wilhelm von Herrmann, appeared, for the first time, in 1975 as volume 24 of the multivolumed Martin Heidegger *Gesamtausgabe* presently in preparation (Frankfurt: Vittorio Klostermann).

In the Editor's Epilogue, which follows the text, Professor von Herrmann explains that the book was composed, under Heidegger's direction, by putting together Heidegger's manuscript of the lectures and his typewritten copy, including his marginalia and insertions, with a contemporaneous transcription of the lectures by Simon Moser, a student in the course. The editor made decisions regarding a number of matters such as the division into parts and their headings; the treatment of insertions, transformations, changes, expansions, and omissions; and the inclusion of recapitulations at the beginning of lecture sessions. The resulting work is therefore only one possible version of the 1927 lecture course. But it is surely a very ample one, containing almost the whole of what was spoken and also much of what was not spoken at the time.

This volume represents the way in which Heidegger himself visualized the printed shape of these early lectures. Whatever imperfections the present text may contain, *The Basic Problems of Phenomenology* is a work of major importance, indispensable for obtaining a clear outlook upon the ontological-phenomenological region toward which Heidegger was heading when he prepared *Being and Time,* of which this is the designed and designated sequel. In it, one form of the Heideggerian Kehre took place—a turning-around, from concentration upon the human being as Dasein, which in older thought was concentration upon the subject, to the passionately sought new focusing upon—not any mere object correlative to a subject but—being itself.

In the Translator's Introduction I have tried to provide a preparatory description of some of the thinking that leads up to and into this turn. Heidegger's conception of the need for his own thought, like all philosophical thought (in the West at least), to orient itself first to the subject, the human Dasein, is even better understood in *Basic Problems* than it was in *Being and Time,* as due to the ontical-ontological priority of the Dasein, its being that being which, among all beings, has understanding-of-being, so that only by ontological analysis of the Dasein can we elucidate the conditions of possibility of a truly conceptualized understanding-of-being, that is to say, ontology, as science of being.

In *Basic Problems* the journey from this preliminary Daseinsanalytik toward the central region of the science of being accomplishes its first stages: (1) presentation of the basic problems of ontology (philosophy, phenomenology) by way of an examination of several historical attempts to deal with them, and (2) initiation of ontology by pressing on toward the final horizon upon which being can be projected in the understanding-of-being, namely, the horizon of temporality in a specific role designated as Temporality. The voyage has been made from being-and-time to time-and-being, from the first questioning about being which leads to the search for time, to the search through time to the horizon within it for being.

From this point onward it becomes possible to turn to ontology itself in its own name, fundamental ontology in the sense of having been founded, and to head toward the elucidation of the fundamental problematic subjects exhibited in *Basic Problems:* the ontological difference, the articulation of being, the multiplicity and unity of being, and the truthcharacter of being—all of them coming into integral unity in response to the one supreme question, that of the meaning of being in general. Readers of Heidegger will recognize developments of all these directional strains in the published writings from the thirties onward.

The present translation is intended to provide a maximally exact rendering of the text as published. I have resisted every temptation to transform or elucidate the text so as to make it more readable or (supposedly) more perspicuous in English than it is in German. It is my hope that a quotation can be made from this translation, from anywhere within it, with the confidence that one is quoting what the text says—not what it might say in English, were that its original language, but what it actually says in a German that is faithfully translated into English. I hope and believe that no tailoring has been done, whether by deletion, addition, or transposition.

The *Gesamtausgabe* is admittedly not a historical-critical edition. Footnotes in *Die Grundprobleme* are minimal, and with few exceptions they are restricted to bibliographical references to points in the text. Even these are often less than complete and do not always cite the best editions. Although the present translation reproduces the notes in the German text, I have corrected errors and added bibliographical information as needed. The numbered footnotes are translations of those that appear in *Die Grundprobleme;* additional remarks by the translator are appended in square brackets. Notes added by the translator are preceded by asterisks. The *Grundprobleme* text does not indicate which of the notes, or which parts of them, were supplied by Heidegger himself and which by the editor.

This translation carries the pagination of the German edition in brackets in the running heads and preserves its paragraphing. In the text, the contents of both parentheses (except in quoted matter) and square brackets are Heidegger's own; italic square brackets enclose the translator's interpolations.

The Lexicon, at the end of the book, was designed and compiled by the translator to aid the reader who wishes to follow topics that are significant in the thought-structure of the work. Toward this end, the Lexicon includes the various senses and contexts in which terms appear as well as a substantial number of descriptive quotations. For example, if the reader wishes to understand Heidegger's doctrine of intentionality, or his doctrine of transcendence, or the relationship between the two, I believe that he or she will most readily reach this goal by pursuing the indications in the Lexicon.

I have received very generous help from Professor Theodore Kisiel, whose scrutiny of the translation has been thoughtful and careful.

It is with genuine pleasure as well as gratitude that I am able to acknowledge here the liberal assistance I have received from John D. Caputo, Hubert Dreyfus, James Edie, Hans-Georg Gadamer, Elisabeth Hirsch, John Haugeland, Werner Marx, Carlos Norena, William Richardson, John Sallis, Thomas J. Sheehan, and Michael E. Zimmerman.

In a separate place acknowledgment has been made of aid from the National Endowment for the Humanities, which allowed me to take an early retirement in order to bring this task to its conclusion. It is fitting here, however, that the kind co-operation of Susan Mango should receive particular notice.

I owe special debts to Gail Mensh for her assistance during the time I was on the Graduate Faculty of the New School for Social Research in New York City, and to Joan Hodgson for her aid in locating needed materials in libraries beyond Santa Cruz.

During this period of effort I have received the faithful and encouraging support of my son and daughter-in-law, Marc E. Hofstadter and Jill Deikman. And always inestimable is my debt to my wife, Manya, steady stay in all trouble and cheerful partner in all happiness, whose marvelous music sounds through the whole.

Santa Cruz, California   ALBERT HOFSTADTER
January 1, 1981

articulation. Heidegger's effort in dealing with the second thesis is to show that this way of construing the articulation of being is faulty and that there must be different ways of differentiating a so-called essential and a so-called existential aspect of being. Thus in the case of the Dasein there is no what or essence in the ordinary and traditional sense, and the Dasein's existence is not the extantness (presence, at-handness) of the traditional ontology, whose thinking of being was indifferent as regards the being of a stone and the being of the Dasein. Instead, the Dasein's mode of being is Existenz—the specific mode of being that belongs to a transcending, intentionalistic being which projects world and thus whose being-in-the-world differs from the mere being within a world of natural beings. The articulation of being is correlative with the ways or modes of being.

(3) Being is differentiable in another way, just mentioned: namely, there are different ways or modes of being. Modern ontology, beginning at least with Descartes, had come to the conclusion that natural beings are in a way different from mental beings. The basic ways-of-being, as Heidegger formulates it, are thought of as res extensa and res cogitans, natural being and mental being. This conviction is shared in the modern tradition from Descartes through Kant to Hegel, according to Heidegger, and he chooses Kant as the middle member of the movement to examine for the nature, meaning, and ontological roots of the distinction. This becomes another step in the de-construction of the tradition and the guidance of thinking into a new ontology. What are the multiply possible *ways*-of-being of beings? But, too, in what way can they be conceived as ways-of-*being?* How can we conceive being as unitary, given this multiplicity of its ways? The ancient problem of the one and the many, or of the universal and the particular, shows itself here in the specific (and radicalized) modality of being and ways-of-being.

(4) Finally there is the mystery of the connection between being and truth. We speak about being in ontology. Ontology is supposed to be a science. We aim to express our thoughts about being in the shape of uttered and utterable propositions about being, ontological propositions. Languages differ in how they express the meaning of being. In our Indo-European tongues we use the copula "is." We express *what* things are and *how* they are. We say what the whatness or the whoness of a being is, what its way-of-being is, what differentiations there are in modes and ways of being. We say that things are. In ontology we say that being *is not* a being. We thereby seem to attribute its own being to being. We also say that being is, just as we say that truth exists. In the course of such assertions the very act of asserting supposes what it asserts to be true. It supposes that that about which it is asserting can exhibit itself (or hide itself!) as being, or as not being, what it is asserted to be. Assertion is apophantic, exhibitive: it shows and displays. What is shown must itself show, exhibit itself, appear—that is to say, it must be "true." Falsehood and concealment belong here, too. How then does *being* show itself? What is the relationship between being and its showing-as-being? What is the truth-character of being? If *beings* appear in the light of being (projected upon the horizon of being)

and are only thus understandable as beings, in what light does *being* itself show (upon what horizon is being itself projectible) so as to be understandable as being?

Here then are four *basic problems of phenomenology*. Nowhere in these lectures does Heidegger demonstrate that there are and must be just these four problems, formulable in just these ways, as the basic problems. Indeed, with whatever assurance Heidegger speaks throughout, there remains the constant realization of the possibility of error: "In the end, . . . faulty interpretations *must* be made, so that the Dasein may reach the path to the true phenomena by correcting them. Without our knowing where the faulty interpretation lies, we can be quietly persuaded that there is also a faulty interpretation concealed within the Temporal interpretation of being as such, and again no arbitrary one. It would run counter to the sense of philosophizing and of science if we were not willing to understand that a fundamental untruth can dwell with what is actually seen and genuinely interpreted" (p. 322). Nevertheless, this is the way the basic problems are seen. They are basic problems as the different aspects of the single basic problem, the question of the meaning of being in general. This central problem cannot be adequately solved unless they are solved and, reciprocally, they cannot be adequately solved except with the pervasive working of the thinking of being in general.

Heidegger had this picture before him. We could make our way toward the full opening-up of the meaning of being in general by developing each of these basic problems and working at their solution. The entire process would be guided by our pre-ontological understanding of being but also by what we have already attained of insight into the meaning of being—and this means, since *Being and Time,* the fundamental horizon of the understanding of being, temporality. That must be our guiding clue. Once having attained a grasp of time and temporality in their original constitution, we should be able to proceed to deal with each of the four basic problems while throughout expanding and deepening our understanding of being in general.

The plan of *Basic Problems* therefore was clear. It is outlined in §6, pages 23−24. Part One would be a new version of the "destruction of the ontological tradition." Since the basic problem of ontology self-differentiates into four basic problems, we turn to the philosophical tradition for outstanding instances of the attempt to deal with these problems in traditional terms. Tradition provides us with four theses: those of Kant, the Middle Ages (and antiquity), the modern period, and logic. Kant's criticism of the ontological argument for God's existence led him to declare that being is not a real predicate. In the background the ontological difference, the distinction between being and beings, is clearly making itself felt here. Our task is to penetrate to the origins of Kant's view, unveil his ontological misapprehension of the nature of being, and thus de-construct the traditional thought with which he operates, leading the way to a new and truer understanding of being. We begin with the first ontological thesis, the Kantian thesis (negative: being is not a real predicate; positive: being is position, existence is absolute position), and we examine it in this way. The examination leads to our initial comprehension of the first ontological problem, that of the ontological difference. We first clearly confront the necessity of differentiating being from beings.

So with the other basic problems. In each case a thesis about being, drawn from the tradition, offers itself for destructive de-construction (Ab-bildung) so as to lead us back (re-duction) not only from beings but now from the traditionally misapprehended nature of being to a more original conception of the real problem and a sense of what would be needed to solve it.

Given the historico-analytic achievement of Part One, we should be ready to proceed to Part Two, which also is fourfold, since it is concerned with the four basic problems taken as such on their own account as the basic problems of ontology. Heidegger classifies them and projects the assignment of a chapter to each of them: ontological difference, basic articulation of being, modifications and unity of being, truth-character of being. As may be seen, he did not get beyond the first of these proposed chapters—no semester could be long enough to bear the burden! It turned out to be the largest in size of all the chapters in the work.

In addition to this projected treatment of the four problems Heidegger had in view a third part, also with four chapters, which would have supervened on the actual ontology produced in Part Two, since it was to have taken ontology itself for subject-matter: its foundation, the possibility and structure of it as knowledge, the basic methodology it must employ, and what it is, seen as the outcome of all these. It would have constituted, so to say, the ontology of ontology itself—the circling of ontological method (phenomenology) back into itself.

If Heidegger examines four traditional theses about being and disentangles four basic ontological problems connected with them, this effort is still preliminary toward the attack upon the main problem, the question of the meaning of being. It is Heidegger's contention here, as it was in *Being and Time,* that this primary problem can be resolved only by the *temporal approach* to ontology. A full explanation of his meaning here would require a concentrated analysis of this volume as well as *Being and Time* and subsequent works, including a concentrated statement about the meaning of being itself as Heidegger grasped it in these works. That explanation goes beyond the function of this introduction. But it is possible to indicate the direction in which Heidegger's thinking heads on this matter if we examine his notion of *fundamental ontology* and come to see how *Basic Problems,* in elaborating the discussion of time and being which had been planned for *Being and Time,* is an articulation of fundamental ontology.

The following observation may usefully be prefaced. The basic question, that is, the *fundamental question of ontology,* is, What is the meaning of being in general? The *question of fundamental ontology* is frequently stated by Heidegger as being this: How is the understanding-of-being possible? The former question has to do with being: it seeks the understanding of being. The latter question has to do with this understanding of being: it seeks to discover the condition of its possibility. The two questions appear to be different, even radically different, since the first requests a certain knowledge, the knowledge of being as such, whereas the second requests reflection on the possibility of that knowledge. Nevertheless, we should not be taken in by the verbal (and associated conceptual) difference. Solution of the question of fundamental ontology—learning how the understanding-of-being is possible—is the first step in solving the fundamental question of ontology, the question of the meaning of being. The difference is essentially a difference of stage in the process of ontological inquiry. In a genuine sense the basic question of ontology *is* the question of fundamental ontology, as fundamental ontology develops its own fullness of being. It is to be hoped that the following discussion of Heidegger's notion of fundamental ontology will help to make this observation plausible and clear.

If the term "fundamental ontology" means what it says, then it would seem to be designating that part of ontology which provides the fundamentum, the foundation, for the whole of ontology. What could such a foundational part of ontology be? If we were thinking in traditional terms, under the guidance of traditional conceptions of being, it would be natural to conceive of the first, basic, part of ontology as dealing with being in general, the fundamental concept of being, before all modifications of it into special kinds of being, and so forth. Or, in a more Hegelian dialectical manner, we might think of it as the initial part of the entire sweep of philosophy, the logic of being as the indeterminate immediate developing its full form as idea, and so forth. But that manner of thinking of the science of being would be, in Heidegger's eyes, an illustration of what happens to philosophy when it forgets the basic distinction between the being of natural things and the being of the human Dasein. These cannot be reduced to a single, indefinite, indeterminate, concept of being, without essential loss of meaning. The true concept of being cannot be an average concept of what belongs in abstract generality to all modes of the being of beings. Being has to be understood in its multiplicity of ways, and its unity can be grasped only with that multiplicity clearly in evidence. To think of the human Dasein's being as basically and in general the same as that of a stone, to think of the existentia of a stone as fundamentally identical with the Existenz of the Dasein, would be, for Heidegger, to cover up the truth about Existenz, to mistake it and thereby to misinterpret the nature of being.

The question that stares us in the face and confronts us at the beginning of the path of thinking toward being is, How are we to get to be able to understand being? Or, speaking with less personal urgency: How is the understanding-of-being possible? This is a unique and peculiar question. It is not the same as asking how the understanding of *beings* is possible. In a sense we already know the answer to that question. It is possible to understand this or that being as a being and as the being that it is, if and only if we already understand the being of that being. So for instance: it is possible to understand a piece of equipment, such as a hammer, only if we already understand hammering, the letting-function of a thing as a hammer;

and to understand this letting-function we must understand the integral functionality-contexture and functionality-relations which permit a being to be a hammer, to be allowed to function as a hammer. But we can understand functionality-contextures and -relations only if we antecedently understand functionality itself: that specific mode of being in virtue of which there can be contextures and relations of functionality and a letting-function of things within these contextures and relations. The understanding-of-being question is *unique* because it is a question about *being*, not about beings, and because the answer to such a question is still not clear to us. For, we may ask, How is it possible to understand the like of functionality? Whence do we derive the concept of functionality, if we must already have it *before* we can encounter any piece of equipment as functionally significant in its being? What is the a priori source of the concept of functionality?

The question about the understanding-of-being is also a *peculiar* one. For it is not only about being but about the *understanding* of being. It is not possible to undertake here an account of Heidegger's doctrine of understanding, nor is it necessary; we need only take note that on his view understanding-of-being belongs to the human being—properly, the human Dasein—alone, among all beings. When the human Dasein comports itself toward any being it always does so, and must by its very constitution do so, through an understanding of the being of that being. When the farmer reaps his corn, he deals with the corn as the vegetable being that it is; he understands it as plant, with the being that belongs to plant, and to this particular kind of plant. Human behavior is mediated by the understanding-of-being. If ontological means "of or belonging to the understanding of being," then the human Dasein is by its very constitution an ontological being. This does not mean that the human being has an explicit concept of being, which he then applies in every encounter with beings; it means rather that before all ontology as explicit discipline of thinking, the human Dasein always already encounters beings in terms of a pre-ontological, pre-conceptual, non-conceptual grasp of their being. Ontology as a scientific discipline is then nothing but the unfolding, in the light proper to thought and therefore in conceptual form, of this pre-conceptual understanding-of-being, Seinsverständnis. It is the Begreifen, the conceptual comprehension, of what earlier was grasped only in the immediateness of the living encounter.

We must not think of being, Sein, as a being, ein Seiendes—as, for example, some deep principle behind all other beings, serving as their source, their ground, their creator. This confusion started with the beginning of philosophy in the West, with Thales (see Lexicon), and has continued down to the present. But the basic ontological principle called the ontological difference is precisely this, that being and beings are to be distinguished, that being is not any being. The necessary implication is that being cannot be understood in the same way as beings. I can understand the hammer by understanding functionality; but functionality is not another being, on a higher plane than the hammer, which then has still another mode of being on a higher plane as its being, by which it is to be understood. There is, as Heidegger makes out, a sequence of projections by which beings are projected upon their being to be understood, and then being is itself projected upon *its own horizon* for it to be understood as being. But the sequence terminates there; no further horizon is needed. This does not make being a being; but it does indicate that the understanding of being is a *peculiar* matter which needs special consideration if ontology, the conceptualized unfolding of the understanding-of-being, is to be understood in its possibility.

The human Dasein is distinguished in Heidegger's view from all other beings in that it is the ontological being, the being which alone has understanding-of-being and is thus the only being which could possibly have ontology as a science. "Have" is an unfortunate word. The Dasein doesn't have understanding as a property. The Dasein *is* its understanding. And if and when it develops ontology, the Dasein is ontological in this peculiar way: it *is* its ontology, it *exists* its understanding-of-being within its life-comportments.

If the human Dasein is the ontological being, this means that the understanding-of-being, whose existence is the condition of possibility of ontology as a science, can be found only in the Dasein's constitution. If we wish to understand how the understanding-of-being is possible, then, we must look to the Dasein and examine its understanding and, in particular, its understanding-of-being. By unfolding the nature and constitution of this understanding-of-being we should be able to see how being is understood, what factors and processes are essential to this mode of understanding.

It is Heidegger's claim that being is not a being; it is not, especially, a being which, like the beings of nature, could also *be* if and when there is no human Dasein. The earth was, as a natural being, before man evolved to inhabit it. But being is not something like the earth. It is not an entity of such a sort that, in comparison with the earth's finite being, it might have, say, a supra-finite being, an eternal, supra-temporal being. It is not an entity at all. If we use the word "is" about being, saying that it is this or that, is not this or that, or even that it just is, or just is not, then this "is" does not have the same significance as the "is" in assertions about beings. Heidegger sometimes uses the existential phrase "es gibt" in regard to being, with the sense that being is *given,* so that one can raise the question about whether and how being is given to us. If being is understood by us, then being has to be given in some way to us. If understanding-of-being is possible, then the givenness-of-being must be possible; and if we are to understand the former possibility, then we must gain insight into the latter possibility.

How is being given to us? How *can* being be given? Heidegger's answer is, Not in some high mode of intuition, not by our being spectators of some resplendent being, some radiant entity at the height of all beings, say, like Plato's Idea of the Good. His claim is that all that is given is given only as projected upon a horizon. Projection, which is always also self-projection, is the fundamental nature of all understanding. For Heidegger it essentially involves and itself is transcendence, the self-transcendence that constitutes the basic nature of the human Dasein. The horizon is the outness upon which every out-there can show up so as to be given, taken in, understood. Being is itself the horizon for beings: they are encountered and understood only as they are projected upon their own being as horizon. But being itself requires another horizon to be projected upon if it is to be understood as being. The unique and peculiar and specific character of Heidegger's ontological thought here is given with the doctrine that it is *time* which is this horizon upon which being itself is projected.

In his own language, being is projected upon the horizon of the Dasein's temporality. In order for the Dasein to exist as temporalizing time, as the temporal being par excellence, it has to have the horizon upon which to project future, past, and present and their unity, which is temporality. This horizon is named by the term "Temporality." Each "ecstasis" of time—future, past, present—has its own horizon. The present has, for example, the horizon that Heidegger calls praesens, upon which the Dasein, in the temporalizing act of enpresenting, can project in order to have the presence that belongs to the present. The unity of these horizons of future, past, and present is the essential unitary horizon of all projection of temporality.

Being can be given only as projected upon this fundamental horizon, the transcendental horizon, Temporality. Therefore, being is understandable only by way of time. If we are to think being and speak of being, and do it properly without confusing being with any beings, then we have to think and speak of it in temporal concepts and terms. Ontology is a temporal—that is to say, a Temporal—science; all its propositions are Temporal propositions (p. 323).

In this introduction I do not need to try to outline for the reader the actual procedure by which Heidegger develops his argument for this thesis. That is what the book itself is for. But it is fitting to emphasize this specific temporal interpretation of the meaning of being. It is what Heidegger headed for from the very first words of *Being and Time* and what he arrived at in the final chapter of *Basic Problems of Phenomenology*.

The horizon upon which something is projected is what gives understandability to the projected. Projection is understanding, understanding is projection. The horizon is that which, in the projecting, *enables understanding*. It is the source of meaningfulness—not meaningfulness as some floating semantic attachment to what is supposed to be meaningful, but meaningfulness as the very being of the meaningful being.[5] Thus if being is understandable only as projected upon the

---

5. Among the complaints one might make against Heidegger's procedure in this work there could well be this, that he did not turn specifically to the concept of horizon with sufficient scope and depth to make it fully explicit as a fundamental functioning concept in his mode of thought. It is obviously taken over from Husserl, but in Heidegger's new phenomenology it required to be reviewed and re-explicated.

horizon of Temporality, the constitution of being itself must in some way be temporal.

This conclusion would appear to have drastic consequences. In *Basic Problems,* as in *Being and Time,* Heidegger places great emphasis on the doctrine that there are no eternal truths, that truth exists in the manner of the Dasein's Existenz, because truth is the disclosedness which belongs to and constitutes the Da of the Dasein. But, then, might one say something similar about being? If being is essentially temporal, if even the being that is constituted as extantness (the mere presence, presence-at-hand, or at-handness of natural beings) is essentially temporal—and so it would be if it were just plain presence, Anwesenheit—then what would happen to being if the Dasein were to cease to be? Being could no longer be given, since temporality would no longer be and there would no longer be any temporal horizon upon which being might be projected so as to be able to be given as being. And then what would happen to the being of the natural beings, which nevertheless are supposed to be able to be even without the being of the Dasein?

Whether these questions are legitimate in Heidegger's terms and how they are to be answered may well be left to the reader. We must now finally return to the matter of fundamental ontology and its place in the present work.

The significance of what Heidegger calls fundamental ontology now begins to become clear. Unless we come to see that and how temporality is the horizon upon which being is projected in the understanding of being, we shall not be able to make the first proper step in ontology. Until we come to grasp the original temporality which is the source of all possibilities of projection of being, we shall not be able to reach to the true meaning of being, the original meaning of which those that are presently current are defective modifications. The beginning of ontology which would be its true fundamentum is the beginning with the Dasein. For it is only in the Dasein that this original temporality can be found, this temporality which is the being of the Dasein itself. If the Dasein's being is being-in-the-world, then examination of it shows that this being-in-the-world is essentially care; and the structural differentiation and unity of care is precisely that of temporality: expecting-retaining-enpresenting as the temporalizing by which temporality has the shape of existence.

We cannot begin in ontology with some abstractly universal and indifferent notion of being, which might then be broken down into its different kinds, and so forth. That notion, the traditional one, stems from the degenerate modification of being which we have in mind when we treat every being as an instance of extantness, presence-at-hand, the being characteristic of natural things. The only proper beginning in ontology is with the original horizon for the projection of being and with an equally original projecting of being upon that horizon. We must first get to the horizon.

Therefore, the only proper beginning in ontology is with the being, the Dasein, in whose existence the horizon exists. Temporality is the Dasein's basic constitution:

the ecstatic opening of future-past-present through expecting-retaining-enpresent-ing. In this opening, future is projected upon temporality in its futural way, past in its retentive way, and present in its enpresenting way. The entire unity of time is projected in its entire unity upon the unity of these ecstatic horizons, the ultimate ecstatic Temporal horizon upon which alone being can be projected. The ultimate transcendental horizon of being is found in the basic temporal constitution of the Dasein.

Ontology can only be a temporal science. The beginning of ontology is the opening of the path toward Temporality as transcendental horizon. The fundamentum on which ontology can begin to be realized is that specific ontology which discloses to us temporality as the being of the Dasein. Once we have attained to a comprehension of temporality as possible horizon, that is, of Temporality, we are in a position to investigate being in general and the different aspects of its structure: articulation, modifications and unity, truth-character. We are able to comprehend and formulate in conceptual terms the true being that belongs, for instance, to equipment, and to differentiate from that and to comprehend in its own temporal terms the being that belongs, for instance, to the cultural works of human beings, such as their works of art or their forms of religion.

Accordingly, Heidegger defines fundamental ontology as being the analytic of the Dasein. He says in so many words: "Ontology has for its fundamental discipline the analytic of the Dasein" (p. 19). This fundamental discipline is the founding discipline in ontology. As such it is "the foundation for all further inquiry, which includes the question of the being of beings and the being of the different regions of being" (p. 224). In its founding role the analytic of the Dasein prepares the ground for ontology. In this role it is a "preparatory ontological investigation" which serves as the foundation. It is preparatory: it alone first leads to the illumination of the meaning of being and of the horizon of the understanding of being (p. 224). It is only preparatory: it aims only at establishing the foundation for "a radical ontology" (p. 224). This radical ontology is presumably the ontology which goes to the root of the problem of being: it goes to the Temporal horizon of ontological projection. Once the radicalizing of ontology has been reached, what was before only a preparatory and provisional ontological analytic of the Dasein *must be repeated at a higher level* (p. 224). The course of investigation is circular and yet not viciously so. The illumination that is first reached in a preliminary way lights the way for the brighter illumination and firmer comprehension of the second, higher, achievement of understanding of being in and through the understanding of the Dasein's being.

When fundamental ontology is conceived in this way it exhibits three aspects corresponding to three tasks that it performs.

(1) The first task is to serve as the inauguration, the preparatory ontological investigation which initiates scientific ontology, bringing us to the gateway into it. This is the shape it takes in *Being and Time*, part 1, division 1: "Preparatory

Fundamental Analysis of the Dasein," which opens the inquiry, outlines the nature of being-in-the-world, worldhood, being-with, being-one's-self, the They, being-in (including the very important account of the being of the Da), and advances to the structure of the Dasein's being as care.

(2) The second task is to serve as the mediating pathway which takes us from the gateway of ontology into its authentic precinct. This is accomplished in *Being and Time*, part 1, division 2: "The Dasein and Temporality." Examination of the Dasein as care already disclosed the threefold unity of its structure due to its constitution by temporality, without disentangling the temporality of which it is the manifestation. By proceeding to the Dasein's possibilities of wholeness, being-toward-death, authenticity of can-be, and resoluteness as the original authentic existential mode of the Dasein's existence, temporality could be unveiled as the ontological meaning of care. And then *Being and Time* proceeded to interpret anew the nature of the Dasein's everyday existence and to confront it with the real historical nature of Existenz, all of which could be done because of the initial illumination of being in general and the being of the Dasein in particular that had been gained by the preparatory and intermediate analysis of the Dasein. The second task was concluded with a first account of the Dasein's common conception of time, which is itself an expression of the Dasein's fallen mode of temporalizing when it exists as fascinated by the world and intraworldly entities.

(3) We are now ready for the third task, which is to bring to conceptual comprehension the fundamental portions of ontology: the basic meaning of being in general and the four basic aspects of being—its difference from beings, its articulation into opposed moments (such as essentia and existentia, whoness and existence), its modifications and unity (such as the differentiation of the being of natural beings and the being of the Dasein, and their unity in terms of being itself), and its truth-character (such as, for instance, is revealed in the Da of the Dasein). On this third task, which falls wholly within the precinct of ontology, *Basic Problems of Phenomenology* makes the beginning. The destruction of the four traditional theses about being, each associated with one of the just-mentioned basic aspects, clears the path for the account to follow of the four basic problems. Of these, the first problem is examined. In attaining to the examination, the account of the Dasein's being and especially of its constitution by temporality, which was started in *Being and Time*, is continued and developed. For the first time the whole structure, constitution, and meaning of temporality is unfolded. Step by step, the analysis probes more deeply into the existential constitution of time and the explanation of how time as ordinarily conceived and used is derivative from its origins in existential temporality. The ultimate transcendental horizon for the projection of being is reached in Temporality, of which praesens is exhibited as an example—the horizon for projection of time's present, die Gegenwart. This third task was not completed in *Basic Problems*. All four of the basic problems would have needed investigation. After that, it would have been possible to proceed to the planned inquiry into the

nature of ontology itself. What its constitution would be, how it would be related to the role of fundamental ontology, how far it would have taken us around back into the analysis of the Dasein at a higher level—these matters can only be the subject of speculation.[6]

Two further and connected points are all that need occupy us in this Introduction: the ontical foundation of ontology in fundamental ontology and the obvious orientation of ontology to the Dasein, that is, in traditional language, to the subject, the apparent subjectivism which is thus introduced into ontology.

Heidegger is very definite and clear on the doctrine that the foundation of ontology, the science of being, lies in *a* being, namely, the human Dasein. Although the ontological difference draws a sharp line of distinction between being and beings, nevertheless, the foundation of the science of being is supposed to lie in the science of one particular being. Ordinarily Heidegger clearly separates ontology from the sciences which deal, not with being as such, but with beings. The sciences of beings are all positive sciences; philosophy is not a positive science. The sciences are positive because they posit the beings with which they are occupied. Ontology does not posit any beings, and hence is not a positive science. (See the Lexicon: Science.)

Nevertheless, if the foundation of ontology lies in the being of the Dasein, then ontology in its beginning and in its foundation, and in the end, too, has to be concerned with *a* being. In an essential and not merely accidental way it is ontical— pertaining to beings—as well as ontological. To be sure, although fundamental ontology must turn to the Dasein, it is not a positive science in the sense that it would be concerned to establish in a positive manner the various properties, relationships, laws of behavior, etc., of the Dasein. Fundamental ontology is not anthropology, psychology, or unified social-humanistic science. Even as regards so-called philosophical anthropology, fundamental ontology is concerned only to extract from its investigation of the Dasein the a priori structures that determine the transcendental horizon of being in temporality. Still, with all this qualification, ontology remains bound to a being, this particular being called the human Dasein, and precisely because of the inescapable necessity placed on it by existence: the horizon for the projection (understanding) of being lies in this being, the Dasein. Being discloses itself only by way of this select being, the Dasein. Ontology is not another abstract positive science like mathematics. It is not an abstract non-positive science—there is none, unless the tautologies of formal logic

---

6. Three senses of the phrase "fundamental ontology" are indicated in the following groups of passages. (1) Passages stressing the ontical founding of ontology: *Sein und Zeit*, pp. 13, 194, 268, 301, 377. (2) Passages stressing the transition to scientific ontology: *Sein und Zeit*, pp. 37–38, 200, 213, 231, 316, 403. (3) Passages in which fundamental ontology deals with the fundamental question of the meaning of being in general: *Sein und Zeit*, pp. 183, 196, 406.
See the Lexicon for occurrences of the phrase "fundamental ontology" in *Basic Problems*.

qualify it for that role. Ontology is the doctrine of the revelation of being through the temporality which is the being of a certain being, the Dasein.

Does this not introduce an unavoidable subjectivism into ontology, causing being to be impregnated throughout with the subjectivity of the human being, labeled the Dasein in these pages? Heidegger often recurs to the point that all of philosophy is, as he puts it, "oriented to the subject." Even what seems the most naively and immediately objectivistic thought, ancient Greek ontology, is nonetheless oriented to the subject. For Parmenides, being is identical with thinking. For Heraclitus, being is intelligible only as the logos—thinking, thought, and the words which express thinking and thought. Heidegger analyzes the fundamental ontological categories of Platonic and Aristotelian thought and discovers that all of them make sense only as expressing being by way of the human being's productive comportment. Medieval ontology takes over these categories and modifies them by its concept of God as absolute creator, but the reference in the categories remains to the subject. Kant, as representative of modern thought, interprets being in terms of perception and, more basically, in terms of position, positing—both of them comportments of the Dasein as subject. German idealism, reaching its denouement in Hegel, transforms all being into the being of the subject.

Although Heidegger wishes to destroy this entire tradition, the destruction is to be done not by removing the orientation to the subject but by correcting it. The subject which dominates all these categories of the tradition, ancient, medieval, and modern, is the subject conceived of as producer, doer, maker, realizer. The beings which are, are products, and their being is that of a product or of an entity involved in production; it is the being of the product as equipment, handiness, or of the product as simply released from the productive process or as merely ready and available (or not-available) for production, extantness, being-present-at-hand. Both types of being are understood as presence, Anwesenheit, in their own special ways, whether the presence characteristic of equipment (functional presence) or the presence of merely natural things. Energeia, entelecheia, actualitas, Wirklichkeit, actuality, all these expressions for being (on the side of way-of-being) are derivative from the subjectivity of the producer, his products, and the consumer of them.

Philosophy must start from the so-called subject. That is the very conception of fundamental ontology: that the meaning of being is revealed, that being is given, only as projected upon the horizon of temporality, and that temporality is the constitutive being of the so-called subject, the Dasein. That is why, without explicitly realizing what it was doing and why, traditional philosophy too started from the subject. If philosophy is to live up to its responsibility as the science of being, then it has to make its way through every concealing, limiting, distorting form of understanding of being and press on toward the ultimate origin of all possible understanding of being, where being can then be projected in the luminous clarity of original temporality. Philosophy has to be "oriented to the subject" in an authentic way, in which the Dasein does not lose itself in the world and does not lose its thinking to be captured by the beings of the world.

Subjectivism is a confusion if it identifies being with the subject or some component of the subject. But being is not a being; being is not even that being, the Dasein, which we ourselves are, each of us. We are here only as the Da in and through which beings and their being can be unveiled. Being needs us to be given—the only sense in which one can say that being "is." But being is not given as the subject. It is given in ways which vary with the age and the understanding-of-being allotted to the Dasein: as ousia, entelecheia, actualitas, position, absolute Idea, Geist, and in the modern world, according to Heidegger's later thinking, under the aegis of Gestell—that enframing, placing, positioning in which all beings are exhibited as stock, resource for processing.

"Philosophy must perhaps start from the 'subject' and return to the 'subject' in its ultimate questions, and yet for all that it may not pose its questions in a one-sidedly subjectivistic manner" (p. 155). Philosophy, so far as it looks at beings, sees them in themselves, in the being that is their own, not in the being that belongs to the subject. Being and the Dasein belong together, they enter into their own peculiar identity, because the Dasein's being is temporality; but by way of temporality what is disclosed is all being, not the Dasein's being alone.

THE BASIC
PROBLEMS OF
PHENOMENOLOGY

Introduction

§1. Exposition and general division of the theme

This course[1] sets for itself the task of posing *the basic problems of phenomenology*, elaborating them, and proceeding to some extent toward their solution. Phenomenology must develop its concept out of what it takes as its theme and how it investigates its object. Our considerations are aimed at the *inherent content* and *inner systematic relationships* of the basic problems. The goal is to achieve a fundamental illumination of these problems.

In negative terms this means that our purpose is not to acquire historical knowledge about the circumstances of the modern movement in philosophy called phenomenology. We shall be dealing not with phenomenology but with what phenomenology itself deals with. And, again, we do not wish

---

1. A new elaboration of division 3 of part 1 of *Being and Time*. [The 7th edition of *Sein und Zeit* (Tübingen: Max Niemeyer, 1953) carries the following prefatory remark:

"The treatise *Sein und Zeit* first appeared in the spring of 1927 in the *Jahrbuch für Philosophie und phänomenologische Forschung,* volume 8, edited by E. *Husserl,* and simultaneously as a separate printing.

"The new impression presented here as the seventh edition is unaltered in its text, although quotations and punctuation have been revised. The page numbers of the new impression agree down to slight variations with those of earlier editions.

"The caption 'First Half,' affixed to the previous editions, has been dropped. After a quarter of a century, the second half could no longer be added without giving a new exposition of the first. Nevertheless, the path it took still remains today a necessary one if the question of being is to move our own *Dasein.*

"For the elucidation of this question the reader is referred to the book *Einführung in die Metaphysik,* which is appearing simultaneously with this new printing under the same imprint. It contains the text of a lecture course given during the summer semester of 1935."

See Martin Heidegger, *Einführung in die Metaphysik* (Tübingen: Max Niemeyer, 1953), trans. Ralph Manheim, *Introduction to Metaphysics* (New Haven: Yale University Press, 1959; Garden City, New York: Doubleday, Anchor Books, 1961).]

1

merely to take note of it so as to be able to report then that phenomenology deals with this or that subject; instead, the course deals with the subject itself, and you yourself are supposed to deal with it, or learn how to do so, as the course proceeds. The point is not to gain some knowledge about philosophy but to be able to philosophize. An introduction to the basic problems could lead to that end.

And these basic problems themselves? Are we to take it on trust that the ones we discuss do in fact constitute the inventory of the basic problems? How shall we arrive at these basic problems? Not directly but by the round-about way of *a discussion of certain individual problems.* From these we shall sift out the basic problems and determine their systematic interconnection. Such an understanding of the basic problems should yield insight into the degree to which philosophy as a science is necessarily demanded by them.

The course accordingly divides into *three parts.* At the outset we may outline them roughly as follows:

1. Concrete phenomenological inquiry leading to the basic problems
2. The basic problems of phenomenology in their systematic order and foundation
3. The scientific way of treating these problems and the idea of phenomenology

The *path* of our reflections will take us from certain individual problems to the basic problems. The question therefore arises, How are we to gain the *starting point* of our considerations? How shall we select and circum-scribe the individual problems? Is this to be left to chance and arbitrary choice? In order to avoid the appearance that we have simply assembled a few problems at random, an introduction leading up to the individual prob-lems is required.

It might be thought that the simplest and surest way would be to derive the concrete individual phenomenological problems from the concept of phenomenology. Phenomenology is essentially such and such; hence it en-compasses such and such problems. But we have first of all to arrive at the concept of phenomenology. This route is accordingly closed to us. But to circumscribe the concrete problems we do not ultimately need a clear-cut and fully validated concept of phenomenology. Instead it might be enough to have some acquaintance with what is nowadays familiarly known by the name "phenomenology." Admittedly, within phenomenological inquiry there are again differing definitions of its nature and tasks. But, even if these differences in defining the nature of phenomenology could be brought to a consensus, it would remain doubtful whether the concept of phe-nomenology thus attained, a sort of average concept, could direct us toward the concrete problems to be chosen. For we should have to be certain beforehand that phenomenological inquiry today has reached the center of philosophy's problems and has defined its own nature by way of their possibilities. As we shall see, however, this is not the case—and so little is it the case that one of the main purposes of this course is to show that, conceived in its basic tendency, phenomenological research can represent nothing less than the more explicit and more radical understanding of the idea of a scientific philosophy which philosophers from ancient times to Hegel sought to realize time and again in a variety of internally coherent endeavors.

Hitherto, phenomenology has been understood, even within that discipline itself, as a science propaedeutic to philosophy, preparing the ground for the proper philosophical disciplines of logic, ethics, aesthetics, and philosophy of religion. But in this definition of phenomenology as a preparatory science the traditional stock of philosophical disciplines is taken over without asking whether that same stock is not called in question and eliminated precisely by phenomenology itself. Does not phenomenology contain within itself the possibility of reversing the alienation of philosophy into these disciplines and of revitalizing and reappropriating in its basic tendencies the great tradition of philosophy with its essential answers? We shall maintain that phenomenology is not just one philosophical science among others, nor is it the science preparatory to the rest of them; rather, *the expression "phenomenology"* is the name for the *method of scientific philosophy in general.*

Clarification of the idea of phenomenology is equivalent to exposition of the concept of scientific philosophy. To be sure, this does not yet tell us what phenomenology means as far as its content is concerned, and it tells us even less about how this method is to be put into practice. But it does indicate how and why we must avoid aligning ourselves with any contemporary tendency in phenomenology.

We shall not deduce the concrete phenomenological problems from some dogmatically proposed concept of phenomenology; on the contrary, we shall allow ourselves to be led to them by a more general and preparatory discussion of the concept of scientific philosophy in general. We shall conduct this discussion in tacit apposition to the basic tendencies of Western philosophy from antiquity to Hegel.

In the early period of ancient thought philosophia means the same as science in general. Later, individual philosophies, that is to say, individual sciences—medicine, for instance, and mathematics—become detached from philosophy. The term philosophia then refers to a science which underlies and encompasses all the other particular sciences. Philosophy becomes science pure and simple. More and more it takes itself to be the first and highest science or, as it was called during the period of German idealism, absolute science. If philosophy is absolute science, then the expression "scientific philosophy" contains a pleonasm. It then means scientific absolute science. It suffices simply to say "philosophy." This already implies science pure and simple. Why then do we still add the adjective "scientific" to the expression "philosophy"? A science, not to speak of absolute science, is scientific by the very meaning of the term. We speak of "scientific philosophy" principally because conceptions of philosophy prevail which not only imperil but even negate its character as science pure and simple. These conceptions of philosophy are not just contemporary but accompany the development of scientific philosophy throughout the time philosophy has existed as a science. On this view philosophy is supposed not only, and not in the first place, to be a theoretical science, but to give practical guidance to our view of things and their interconnection and our attitudes toward them, and to regulate and direct our interpretation of existence and its meaning. Philosophy is wisdom of the world and of life, or, to use an expression current nowadays, philosophy is supposed to provide a Weltanschauung, a world-view. Scientific philosophy can thus be set off against philosophy as world-view.

We shall try to examine this distinction more critically and to decide whether it is valid or whether it has to be absorbed into one of its members. In this way the concept of philosophy should become clear to us and put us in a position to justify the selection of the individual problems to be dealt with in the first part. It should be borne in mind here that these discussions concerning the concept of philosophy can be only provisional—provisional not just in regard to the course as a whole but provisional in general. For the concept of philosophy is the most proper and highest result of philosophy itself. Similarly, the question whether philosophy is at all possible or not can be decided only by philosophy itself.

§2. *The concept of philosophy* *Philosophy and world-view*

In discussing the difference between scientific philosophy and philosophy as world-view, we may fittingly start from the latter notion and begin with the term "Weltanschauung," "world-view." This expression is not a translation from Greek, say, or Latin. There is no such expression as kosmotheoria. The word "Weltanschauung" is of specifically German coinage; it was in fact coined within philosophy. It first turns up in its natural meaning in Kant's *Critique of Judgment*—world-intuition in the sense of contemplation of the world given to the senses or, as Kant says, the mundus sensibilis—a beholding of the world as simple apprehension of nature in the broadest sense. Goethe and Alexander von Humboldt thereupon use the word in this way. This usage dies out in the thirties of the last century under the influence of a new meaning given to the expression "Weltanschauung" by the Romantics and principally by Schelling. In the *Einleitung zu dem Entwurf eines Systems der Naturphilosophie* *[*Introduction to the draft of a system of philosophy of nature*]* (1799), Schelling says: "Intelligence is productive in a double manner, either blindly and unconsciously or freely and consciously; it is unconsciously productive in Weltanschauung and consciously productive in the creation of an ideal world."[1] Here Weltanschauung is directly assigned not to sense-observation but to intelligence, albeit to unconscious intelligence. Moreover, the factor of productivity, the independent formative process of intuition, is emphasized. Thus the word approaches the meaning we are familiar with today, a self-realized, productive as well as conscious way of apprehending and interpreting the universe of beings. Schelling speaks of a schematism of Weltanschauung, a schematized form for the different possible world-views which appear and take shape in fact. A view of the world, understood in this way, does not have to be produced with a theoretical intention and with the means of theoretical science. In his *Phänomenologie des Geistes* *[*Phenomenology of Spirit*]*, Hegel speaks of a "moral world-view."[2] Görres makes use of the expression "poetic world-view." Ranke speaks of the "religious and Christian world-view." Mention is made sometimes of the democratic, sometimes of the pessimistic world-view or even of the medieval world-view. Schleiermacher says: "It is only our world-view that makes our knowledge of God complete." Bismarck at one point writes to his bride: "What strange views of the world there are among clever people!" From the forms and possibilities of world-view thus enumerated it becomes clear that what is meant by this term is not only a conception of the contexture of natural things but at the same time an interpretation of the sense and purpose of the human Dasein and hence of history. A world-view always includes a view of life. A world-view grows out of an all-inclusive reflection on the world and the human Dasein, and this again happens in different ways, explicitly and consciously in individuals

---

1. [In Friedrich Wilhelm Joseph von] Schelling, *Schellings Werke*, ed. Manfred Schröter, vol. 2, p. 271. [The German text erroneously cites volume 3, which was the number in the original edition of Schelling's works. Schröter rearranged the order in his edition (Munich: Beck and Oldenbourg, 1927). A new historical-critical edition of Schelling's works is in process of preparation and publication, commissioned by the Schelling Commission of the Bavarian Academy of Sciences (Stuttgart-Bad Cannstatt: Frommann (Holzboog), 1979 –). The work from which Heidegger quotes is not yet available in this edition.]

2. [In Georg Wilhelm Friedrich] Hegel, *Sämtliche Werke*, ed. Hermann Glockner, vol. 2, p. 461 ff. [This is the Jubilee edition, edited by Glockner on the basis of the original edition produced by "Friends of the Deceased," Berlin, 1832 – 1845, and rearranged in chronological order (Stuttgart-Bad Cannstatt: Frommann (Holzboog)). The first printing was in 1927, opening the possibility that Heidegger might personally have used this edition. Glockner's is not a critical edition.]

or by appropriating an already prevalent world-view. We grow up within such a world-view and gradually become accustomed to it. Our world-view is determined by environment—people, race, class, developmental stage of culture. Every world-view thus individually formed arises out of a natural world-view, out of a range of conceptions of the world and determinations of the human Dasein which are at any particular time given more or less explicitly with each such Dasein. We must distinguish the individually formed world-view or the cultural world-view from the natural world-view.

A world-view is not a matter of theoretical knowledge, either in respect of its origin or in relation to its use. It is not simply retained in memory like a parcel of cognitive property. Rather, it is a matter of a coherent conviction which determines the current affairs of life more or less expressly and directly. A world-view is related in its meaning to the particular contemporary Dasein at any given time. In this relationship to the Dasein the world-view is a guide to it and a source of strength under pressure. Whether the world-view is determined by superstitions and prejudices or is based purely on scientific knowledge and experience or even, as is usually the case, is a mixture of superstition and knowledge, prejudice and sober reason, it all comes to the same thing; nothing essential is changed.

This indication of the characteristic traits of what we mean by the term "world-view"may suffice here. A rigorous definition of it would have to be gained in another way, as we shall see. In his *Psychologie der Weltanschauungen,* Jaspers says that "when we speak of world-views we mean Ideas, what is ultimate and total in man, both subjectively, as life-experience and power and character, and objectively, as a world having objective shape."[3] For our purpose of distinguishing between philosophy as world-view and scientific philosophy, it is above all important to see that the world-view, in its meaning, always arises out of the particular factical existence of the human being in accordance with his factical possibilities of thoughtful reflection and attitude-formation, and it arises thus *for* this factical Dasein. The world-view is something that in each case exists historically from, with, and for the factical Dasein. A philosophical world-view is one that expressly and explicitly or at any rate preponderantly has to be worked out and brought about by philosophy, that is to say, by theoretical speculation, to the exclusion of artistic and religious interpretations of the world and the Dasein. This world-view is not a by-product of philosophy; its cultivation, rather, is the proper goal and nature of philosophy itself. In its very concept philosophy is world-view philosophy, philosophy as world-view. If philosophy in the form of theoretical knowledge of the world aims at what is

---

3. Karl Jaspers, *Psychologie der Weltanschauungen,* 3rd ed. (Berlin: [Springer,] 1925), pp. 1–2.

universal in the world and ultimate for the Dasein—the whence, the whither, and the wherefore of the world and life—then this differentiates it from the particular sciences, which always consider only a particular region of the world and the Dasein, as well as from the artistic and religious attitudes, which are not based primarily on the theoretical attitude. It seems to be without question that philosophy has as its goal the formation of a world-view. This task must define the nature and concept of philosophy. Philosophy, it appears, is so essentially world-view philosophy that it would be preferable to reject this latter expression as an unnecessary overstatement. And what is even more, to propose to strive for a scientific philosophy is a misunderstanding. For the philosophical world-view, it is said, naturally ought to be scientific. By this is meant: first, that it should take cognizance of the results of the different sciences and use them in constructing the world-picture and the interpretation of the Dasein; secondly, that it ought to be scientific by forming the world-view in strict conformity with the rules of scientific thought. This conception of philosophy as the formation of a world-view in a theoretical way is so much taken for granted that it commonly and widely defines the concept of philosophy and consequently also prescribes for the popular mind what is to be and what ought to be expected of philosophy. Conversely, if philosophy does not give satisfactory answers to the questions of world-view, the popular mind regards it as insignificant. Demands made on philosophy and attitudes taken toward it are governed by this notion of it as the scientific construction of a world-view. To determine whether philosophy succeeds or fails in this task, its history is examined for unequivocal confirmation that it deals knowingly with the ultimate questions—of nature, of the soul, that is to say, of the freedom and history of man, of God.

If philosophy is the scientific construction of a world-view, then the distinction between "scientific philosophy" and "philosophy as world-view" vanishes. The two together constitute the essence of philosophy, so that what is really emphasized ultimately is the task of the world-view. This *seems* also to be the view of Kant, who put the scientific character of philosophy on a new basis. We need only recall the distinction he drew in the introduction to the *Logic* between the *academic* and the *cosmic conceptions of philosophy*.[4] Here we turn to an oft-quoted Kantian distinction which apparently supports the distinction between scientific philosophy and philosophy as world-view or, more exactly, serves as evidence for the fact that

---

4. In *Immanuel Kants Werke*, ed. Ernst Cassirer, vol. 8, p. 342 ff. [Edited by Ernst Cassirer with the collaboration of Hermann Cohen, Artur Buchenau, Otto Buek, Albert Görland, and B. Kellermann, 11 vols. (Berlin: Bruno Cassirer, 1912; reprinted, 1922; reissued, Hildesheim: Gerstenberg, 1973). In the Cassirer edition, Kant's *Logik*, edited by Artur Buchenau, is entitled *Vorlesungen Kants über Logik* [Kant's lectures on logic].]

Kant himself, for whom the scientific character of philosophy was central, likewise conceives of philosophy as philosophical world-view.

According to the *academic concept* or, as Kant also says, in the scholastic sense, philosophy is the doctrine of the skill of reason and includes two parts: "first, a sufficient stock of rational cognitions from concepts; and, secondly, a systematic interconnection of these cognitions or a combination of them in the idea of a whole." Kant is here thinking of the fact that philosophy in the scholastic sense includes the interconnection of the formal principles of thought and of reason in general as well as the discussion and determination of those concepts which, as a necessary presupposition, underlie our apprehension of the world, that is to say, for Kant, of nature. According to the academic concept, philosophy is the whole of all the formal and material fundamental concepts and principles of rational knowledge.

Kant defines the *cosmic concept* of philosophy or, as he also says, philosophy in the cosmopolitan sense, as follows: "But as regards philosophy in the cosmic sense (in sensu cosmico), it can also be called a science of the supreme maxims of the use of our reason, understanding by 'maxim' the inner principle of choice among diverse ends." Philosophy in the cosmic sense deals with that for the sake of which all use of reason, including that of philosophy itself, is what it is. "For philosophy in the latter sense is indeed the science of the relation of every use of knowledge and reason to the final purpose of human reason, under which, as the supreme end, all other ends are subordinated and must come together into unity in it. In this cosmopolitan sense the field of philosophy can be defined by the following questions: 1) What can I know? 2) What should I do? 3) What may I hope? 4) What is man?"[5] At bottom, says Kant, the first three questions are concentrated in the fourth, "What is man?" For the determination of the final ends of human reason results from the explanation of what man is. It is to these ends that philosophy in the academic sense also must relate.

Does this Kantian separation between philosophy in the scholastic sense and philosophy in the cosmopolitan sense coincide with the distinction between scientific philosophy and philosophy as world-view? Yes and no. Yes, since Kant after all makes a distinction within the concept of philosophy

---

5. Ibid. Cf. Immanuel Kant, *Critique of Pure Reason*, B833. [By custom, Kant's first and second editions of the *Kritik der reinen Vernunft* are labeled A and B, respectively. Raymund Schmidt's edition (2nd ed. revised, 1930; Philosophische Bibliothek, vol. 37a, Hamburg: F. Meiner, 1976), which collates the two German texts, is both good and accessible. Norman Kemp Smith's translation, *Critique of Pure Reason*, 2nd ed. (London: Macmillan; New York: St. Martin's Press, 1933) is standard. Since both Schmidt and Smith give marginal references to both editions, further citations of this work will give only the English title and the *Grundprobleme*'s references.]

and, on the basis of this distinction, makes the questions of the end and limits of human existence central. No, since philosophy in the cosmic sense does not have the task of developing a world-view in the designated sense. What Kant ultimately has in mind as the task of philosophy in the cosmic sense, without being able to say so explicitly, is nothing but the a priori and therefore ontological circumscription of the characteristics which belong to the essential nature of the human Dasein and which also generally determine the concept of a world-view.[6] As the most fundamental a priori determination of the essential nature of the human Dasein Kant recognizes the proposition: Man is a being which exists as its own end.[7] Philosophy in the cosmic sense, as Kant understands it, also has to do with determinations of essential nature. It does not seek a specific factual account of the merely factually known world and the merely factually lived life; rather, it seeks to delimit what belongs to world in general, to the Dasein in general, and thus to world-view in general. Philosophy in the cosmic sense has for Kant exactly the same methodological character as philosophy in the academic sense, except that for reasons which we shall not discuss here in further detail Kant does not see the connection between the two. More precisely, he does not see the basis for establishing both concepts on a common original ground. We shall deal with this later on. For the present it is clear only that, if philosophy is viewed as being the scientific construction of a world-view, appeal should not be made to Kant. Fundamentally, Kant recognizes only philosophy as science.

A world-view, as we saw, springs in every case from a factical Dasein in accordance with its factical possibilities, and it is what it is always for this particular Dasein. This in no way asserts a relativism of world-views. What a world-view fashioned in this way says can be formulated in propositions and rules which are related in their meaning to a specific really existing world, to the particular factically existing Dasein. Every world-view and life-view posits; that is to say, it is related being-ly to some being or beings. It posits a being, something that *is;* it is positive. A world-view belongs to each Dasein and, like this Dasein, it is always in fact determined historically. To the world-view there belongs this multiple positivity, that it is always

---

6. See Kant, *Critique of Pure Reason,* B844.

7. See Kant, *Critique of Pure Reason,* B868. [Heidegger's formulation is "Der Mensch ist ein Seiendes, das als Zweck seiner selbst existiert." He does not set it within quotation marks, so presumably it is not intended to be an exact reproduction of Kant's statement. In the passage cited, Kant does not use the phrase "als Zweck seiner selbst," "as its own end." What he says is: "Essential ends are not yet the highest ends; there can be only one highest end (in the complete systematic unity of reason). Therefore, they are either the final end or else they are subordinate ends belonging as means to the final end. The former is none other than the whole determination of man, and the philosophy of it is called moral philosophy." Bestimmung, which I have translated here as determination, also connotes vocation.]

rooted in a Dasein which is in such and such a way; that as such it relates to the existing world and points to the factically existent Dasein. It is just because this positivity—that is, the relatedness to beings, to world that *is,* Dasein that *is*—belongs to the essence of the world-view, and thus in general to the formation of the world-view, that the formation of a world-view cannot be the task of philosophy. To say this is not to exclude but to include the idea that philosophy itself is a distinctive primal form of world-view. Philosophy can and perhaps must show, among many other things, that something like a world-view belongs to the essential nature of the Dasein. Philosophy can and must define what in general constitutes the structure of a world-view. But it can never develop and posit some specific world-view qua just this or that particular one. Philosophy is not essentially the formation of a world-view; but perhaps just on this account it has an elementary and fundamental relation to all world-view formation, even to that which is not theoretical but factually historical.

The thesis that world-view formation does not belong to the task of philosophy is valid, of course, only on the presupposition that philosophy does not relate in a positive manner to some being qua this or that particular being, that it does not posit a being. Can this presupposition that philosophy does not relate positively to beings, as the sciences do, be justified? What then is philosophy supposed to concern itself with if not with beings, with that which is, as well as with the whole of what is? What is not, is surely the nothing. Should philosophy, then, as absolute science, have the nothing as its theme? What can there be apart from nature, history, God, space, number? We say of each of these, even though in a different sense, that it *is.* We call it a being. In relating to it, whether theoretically or practically, we are comporting ourselves toward a being. Beyond all these beings *there is nothing.* Perhaps there *is* no other being beyond what has been enumerated, but perhaps, as in the German idiom for "there is," *es gibt* /literally, it gives/, still something else *is given,* something else which indeed *is* not but which nevertheless, in a sense yet to be determined, *is given.* Even more. In the end something is given which *must* be given if we are to be able to make beings accessible to us as beings and comport ourselves toward them, something which, to be sure, is not but which must be given if we are to experience and understand any beings at all. We are able to grasp beings as such, as beings, only if we understand something like *being.* If we did not understand, even though at first roughly and without conceptual comprehension, what actuality signifies, then the actual would remain hidden from us. If we did not understand what reality means, then the real would remain inaccessible. If we did not understand what life and vitality signify, then we would not be able to comport ourselves toward living beings. If we did not understand what existence and existentiality signify, then we ourselves would not be able to exist as Dasein. If we did not understand what permanence and constancy signify, then constant geometric relations or numerical proportions would remain a secret to us. We must understand actuality, reality, vitality, existentiality, constancy in order to be able to comport ourselves positively toward specifically actual, real, living, existing, constant beings. We must understand being so that we may be able to be given over to a world that *is,* so that we can exist in it and be our own Dasein itself as a being. We must be able to understand actuality *before* all factual experience of actual beings. This understanding of actuality or of being in the widest sense as over against the experience of beings is in a certain sense *earlier* than the experience of beings. To say that the understanding of being precedes all factual experience of beings does not mean that we would first need to have an explicit concept of being in order to experience beings theoretically or practically. We must understand being—being, which may no longer itself be called a being, being, which does not occur as a being among other beings but which nevertheless must be given and in fact is given in the understanding of being.

§3. *Philosophy as science of being*

We assert now that *being is the proper and sole theme of philosophy.* This is not our own invention; it is a way of putting the theme which comes to life at the beginning of philosophy in antiquity, and it assumes its most grandiose form in Hegel's logic. At present we are merely asserting that being is the proper and sole theme of philosophy. Negatively, this means that philosophy is not a *science of* beings but of *being* or, as the Greek expression goes, *ontology.* We take this expression in the widest possible sense and not in the narrower one it has, say, in Scholasticism or in modern philosophy in Descartes and Leibniz.

A discussion of the basic problems of phenomenology then is tantamount to providing fundamental substantiation for this assertion *that* philosophy is the science of being and establishing *how* it is such. The discussion should show the possibility and necessity of the absolute science of being and demonstrate its character in the very process of the inquiry. Philosophy is the theoretical conceptual interpretation of being, of being's structure and its possibilities. Philosophy is ontological. In contrast, a world-view is a positing knowledge of beings and a positing attitude toward beings; it is not ontological but ontical. The formation of a world-view falls outside the range of philosophy's tasks, but not because philosophy is in an incomplete condition and does not yet suffice to give a unanimous and universally cogent answer to the questions pertinent to world-views; rather, the formation of a world-view falls outside the range of philosophy's tasks because philosophy in principle does not relate to beings. It is not because of a defect that philosophy renounces the task of forming a world-view but because of a distinctive priority: it deals with what every positing of beings, even the positing done by a world-view, must already *presuppose* essentially. The distinction between philosophy as science and philosophy as world-view is untenable, not—as it seemed earlier—because scientific philosophy has as its chief end the formation of a world-view and thus would have to be elevated to the level of a world-view philosophy, but because the notion of a world-view philosophy is simply inconceivable. For it implies that philosophy, as science of being, is supposed to adopt specific attitudes toward and posit specific things about beings. To anyone who has even an approximate understanding of the concept of philosophy and its history, the notion of a world-view philosophy is an absurdity. If one term of the distinction between scientific philosophy and world-view philosophy is inconceivable, then the other, too, must be inappropriately conceived. Once it has been seen that world-view philosophy is impossible in principle if it is supposed to be philosophy, then the differentiating adjective "scientific" is no longer necessary for characterizing philosophy. That philosophy is scientific is implied in its very concept. It can be shown historically that at bottom all the great philosophies since antiquity more or less explicitly took themselves to be, and as such sought to be, ontology. In a similar way, however, it can also be shown that these attempts failed over and over again and why they had to fail. I gave the historical proof of this in my courses of the last two semesters, one on ancient philosophy and the other on the history of philosophy from Thomas Aquinas to Kant.* We shall not now refer to this historical demonstration of the nature of philosophy, a demonstration having its own peculiar character. Let us rather in the whole of the present course try to establish philosophy on its own basis, so far as it is a work of human freedom. Philosophy must legitimate by its own resources its claim to be universal ontology.

In the meantime, however, the statement that philosophy is the science of being remains a pure assertion. Correspondingly, the elimination of world-view formation from the range of philosophical tasks has not yet been warranted. We raised this distinction between scientific philosophy and world-view philosophy in order to give a provisional clarification of the con-

---

* The texts of these courses, given in the summer semester 1926 and the winter semester 1926–1927, respectively, are planned for publication, as the two volumes numerically preceding the volume translated here, in the Marburg University Lectures, 1923–1928 section of the Lectures, 1923–1944 division of the collected works: Martin Heidegger, *Gesamtausgabe*, vol. 22, *Grundbegriffe der antiken Philosophie*, and vol. 23, *Geschichte der Philosophie von Thomas v. Aquin bis Kant* (Frankfurt: Vittorio Klostermann).

cept of philosophy and to demarcate it from the popular concept. The clarification and demarcation, again, were provided in order to account for the selection of the concrete phenomenological problems to be dealt with next and to remove from the choice the appearance of complete arbitrariness.

Philosophy is the science of being. For the future we shall mean by "philosophy" scientific philosophy and nothing else. In conformity with this usage, all non-philosophical sciences have as their theme some being or beings, and indeed in such a way that they are in every case antecedently given as beings to those sciences. They are posited by them in advance; they are a positum for them. All the propositions of the non-philosophical sciences, including those of mathematics, are positive propositions. Hence, to distinguish them from philosophy, we shall call all non-philosophical sciences positive sciences. Positive sciences deal with that which is, with beings; that is to say, they always deal with specific domains, for instance, nature. Within a given domain scientific research again cuts out particular spheres: nature as physically material lifeless nature and nature as living nature. It divides the sphere of the living into individual fields: the plant world, the animal world. Another domain of beings is history; its spheres are art history, political history, history of science, and history of religion. Still another domain of beings is the pure space of geometry, which is abstracted from space pre-theoretically uncovered in the environing world. The beings of these domains are familiar to us even if at first and for the most part we are not in a position to delimit them sharply and clearly from one another. We can, of course, always name, as a provisional description which satisfies practically the purpose of positive science, some being that falls within the domain. We can always bring before ourselves, as it were, a particular being from a particular domain as an example. Historically, the actual partitioning of domains comes about not according to some preconceived plan of a system of science but in conformity with the current research problems of the positive sciences.

We can always easily bring forward and picture to ourselves some being belonging to any given domain. As we are accustomed to say, we are able to think something about it. What is the situation here with philosophy's object? Can something like being be imagined? If we try to do this, doesn't our head start to swim? Indeed, at first we are baffled and find ourselves clutching at thin air. A being—that's something, a table, a chair, a tree, the sky, a body, some words, an action. A being, yes, indeed—but being? It looks like nothing—and no less a thinker than Hegel said that being and nothing are the same. Is philosophy as science of being the science of nothing? At the outset of our considerations, without raising any false hopes and without mincing matters, we must confess that under the heading of being we can at first think to ourselves nothing. On the other hand, it is just as certain that we are constantly thinking being. We think being just as often as, daily, on innumerable occasions, whether aloud or silently, we say "This *is* such and such," "That other *is not* so," "That *was*," "It *will be*." In each use of a verb we have already thought, and have always in some way understood, being. We understand immediately "Today is Saturday; the sun is up." We understand the "is" we use in speaking, although we do not comprehend it conceptually. The meaning of this "is" remains closed to us. This understanding of the "is" and of being in general is so much a matter of course that it was possible for the dogma to spread in philosophy uncontested to the present day that being is the simplest and most self-evident concept, that it is neither susceptible of nor in need of definition. Appeal is made to common sense. But wherever common sense is taken to be philosophy's highest court of appeal, philosophy must become suspicious. In "Über das Wesen der philosophischen Kritik überhaupt" *["On the Essence of Philosophical Criticism"]*, Hegel says: "Philosophy by its very nature is esoteric; for itself it is neither made for the masses nor is it susceptible of being cooked up for them. It is philosophy only because it goes exactly contrary to the understanding and thus even more so to 'sound common sense,' the so-called healthy human understanding, which actually means the local and temporary vision of some limited generation of human beings. To that generation the world of philosophy is in and for itself a topsy-turvy, an inverted, world."[1] The demands and standards of common sense have no right to claim any validity or to represent any authority in regard to what philosophy is and what it is not.

What if being were the most complex and most obscure concept? What if arriving at the concept of being were the most urgent task of philosophy, a task which has to be taken up ever anew? Today, when philosophizing is so barbarous, so much like a St. Vitus' dance, as perhaps in no other period of the cultural history of the West, and when nevertheless the resurrection of metaphysics is hawked up and down all the streets, what Aristotle says in one of his most important investigations in the *Metaphysics* has been

---

1. In Hegel, *Sämtliche Werke,* ed. Glockner, vol. 1, pp. 185–186. [The quotation departs from the cited text in two minute points—the entire passage is at the top of p. 185, and a comma is omitted after the word "Verstand." The phrase "eine verkehrte Welt," "a topsy-turvy, an inverted, world," anticipates Hegel's later use of it in the *Phenomenology* in a section (A, 3) entitled "Force and Understanding: Appearance and the Supersensible World." It is precisely by going contrary to the understanding that the inverted world makes possible the passage from consciousness to self-consciousness, and eventually to subject, reason, and spirit. It is of interest that Hegel was already using this phrase by 1802, and indeed as the characteristic of what is specifically philosophical in comparison with ordinary scientific understanding, and that Heidegger chooses this early passage, with its reverberations, in the present context of the discussion of the nature of philosophical thinking. Heidegger employs the phrase several times in these lectures; see Lexicon: inverted world. More idiomatically one could simply say, "Philosophy's world is a crazy world."]

completely forgotten. Kai de kai to palai te kai nun kai aei zetoumenon kai aei aporoumenon, ti to on, touto esti tis he ousia.[2] "That which has been sought for from of old and now and in the future and constantly, and that on which inquiry founders over and over again, is the problem What is being?" If philosophy is the science of being, then the first and last and basic problem of philosophy must be, What does being signify? Whence can something like being in general be understood? How is understanding of being at all possible?

§4. The four theses about being and the basic problems of phenomenology

Before we broach these fundamental questions, it will be worthwhile first to make ourselves familiar for once with discussions about being. To this end we shall deal in the first part of the course with some characteristic theses about being as individual concrete phenomenological problems, theses that have been advocated in the course of the history of Western philosophy since antiquity. In this connection we are interested, not in the historical contexts of the philosophical inquiries within which these theses about being make their appearance, but in their specifically inherent content. This content is to be discussed critically, so that we may make the transition from it to the above-mentioned basic problems of the science of being. The discussion of these theses should at the same time render us familiar with the phenomenological way of dealing with problems relating to being. We choose four such theses:

1. Kant's thesis: Being is not a real predicate.
2. The thesis of medieval ontology (Scholasticism) which goes back to Aristotle: To the constitution of the being of a being there belong (a) whatness, essence (Was-sein, essentia), and (b) existence or extantness (existentia, Vorhandensein).
3. The thesis of modern ontology: The basic ways of being are the being of nature (res extensa) and the being of mind (res cogitans).
4. The thesis of logic in the broadest sense: Every being, regardless of its particular way of being, can be addressed and talked about by means of the "is." The being of the copula.

These theses seem at first to have been gathered together arbitrarily. Looked at more closely, however, they are interconnected in a most intimate way. Attention to what is denoted in these theses leads to the insight that

---

2. Aristotle, *Metaphysica*, book Zeta, 1.1028[b]2 ff.

they cannot be brought up adequately—not even as problems—as long as the *fundamental question* of the whole science of being has not been put and answered: *the question of the meaning of being in general.* The second part of our course will deal with this question. Discussion of the basic question of the meaning of being in general and of the problems arising from that question constitutes the entire stock of basic problems of phenomenology in their systematic order and their foundation. For the present we delineate the range of these problems only roughly.

On what path can we advance toward the meaning of being in general? Is not the question of the meaning of being and the task of an elucidation of this concept a pseudo-problem if, as usual, the opinion is held dogmatically that being is the most general and simplest concept? What is the source for defining this concept and in what direction is it to be resolved?

Something like being reveals itself to us in the understanding of being, an understanding that lies at the root of all comportment toward beings. Comportment toward beings belongs, on its part, to a definite being, the being which we ourselves are, the human Dasein. It is to the human Dasein that there belongs the understanding of being which first of all makes possible every comportment toward beings. The understanding of being has itself the mode of being of the human Dasein. The more originally and appropriately we define this being in regard to the structure of its being, that is to say, ontologically, the more securely we are placed in a position to comprehend in its structure the understanding of being that belongs to the Dasein, and the more clearly and unequivocally the question can then be posed, What is it that makes this understanding of being possible at all? Whence—that is, from which antecedently given horizon—do we understand the like of being?

The analysis of the understanding of being in regard to what is specific to this understanding and what is understood in it or its intelligibility presupposes an analytic of the Dasein ordered to that end. This analytic has the task of exhibiting the basic constitution of the human Dasein and of characterizing the meaning of the Dasein's being. In this ontological analytic of the Dasein, the original constitution of the Dasein's being is revealed to be *temporality.* The interpretation of temporality leads to a more radical understanding and conceptual comprehension of time than has been possible hitherto in philosophy. The familiar concept of time as traditionally treated in philosophy is only an offshoot of temporality as the original meaning of the Dasein. If temporality constitutes the meaning of the being of the human Dasein and if understanding of being belongs to the constitution of the Dasein's being, then this understanding of being, too, must be possible only on the basis of temporality. Hence there arises the prospect of a possible confirmation of the thesis that time is the horizon from which something like being becomes at all intelligible. We interpret being by way of time (tempus). The interpretation is a Temporal one.* The fundamental subject of research in ontology, as determination of the meaning of being by way of time, is *Temporality*.

We said that ontology is the science of being. But being is always the being of a being. Being is essentially different from a being, from beings. How is the distinction between being and beings to be grasped? How can its possibility be explained? If being is not itself a being, how then does it nevertheless belong to beings, since, after all, beings and only beings *are*? What does it mean to say that being *belongs* to beings? The correct answer to this question is the basic presupposition needed to set about the problems of ontology regarded as the science of being. We must be able to bring out clearly the difference between being and beings in order to make something like being the theme of inquiry. This distinction is not arbitrary; rather, it is the one by which the theme of ontology and thus of philosophy itself is first of all attained. It is a distinction which is first and foremost constitutive for ontology. We call it the *ontological difference*—the differentiation between being and beings. Only by making this distinction—krinein in Greek—not between one being and another being but between being and beings do we first enter the field of philosophical research. Only by taking this critical stance do we keep our own standing inside the field of philosophy. Therefore, in distinction from the sciences of the things that are, of beings, ontology, or philosophy in general, is the critical science, or the science of the inverted world. With this distinction between being and beings and the selection of being as theme we depart in principle from the domain of beings. We surmount it, transcend it. We can also call the science of being, as critical science, *transcendental science*. In doing so we are not simply taking over unaltered the concept of the transcendental in Kant, although we are indeed adopting its original sense and its true tendency, perhaps still concealed from Kant. We are surmounting beings in order to reach being. Once having made the ascent we shall not again descend to a being, which, say, might lie like another world behind the familiar beings. The transcendental science of being has nothing to do with popular metaphysics, which deals with some being behind the known beings; rather, the scientific concept of metaphysics is identical with the concept of philosophy in general—critically transcendental science of being, ontology. It is easily seen that the ontological difference can be cleared up and carried out unambiguously for ontological inquiry only if and when the meaning of being in general has been explicitly brought to light, that is to say, only when it has been shown

---

* In its role as condition of possibility of the understanding of being, temporality is Temporality. See Lexicon: Temporality.

how temporality makes possible the distinguishability between being and beings. Only on the basis of this consideration can the Kantian thesis that being is not a real predicate be given its original sense and adequately explained.

Every being is *something;* it has its *what* and as such has a specific possible *mode of being.* In the first part of our course, while discussing the second thesis, we shall show that ancient as well as medieval ontology dogmatically enunciated this proposition—that to each being there belongs a what and a way of being, essentia and existentia—as if it were self-evident. For us the question arises, Can the reason every being must and can have a what, a ti, and a possible way of being be grounded in the meaning of being itself, that is to say, Temporally? Do these characteristics, whatness and way-of-being, taken with sufficient breadth, belong to being itself? "Is" being articulated by means of these characteristics in accordance with its essential nature? With this we are now confronted by *the problem of the basic articulation of being,* the question of the necessary belonging-together of *whatness* and *way-of-being* and of *the belonging of the two of them in their unity to the idea of being in general.*

Every being has a way-of-being. The question is whether this way-of-being has the same character in every being—as ancient ontology believed and subsequent periods have basically had to maintain even down to the present—or whether individual ways-of-being are mutually distinct. Which are the basic ways of being? Is there a multiplicity? How is the variety of ways-of-being possible and how is it at all intelligible, given the meaning of being? How can we speak at all of a unitary concept of being despite the variety of ways-of-being? These questions can be consolidated into *the problem of the possible modifications of being and the unity of being's variety.*

Every being with which we have any dealings can be addressed and spoken of by saying *"it is"* thus and so, regardless of its specific mode of being. We meet with a being's being in the understanding of being. It is understanding that first of all opens up or, as we say, discloses or reveals something like being. Being is given only in the specific disclosedness that characterizes the understanding of being. But we call the disclosedness of something truth. That is the proper concept of truth, as it already begins to dawn in antiquity. Being is given only if there is disclosure, that is to say, if there is truth. But there is truth only if a being exists which opens up, which discloses, and indeed in such a way that disclosure itself belongs to the mode of being of this being. We ourselves are such a being. The Dasein itself exists in the truth. To the Dasein there belongs essentially a disclosed world and with that the disclosedness of the Dasein itself. The Dasein, by the nature of its existence, is "in" truth, and only because it is "in" truth does it have the possibility of being "in" untruth. Being is given only if truth, hence if the Dasein, exists. And only for this reason is it not merely possible to address beings but within certain limits sometimes—presupposing that the Dasein exists—necessary. We shall consolidate these problems of the interconnectedness between being and truth into *the problem of the truth-character of being* (veritas transcendentalis).

We have thus identified four groups of problems that constitute the content of the second part of the course: the problem of the ontological difference, the problem of the basic articulation of being, the problem of the possible modifications of being in its ways of being, the problem of the truth-character of being. The four theses treated provisionally in the first part correspond to these four basic problems. More precisely, looking backward from the discussion of the basic problems in the second half, we see that the problems with which we are provisionally occupied in the first part, following the lead of these theses, are not accidental but grow out of the inner systematic coherence of the general problem of being.

§5. *The character of ontological method*
The three basic components of phenomenological method

Our conduct of the ontological investigation in the first and second parts opens up for us at the same time a view of the way in which these phenomenological investigations proceed. This raises the question of the character of method in ontology. Thus we come to the third part of the course: the scientific method of ontology and the idea of phenomenology.

The method of ontology, that is, of philosophy in general, is distinguished by the fact that ontology has nothing in common with any method of any of the other sciences, all of which as positive sciences deal with beings. On the other hand, it is precisely the analysis of the truth-character of being which shows that being also is, as it were, based in a being, namely, in the Dasein. Being is given only if the understanding of being, hence the Dasein, exists. This being accordingly lays claim to a distinctive priority in ontological inquiry. It makes itself manifest in all discussions of the basic problems of ontology and above all in the fundamental question of the meaning of being in general. The elaboration of this question and its answer requires a general analytic of the Dasein. Ontology has for its fundamental discipline the analytic of the Dasein. This implies at the same time that ontology cannot be established in a purely ontological manner. Its possibility is referred back to a being, that is, to something ontical—the Dasein. Ontology has an ontical foundation, a fact which is manifest over and over again in the history of philosophy down to the present. For example, it is expressed as early as Aristotle's dictum that the first science, the science of being, is theology. As the work of the freedom of the human Dasein, the possibilities and destinies of philosophy are bound up with man's existence, and thus with temporality and with historicality, and indeed in a more original sense than is any other science. Consequently, in clarifying the scientific character of ontology, *the first task is the demonstration of its ontical foundation* and the characterization of this foundation itself.

The *second* task consists in distinguishing the mode of knowing operative in ontology as science of being, and this requires us to *work out the methodological structure of ontological-transcendental differentiation.* In early antiquity it was already seen that being and its attributes in a certain way underlie beings and precede them and so are a proteron, an earlier. The term denoting this character by which being precedes beings is the expression a priori, *apriority,* being earlier or prior. As a priori, being is earlier than beings. The meaning of this a priori, the sense of the earlier and its possibility, has never been cleared up. The question has not even once been raised as to why the determinations of being and being itself must have this character of priority and how such priority is possible. To be earlier is a determination of time, but it does not pertain to the temporal order of the time that we measure by the clock; rather, it is an earlier that belongs to the "inverted world." Therefore, this earlier which characterizes being is taken by the popular understanding to be the later. Only the interpretation of being by way of temporality can make clear why and how this feature of being earlier, apriority, goes together with being. The a priori character of being and of all the structures of being accordingly calls for a specific kind of approach and way of apprehending being—*a priori cognition.*

The basic components of a priori cognition constitute what we call *phenomenology.* Phenomenology is the name for the method of ontology, that is, of scientific philosophy. Rightly conceived, phenomenology is the concept of a method. It is therefore precluded from the start that phenomenology should pronounce any theses about being which have specific content, thus adopting a so-called standpoint.

We shall not enter into detail concerning which ideas about phenomenology are current today, instigated in part by phenomenology itself. We shall touch briefly on just one example. It has been said that my work is Catholic phenomenology—presumably because it is my conviction that thinkers like Thomas Aquinas and Duns Scotus also understood something of philosophy, perhaps more than the moderns. But the concept of a Catholic phenomenology is even more absurd than the concept of a Protestant mathematics. Philosophy as science of being is fundamentally distinct in method from any other science. The distinction in method between, say, mathematics and classical philology is not as great as the difference between mathematics and philosophy or between philology and philosophy. The breadth of the difference between philosophy and the positive sciences, to which mathematics and philology belong, cannot at all be estimated quantitatively. In ontology, being is supposed to be grasped and comprehended conceptually by way of the phenomenological method, in connection with which we may observe that, while phenomenology certainly arouses lively interest today, what it seeks and aims at was already vigorously pursued in Western philosophy from the very beginning.

Being is to be laid hold of and made our theme. Being is always being of beings and accordingly it becomes accessible at first only by starting with some being. Here the phenomenological vision which does the apprehending must indeed direct itself toward a being, but it has to do so in such a way that the being of this being is thereby brought out so that it may be possible to thematize it. Apprehension of being, ontological investigation, always turns, at first and necessarily, to some being; but then, *in a precise way, it is led away from that being and led back to its being.* We call this basic component of phenomenological method—the leading back or re-duction of investigative vision from a naively apprehended being to being—*phenomenological reduction.* We are thus adopting a central term of Husserl's phenomenology in its literal wording though not in its substantive intent. *For Husserl* the phenomenological reduction, which he worked out for the first time expressly in the *Ideas Toward a Pure Phenomenology and Phenomenological Philosophy* (1913), is the method of leading phenomenological vision from the natural attitude of the human being whose life is involved in the world of things and persons back to the transcendental life of consciousness and its noetic-noematic experiences, in which objects are constituted as correlates of consciousness. *For us* phenomenological reduction means leading phenomenological vision back from the apprehension of a being, whatever may be the character of that apprehension, to the understanding of the being of this being (projecting upon the way it is unconcealed). Like every other scientific method, phenomenological method grows and changes due to the progress made precisely with its help into the subjects under investigation. Scientific method is never a technique. As soon as it becomes one it has fallen away from its own proper nature.

Phenomenological reduction as the leading of our vision from beings to being nevertheless is not the only basic component of phenomenological method; in fact, it is not even the central component. For this guidance of vision back from beings to being requires at the same time that we should bring ourselves forward toward being itself. Pure aversion from beings is a merely negative methodological measure which not only needs to be supplemented by a positive one but expressly requires us to be led toward being; it thus requires guidance. Being does not become accessible like a being. We do not simply find it in front of us. As is to be shown, it must always be brought to view in a free projection. This projecting of the antecedently given being upon its being and the structures of its being we call *phenomenological construction.*

But the method of phenomenology is likewise not exhausted by phenomenological construction. We have heard that every projection of being occurs in a reductive recursion from beings. The consideration of being takes its start from beings. This commencement is obviously always determined by the factual experience of beings and the range of possibilities of experience that at any time are peculiar to a factical Dasein, and hence to the historical situation of a philosophical investigation. It is not the case that at all times and for everyone all beings and all specific domains of beings are accessible in the same way; and, even if beings are accessible inside the range of experience, the question still remains whether, within naive and common experience, they are already suitably understood in their specific mode of being. Because the Dasein is historical in its own existence, possibilities of access and modes of interpretation of beings are themselves diverse, varying in different historical circumstances. A glance at the history of philosophy shows that many domains of beings were discovered very early—nature, space, the soul—but that, nevertheless, they could not yet be comprehended in their specific being. As early as antiquity a common or average concept of being came to light, which was employed for the interpretation of all the beings of the various domains of being and their modes of being, although their specific being itself, taken expressly in its structure, was not made into a problem and could not be defined. Thus Plato saw quite well that the soul, with its logos, is a being different from sensible being. But he was not in a position to demarcate the specific mode of being of this being from the mode of being of any other being or non-being. Instead, for him as well as for Aristotle and subsequent thinkers down to Hegel, and all the more so for their successors, all ontological investigations proceed within an average concept of being in general. Even the ontological investigation which we are now conducting is determined by its historical situation and, therewith, by certain possibilities of approaching beings and by the preceding philosophical tradition. The store of basic philosophical concepts derived from the philosophical tradition is still so influential today that this effect of tradition can hardly be overestimated. It is for this reason that all philosophical discussion, even the most radical attempt to begin all over again, is pervaded by traditional concepts and thus by traditional horizons and traditional angles of approach, which we cannot assume with unquestionable certainty to have arisen originally and genuinely from the domain of being and the constitution of being they claim to comprehend. It is for this reason that there necessarily belongs to the conceptual interpretation of being and its structures, that is, to the reductive construction of being, a *destruction—*

a critical process in which the traditional concepts, which at first must necessarily be employed, are de-constructed down to the sources from which they were drawn. Only by means of this destruction can ontology fully assure itself in a phenomenological way of the genuine character of its concepts.

These three basic components of phenomenological method—reduction, construction, destruction—belong together in their content and must receive grounding in their mutual pertinence. Construction in philosophy is necessarily destruction, that is to say, a de-constructing of traditional concepts carried out in a historical recursion to the tradition. And this is not a negation of the tradition or a condemnation of it as worthless; quite the reverse, it signifies precisely a positive appropriation of tradition. Because destruction belongs to construction, philosophical cognition is essentially at the same time, in a certain sense, historical cognition. History of philosophy, as it is called, belongs to the concept of philosophy as science, to the concept of phenomenological investigation. The history of philosophy is not an arbitrary appendage to the business of teaching philosophy, which provides an occasion for picking up some convenient and easy theme for passing an examination or even for just looking around to see how things were in earlier times. Knowledge of the history of philosophy is intrinsically unitary on its own account, and the specific mode of historical cognition in philosophy differs in its object from all other scientific knowledge of history.

The method of ontology thus delineated makes it possible to characterize the idea of phenomenology distinctively as the scientific procedure of philosophy. We therewith gain the possibility of defining the concept of philosophy more concretely. Thus our considerations in the third part lead back again to the starting point of the course.

§6. *Outline of the course*

The path of our thought in the course will accordingly be divided into three parts:

Part One.　Phenomenological-critical discussion of several traditional theses about being

Part Two.　The fundamental-ontological question about the meaning of being in general. The basic structures and basic ways of being

Part Three. The scientific method of ontology and the idea of phenomenology

Part One consists of *four chapters:*

1. Kant's thesis: Being is not a real predicate.
2. The thesis of medieval ontology which goes back to Aristotle: To the being of a being there belong whatness (essentia) and existence (existentia, extantness).
3. The thesis of modern ontology: The basic ways of being are the being of nature (res extensa) and the being of mind (res cogitans).
4. The thesis of logic: Every being, regardless of its particular way of being, can be addressed and talked about by means of the "is." The being of the copula.

Part Two correspondingly has a *fourfold division:*

1. The problem of the ontological difference (the distinction between being and beings).
2. The problem of the basic articulation of being (essentia, existentia).
3. The problem of the possible modifications of being and the unity of its manifoldness.
4. The truth-character of being.

Part Three also divides into *four chapters:*

1. The ontical foundation of ontology and the analytic of the Dasein as fundamental ontology.
2. The apriority of being and the possibility and structure of a priori knowledge.
3. The basic components of phenomenological method: reduction, construction, destruction.
4. Phenomenological ontology and the concept of philosophy.

PART ONE

Critical Phenomenological Discussion of
Some Traditional Theses about Being

Chapter One

Kant's Thesis: Being Is Not a Real Predicate

§7. The content of the Kantian thesis

Kant discusses his thesis that being is not a real predicate in two places. One is a small essay, *Der einzig mögliche Beweisgrund zu einer Demonstration des Daseins Gottes* [The sole possible argument for a demonstration of God's existence] (1763). This work belongs to Kant's so-called pre-critical period, the period before the *Critique of Pure Reason* (1781). It falls into three parts. Our thesis is dealt with in the first part, which discusses the basic questions and divides into four considerations: (1) "On existence in general"; (2) "On inner possibility insofar as it presupposes an existence"; (3) "On absolutely necessary existence"; (4) "Argument for a demonstration of God's existence."

Kant discusses the thesis again in his *Critique of Pure Reason* (first edition, A, 1781; second edition, B, 1787), specifically in the "Transcendental Logic." Our citations will henceforth be from the second edition (B). "Transcendental logic," or, as we may also say, the ontology of nature, falls into two parts: "transcendental analytic" and "transcendental dialectic." In the transcendental dialectic, book 2, chapter 3, section 4 (B 620 ff), Kant again takes up the thesis he discusses in the *Beweisgrund* essay. The section is entitled "The Impossibility of an Ontological Proof of the Existence of God."

In both places, in the *Beweisgrund* and in the *Critique,* the thesis is treated in the same way. For the purpose of our exposition, in which we propose to examine this thesis in detail, we shall refer to both these works. We may cite them briefly as *Beweisgrund* and *Critique,* references to the former being made according to Ernst Cassirer's edition of Kant's works. Before we elucidate the content of the Kantian thesis, let us characterize

27

briefly the pertinent essentials of the context in which it is discussed in
both places.

First of all, however, a general terminological observation is required. As
the title of the *Beweisgrund* indicates, Kant is speaking of the *existence of
God*. He speaks similarly of the *existence of things* outside us, of the *existence
of nature*. This concept of existence, Dasein, corresponds in Kant to the
Scholastic term existentia. Kant therefore often uses the expression "Existenz"—"actuality" *["Wirklichkeit"]*—instead of "Dasein." In contrast, our
own terminological usage is a different one, which, as will appear, is
grounded in the nature of the case. For what Kant calls existence, using
either Dasein or Existenz, and what Scholasticism calls existentia, we employ the terms "Vorhandensein," "being-extant," "being-at-hand," or "Vorhandenheit," "extantness." These are all names for the way of being of
natural things in the broadest sense. As our course proceeds, the choice of
these expressions must itself be validated on the basis of the specific sense
of this way of being—a way of being that demands these expressions: things
extant, extantness, being-at-hand. In his terminology Husserl follows Kant
and thus utilizes the concept of existence, Dasein, in the sense of being
extant. For us, in contrast, the word "Dasein" does not designate, as it does
for Kant, the way of being of natural things. It does not designate a way of
being at all, but rather a specific being which we ourselves are, the *human
Dasein*. We are at every moment Dasein. This being, the Dasein, like every
other being, has a specific way of being. To this way of the Dasein's being
we assign the term *"Existenz,"* "existence"; and it should be noted here that
existence or the expression "the Dasein exists" is not the sole determination
of the mode of being belonging to us. We shall become acquainted with a
threefold determination of this kind, which is of course rooted in a specific
sense in existence. For Kant and Scholasticism existence is the way of being
of natural things, whereas for us, on the contrary, it is the way of being of
the Dasein. Therefore, we might, for example, say "A body does not exist;
it is, rather, extant." In contrast, Daseins, we ourselves, are not extant; the
Dasein exists. But the Dasein and bodies as respectively existent or extant
at each time *are*. Accordingly, not every being is an extant entity, but also
not everything which is not an extant entity is therefore also a non-being
or something that *is not*. Rather, it can exist or, as we have yet to see, subsist
or have some other mode of being.

The Kantian or the Scholastic concept of *reality* must be sharply distinguished from the Kantian concept of existence as a way of being of things
and from our own terminology of extantness. In Kant as well as in Scholasticism, which he follows, the expression "reality" does not mean what is
commonly understood today by the concept of reality in speaking, for
example, about the reality of the external world. In contemporary usage

reality is tantamount to actuality or existence. The Kantian concept of reality is altogether different, as we shall see. Understanding the thesis that being is not a real predicate depends on understanding this Kantian concept of reality.

Before beginning the interpretation of this thesis, it will be worthwhile to characterize briefly the pertinent context in which it appears. This context strikes the eye on reading the title of the work first mentioned as well as the heading of the relevant section of the *Critique of Pure Reason*. It deals with the proof of the existence, actuality, and—in our terms—extantness of God. We are confronted by the striking fact that Kant discusses the most general of all the concepts of being where he is dealing with the knowability of a wholly determinate, distinctive being, namely, God. But, to anyone who knows the history of philosophy (ontology), this fact is so little surprising that it rather just makes clear how directly Kant stands in the great tradition of ancient and Scholastic ontology. God is the supreme being, summum ens, the most perfect being, ens perfectissimum. What most perfectly *is,* is obviously most suited to be the exemplary being, from which the idea of being can be read off. God is not merely the basic ontological example of the being ·of a being; he is at the same time the primal ground of all beings. The being of the non-divine, created entity must be understood by way of the being of the supreme being. Therefore, it is no accident that the science of being is oriented in a distinctive sense toward the being which is God. This goes so far that Aristotle called the prote philosophia, first philosophy, by the name of theologia.[1] We should take note here that this concept of theology has nothing to do with the present-day concept of Christian theology as a positive science. They have only the name in common. This orientation of theology toward the idea of God came to have a decisive significance for the subsequent history of ontology and for ontology's destiny. It is not our present concern to deal here with the legitimacy of this orientation. It is enough that there is nothing surprising about the fact that Kant discussed the concept of being or existence in the context of the possibility of our knowledge of God. More precisely, what Kant was occupied with was the possibility of that proof of the existence of God which he was the first to call the ontological proof. There comes to light here a remarkable phenomenon which we shall repeatedly encounter in philosophy before Kant and also in post-Kantian philosophy, and in its most extreme form in Hegel, namely, that the problem of being in general is most closely bound up with the problem of God, the problem of defining his essence and demonstrating his existence. We cannot here discuss the reason for this remarkable connection, which nevertheless is in the first instance not at all a mere matter of course, for that would require

---

1. Aristotle, *Metaphysica,* book Epsilon, 1.1026ª19; book Kappa, 7.1064ᵇ3.

us to discuss the foundations of ancient philosophy and metaphysics. The fact persists even in Kant and it proves, quite externally to begin with, that Kant's mode of inquiry still proceeds wholly within the channel of traditional metaphysics. In the places mentioned Kant deals with the possibility of the ontological proof. A peculiar feature of this proof is that it tries to infer God's existence from his *concept*. The philosophical science which in Kant's opinion starts purely from concepts and tries dogmatically to settle something about that which *is*, is ontology or, in traditional language, metaphysics. That is why Kant calls this proof from the concept of God the ontological proof, where "ontological" is equivalent in signification to dogmatical, metaphysical. Kant does not himself deny the possibility of metaphysics but is in search precisely of a scientific metaphysics, a scientific ontology, the idea of which he defines as a system of transcendental philosophy.

The ontological proof is old. It is commonly traced back to Anselm of Canterbury (1033–1109). Anselm proposed his proof in a short treatise, *Proslogium seu alloquium de Dei existentia* [Proslogium, or discourse on the existence of God]. In chapter 3, "Proslogium de Dei existentia," the real core of the proof is presented. In the literature this proof is frequently called the Scholastic proof of God's existence. The term is inappropriate because in many cases it was precisely medieval Scholasticism which challenged the logical validity and cogency of this proof. It was not Kant but Thomas Aquinas who first contested the logical validity of this proof, whereas Bonaventura and Duns Scotus admit the proof. But the Kantian refutation of the possibility of the ontological proof is much more radical and thoroughgoing than that given by Thomas.

The characteristic feature of this proof is the attempt to infer God's existence from his concept. The determination that God is the most perfect being, ens perfectissimum, belongs to his concept, the idea of him. The most perfect being is the one that can lack no possible positive characteristic and that possesses every positive characteristic in an infinitely perfect way. It is impossible that the most perfect being, such as we think God to be in our concept of him, should not have any given positive characteristic. In conformity with the concept of it, every defect is excluded from this being. Therefore also, manifestly, or even before all else, that it *is*, its existence, belongs to the perfection of the most perfect *being*. God is not *what* he is, in accordance with his essential nature as the most perfect being, unless he exists. That God exists thus follows from the concept of God. The proof declares: If God is thought according to his essence, that is to say, according to his concept, then his existence must be thought along with it. This readily suggests the question, Does it follow therefrom that we must *think* God as existing, think his existence? We cannot here go into the provenance of this proof, which reaches back beyond Anselm to Boethius and Dionysius the Areopagite, and thus to Neoplatonism; nor can we examine the various modifications it has undergone and the attitudes that have been taken toward it in the history of philosophy. We shall only in passing describe the view of Thomas Aquinas because it is suitable as a background against which to bring the Kantian refutation into sharpest outline.

Thomas Aquinas discusses and criticizes the possibility of the ontological proof of God's existence, which he does not yet call by this name, in four places: (1) the *Commentary on the Sentences of Peter Lombard*, Sentences 1, dist. 3, qu. 1, art. 2 ad 4; (2) *Summa theologica* 1, qu. 2, art. 1; (3) *Summa contra gentiles* 1, chaps. 10–11; (4) *De veritate*, qu. 10, art. 12. The last mentioned is the most lucid of these accounts. In this place Thomas raises the question utrum deum esse sit per se notum menti humanae, sicut prima principia demonstrationis, quae non possunt cogitari non esse; "whether God is known to the human mind by himself and in himself like the first principles of demonstration [the law of identity, the law of contradiction], which cannot be thought as not being." Thomas asks: Do we know about God's existence with the aid of God's concept, according to which he cannot not exist? In section 10 we read: Ad hoc autem quod sit per se notum, oportet quod nobis sit cognita ratio subjecti in qua concluditur praedicatum. In Thomas' discussion, too, something like a predicate appears, just as it does in the Kantian thesis that being is not a real predicate. "For something to be known in itself, to be intelligible of itself, nothing else is required save that the predicate which is asserted of the being in question is de ratione subjecti, from the concept of the subject." Ratio is equivalent in meaning to essentia or natura or, as we shall see, reality. In this case the subject cannot be thought without that which appears in the predicate. But in order for us to have such a cognition, which Kant later called an analytic cognition, that is to say, in order for us to be able to infer a thing's characteristics immediately from its essence, it is necessary that the ratio subjecti, the concept of the thing, should be known to us. For the proof of God's existence this implies that the concept of God, his whole essence, must be discernible to us. Sed quia quidditas Dei non est nobis nota, ideo quoad nos Deum esse non est per se notum, sed indiget demonstratione. Ideo nobis necessarium est, ad hoc cognoscendum, demonstrationes habere ex effectibus sumptas. But since the quidditas, what God is, his whatness, his essence, is not known to us, since with respect to us God is not transparent in his essence, but requires proof based on the experience of what he has created, therefore, the demonstration of God's existence from his concept lacks adequate grounding of the starting-point of the proof, namely, the concept.

According to Thomas the ontological proof is impossible because, starting out from ourselves, we are not in a position to expound the pure concept of God so as to demonstrate from it the necessity of his existence. We shall see that it is at a different place that Kant tackles the ontological proof critically, attacks its real nerve, and thus first really unhinges it.

In order to discern more clearly this place in the ontological proof on which the Kantian *Critique* makes its assault, we shall give to this proof the formal shape of a syllogism.

> Major premise: God, by his concept, is the most perfect being.
> Minor premise: Existence belongs to the concept of the most perfect being.
> Conclusion: Therefore God exists.

Now Kant does not dispute that by his concept God is the most perfect being, nor does he contest the existence of God. With regard to the form of the syllogism, this means that Kant leaves undisturbed the major premise and the conclusion. If he nevertheless attacks the proof, the attack can bear only upon the minor premise, which says that existence belongs to the concept of the most perfect being. The thesis of Kant, whose phenomenological interpretation we are taking as our theme, is nothing but the fundamental denial of the possibility of the assertion laid down in the minor premise of the ontological proof. Kant's thesis that being or existence is not a real predicate does not assert merely that existence cannot belong to the concept of the most perfect being or that we cannot know it to belong to that concept (Thomas). It goes further. It says, fundamentally, that something like existence does not belong to the determinateness of a concept at all.

We must first show how Kant argues for his thesis. In this way it will become clear of itself how he explicates the concept of existence in our sense of extantness.

The first section of the *Beweisgrund* divides into four disquisitions, the first of which is "On existence in general." It discusses three theses or questions: (1) "Existence is not a predicate or determination of any thing at all"; (2) "Existence is the absolute position of a thing and thereby differs from any sort of predicate, which, as such, is posited at each time merely relatively to another thing"; (3) "Can I really say that there is more in existence than in mere possibility?"

The first proposition, "Existence is not a predicate or determination of any thing at all," is a negative characterization of the nature of existence. The second proposition gives a positive definition of the ontological sense of existence—existence equals absolute position. The question enunciated in the third place takes a stand toward a contemporary explication of the concept of existence, such as was given by Wolff or his school, according to which existence signifies *complementum possibilitatis*: the actuality of a thing, or its existence, is the complement of its possibility.

A more concise treatment of the same thesis is to be found in the *Critique of Pure Reason.*[2] The first proposition from the *Beweisgrund* coincides with the proposition in the *Critique* which we chose as a formulation of the first thesis and which reads in full as follows: "Being is manifestly not a real predicate, that is, a concept of something that could be added to the concept of a thing." This proposition is followed by another, which defines the nature of being or existence positively and likewise coincides with the second proposition of the *Beweisgrund*. Being "is merely the position of a thing or of certain determinations in themselves." No distinction is made to begin with between being in general and existence.

First of all, what is meant by the *negative thesis* that being is not a real predicate or, as Kant also says, that being is not at all a predicate of a thing? That being is not a *real* predicate signifies that it is not a predicate of a *res*. It is not a predicate at all, but mere position. Can we say that existence is not a predicate at all? Predicate means that which is asserted in an assertion (judgment). But then existence is surely asserted when I say "God exists" or, in our terminology, "The mountain is extant." Being extant and existing are certainly *asserted* here. This *seems* to be the case and Kant himself stresses it. "This statement [Existence is not at all a predicate of any thing whatsoever] seems strange and paradoxical, yet it is undoubtedly certain."[3]

What about the question whether existence is or is not asserted, is or is not a predicate? How does Kant define the nature of predication? According to him the formal concept of assertion is the combining of something with something. The basic action of the understanding, according to him, is the "I combine." This characterization of the nature of assertion is a purely formal definition or, as Kant also says, a formal-logical characterization, in which abstraction is made from *what* it is that is combined with something else. Each predicate is always something determinate, material. Formal logic thematizes only the form of predication in general, relation, combination, separation. As we say, abstraction is made in it from any real content the predicate may have, and similarly with the subject. It is a logical char-

---

2. Kant, *Critique of Pure Reason,* B626 ff. [The text's note here cites R. Schmidt as editor and F. Meiner as publisher.]

3. Kant, *Beweisgrund,* in *Immanuel Kants Werke,* ed. Ernst Cassirer, vol. 2, p. 76. [*Der einzig mögliche Beweisgrund zu einer Demonstration des Daseins Gottes* (The sole possible argument for a demonstration of God's existence). This work appears in volume 2 of the Cassirer edition. It may be found also in volume 2 of the Academy edition: *Gesammelte Schriften,* begun in 1902 by the Prussian Academy of Sciences and continued by the German Academy of Sciences, Berlin, and the Academy of Sciences, Göttingen, 28 vols. in 32 (Berlin and New York: W. de Gruyter, 1978–); this is a critical edition.]

acterization of assertion with regard to its emptiest form, that is to say, formally, as a relating of something to something or as a combining of the two.

If we orient ourselves in this way toward the formal-logical concept of predication and the predicate, we cannot yet decide whether existence is a predicate. For existence has a specific content; it says something. Therefore, we must ask more precisely: Is existence a real predicate or, as Kant says more concisely, a *determination?* A determination, he says, is a predicate that is added to the concept of the subject from *beyond* it and thus enlarges it. The determination, the predicate, must not already be contained in the concept. A determination is a real predicate that enlarges the thing, the Sache, res, in its content. This concept of the real and of reality must be held in mind from the beginning if we wish to understand correctly Kant's thesis that existence is not a real predicate, not a determination of the real content of a thing. The concept of reality and the real in Kant does not have the meaning most often intended nowadays when we speak of the reality of the external world or of epistemological realism. Reality is not equivalent to actuality, existence, or extantness. It is not identical with existence, although Kant indeed uses the concept "objective reality" identically with existence.

The Kantian meaning of the term "reality" is the one that is appropriate to the literal sense of the word. In one place Kant translates "reality" very fittingly by "thingness," "thing-determinateness."[4] The real is what pertains to the res. When Kant talks about the omnitudo realitatis, the totality of all realities, he means not the whole of all beings actually extant but, just the reverse, the whole of all possible thing-determinations, the whole of all thing-contents or real-contents, essences, possible things. Accordingly, realitas is synonymous with Leibniz' term possibilitas, possibility. Realities are the what-contents of possible things in general, without regard to whether or not they are actual, or "real" in our modern sense. The concept of reality is equivalent to the concept of the Platonic idea as that pertaining to a being which is understood when I ask: Ti esti, *what* is the being? The what-

---

4. *Critique of Pure Reason,* B182. [Kant's terms are Sachheit, Sachbestimmtheit. Sache and its derivatives are hardly translatable by a single English equivalent throughout. Sache itself is close to the English word "thing," but ranges widely in a very general way: object, cause, legal case, matter, affair, fact, etc. Later in his career Heidegger wrote about "die Sache des Denkens," "the matter of thought," "thinking's thing." Often Sache has the sense of the essential thing, and in Heidegger's interpretation it becomes linked with the medieval concept of res, where realitas is to res as Sachheit is to Sache: the essence to the being whose essence it is. Because of this manner of association, the adjectival form, sachlich, whose literal translation, thingly, could be significant but would hardly be understood, is rendered most frequently as inherent or intrinsic. Its use in other contexts would be closer to senses like essential, material, pertinent, to the point, objective.]

content of the thing, which Scholasticism called the res, then gives me the answer. Kant's terminology relates directly to the usage of Baumgarten, a disciple of Wolff. Kant often took as text for his lectures Baumgarten's compendium of metaphysics, that is, of ontology, and he accordingly adopted its terminology.

In discussing the Kantian thesis and also in dealing with Kant in other matters, we should not hesitate to concern ourselves with terminological points down even to a certain degree of fussiness about detail. For it is exactly in Kant that concepts are clearly defined and determined with a sharpness that undoubtedly no philosophy ever reached before or after him, although this does not imply that the real contents of the concepts and what is therewith intended by them correspond radically in every respect to the interpretation. Precisely with regard to the expression "reality," understanding Kant's thesis and his position is hopeless unless the terminological sense of this expression, which traces back to Scholasticism and antiquity, has been clarified. The immediate source for the term is Baumgarten, who was not only influenced by Leibniz and Descartes, but derives directly from Scholasticism. This connection of Kant with Baumgarten will be treated with regard to other problems that become thematic in these lectures.

In the section in which he defines ens, that which *is* in general, Baumgarten says: Quod aut ponitur esse A, aut ponitur non esse A, determinatur;[5] "that which is posited as being A or is posited as being not-A is determined." The A thus posited is a determinatio. Kant speaks of the determination that is added to the what of a thing, to the res. Determination, determinatio, means the determinant of a res; it is a real predicate. Hence Baumgarten says: Quae determinando ponuntur in aliquo, (notae et praedicata) sunt determinationes;[6] "what is posited in any thing in the way of determining (marks and predicates) is a determination." When Kant says that existence is not a determination, this expression is not arbitrary but is terminologically defined: determinatio. These determinations, determinationes, can be twofold. Altera positiva, et affirmativa, quae si vere sit, est realitas, altera negativa, quae si vere sit, est negatio;[7] "the determinant which posits positively or affirmatively is, if the affirmation is correct, a reality; the other, negative, determination, if it is correct, is a negation." Accordingly, reality is the real determination, determinatio, that has real content and is the correct one,

---

5. Baumgarten, *Metaphysica* (1743), §34. [*Metaphysica Alexandri Baumgarten*, Halae Magdeburicae, impensis C. H. Hemmerde (1st ed., 1739; 3rd ed., 1763; reprint of 3rd ed., Hildesheim: G. Olms, 1963). Alexander Gottlieb Baumgarten (1714–1762) is the most important representative of the school of Leibniz-Wolff, whose writings Kant used as texts for courses.]

6. Ibid., §36.

7. Ibid.

belonging to the thing, res, itself, to its concept. The opposite of reality is negation.

Kant not only adheres to these definitions in his pre-critical period but continues to do so in his *Critique of Pure Reason*. Thus he speaks of the concept of a thing and puts in brackets "of a real," which does not mean of an actual.[8] For reality means the affirmatively posited predicate having real content. Every predicate is at bottom a real predicate. Therefore Kant's thesis reads: Being is not a real predicate, that is, being in general is not a predicate of any thing at all. It is from the table of judgments that Kant derives the table of categories to which reality as well as existence belongs. Viewed formally, judgments are combinations of subject and predicate. All combining comes about in each instance in regard to a possible unity. In every uniting the idea of a unity is entertained, even if it is not also thematically realized. The different possible forms of the unity that is had in mind in judging, in uniting these possible respects or contents of the respects for judgmental combination, are the categories. This is the logical concept of the category in Kant. It arises out of a purely phenomenological analysis if we merely follow out what Kant means. The category is not a kind of form with which any pre-given material is molded. A category represents the idea of unity with regard to judgmental union; the categories are the possible forms of unity of combination. If the table of judgments, or the sum total of all possible forms of union, is given to me, then I can read off from this table the idea of unity presupposed in each form of judgment; thus from it I can deduce the table of categories. Kant here makes the presupposition that the table of judgments is intrinsically certain and valid, which is surely questionable. The categories are forms of unity of the possible unions in judgment. Reality belongs to these forms of unity as does also existence. We can infer clearly the disparity between these two categories, reality and existence, from their belonging to entirely different classes of categories. Reality belongs among the categories of quality. Existence or actuality belongs, in contrast, among the categories of modality. Reality is a category of quality. By quality Kant refers to that character of judgmental positing which indicates whether a predicate is ascribed to a subject, whether it is affirmed of the subject or opposed to it, that is, denied

---

8. *Critique of Pure Reason,* B286. [The passage in the *Kritik* actually reads: "Da sie aber gleichwohl doch immer synthetisch sind, so sind es es nur subjektiv, d.i., sie fügen zu dem Begriffe eines Dinges (Realen,) von dem sie sonst nichts sagen." The noun "Realen" appears in B instead of the adjective "realen" of A. In his translation, Norman Kemp Smith renders the passage thus: "But since they are none the less synthetic, they are so subjectively only, that is, they add to the concept of a thing (of something real), of which otherwise they say nothing." Heidegger prefers the shift from the phrase "of a real thing" to the phrase "of a real," where "real" is now a substantive on its own account, although we must presume from the construction that it is still a *Ding* about which Kant is talking.]

of it. Reality is accordingly the form of unity of the affirming, affirmative, positing, positive judgment. This is precisely the definition that Baumgarten gives of reality. In contrast, existence, or actuality, belongs to the class of categories of modality. Modality expresses the attitude of the cognizing subject to that which is judged in the judgment. The concept complementary to existence or actuality is not negation, as in the case of reality, but either possibility or necessity. As a category, existence corresponds to the assertoric judgment, which is simply assertive, whether positive or negative. The expression "reality" functions in the already defined sense of real content *["thing-", "res-," what-content]*, also in the term which traditional ontology often used to refer to God—ens realissimum or, as Kant always says, the most real of all beings *[allerrealstes Wesen]*. This expression signifies, not something actual with the highest degree of actuality, but the being with the greatest possible real contents, the being lacking no positive reality, no real determination, or, in Anselm of Canterbury's formulation, aliquid quo maius cogitari non potest.[9]

The Kantian concept of *objective reality*, which is identical with actuality, must be distinguished from the concept of reality as thus elucidated. The realness or being-something that is fulfilled in the object thought in it, in its object, is called objective reality. That is to say, it is the reality exhibited in the experienced entity as an actual existent entity. In reference to objective reality and reality in general, Kant says: "As regards reality, we obviously cannot think it in concreto without calling experience to our aid. For reality can only relate to sensation as material of experience and is not concerned with the form of the relationship, whereas, if we so chose, this form could be made subject to a play of fictions."[10] Kant here separates objective reality as actuality from possibility. If I devise or invent some possible thing, then in doing so I am occupied with this imagined thing's pure relationships having real content, though without thinking of this object with these relations as being actual, presently existent. In retrospect, this use of reality occurs also in Descartes. Descartes says, for instance, that error, and in general everything that has negative value, everything malum, non esse quid reale, is not real.[11] This does not mean that error does not actually exist; instead, error is surely actual, but it and everything evil and bad is not a res in the sense that it would be an independent real content for itself.

---

9. Anselm of Canterbury, *Proslogion*, chap. 3. [A recent and accessible translation of this work is *St. Anselm's Proslogion*, with a reply on behalf of the fool by Gaunilon and the author's reply to Gaunilon, trans. with an introduction and philosophical commentary by M. J. Charlesworth, with Latin texts (Oxford and London: Clarendon Press, 1965).]

10. *Critique of Pure Reason*, B270.

11. Descartes, *Meditationes de prima philosophia*, Latin-German edition (Felix Meiner, 1959), Meditation 4, p. 100.

It is always only derivative and it *is* only by means of the negation of an independent real content, by the negation of the good. Similarly in the proof for God's existence in the third meditation, when he is speaking of realitas objectiva and realitas actualis, Descartes here, too, takes reality in the sense mentioned above—the sense of realness or res-ness, German Sachheit—equivalent to the Scholastic quidditas /whatness, something-ness/. Realitas objectiva is not identical with the Kantian objective reality but just the opposite. In Descartes realitas objectiva means, following Scho-lasticism, the objectified what, which is held over against me only in pure representation, the essence of a thing. Realitas objectiva equals possibility, possibilitas. In contrast, what corresponds to the Kantian concept of objec-tive reality, or actuality, is the Cartesian and Scholastic concept of realitas actualis—the what which is actualized (actu). This noteworthy distinction between the Cartesian concept of realitas objectiva as tantamount to sub-jectively represented possibility and the Kantian concept of objective reality, or that which is in itself, is connected with the fact that the concept of the objective was turned into its exact opposite during this period. The objec-tive, namely, that which is merely held over against me, is in Kantian and modern language the subjective. What Kant calls the subjective is for the Scholastics that which lies at the basis, hupokeimenon, the objective, thus corresponding to the literal sense of the expression "subject."

Kant says that existence is not a reality. This means that it is not a determination of the concept of a thing relating to its real content or, as he says succinctly, not a predicate of the thing itself.[12] "A hundred actual thalers contain not the least bit more than a hundred possible thalers."[13] A hundred possible thalers and a hundred actual thalers do not differ in their reality. Everything gets confused if we do not keep in mind Kant's concept "reality" but alter its meaning so as to give it the modern sense of actuality. It could then be said that a hundred possible thalers and a hundred actual thalers are after all indubitably different with regard to their reality, for the actual thalers are precisely actual, whereas the possible thalers have no reality in the non-Kantian sense. In contrast, Kant says in his own language that a hundred possible thalers and a hundred actual thalers do not differ in their *reality.* The what-content of the concept "a hundred possible thalers" coincides with that of the concept "a hundred actual thalers." No more thalers are thought in the concept "a hundred actual thalers," no greater reality, but exactly the same amount. What is possible is also the same thing actually as far as its what-content is concerned; the what-content, the reality, of the possible and the actual thing must be the same. "When therefore I

---

12. *Beweisgrund,* p. 76.
13. *Critique of Pure Reason,* B627.

think of a thing, by whatever and by however many predicates I please (even in an exhaustive determination of it), nevertheless my proceeding further to think that this thing *is* [exists] makes not the least addition to the thing [that is, to the res]. For, otherwise, what would exist would be not exactly the same but more than I had thought in the concept, and I could not say that the exact object of my concept exists."[14]

On the other hand, the fact nevertheless remains that this "exists"—a thing exists—occurs as a predicate in common linguistic usage.[15] What is more, the expression "is" in the broadest sense is involved in every predication, even when I do not posit as existent that about which I am judging and predicating, even when I merely say "Body, by its very nature, is extended"—whether a body exists or not. Here I am also using an "is," the "is" in the sense of the copula, which is distinct from the "is" when I say "God is," that is, "God exists." Being as copula, as linking concept, and being in the sense of existence must consequently be distinguished.

How does Kant explain this distinction? If being or existence is not a real predicate, then *how can being be determined positively* and how does the concept of existence differ from the concept of being in general? Kant says: "The concept of position is utterly simple and is one and the same as the concept of being. Now something can be thought as posited merely relatively, or, better, we can think merely the relation (respectus logicus) of something as a mark to a thing, and then being, that is, the position of this relation ["A is B"], is nothing but the combining concept in a judgment. If what is had in view is not merely this relation [that is, if being and "is" are used not merely in the sense of the copula, "A is B"] but instead the thing is posited in and for itself, then this being is tantamount to existence [that is, Vorhandensein]."[16] Existence "is thereby also distinguished from every predicate, which qua predicate is always posited merely relatively to another thing."[17] Being in general is one and the same as position in general. In this sense Kant speaks of the mere positions (realities) of a thing, which constitute its concept, that is, its possibility, and which must not be mutually contradictory, since the principle of contradiction (non-contradiction) is the criterion of logical possibilities.[18] By its very concept, every predicate is always posited merely relatively. When, on the other hand, I say "Something exists," in this positing I am not making a relational reference to any other thing or to some other characteristic of a thing, to some other real being; instead, I am here positing the thing in and for itself, free of relation; I am

14. Ibid., B628.
15. *Beweisgrund*, p. 76.
16. Ibid., p. 77.
17. Ibid.
18. *Critique of Pure Reason*, B630.

positing here without relation, non-relatively, absolutely. In the proposition
"A exists," an absolute positing is involved. Being qua existence must not
be confused with being in the sense of "mere position" (being something).
Whereas in the *Beweisgrund* (p. 77) Kant characterizes existence as absolute
position, he says in the *Critique:* "It is merely the position of a thing, or of
certain determinations in themselves. In logical use it is merely the copula
of a judgment."[19] Existence is not "mere position." When Kant says that
it is *merely* position, this limitation holds with regard to the fact that it is
not a real predicate. In this context "merely" means "not relatively." Being
is not a real predicate either in the sense of "mere position" or in that of
"absolute position." In the passages cited, Kant defines the meaning of being
as position only with regard to being qua existence. He is elucidating the
concept of absolute position in the context of the problem of the proof of
God's existence.

The preliminary interpretation of being as "mere position" and of existence as "absolute position" should be kept in mind. In the citation from
Baumgarten the expression ponitur, position, also appeared. For the real,
too, the mere what of a thing, is posited in the pure representing of the
thing as in a certain way in itself. But this positing is merely the positing
of the possible, "mere position." In one place Kant says that "as possibility
was . . . merely a position of the thing in relation to the understanding, so
actuality [existence] is at the same time a combining of it [the thing] with
perception."[20] Actuality, existence, is absolute position; possibility, in
contrast, is mere position. "The proposition 'God is omnipotent' contains
two concepts, each of which has its object: God and omnipotence; the little
word 'is' is not, in addition, a predicate but only posits the predicate *relatively*
to the subject."[21] In this positing of "is," of mere position, nothing is asserted
about existence. Kant says: "Hence also this being [of the copula] is used
quite correctly even in the case of the relations which impossible things have to
each other,"[22] as when, for example, I say "The circle is square." "If
now I take the subject (God) together with all of its predicates (among which is
omnipotence) and I say 'God is,' or 'There is a God,' then I am not positing
a new predicate as added to the concept of God; rather, I am positing only
the subject in itself with all its predicates, and indeed I am positing [now
absolute position is more precisely discussed] the object [by this Kant means
the actual being] in relation to my concept."[23] The object, the actual existent
entity corresponding to the concept, is added synthetically to my concept

19. Ibid., B626.
20. Ibid., B287 n.; see also *Beweisgrund,* p. 79.
21. *Critique of Pure Reason,* B626–627.
22. *Beweisgrund,* p. 78.
23. *Critique of Pure Reason,* B627.

in the assertion "God exists," without my concept being in the least aug-
mented by this being [Sein], this existence outside my concept. It follows
that in the existential assertion, "God exists," "A exists," a synthesis is also
involved, and exactly so, that is, a positing of a relation; but it has an essentially different character from the synthesis of predication, "A is B." The
synthesis of existential assertion does not concern real characteristics of the
thing and their relationships; rather, what is posited in existential assertion
and is added to the mere representation, to the concept, is "a relation of the
actual thing to my own self." The relation that is posited is that of the entire
conceptual content, the full reality of the concept, to the object of the concept. The thing intended in the concept is posited absolutely in and for
itself. Predicative synthesis operates with real relationships. Existential synthesis concerns the whole of these real relationships in their relation to their
object. This object is posited absolutely. In positing existence we have to go
outside the concept. The relation of the concept to the object, to the actual
being, is what gets added, or ap-posited, synthetically to the concept.

In positing an actual, existent thing, I can ask two questions, according
to Kant: *What* is posited and *how* is it posited?[24] To the question *What* is
posited? the answer is, Nothing more and nothing other than in the positing
of a possible thing, indeed exactly the same what-content, as the example
of the thalers shows. But I can also ask: *How* is it posited? It must then be
said that certainly by actuality something *more* is posited.[25] Kant sums up
the difference in brief. "Nothing more is posited in an existent than in
something merely possible (for in this case we are speaking of its predicates);
but more is posited by an existent than by something merely possible, for
this [existent] also goes to the absolute position of the thing itself."[26]

In this way the concept of existence is explained or indicated by Kant in
the sense of absolute position, and from it something like existence, or
being in general, can be elucidated. The relation posited in absolute position
is the relation of the existent object itself to its concept. But if, according
to Kant, existence occurs "in common linguistic usage" as a predicate, so
that here there is a fact controverting Kant's thesis that existence is not a
predicate, it is not so much a predicate of the thing itself, says Kant, as
rather of the thought we have, in the first instance, of the thing. "For
example, existence belongs to the sea-unicorn [narwhal]." This means, according to Kant, that "the idea of the sea-unicorn is an experiential concept,
the idea of an existent thing."[27] "God exists" would mean, more precisely

---

24. *Beweisgrund*, p. 79.
25. Ibid.
26. Ibid., p. 80.
27. Ibid., pp. 76–77.

expressed, "Something existing is God."[28] Kant wishes to indicate by this conversion of the proposition that existence is thought not in the predicate of the proposition but in its subject.

Application of this explanation of his thesis to the possibility of the ontological proof of God's existence follows of itself. Existence in general is not a real predicate and thus essentially cannot belong to the concept of a thing; therefore, on the strength of thinking the pure conceptual content, I can never be assured of the existence of what is thought in the concept, unless I already co-posit and presup-pose the thing's actuality in its concept; but then, says Kant, this alleged proof is nothing but a miserable tautology.[29]

Kant attacks the minor premise in the ontological argument. He assails this premise fundamentally by saying that existence does not at all belong to the concept of a thing. Exactly what Kant calls in question—that existence might be a real predicate—is self-evidently certain according to Thomas. Except that Thomas finds another difficulty: we are not in a position to know this belonging of the predicate of existence to God's essence along with other determinations so perspicuously that we could derive from it a proof of the actual existence of the object thought. The Thomistic refutation has regard to the incompetence and finiteness of our understanding, whereas the Kantian refutation is fundamental, relating to what the proof lays claim to in its minor premise, which is the pivot of any syllogism.

What interests us here is not the problem of the proof of God's existence but the Kantian explication of the concept of being or of the concept of existence: being equals position, existence equals absolute position. We are not at all asking yet whether this interpretation of the meaning of being and existence is tenable but solely whether the explication Kant gives of the concept of existence is satisfactory. Kant himself stresses in one place the "this concept [existence, being] is so simple that nothing can be said in explication of it, except to take careful note that it must not be confused with the relationships things have with their distinctive marks."[30] Obviously, this can only mean that the concept of being and existence is indeed to be protected from confusion, that it is delimitable negatively but is accessible positively only directly in a simple understanding. For us the question arises whether we can push this understanding of being and existence—being equals position—still further in the direction of Kant's account. Can we reach a greater degree of clarity within the Kantian approach itself? Can it be shown that the Kantian explanation does not really have the clarity it

28. Ibid., p. 79.
29. *Critique of Pure Reason*, B625.
30. *Beweisgrund*, pp. 77-78.

claims? Does the thesis that being equals position, existence equals absolute position, perhaps lead us into the dark?

§8. *Phenomenological analysis of the explanation of the concept of being or of existence given by Kant*

a) Being (existence /Dasein, Existenz, Vorhandensein/), absolute position, and perception

We have made clear to ourselves the content of the Kantian thesis according to which being, or existence, is not a real predicate. At the center of the explanation of this thesis stood the definition of the concept *reality.* Definition of this concept is all the more necessary as the contemporary philosophical concept of this term is different from the Kantian, which on its part agrees with the whole of the antecedent tradition. In conformity with that tradition, reality means for Kant the same as Sachheit /literally thinghood, taking "thing" in the sense of res/. That is real which belongs to a res, to a thing in the sense of a Sache, to its inherent or essential content, its whatness. To the thing "house" belong its foundation wall, roof, door, size, extension, color—real predicates or determinations, real determinations of the thing "house," regardless of whether it is actually existent or not. Now Kant says, the actuality of something actual, the existence of an existent, is not a real predicate. A hundred thalers do not differ in their what-contents whether they be a hundred possible or a hundred actual thalers. Actuality does not affect the *what,* the reality, but the *how* of the being, whether possible or actual. Nevertheless, we still say that the house exists or, in our terminology, is extant. We ascribe to this thing something like existence. The question arises, What sort of determination then is existence and actuality? Negatively, Kant says that actuality is not a real determination. As we shall see later, the meaning of this negative proposition is that actuality, existence, is not itself anything actual or existent; being is not itself a being.

But how does Kant define the meaning of existence *positively?* He makes existence equivalent to absolute position, and he identifies being with position in general. Kant himself undertook this investigation only for the purpose of clearing up the concept of existence, with a view to the possibility of the ontological proof of God's existence. When he says that existence is not a real predicate, he therewith denies the possible meaning of the minor premise of the ontological argument: existence belongs to God's essence, that is, to his reality. But if the possibility of this minor premise is shaken in principle, the entire proof is therewith shown to be impossible. It is not the question of the proofs of God's existence that interests us here but the

problem of the interpretation of being. We ask, How is the Kantian interpretation—being equals position, existence equals absolute position—to be
understood? Is it valid? What does a more detailed rational argument for
this interpretation demand? We shall attempt a phenomenological analysis
of the explanation Kant gives of the concepts of being and existence.

There is a methodological maxim which seems to be opposed to our
attempt to press still further in the interpretation of the concept of being
and accordingly to clarify even the Kantian clarification itself—exactly the
maxim with which Kant prefaced his explication of the concept of being.
As opposed to the exaggerated rage for method which proves everything
and in the end proves nothing, Kant wants to take as his methodological
principle "caution" in the explication and analysis of concepts; he does not
wish to begin with a "formal definition" that already decides "what the fully
determinate concept [of existence] is supposed to consist in."[1] Instead he
wants to assure himself beforehand about "what can be said with certainty,
affirmatively or negatively, about the object of the definition,"[2] for "as regards the flattering idea we have of ourselves that with greater clear-sight-
edness we shall have better success than others, we understand quite well
that all those who have wanted to draw us from an alien error into their
own error have always talked in this way."[3] Kant nevertheless does not
exempt himself from the task of clarifying the concept of existence. He
says—to be sure, with a certain fussy circumstantiality characteristic of
him—"I am concerned about becoming unintelligible because of a too long-
winded discussion of such a simple idea [as that of being]. I could also be
fearful of offending the delicacy of those who complain essentially about
dullness. But without holding this fault to be a trifling thing, I must insist
on permission to be guilty of it this time. For although I have as little taste
as anyone else for the superfine wisdom of those who heat up, distil, and
refine assured and useful concepts in their logical smelting furnaces for such
a long time that they evaporate into gases and volatile salts, still the object
of contemplation I have before me is of such a sort that either we have to
give up completely ever attaining to a demonstrative certainty about it or
else we must put up with dissolving our concepts into these atoms."[4] Kant
points expressly to the fact that the whole of our knowledge ultimately leads
to unanalyzable concepts. "When we see that the whole of our knowledge
finally ends in unanalyzable concepts, we also realize that there will be some
that are well-nigh unanalyzable, that is, where the marks are only very little
clearer and simpler than the thing itself. This is the case with our definition

---

1. *Beweisgrund,* p. 75.
2. Ibid.
3. Ibid.
4. Ibid., p. 79.

of existence. I admit readily that the definition of the concept clarifies it only in a very small degree. However, the nature of the object in relation to our understanding's capacities likewise does not allow of any higher degree."[5] From this admission by Kant it appears as though the clarification of being and existence in fact cannot be pushed farther than the characterization: being equals position, existence equals absolute position. Therefore, we too shall not at first attempt to do any better than Kant. Rather, we shall stay with Kant's explication, with what he hit upon, and ask merely whether, in fact, intrinsically and regardless of any other standard, it affords "no higher degree" of clarity.

Is this clarification, being equals position, crystal clear in every respect? Does everything stand in the clear, or does it stand in the dark as a result of the statement that being equals position? Does not everything lapse into indeterminateness? What does "position" mean? What can this expression signify? We shall first attempt to gain from Kant himself a clarification of this definition of the concept, and then we shall ask whether the phenomena thus drawn on for the purposes of clarification are themselves clearly transparent and whether the explication itself is specified with respect to its methodical character and is well founded in its right and in its necessity.

We saw that there is also a synthesis present in the experience of an existent, even though it is not the synthesis of predication, of the addition of a predicate to a subject. In the proposition "A is B," B is a real predicate adjoined to A. In contrast, in the statement "A exists," A is posited absolutely, and indeed with the sum total of its real determinations B, C, D, and so forth. This positing is added to A, but not in the way B is added to A in the previous example. What is this added position? Plainly it is itself a relation, although not a real-relationship, not a thing-relationship, within the real determinations of the thing, of A, but the reference of the whole thing (A) to my thought of the thing. By means of this reference what is thus posited comes into relation to my ego-state. Since the A, which is at first merely thought, already stands in relation to me in this thought-reference of mere thought, plainly this mere thought-reference, the mere representing of A, becomes different due to the addition of the absolute positing. In absolute position the object of the concept, the actual being corresponding to it, is put into relation, as actual, to the concept that is merely thought.

Existence consequently expresses a relationship of the object to the cognitive faculty. At the beginning of the explanation of the "postulates of empirical thinking in general" Kant says: "The categories of modality [possibility, actuality, necessity] have in themselves the peculiarity that they do not in the least augment the concept to which they are attached as

---

5. Ibid., p. 78.

predicates, by determining its object, but express only the relationship [of the object] to the faculty of knowledge."[6] In contrast, real predicates express the real relationships immanent in the thing. Possibility expresses the relationship of the object with all its determinations, that is, of the entire reality, to the understanding, to mere thinking. Actuality, that is, existence, expresses the relationship to the empirical use of the understanding or, as Kant also says, to the empirical faculty of judgment. Necessity expresses the relationship of the object to reason in its application to experience.

We restrict ourselves to defining in further detail the relationship of the object to the empirical use of understanding expressed by actuality. Actuality, existence, according to Kant, has to do "only with the question whether such a thing [as we can think it solely according to its possibility] is given to us in such a way that the perception of it can possibly precede the concept."[7] "The perception, however, which supplies the material to the concept is the sole character of actuality."[8] "Our knowledge of the existence of things, therefore, reaches also up to the point where perception and what is attached to it according to empirical laws reach."[9] It is perception which intrinsically bears within itself the reach to the actuality, the existence or, in our terminology, the extantness, of things. Thus the *specific character of absolute position*, as Kant defines it, reveals itself as *perception*. Actuality, possibility, necessity—which can be called predicates only in an improper sense—are not real-synthetic; they are, as Kant says, "merely subjective." They "add to the concept of a thing (of something real) . . . the faculty of knowledge."[10] The predicate of actuality adds perception to the concept of a thing. Kant thus says in short: actuality, existence, equals absolute position equals perception.

But what is it supposed to mean when we say that in apprehending the thing as existent the faculty of knowledge, or perception, is added to it? For example, I think of a window with all its attributes. I represent something of the sort. In mere representation I imagine a window. To what is thus represented I now add not further real predicates—the color of the frame,

---

6. *Critique of Pure Reason*, B266.

7. Ibid., B272–273.

8. Ibid., B273.

9. Ibid. [Norman Kemp Smith, with Emil Wille ("Neue Konjekturen zu *Kants Kritik der reinen Vernunft*," *Kant-Studien* 4 [1900]:450), reads Fortgang for Anhang. In his translation, Smith accordingly renders this sentence as: "Our knowledge of the existence of things reaches, then, only so far as perception and *its advance* according to empirical laws can extend." (Italics mine.) Heidegger retains Anhang, which (despite Wille's argument) makes sense, since the idea of the sentence is that perception, along with *whatever is connected with it* by empirical laws, is the decisive focus for the concept of actuality, whereas the notion of an "advance" according to empirical laws of perception introduces a strained concept out of keeping with the remainder of the passage.]

10. *Critique of Pure Reason*, B286.

the hardness of the glass—but something subjective, something taken from the subject, the faculty of knowledge, perception. Is this added perception or this addition of perception supposed to constitute the existence of the window? Kant says literally: "Perception . . . is the sole character of actuality."[11] How am I to provide something thought, the thing called "window," with a perception? What does adding a "subjective cognitive faculty" to an object mean? How should the existence of the object receive expression by this means? What is a window with a perception attached to it, a house furnished with an "absolute position"? Do any such structures exist? Can even the most powerful imagination conceive such a monstrosity as a window with a perception attached?

But perhaps, by this crude talk of adding my cognitive capacity, perception, to the thing, Kant means something else, even though his interpretation of existence provides no further explicit information about it. What does he basically mean and what alone can he mean? Plainly, only one thing. To say that the perception that belongs to the subject as its manner of comportment is added to the thing means the following: The subject brings itself perceivingly to the thing in a relation that is aware of and takes up this thing "in and for itself." The thing is posited in the relationship of cognition. In this perception the existent, the extant thing at hand, gives itself in its own self. The real exhibits itself as an actual entity.

But is the concept of existence elucidated by recourse to the perception that apprehends an existent? What gives Kant the authority to say—and he says this constantly—that existence equals absolute position equals perception, that perception and absolute position are the sole character of actuality?

b) Perceiving, perceived, perceivedness. Distinction between perceivedness and extantness of the extant

Something like existence is surely not a perception. Perception is itself something that *is,* a being, an action performed by the ego, something actual in the actual subject. This actual thing in the subject, perception, is surely not actuality, and this actual thing in the subject is not at all the actuality of the object. Perception as *perceiving* cannot be equated with existence. Perception is not existence; it is what perceives the existent, the extant, and relates itself to what is perceived. What is thus perceived in perception we also customarily call perception, for short. Perhaps Kant is taking the expression "perception," when he identifies actuality and perception, in the sense of the *perceived,* as when we say "The perception I had

---

11. Ibid., B273.

to have there was painful." Here I do not mean that the perception as an act of seeing caused me pain but that what I experienced, the perceived, oppressed me. Here we take perception not in the sense of the perceptual act but in that of the perceived, and we ask: Can perception in this sense be equated with existence, actuality? In this case it would itself be a being, something real. But the uncontested negative import of the Kantian thesis says that existence is not such a being. The Kantian thesis excludes equating actuality with the perceived actual entity.

It follows that existence is not equal to perception, either in the sense of perceiving or in that of the perceived. What remains then in the Kantian equation of perception with actuality (existence)?

Let us take another step in meeting Kant halfway and interpreting him favorably. Existence cannot be equated with the perceived existent, but it can quite well, perhaps, be equated with the *being-perceived* of the perceived, its *perceivedness*. It is not the existent, extant, window that is existence, extantness, but perhaps the window's being-extant is expressed in the factor of being-perceived, in consequence of which the thing is encountered by us as perceived, as uncovered, and so is accessible to us as extant by way of the perceiving. Perception in Kant's language would then mean the same thing as perceivedness, uncoveredness in perception. Kant himself says nothing on this matter, any more than he gives unambiguous information about whether he understands perception in the sense of the act of perceiving or in the sense of the perceived as object. Hence incontestably there is to begin with this one result: Kant's discussion of the concept of existence, actuality, as perception is in any case unclear and to that extent it is susceptible of a greater degree of clarity in comparison with his intention, especially since it can and must be decided whether perception should be understood here as perceiving or as perceived or as the perceivedness of the perceived, or whether indeed all three meanings are intended in their unity, and what this then means.

The obscurity present in the concept "perception" is found also in the more generally formulated interpretation Kant gives of being and existence when he equates being with position and existence with absolute position. In the sentences quoted from the *Beweisgrund,* Kant says: "The concept of position is . . . one and the same as that of being in general."[12] We ask, Does "position" mean *positing* as an action of the subject, or does it mean the *posited,* the object, or even the *positedness* of the posited object? Kant leaves this in the dark.

Suppose we overlook for the while this lack of clarity, so insupportable for a concept as fundamental as that of existence. Let us for the while adopt the interpretation of perception or of position most favorable to Kant and

---

12. *Beweisgrund,* p. 77.

identify existence with perceivedness or with positedness and, correspondingly, being in general with positedness in general. We then ask whether something is existent by virtue of its being perceived. Does the perceivedness of a being, of an existent, constitute its existence? Are existence, actuality, and perceivedness one and the same? The window, however, surely does not receive existence from my perceiving it, but just the reverse: I can perceive it only *if* it exists and *because* it exists. In every case, perceivedness presupposes perceivability, and perceivability on its part already requires the *existence* of the perceivable or the perceived being. Perception or absolute position is at most the *mode of access* to the existent, the extant; it is the way it is uncovered; uncoveredness, however, is not the extantness of the extant, the existence of the existent. This extantness, or existence, belongs to the extant, the existent, without its being uncovered. That alone is why it is uncoverable. Similarly, position in the sense of positedness is not the being of beings and one and the same with it; rather, it is at most the *how of the being apprehended* of something posited.

Thus the provisional analysis of the Kantian interpretation of existence yields a double result. First, not only is this interpretation unclear and thus in need of greater clarity, but, secondly, it is questionable even when given the most favorable reading, being equals perceivedness.

Are we to remain with this negative critical statement? A merely negative, carping criticism would be an unworthy undertaking against Kant and at the same time an unfruitful occupation with regard to the goal toward which we are striving. We wish to reach a positive explanation of the concepts of existence and being in general and to do it in such a way that we are not simply counterposing to Kant our own, and hence an alien, meaning. Rather, we wish to pursue Kant's own approach, the interpretation of being and existence, further in the direction of his own vision. In the end Kant is surely moving in the right direction in his attempt to clarify existence. But he does not see sufficiently clearly the horizon from which and within which he wants to carry through the elucidation because he did not assure himself of this horizon in advance and prepare it expressly for his explication. What follows from this we discuss in the next paragraph.

§9. Demonstration of the need for a more fundamental formulation of the problem of the thesis and of a more radical foundation of this problem

a) The inadequacy of psychology as a positive science for the ontological elucidation of perception

We ask, Is it an accident and a mere whim of Kant's that in attempting an elucidation of being, existence, actuality, he resorts to things like position and perception? In what direction is he looking in following this course? Whence does he get the marks of the concepts of existence that provide clarification here? Whence does something like position derive? What is it in the source that is necessarily conceived as making something like position possible? Did Kant himself adequately define these conditions of the possibility of position in general and thus clarify the essential nature of position and place what is thus clarified—being, actuality—itself in the light?

We saw that the perceivedness, uncoveredness, of the existent is not the same as the existence of the existent. But in every uncovering of the existent it is uncovered as existent, in its existence. Accordingly, in the perceivedness, or the uncoveredness, of something existent, existence is somehow disclosed, or uncovered, along with it. Being, to be sure, is not identical with positedness, but positedness is the how in which the positing of an entity assures itself of the being of this posited entity. Perhaps from sufficient analysis of perceivedness and positedness the being, or the actuality, discovered in them and its meaning can be elucidated. If we succeed, therefore, in elucidating perception and absolute positing in all their essential structures as the uncovering of things existent, then it must also be possible to meet with existence, extantness and the like along the way. The question arises, How can we attain an adequate determination of the phenomena of perception and position, which Kant draws on for the clarification of actuality and existence? We have shown that the concepts with which Kant tries to elucidate the concepts of being and existence are themselves in need of elucidation, for one thing because the concepts of perception and position are ambiguous and it is still undecided in which sense Kant takes them or the thing meant by them, and for another because even on the most favorable interpretation it is doubtful whether being can really be interpreted as position, or existence as perception. These phenomena, perception and position, are themselves in need of elucidation and it is a question how this is to be achieved. Plainly, by recourse to what makes perception, position, and similar cognitive powers possible, what lies at the basis of perception, position, what determines them as comportments of the being to whom they belong.

According to Kant all thinking, all positing, is an I-think. The ego and its states, its behaviors, what is generally called the psychical, require a preliminary clarification. The reason for the deficiency of the Kantian explication of concepts regarding existence apparently lies open to view: Kant is still working with a very crude psychology. It might be supposed that, had he had the possibility that exists today of investigating perception exactly and, instead of operating with empty acuteness and dualistic conceptual constructions, had he placed himself on a factual basis, then he, too, might have drawn from that a different insight into the essential nature of existence.

But what about this call for a scientific psychology based on facts as foundation for the Kantian problem—and this means by implication for every philosophical problem? We must briefly discuss whether psychology is in a position fundamentally, and not just in this or that direction of its work, to prepare the soil for the Kantian problem and to provide the means for its solution.

Psychology takes its stand on the basis of facts; it rightly lays claim to this as its advantage. As an exact inductive investigation of facts, it has its model in mathematical physics and chemistry. It is a positive science of a specific being, a science which also took mathematical physics as the prototype of science during its historical development, particularly in the nineteenth century. In all its tendencies, which diverge almost solely in terminology, whether it be Gestalt psychology or developmental psychology or the psychology of thinking or eidetics, contemporary psychology says: Today we are beyond the naturalism of the previous century and the previous decades. The object of psychology for us now is life, no longer merely sensations, tactual impressions, and memory performances. We investigate life in its full actuality, and when we are conducting this inquiry we awaken life in ourselves. Our science of life is at the same time the true philosophy, because it cultivates life itself by this means and is a life-view and a world-view. This investigation of life settles in the domain of facts; it builds from the ground up and does not move in the airy space of customary philosophy. Not only is there nothing exceptionable in a positive science of life phenomena, biological anthropology, but, like every other positive science, it has its own right and its own significance. That in its anthropological orientation, which has been developing in all its tendencies for a number of years, contemporary psychology goes further and assigns to itself more or less expressly and programmatically a philosophical significance in addition, because it believes that it is working for the development of a vital life-view and for a so-called proximity to life of science, and consequently calls biological anthropology by the name of philosophical anthropology—this is an irrelevant phenomenon which repeatedly accompanies the positive sciences and above all the natural sciences. We need only recall Häckel or contemporary attempts to establish and proclaim a world-view or a philosophical standpoint with the aid, say, of the physical theory called relativity theory.

With respect to psychology as such and completely without regard to any particular school, two questions are important for us. First, when contemporary psychology says that it has now gotten beyond the naturalism of the previous decades, it would be a misunderstanding to believe that psychology had brought itself beyond naturalism. Where psychology stands today, fundamentally, in all its tendencies, with its emphasis on the anthropological problem, Dilthey already stood with absolute clarity more than three decades ago, except that the psychology presumed to be scientific in his time, the predecessor of today's version, opposed and rejected him most vehemently as unscientific. As to the latter, compare Ebbinghaus' criticism of Dilthey. Psychology brought itself to where it stands today not on the strength of its results but by a more or less consciously effected fundamental change of attitude toward the totality of life phenomena. It could no longer avoid this shift in position since for decades it had been demanded by Dilthey and phenomenology. The change is necessary if psychology is not to become philosophy but to come into its own as a positive science. This new type of inquiry in contemporary psychology, whose significance should not be over-estimated, must naturally lead to new results within the positive psycholog-ical science of life, as compared with the old type of inquiry. For nature, physical as well as psychical, always replies in an experiment only to that which it is interrogated about. The result of positive inquiry can always corroborate only the fundamental mode of inquiry in which it moves. But it cannot substantiate the fundamental mode of inquiry itself and the manner of thematizing entities that is implicit in it. It cannot even ascertain their meaning.

With this we come upon the second fundamental question regarding psychology. If psychology is today extending its investigative work to the field which Aristotle assigned to it in its wholeness, namely, the whole of life phenomena, then this expansion of its domain is only the completion of the domain that belongs to psychology; what was a standing deficiency is simply being set aside. In this newer form, psychology still remains what it is; it is first really becoming what it can be: a science of a specific sphere of beings, of life. It remains a positive science. But as such, like every other positive science, it is in need of a preliminary description of the constitution of the being of the beings it takes for its theme. The ontological constitution of its domain, which psychology—like every other positive science: physics, chemistry, biology in the narrower sense, but also philology, art history—tacitly presupposes, is itself inaccessible in its meaning to positive science, if indeed being is not a being and correspondingly requires a fundamentally different mode of apprehension. The positive positing of any being includes within itself an a priori knowledge and an a priori understanding of the being's being, although the positive experience of such a being knows nothing of this understanding and is incapable of bringing what is understood by it into the form of a concept. The constitution of the being of beings is acces-sible only to a totally different science: philosophy as science of being. All positive sciences of beings, as Plato says somewhere, can only dream of that which is, that is to say, of their thematic object; positive science is not awake to what makes a being what it is as a being, namely, being. Nevertheless, along with the beings that are its objects, being is given in a certain way for positive science, namely, in a dreamlike way. Plato alludes to this distinction between the sciences that dream—indeed, not accidentally but necessarily—and philosophy with regard to the relationship of geometry to philosophy.

Geometry is a science which, corresponding to its method of knowing, seems to coincide with philosophy. For it is, not an experiential science in the sense of physics or botany, but a priori knowledge. Therefore, it is no accident that modern philosophy strove to formulate as well as to solve its problems more geometrico, according to mathematical method. Kant himself emphasizes that a positive science is science only as far as it contains mathematics. Plato says, however, that although geometry is a priori knowledge it still differs in principle from philosophy, which is also a priori knowledge and which has the a priori as its theme. Geometry has as its object a specific being with a specific what-content, pure space; this indeed does not exist like a physical material thing, and it also does not exist like a living being, life; instead, it exists in the manner of subsistence. Plato says in the *Republic:* Hai de loipai, has tou ontos ti ephamen epilambanesthai, geometrias te kai tas taute hepomenas, horomen hos oneirottousi men peri to on, hupar de adunaton autais idein, heos an hupothesesi chromenai tautas akinetous eosi, me dunamenai logon didonai auton.[1] The other technai— modes of commerce with beings, of which we said that they always apprehend thematically a piece of what *is,* as such, that is, the sciences of beings, geometry and those sciences that, following it, make use of it—dream about beings; but they are not in a position to see a being as something sighted in waking vision, idein, idea, that is, to apprehend the being of such a being. They are not in a position to do this as long as they make use of presuppositions about what *is,* about its ontological constitution, and leave these presuppositions unmoved, akinetous, do not run through them in philosophical knowledge, in *dialectic.* But for this they are fundamentally unqualified, since they are not capable of exhibiting what a being is in its own self. They are unable to give an account of what a being is as a being. The concept of being and of the constitution of the being of beings is a mystery to them. Plato makes a distinction regarding the way in which that which *is,* the on, is accessible for what we today call positive sciences and for philosophy. The on is accessible for positive sciences in dreaming. For this the Greeks have a brief expression, onar. But for them the on is not accessible as a waking vision, hupar. Among the sciences which merely dream about their object Plato reckons geometry, too. Thus at the basis of what geometry deals with a priori there lies a still further a priori to which geometry itself

---

1. Plato (Burnet), *Politeia,* 7.533^{b}6 ff. [In *Platonis opera,* ed. John Burnet, 5 vols., Scriptorum classicorum bibliotheca Oxoniensis (Oxford: Clarendon Press, 1899). *Politeia (Respublica)* is in volume 4.]

is not awake, not just contingently, but to which it cannot be awake, in correspondence with its character as science, any more than, say, arithmetic can understand and explain in its peculiar nature the law of contradiction, which it makes use of constantly. I cannot elucidate the law of contradiction either arithmetically or otherwise. If even a priori sciences like geometry, which never deal with empirical facts, still presuppose something that is inaccessible to them, the constitution of the being of their thematic domain, then this holds all the more for all factual sciences and consequently also for psychology as a science of life or, as is often said now in imitation of Dilthey, anthropology, the science of living humans. Each psychology merely dreams about man and human existence, because it must necessarily make presuppositions about the constitution of the being of the human Dasein and of its way of being, which we call existence. These ontological presuppositions remain closed off for all eternity to psychology as an ontical science. Psychology must let them be given to it by philosophy as ontology. The positive sciences, however—and this is what is remarkable—arrive at their results precisely while dreaming in this way. They do not need to become philosophically awake, and even if they were to become so they would themselves never become philosophy. The history of all the positive sciences shows that it is only momentarily that they awaken from their dreaming and open their eyes to the being of *the* beings *which* they investigate. That is our situation today. The basic concepts of the positive sciences are in a state of flux. It is demanded that they be revised by recourse to the original sources from which they sprang. To speak more precisely, we just recently were in such a situation. Anyone who listens more precisely and detects the true movements of the sciences above the external din and the busy activity of the industry of science must see that they are already dreaming again, which naturally should not be any objection to science, say, from the lofty standpoint of philosophy; it must rather be recognized that they are already returning to the state that is suited and familiar to them. It is too uncomfortable to sit on a powder keg, knowing that the basic concepts are just well-worn opinions. People have already had their fill of inquiry into the basic concepts; they want to have some respite from it. Philosophy as science of the "inverted world" is uncomfortable for the common understanding. Thus the concept of philosophy is governed not by philosophy's idea but by the needs and the possibilities of understanding belonging to what Kant calls the common understanding, which is impressed by nothing so much as facts.

These reflections on the relationship of the positive sciences to philosophy in connection with the Platonic statement should make it clear that, even if Kant had had an exact psychology of perception and knowledge, it would not in the least have expedited the task of a clarification of the concept of existence. Kant's explanation of the concept in question made no progress, not because the psychology of his time was not exact and empirical enough, but because it was not founded in an adequately a priori manner—because the ontology of the human Dasein was lacking. Psychology can in no way remedy the defect—which has yet to be discussed more precisely—of the Kantian interpretation of existence as perception and position, because it itself is in need of aid. Making anthropology, in the sense of psychology as a positive science, the foundation of philosophy—for example, of logic—is basically even more absurd than wishing to attempt to establish geometry with the aid of the chemistry and physics of corporeal things. Whatever the stage of development of this science of anthropological psychology, we can expect no help from it for the elucidation of a philosophical problem. It is hardly necessary to observe that what has been said about psychology cannot mean that it is not a science. On the contrary, the fundamental determination of the scientific character of psychology as being a positive, or non-philosophical, science speaks not against psychology but rather in its favor, with the aim of extricating it from its current confusion.

When Kant interprets existence or extantness as perception, this phenomenon "perception" cannot itself be made clear by means of psychology. Psychology, rather, must already know what perception in general is, if it does not wish to grope about blindly in its investigation of perception in its factual processes and genesis.

b) The ontological constitution of perception. Intentionality and transcendence

From what Kant leaves unexplained in the phenomena "perception" and "position" and allows to become blurred in the ambiguity indicated, we shall now attempt to infer which investigation of which interrelationships is provisionally required in order to provide a solid basis, a clear horizon, and assured access for the task of an interpretation of existence, extantness, actuality, being in general.

Kant's thesis that being is not a real predicate cannot be impugned in its negative content. By it Kant basically wants to say that being is not a being. In contrast, Kant's positive interpretation—existence as absolute position (perception), being as position in general—turned out to be unclear as well as ambiguous and at the same time questionable when suitably formulated. We now ask, What does Kant really leave undetermined when he uses perception, position with the ambiguity mentioned? What remains obscured when perceiving, the perceived, and the perceivedness of the perceived are not distinguished but nevertheless taken as belonging homogeneously to perception? Nothing less than the *constitution of the being of perception in general,* that is, its ontological nature, and similarly the *constitution of the being of position.* The ambiguous or the unclear use of the terms "perception" and "position" in Kant is the index of the fact that he leaves altogether undetermined the ontological nature of position and perception. This implies further that in the end the comportments of the ego, of the Dasein in our terminology, are ontologically undefined. The proper explicit ontology of the Dasein, of the being that we ourselves are, is in a bad way. But not only that; it also is not recognized that adequate treatment of the ontology of the Dasein is the presupposition for posing the problem whose solution Kant takes as his task in elucidating the concept of being.

At the outset here we shall not go into the fundamental concept of an ontology of the Dasein. This concept will occupy us in the second and third parts of the course. We shall refrain also from discussing its function as a foundation for philosophical inquiry in general; and still less is it possible to carry out and give an exposition of the ontology of the Dasein even in its main features. I have already offered an attempt at this in the first part of my recently published treatise *Being and Time.* Conversely, by continuing our analysis of the Kantian problem and the Kantian solution, we shall now try to make our way toward the sphere of the ontology of the Dasein as the foundation of ontology in general.

Kant interprets existence—we say, in our terminology, extantness, because we reserve for the human being the term [ordinarily used by Kant for existence] "Dasein"—as perception. The threefold meaning, perceiving, perceived, perceivedness of the perceived, is to be kept in mind. But have we gained anything for the elucidation of the existence concept by taking explicit notice of the ambiguity of the expression "perception" and retaining the different meanings? Have we advanced any further in understanding the phenomenon intended by this expression when we differentiate the three meanings of the word "perception"? You surely do not gain any knowledge of a thing by enumerating what a word can mean in its ambiguity. Of course not. But these differences of meaning of the term "perception" have their ground ultimately in the thing signified by them, in the phenomenon of perception itself. Not only the differences of meaning as explicitly conscious, but also precisely the imprecise usage of the ambiguous word goes back perhaps to the peculiarity of the thing signified. Maybe this ambiguity of the expression "perception" is not accidental but bears witness exactly that the phenomenon intended by it already of itself gives to common experience and understanding the basis for interpreting it sometimes as perceiving, perceptual comportment, sometimes as the perceived in the sense of that to which perceptual comportment relates, sometimes as perceivedness in the sense of the being-perceived of what is perceived in perceptual comportment. It could thus indeed be that the phenomenon meant by perception provides the basis and support for the ambiguity because it is not simple but ambiguous in its own peculiar structure. Possibly what is intended, which is separated into the three meanings, belongs originally to the unitary structure of what we have to understand as perception. Perhaps this unitary structure is viewed in different respects in the individual meanings and in the apprehension which they guide of the thing denoted.

This is in fact the case. What we concisely call perception is, more explicitly formulated, the perceptual *directing of oneself toward* what is perceived, in such a way indeed that the perceived is itself always understood as perceived in its perceivedness. This statement does not seem to express an exceptional piece of wisdom. Perception is perceiving, to which there belongs something perceived in its perceivedness. Is this not an empty tautology? A table is a table. The statement, although provisional, is more than a tautology. In it we are saying that perception and perceived belong together in the latter's perceivedness. In speaking of perceptual directedness-toward or of directing-oneself-toward we are saying that the belonging together of the three moments of perception is in each case a character of this directedness-toward. This directedness-toward constitutes, as it were, the framework of the whole phenomenon "perception."

But that perceiving directs itself toward a perceived or, speaking formally and generally, relates itself to it, is surely too self-evident for such a thing to need to receive special notice. Kant indeed says the same thing when he talks about the thing, the perceived, entering into relation with the cognitive faculty, with perceiving, when he talks about a subjective synthesis. Moreover, this expressly noticed relation of perceiving to the perceived also belongs to other modes of comportment: to mere representing, which relates to the represented, to thinking, which thinks the thought, to judgment, which determines something judged, to love, which relates to a beloved. These, one might think, are unsurpassable trivialities which one ought to shrink from pronouncing. Nevertheless, we shall not deny ourselves the explicit formulation of this discovery. Comportments relate to something: they are directed toward this whereto; or, in formal terms, they are related or referred to it. But what are we to make of this statement of the relation of the comportments to that to which they comport? Is this still philosophy at all? Whether it is or is not philosophy we may leave undecided. We may even admit that it is not or is not yet philosophy. Also, we are not really concerned as to what we are to make of the identification of the alleged trivialities, whether with them we shall be penetrating into the mysteries of the world and of the Dasein. The only thing we care about here is that this trivial identification and what is intended in it should not escape us— that we should perhaps bring it closer to us. Perhaps then the alleged triviality will turn into a total enigma. Perhaps this insignificance will become one of the most exciting problems for him who can philosophize, who has come to understand that what is taken for granted as being self-evident is the true and sole theme of philosophy.

Comportments have the structure of directing-oneself-toward, of being-directed-toward. Annexing a term from Scholasticism, phenomenology calls this structure *intentionality*. Scholasticism speaks of the intentio of the will, of voluntas; it speaks of intentio only in reference to the will. It is far from assigning intentio also to the remaining comportments of the subject or indeed from grasping the sense of this structure at all fundamentally. Consequently, it is a historical as well as a substantive error to say, as is most frequently said today, that the doctrine of intentionality is Scholastic. But, even if it were correct, that would be reason not to reject it but rather only to ask whether it is intrinsically tenable. Nevertheless, Scholasticism does not know the doctrine of intentionality. In contrast, to be sure, Franz Brentano in his *Psychologie vom empirischen Standpunkt* (1874), under the strong influence of Scholasticism, and especially of Thomas and Suarez, gave sharper emphasis to intentionality and said that the sum total of all psychical experiences could and had to be classified with regard to this structure, the manner of directing oneself toward something. The title "Psychology from an Empirical Standpoint" means something quite different from the contemporary expression "empirical psychology." Brentano influenced Husserl, who for the first time elucidated the nature of intentionality in the *Logical Investigations* and carried this clarification further in the *Ideas*. Nevertheless, it must be said that this enigmatic phenomenon of intentionality is far from having been adequately comprehended philosophically. Our inquiry will concentrate precisely on seeing this phenomenon more clearly.

If we recall what we ourselves said about perception, the concept of intentionality can, to begin with, be made clear as follows. Every comportment is a comporting-toward; perception is a perceiving-of. We call this comporting-toward in the narrower sense the intendere or intentio. Every comporting-toward and every being-directed-toward has its specific *whereto of the comporting* and *toward-which of the directedness*. This whereto of comportment and toward-which of directedness belonging to the intentio we call the intentum. Intentionality comprises both moments, the *intentio* and the *intentum,* within its unity, thus far still obscure. The two moments are different in each comportment; diversity of intentio or of intentum constitutes precisely the diversity of the modes of comportment. They differ each in regard to its own peculiar intentionality.

The task is now to pursue this structure of Dasein's comportments with particular regard to perception and to ask how this structure of intentionality itself looks, but above all *how it is grounded ontologically in the basic constitution of the Dasein.* To begin with, intentionality as a structure of the Dasein's comportments must be brought still closer to us; it has to be preserved from natural and constantly importunate misinterpretations. We are thinking here not so much of the misinterpretations contemporary philosophy heaps upon intentionality, all of which arise from preconceived epistemological or metaphysical standpoints. We leave aside specific theories of knowledge, specific philosophical theories in general. We must make the attempt to see the phenomenon of intentionality straightforwardly and without bias. However, even if we avoid the prejudgments that spring from philosophical theories, we are not yet thereby immune to all misinterpretations. On the contrary, the most dangerous and stubborn prejudices relative to the understanding of intentionality are not the explicit ones in the form of philosophical theories but the implicit ones that arise from the natural apprehension and interpretation of things by the Dasein's everyday "good sense." These latter misinterpretations are exactly the ones that are least noticeable and hardest to repulse. We shall not ask wherein these popular prejudices have their ground or to what extent they possess their own right within the everyday Dasein. We shall first attempt to characterize one misinterpretation of intentionality that is based exactly in the naive, natural vision of things. Here we shall orient ourselves again in connection with the intentional character of perception.

"Perception has an intentional character" means first of all that perceiving, its intentio, relates to the perceived, intentum. I perceive the window over there. Let us talk briefly about the relation of the perception to the object. How is this relation to be characterized naturally? The object of perception is the window over there. The relation of the perception of the window manifestly expresses the relation in which the window, extant over there, stands to me as the human being, the subject, extant here. By this presently existent perception of the window there is accordingly created an extant relation between two beings, the extant object and the extant subject. The relation of perception is an extant relation between two extant entities. If I remove one of the members of this relation, say the subject, then the relation itself is also no longer extant. If I let the other member of the relation, the object, the extant window, vanish or if I think it as vanished for me, then also the relation between me and the extant object, and indeed the whole possibility of relation, vanishes with it. For the relation now has, as it were, no further point of support in the extant object. The intentional relation can, it appears, be extant as a relation only if both the relational members are extant, and the relation subsists only so long as these relational members are themselves extant. Put in another way, in order that a possible relation should subsist between the psychical subject and something else, that subject needs the extantness of a physical object. If there were no physical things, then the psychological subject, without this intentional relation, would have to be extant for itself in an isolated way. The intentional relation belongs to the subject by virtue of the object's being extant and conversely. All of this seems obvious.

Nevertheless, in this characterization of intentionality as an extant relation between two things extant, a psychical subject and a physical object, the nature as well as the mode of being of intentionality is completely missed. The mistake lies in the fact that this interpretation takes the intentional relation to be something that at each time accrues to the subject due to the emergence of the extantness of an object. Implied in this is the notion that in itself, as an isolated psychical subject, this subject is without intentionality. In contrast, it is necessary to see that the intentional relation does not first arise through the addition of an object to a subject as, say, something like a distance between two extant bodies first arises and is extant only when a second such body is added to a first. The intentional relation to the object does not first fall to the subject with and by means of the extantness of the object; rather, the subject is structured intentionally within itself. As subject it is directed toward.... Suppose that someone is seized by a hallucination. In hallucinating he sees here and now in this room that some elephants are moving around. He perceives these objects even though they are not extant. He perceives them; he is directed perceptually toward them. We have here a directedness toward objects without their being extant. As we others say, they are given for him as extant merely in an imaginary way. But these objects can be given to the hallucinator in a merely imaginary way only because his perceiving in the manner of hallucination as such is of such a nature that in this perceiving something can be encountered—because perceiving is intrinsically a comporting-toward, a relationship to the object, whether that object is extant actually or only in imagination. Only because the hallucinative perceiving has within itself qua perception the character of being-directed-toward can the hallucinator intend something in an imaginary way. I can apprehend something *imaginarily* only if, as apprehender, I *intend* in general. Only then can intending assume the modification of imaginariness. The intentional relation does not arise first through the actual extantness of objects but lies in the perceiving itself, whether illusionless or illusory. Perceiving must be the perception-of something in order for me to be able to be deceived *about* something.

It thus becomes clear that what is said about the relation of perceiving to an object is ambiguous. It can mean that perceiving, as something psychical in the extant subject, stands in a relation with an extant object, the relation being extant because of these two extant entities. This relation stands and falls accordingly with the extantness of the members of the relation. Or the expression "relation of perception to an object" means that the perceiving is intrinsically, in its own structure, constituted by this relation, whether that to which it comports as object is or is not extant. This second sense in which we might speak about the relation of perception to an object is the one more pertinent to the peculiar nature of intentionality. The expression "relation of perception" means, not a relation into which perception first enters as one of the relata and which falls to perception as in itself free of relation, but rather a relation which perceiving itself is, as such. This relation, which we signify by intentionality, is the *a priori comportmental character* of what we call comporting.

As structure of comportments, intentionality is itself a structure of the self-comporting subject. It is intrinsic to the manner of being of the self-comporting subject as the *comportmental character* of this comportmental relationship. It belongs to the essential nature of comportments, so that to speak of intentional comportment is already a pleonasm and is somewhat equivalent to my speaking of a spatial triangle. Conversely, as long as intentionality is not seen as such, comportments are thought in a confused way, as when I merely represent to myself a triangle without the corresponding idea of space, which is basic to it and makes it possible.

We have thus warded off a misinterpretation of intentionality familiarly present in common sense, but at the same time we have suggested a new misinterpretation to which non-phenomenological philosophy almost universally falls victim. We shall also discuss this *second misinterpretation* without entering more deeply into specific theories.

The result of the foregoing clarification was that intentionality is not an objective, extant relation between two things extant but, as the comportmental character of comporting, a determination of the subject. The comportments are those of the ego. They are also commonly called the subject's experiences. Experiences are intentional and accordingly belong to the ego, or, in erudite language, they are immanent to the subject, they belong to the subjective sphere. But, according to a universal methodological conviction of modern philosophy since Descartes, the subject and its experiences are just that which is given for the subject, the ego itself, as above all solely and indubitably certain. The question arises, How can this ego with its intentional experiences get outside its sphere of experience and assume a relation to the extant world? How can the ego transcend its own sphere and the intentional experiences enclosed within it, and what does this transcendence consist in? More precisely we have to ask, What does the intentional structure of experiences contribute to the philosophical elucidation of transcendence? For intentionality designates a relation of the subject to the object. But we have heard that intentionality is a structure of experiences and thus belongs to the subjective sphere. Thus intentional directing-oneself-toward seems also to remain within the subject's sphere and, taken for itself, it seems to provide no help in elucidating transcendence. How do we proceed from inside the intentional experiences in the subject outward to things as objects? In themselves, it is said, intentional experiences as belonging to the subjective sphere relate only to what is immanent within this sphere. Perceptions as psychical direct themselves toward sensations, representational images, memory residues, and determinations which the thinking that is likewise immanent to the subject adds to what is first given subjectively. Thus the problem that is above all alleged to be the central philosophical problem must be posed: How do experiences and that to which they direct themselves as intentional, the subjective in sensations, representations, relate to the objective?

This way of putting the question seems plausible and necessary; after all, we ourselves said that experiences, which are supposed to have the character of intentionality, belong to the subjective sphere. The succeeding question seems inevitable: How do intentional experiences, belonging as they do to the subjective sphere, relate to transcendent objects? But however plausible this manner of questioning may seem and however widespread it may be even within phenomenology itself and the most closely associated tendencies of recent epistemological realism, as for instance the view of Nicolai Hartmann, this interpretation of intentionality misses out on that phenomenon. It fails because for it theory comes first, before fulfilling the requirement to open our eyes and take the phenomena as they offer themselves as against all firmly rooted theory and even despite it, that is, the requirement to align theory according to the phenomena rather than the opposite, to do violence to the phenomena by a preconceived theory.

What is the central source of this second misinterpretation of intentionality that now has to be clarified? This time it does not lie in the character of the intentio, as with the first misinterpretation, but in that of the intentum, that toward which the comportment—in our case perception—directs itself. Intentionality is said to be a character of experiences. Experiences belong to the subject's sphere. What is more natural and more logical than to infer that, consequently, that toward which immanent experiences are directed must itself be subjective? But however natural and logical this inference may seem and however critical and cautious this characterization of intentional experiences and of that toward which they direct themselves may be, it is after all a theory, in which we close our eyes to the phenomena and do not give an account of them themselves.

Let us take a natural perception without any theory, without any pre-conceived opinion about the relationship of subject to object and other such matters, and let us interrogate this concrete perception in which we live, say, the perception of the window. Toward what does it direct itself in correspondence with the peculiar sense of direction of its intentio? Toward what is the perceiving directed in conformity with the peculiar perceptual sense by which it is guided? In everyday behavior, say, in moving around in this room, taking a look around my environment, I perceive the wall and the window. To what am I directed in this perception? To sensations? Or, when I avoid what is perceived, am I turning aside from representational images and taking care not to fall out of these representational images and sensations into the courtyard of the university building?

To say that I am in the first place oriented toward sensations is all just pure theory. In conformity with its sense of direction, perception is directed toward a being that is extant. It intends this precisely as extant and knows nothing at all about sensations that it is apprehending. This holds also when I am involved in a perceptual illusion. If I have the illusion that the shadow of a tree is a man, it would be wrong to say that this perception is directed toward a tree but takes it to be a man, that the human being is a mere representation and, consequently, in this illusion I am directed toward a representation. On the contrary, the sense of the illusion is precisely that in taking the tree for a man I am apprehending what I perceive and what I believe I am perceiving as something extant. In this perceptual illusion the man himself is given to me and not, say, a representation of the man.

That toward which perception is directed in conformity with its sense is the perceived itself. It is this that is intended. What is implied in an exposition of this kind, not deluded by any theories? Nothing less than that the question as to how subjective intentional experiences can on their part relate to something objectively present is put completely the wrong way. I cannot and must not ask how the inner intentional experience arrives at an outside. I cannot and must not put the question in that way because intentional comportment itself as such orients itself toward the extant. I do not first need to ask how the immanent intentional experience acquires transcendent validity; rather, what has to be seen is that it is precisely intentionality and nothing else in which *transcendence* consists. This does not yet provide an adequate elucidation of intentionality and transcendence, but it does provide the way of putting the question that corresponds to the peculiar inherent content of what is being examined, because it is derived from the thing itself. The usual conception of intentionality misunderstands that toward which—in the case of perception—the perceiving directs itself. Accordingly, it also misconstrues the structure of the self-directedness-toward, the intentio. This misinterpretation lies in *an erroneous subjectivizing* of intentionality. An ego or subject is supposed, to whose so-called sphere intentional experiences are then supposed to belong. The ego here is some-thing with a sphere in which its intentional experiences are, as it were, encapsulated. But, now, we have seen that the transcending is constituted by the intentional comportments themselves. It follows from this that in-tentionality must not be misinterpreted on the basis of an arbitrary concept of the subject and ego and subjective sphere and thus taken for an absurd problem of transcendence; rather, just the reverse, the subject is first of all determined in its essential nature only on the basis of an unbiased view of the character of intentionality and its transcendence. Because the usual separation between a subject with its immanent sphere and an object with its transcendent sphere—because, in general, the distinction between an inner and an outer is constructive and continually gives occasion for further constructions, we shall in the future no longer speak of a subject, of a subjective sphere, but shall understand the being to whom intentional com-portments belong as *Dasein,* and indeed in such a way that it is precisely with the aid of *intentional comportment,* properly understood, that we at-tempt to characterize suitably the being of the Dasein, *one of the Dasein's basic constitutions.* The statement that the comportments of the Dasein are intentional means that the mode of being of our own self, the Dasein, is essentially such that this being, so far as it *is,* is always already dwelling with the extant. The idea of a subject which has intentional experiences merely inside its own sphere and is not yet outside it but encapsulated within itself is an absurdity which misconstrues the basic ontological struc-ture of the being that we ourselves are. When, as earlier remarked, we give the concise name "existence" to the Dasein's mode of being, this is to say that the Dasein exists and is not extant like a thing. A distinguishing feature between the existent and the extant is found precisely in intentionality. "The Dasein exists" means, among other things, that the Dasein is in such a way that in being it comports toward what is extant but not toward it as toward something subjective. A window, a chair, in general anything extant in the broadest sense, does not exist, because it cannot comport toward extant entities in the manner of intentional self-directedness-toward them. An extant being is simply one among others also extant.

With this we have made only a first approach toward preserving the phenomenon of intentionality from the crudest of misinterpretations, bring-ing it to view as yet only approximately. This is the presupposition for expressly making intentionality into a problem, as we shall try to do in the second part of the course.

With the aim of clarifying fundamentally the phenomenon of perception we have first warded off two natural and stubborn misinterpretations of intentionality. We may briefly summarize the two faulty interpretations. First, against the *erroneous objectivizing* of intentionality, it must be said that intentionality is not an extant relation between an extant subject and object but a structure that constitutes the *comportmental character* of the Dasein's behavior. Secondly, in opposition to the *erroneous subjectivizing* of intentionality, we must hold that the intentional structure of comportments is not something which is immanent to the so-called subject and which would first of all be in need of transcendence; rather, the intentional constitution of the Dasein's comportments is precisely the *ontological condition of the possibility of every and any transcendence*. Transcendence, transcending, belongs to the essential nature of the being that exists (on the basis of transcendence) as intentional, that is, exists in the manner of dwelling among the extant. Intentionality is the ratio cognoscendi of transcendence. Transcendence is the ratio essendi of intentionality in its diverse modes.

It follows from these two determinations that intentionality is neither objective, extant like an object, nor subjective in the sense of something that occurs within a so-called subject, where this subject's mode of being remains completely undetermined. Intentionality is neither objective nor subjective in the usual sense, although it is certainly both, but in a much more original sense, since intentionality, as belonging to the Dasein's existence, makes it possible that this being, the Dasein, comports existingly toward the extant. With an adequate interpretation of intentionality, the traditional concept of the subject and of subjectivity becomes questionable. Not only does what psychology means by the subject become questionable but also what psychology itself as a positive science must presuppose implicitly about the idea and constitution of the subject and what philosophy itself has hitherto defined ontologically in an utterly deficient way and left in the dark. The traditional philosophical concept of the subject has also been inadequately determined with regard to the basic constitution of intentionality. We cannot decide anything about intentionality starting from a concept of the subject because intentionality is the essential though not the most original structure of the subject itself.

In view of the misinterpretations mentioned, it is not self-evident what is meant by the trivial statement that perception relates to something perceived. If today under the influence of phenomenology there is much talk about intentionality, whether by that name or another, this does not yet prove that the phenomenon thus designated has been seen phenomenologically. That the comportments of representing, judging, thinking, and willing are intentionally structured is not a proposition that can be noted and known so that, say, inferences can be made from it; rather, it is a directive to bring to mind what is meant by it, namely, the structure of comportments, and, by turning to the phenomena, to assure ourselves ever anew of the legitimacy of this assertion.

The misinterpretations are not accidental. They are not even exclusively and primarily grounded in a superficiality of thought and of philosophical elaboration. They have their ground instead in the natural conception of things itself, as they are present in the Dasein in conformity with its nature. The Dasein has this natural tendency to start by taking every being— whether something extant in the sense of a natural thing or something with the mode of being of the subject—as an extant entity and to understand it in the sense of being extant. This is the basic tendency of ancient ontology and one that has not yet been overcome down to the present day because it belongs with the Dasein's understanding of being and its mode of understanding being. Since, in this taking everything given to be something extant, intentionality is not discoverable as a relation among extant things, it must apparently be referred to the subject: if it is not objective then it is something subjective. The subject, again, is taken with the same ontological indeterminateness to be something extant; this is manifest, for instance, in Descartes' cogito sum. Thus intentionality—whether it is conceived objectively or subjectively—remains something that is in some way extant. On the contrary, precisely with the aid of intentionality and its peculiarity of being neither objective nor subjective, we should stop short and ask: Must not the being to which this phenomenon, neither objective nor subjective, obviously belongs be conceived differently than it thus far has been?

When Kant talks about a relation of the thing to the cognitive faculty, it now turns out that this way of speaking and the kind of inquiry that arises from it are full of confusion. The thing does not relate to a cognitive faculty interior to the subject; instead, the cognitive faculty itself and with it this subject are structured intentionally in their ontological constitution. The cognitive faculty is not the terminal member of the relation between an external thing and the internal subject; rather, its essence is the relating itself, and indeed in such a way that the intentional Dasein which thus relates itself as an existent is always already immediately dwelling among things. For the Dasein there is no outside, for which reason it is also absurd to talk about an inside.

If we modify Kant's ambiguous language about perception and attempt to secure independent standing for perception by distinguishing the perceptual intention and the perceived, then we are not simply correcting verbal meanings and terminologies but going back to the ontological nature of what is meant by perception. Because perception has intentional structure, not only *can* the ambiguity mentioned arise but it *must* necessarily arise with the failure to see this. Wherever he deals with perception Kant himself has to make use of its intentional structure under duress from the things themselves, without expressly recognizing it as such. In one place he speaks of perception as reaching somewhere and says that something actual, extant, can be encountered there where it reaches to.[2] But perception can have a reach only if, in conformity with its own nature, it reaches in some way, stretches out-toward, that is, directs-itself-toward. By their essential nature, perceptions relate to something perceived; they point toward or refer to it, but not in such a way that this referential structure would first have to be procured for them; rather, they have it from the start *as* perceptions. Whether they give correctly what they claim to be giving is another question; but it would be meaningless to discuss this question if the nature of the claim remained in the dark.

c) Intentionality and understanding of being. Uncoveredness (perceivedness) of beings and disclosedness of being

We shall keep the direction of Kant's interpretation of actuality, extantness, and characterize more clearly and suitably only the horizon from and in which he carries out the elucidation. What have we gained so far with our preliminary elucidation of the intentional structure of perception? We shall be returning to the structure of position in general when discussing the fourth thesis. We concede to Kant that he does not wish to equate extantness with perceiving, the intentio, and certainly not with the perceived, the intentum, even though he does not himself introduce this distinction. Consequently, the only possibility remaining is to interpret Kant's equation of actuality with perception in the sense that perception here means perceivedness. To be sure, it turned out to be open to question whether the actuality of something actual (the extantness of something extant) may be identified with its perceivedness. On the other hand, however, we reflected that in the perceivedness (being perceived) of the perceived, and thus of the uncovered actual, its actuality must manifestly be unveiled along with it and in a certain sense the extantness of a perceived extant entity must lie enclosed within its perceivedness—that it must be possible to press ahead in some way toward the extantness of the extant by means of the analysis of the perceivedness of the perceived. This implies, however, that perceivedness is not to be equated with extantness but that it is only a necessary though indeed not a sufficient condition of access to

---

2. Kant, *Critique of Pure Reason*, B273. [This is the same passage that is referred to in n. 9 of §8 above and is quoted on p. 46.]

extantness. This interconnection renders it necessary to attempt a characterization of perceivedness as such.

We therefore ask what the relationship of this character of the perceivedness of something perceived is to what we have been saying hitherto about intentional constitution in general. Perceivedness is of the perceived. How does it belong to it? Can we advance toward the sense of the actuality of something actual by means of the analysis of its perceivedness? Looking to the intentionality of perception, we must say that the perceivedness that belongs to something perceived plainly falls within the intentum, within that toward which the perception is directed. We must first of all pursue further what the intentum of perception is. We have already said that implicit in the intentional directional sense of perceiving there is an intending of the perceived as extant in itself. The intentional directional sense of the perceiving, whether or not it is illusory, itself aims at the extant as extant. In perceiving, I am directed toward the window there as this particular functional thing. This being, this extant entity in the broadest sense, is involved in a particular functionality [Bewandtnis]. It serves to illuminate the room and at the same time to protect it. From its serviceability, from that for which it serves, its characteristic constitution is prescribed—everything that belongs to its determinate reality in the Kantian sense, to its thingness [its Sachheit, what-content, realitas]. We can perceptually describe this extant entity in the everyday way, naively, making pre-scientific statements, but also statements of positive science, about this object. The window is open, it doesn't close tightly, it is seated well in the wall; the frame's color is such and such and it has this or that extension. What we thus find before us in this extant entity is, for one thing, determinations that belong to it as a thing of use or, as we also say, as an *instrument,* and again, determinations like hardness, weight, extendedness, which belong to the window not qua window but as a pure material thing. We can cover over the *instrumental characteristics* that in the first instance confront us in our natural commerce with such a thing as a window, constituting its utilitarian character, and consider the window merely as an extant thing. But in both cases, whether we consider and describe the window as a utilitarian thing, an instrument, or as a pure natural thing, we already understand in a certain way what it means to say "instrument" and "thing." In our natural commerce with the instrument, the tool, the measuring instrument, the vehicular instrument, we understand something like *instrumentality,* and in confrontation with material things we understand something like *thingliness.* We are searching, however, for the perceivedness of the perceived. But we do not find it among all these thing-determinations which constitute the instrumental character of the perceived entity or among the determinations which belong to the general thing-character of something extant. Nevertheless, it surely has this perceivedness. For we surely say that the extant *is* the perceived. Therefore perceivedness is also not a "real predicate." How does it belong to the extant entity? The extant surely doesn't undergo any alteration due to my perceiving it. It doesn't experience any increase or diminution of what it is as this extant thing. It is certainly not damaged and made useless by my perceiving it. On the contrary, implicit in the sense of perceptual apprehension is the aim to uncover what is perceived in such a way that it exhibits itself in and of its own self. Thus perceivedness is nothing objective in the object. But may we then conclude, perhaps, that it is something subjective, belonging not to the perceived, the intentum, but to the perceiving, the intentio?

In the analysis of intentionality we were already puzzled about the legitimacy of this customary distinction between subject and object, subjective and objective. Perceiving, as intentional, falls so little into a subjective sphere that, as soon as we wish to talk about such a sphere, perceiving immediately transcends it. Perceivedness belongs perhaps to the Dasein's intentional comportment; that is to say, it is not subjective and also it is not objective, even though we must always continue to maintain that the perceived being, the extant entity, is perceived, has the character of perceivedness. This perceivedness is a remarkable and enigmatic structure, belonging in a certain sense to the object, to the perceived, and yet not itself anything objective, and belonging to the Dasein and its intentional existence and yet not itself anything subjective. Time and again it becomes necessary to impress on ourselves the methodological maxims of phenomenology not to flee prematurely from the enigmatic character of phenomena nor to explain it away by the violent coup de main of a wild theory but rather to accentuate the puzzlement. Only in this way does it become palpable and conceptually comprehensible, that is, intelligible and so concrete that the indications for the solution of the problem leap out toward us from the enigmatic matter itself. In regard to perceivedness—but also, as will yet appear, correspondingly in regard to other features—the problem arises, How can something belong in a certain sense to the extant without itself being something extant, and how can it belong to the Dasein without signifying something subjective? We shall not solve this problem at present but simply heighten it, in order to show in Part Two that the explanation of the possibility of such a puzzling phenomenon lies in the nature of time.

One thing is clear. The perceivedness of something extant is not itself extant in this thing but belongs to the Dasein, which does not mean that it belongs to the subject and the subject's immanent sphere. Perceivedness belongs to perceptual intentional comportment. This makes it possible that the extant should be encountered in its own self. Perceiving uncovers the extant and lets it be encountered in the manner of a specific *uncovering*.

Perception takes from the extant its coveredness and releases it so that it can show itself in its own self. That is the sense of every natural self-circumspection and every natural self-orientation about something, and indeed because this mode of uncovering is implicit in perceiving, corresponding to its own intentional sense.

Our pointing to the fact that perception refers to a perceived does not adequately delimit it as against mere representation, the mere bringing something to mind. This also refers to something, to a being, in a specific way and, like perception itself, it can even refer to something extant. Thus I can now bring to mind the railway station at Marburg. In doing so I am referring not to a representation and not to anything represented but rather to the railway station as it is actually present there. Nevertheless, in this pure bringing-to-mind, that particular entity is apprehended and given in a different way than in immediate perception. These essential differences of intentionality and intentum are not of interest to us here.

Perceiving is a *release* of extant things which *lets them be encountered.* Transcending is an uncovering. The Dasein exists as uncovering. The uncoveredness of the extant is what makes possible its release as something encountered. *Perceivedness,* that is, the specific release of a being in perceiving, is a *mode of uncoveredness in general.* Uncoveredness is also the determination of the release of something in production or in judgment about....

What is it that belongs to an uncovering of a being, in our case the perceptual uncovering of an extant entity? The mode of uncovering and the mode of uncoveredness of the extant obviously must be determined by the entity to be uncovered by them and by its way of being. I cannot perceive geometrical relations in the sense of natural sense perception. But how is the mode of uncovering to be, as it were, regulated and prescribed by the entity to be uncovered and its mode of being, unless the entity is itself uncovered beforehand so that the mode of apprehension can direct itself toward it? On the other hand, this uncovering in its turn is supposed to adapt itself to the entity that is to be uncovered. The mode of the possible uncoveredness of the extant in perception must already be prescribed in the perceiving itself; that is, the perceptual uncovering of the extant must already understand beforehand something like extantness. In the intentio of the perceiving something like an *understanding of extantness* must already be antecedently present. Is this solely an a priori requirement that we must impose because otherwise the perceptual uncovering of things would remain unintelligible? Or can it be shown that something like an *understanding of extantness is already implicit in the intentionality of perception,* that is, in perceptual uncovering? Not only can this be shown but we have already shown it, or, to speak more cautiously, we have already made use of this understanding of extantness that belongs to the intentionality of perception, but without having yet explicitly characterized this structure.

In the first description of the intentum—that toward which perception directs itself—in opposition to the subjectivistic misinterpretations that perception is directed in the first instance only to something subjective, that is, to sensations, it was necessary to show that perception is directed toward the extant itself. We said then that in order to see this we need only interrogate the tendency of apprehension, or its directional sense, which lies in perception itself. In accord with its directional sense, perceiving intends the extant in its extantness. The extant in its extantness belongs to the directional sense—that is to say, the intentio is directed toward uncovering the extant in its extantness. The intentio itself includes an understanding of extantness, even if it is only pre-conceptual. In this understanding, what extantness means is unveiled, laid open, or, as we say, disclosed. We speak of the *disclosedness* given in the understanding of extantness. This understanding of extantness is present beforehand as pre-conceptual in the intentio of perceptual uncovering as such. This "beforehand" does not mean that in order to perceive, to uncover something extant, I would first expressly have to make clear to myself the sense of extantness. The antecedent understanding of extantness is not prior in the order of measured clock-time. The precedence of the understanding of extantness belonging to perceptual uncovering means rather the reverse. This understanding of extantness, of actuality in the Kantian sense, is prior in such a way—it belongs in such a way to the nature of perceptual comportment—that I do not at all first have to perform it expressly; rather, as we shall see, it is implicit in the basic constitution of the Dasein itself that, in existing, the Dasein also already understands the mode of being of the extant, to which it comports existingly, regardless of how far this extant entity is uncovered and whether it is or is not adequately and suitably uncovered. Not only do intentio and intentum belong to the intentionality of perception but so also does *the understanding of the mode of being of what is intended in the intentum.*

Later we shall occupy ourselves with how this precursory pre-conceptual understanding of extantness (actuality) lies in the uncovering of the extant—what this lying means and how it is possible. What is of concern now is merely to see in general that uncovering comportment toward the extant maintains itself in an understanding of extantness and that the *disclosure of extantness* belongs to this comportment, to the Dasein's existence. This is the condition of the possibility of the *uncoverability of extant things.* Uncoverability, the perceptibility of extant things, presupposes disclosedness of extantness. With respect to its possibility, *perceivedness is grounded in the understanding of extantness.* Only if we bring the perceivedness of the perceived back in this way to its foundations, only if we analyze this understanding of extantness itself which belongs essentially to the full intentionality of perception, do we place ourselves in a position to clarify the sense of the extantness thus understood or, in Kantian terms, the sense of existence.

It is manifestly this understanding of being to which Kant recurs without seeing it clearly when he says that existence, actuality, is equivalent to perception. Without already giving the answer to the question how actuality is to be interpreted, we must keep in mind that over against the Kantian interpretation, actuality equals perception, there is presented a wealth of structures and structural moments of that to which Kant basically recurs. In the first place we meet with intentionality. Not only intentio and intentum but with similar originality a mode of uncoveredness of the intentum uncovered in the intentio belong to it. Not only does its uncoveredness—that it is uncovered—belong to the entity which is perceived in perception, but also the being-understood, that is, the disclosedness of that uncovered entity's mode of being. We therefore distinguish not only terminologically but also for reasons of intrinsic content between the *uncoveredness of a being* and the *disclosedness of its being*. A being can be uncovered, whether by way of perception or some other mode of access, only if the being of this being is already disclosed—only if I already understand it. Only then can I ask whether it is actual or not and embark on some procedure to establish the actuality of the being. We must now manage to exhibit more precisely the interconnection between the uncoveredness of a being and the disclosedness of its being and to show how the disclosedness (unveiledness) of being founds, that is to say, gives the ground, the foundation, for the possibility of the uncoveredness of the being. In other words, we must manage to conceptualize the distinction between uncoveredness and disclosedness, its possibility and necessity. but likewise also to comprehend the possible unity of the two. This involves at the same time the possibility of formulating the distinction between the being /Seienden/ that is uncovered in the uncoveredness and the being /Sein/ which is disclosed in the disclosedness, thus fixing the differentiation between being and beings, the ontological difference. In pursuing the Kantian problem we arrive at the question of the *ontological difference*. Only on the path of the solution of this basic ontological question can we succeed in not only positively corroborating the Kantian thesis that being is not a real predicate but at the same time positively supplementing it by a radical interpretation of being in general as extantness (actuality, existence).

We now clearly see that the possibility of giving an exposition of the ontological difference is interconnected with the necessity of investigating intentionality, the mode of access to beings, although this does not mean that the mode of access to each being represents perception in the Kantian sense.

Kant does not put the elucidation of actuality, existence, in the center when he equates actuality with perception. He stays at the extreme edge of the problem's field and in such a way that this edge even disappears for him into obscurity. Nevertheless the direction of the path he follows, by returning to the subject in its broadest sense, is the only one that is possible and correct. It is the direction of the interpretation of being, actuality, existence that was followed not just by modern philosophy since Descartes, by expressly orienting its philosophical problems to the subject. Direction toward the subject—or toward what is basically meant by it, namely, our Dasein—is also followed by ontological inquiry in antiquity, that of Plato and Aristotle, which was not yet at all oriented subjectivistically in the modern sense. This, however, does not mean that Plato's and Aristotle's basic philosophical tendency may be interpreted somewhat in Kant's sense, as the Marburg School did some years back. In their effort to elucidate being, the Greeks proceed in the same direction as Kant when they go back to the logos. The logos has the peculiarity of making manifest, either of uncovering or of disclosing something, between which two the Greeks distinguished as little as did modern philosophy. As basic comportment of the psuche, the logos is an aletheuein, a making-manifest, which is peculiar to the psuche in the broadest sense or to the nous—terms that are badly understood if they are thoughtlessly translated as soul and mind and oriented to the corresponding concepts. The psuche, says Plato, discourses with itself about being; it discusses being, otherness, sameness, motion, rest, and the like thoroughly with itself; that is, it already of its own self understands being, actuality, and the like. The logos psuches is the horizon to which every procedure that attempts to elucidate being and actuality and the like betakes itself. All philosophy, in whatever way it may view the "subject" and place it in the center of philosophical investigation, returns to the soul, mind, consciousness, subject, ego in clarifying the basic ontological phenomena. Neither ancient nor medieval ontology is, as the customary ignorance of them takes them to be, a purely objective ontology excluding consciousness; rather, what is peculiar to them is precisely that consciousness and the ego are taken to be in the same way as the objective is taken to be. Evidence for this is provided by the fact that ancient philosophy orients its ontology to the logos and it could be said with a certain propriety that ancient ontology is a logic of being. This is correct to the extent that the logos is the phenomenon that is supposed to clarify what being means. However, the "logic" of being does not mean that ontological problems were reduced to logical problems in the sense of academic logic. Reversion to the ego, to the soul, to consciousness, to mind, and to the Dasein is necessary for specific and inherently pertinent reasons.

We can express the unanimity of this tendency in philosophical interpretations of being and actuality by still another formulation of the problem. Being, actuality, existence belong among the most universal concepts that the ego, as it were, brings with it. These concepts were and are therefore called innate ideas, ideae innatae. They reside in the human Dasein from the very outset. On the basis of its ontological constitution the Dasein brings with it a vision, idein, an understanding, of being, actuality, existence. Leibniz says frequently, even if much more crudely and ambiguously than Kant, that we comprehend what being, substance, identity, duration, alteration, cause, and effect are only in reflection upon our own selves. The doctrine of innate ideas is prevalent more or less plainly throughout the whole of philosophy. Nevertheless, it is more of an evasion and an elimination than a solution of the problem. It is too simple a retreat to a being and a property of that being, innateness, which is itself explained no further. However unclearly innateness is conceived, it should not be understood here in the physiological-biological sense. It should be taken instead to mean that being and existence are understood *prior to* beings. This does not, however, mean that being, existence, and actuality are what the individual first realizes in his biological development—that children first of all understand what existence is; rather, this ambiguous expression "innateness" refers only to the earlier, the preceding, the a priori, which was identified with the subjective from Descartes to Hegel. The problem of the elucidation of being can be extricated from this blind alley or first properly posed as a problem only if we ask: What does innateness mean? How is it possible on the basis of the Dasein's ontological constitution? How can it be defined? Innateness is not a physiological-biological fact; instead, its sense lies in the indication that being, existence, is earlier than beings. It must be taken in the philosophical-ontological sense. Hence it is also not to be thought that these concepts and principles are innate because all men recognize the validity of these propositions. The agreement of human beings about the validity of the law of contradiction is solely a *sign* of innateness but not the reason for it. Recourse to universal agreement and assent is not yet a philosophical certification of logical or ontological axioms. In our phenomenological consideration of the second thesis—to each being there belong a what and a way-of-being—we shall see that the same horizon opens up there as well, namely, the attempt to elucidate ontological concepts by recourse to the Dasein of human beings. To be sure, it will also appear that this recourse, precisely with regard to this problem, is not formulated as explicitly in ancient and medieval ontology as it is in Kant. Nevertheless, it is in fact present there.

It has become clear in a number of ways that the critical discussion of the Kantian thesis leads to the necessity of an explicit ontology of the Dasein. For it is only on the basis of the exposition of the basic ontological constitution of the Dasein that we put ourselves in a position to understand adequately the phenomenon correlated with the idea of being, the understanding of being which lies at the basis of all comportment to beings and guides it. Only if we understand the basic ontological constitution of the Dasein can we make clear to ourselves how an understanding of being is possible in the Dasein. It has, however, also become clear that the ontology of the Dasein represents the latent goal and constant and more or less evident demand of the whole development of Western philosophy. But this can be seen and demonstrated only if this demand is itself expressly put and fulfilled in its basic features. The discussion of the Kantian thesis led in particular to a basic ontological problem, the question of the distinction between being and beings, the problem of the ontological difference. In examining the Kantian thesis we touched upon problems at every step without taking note of them expressly as such. Thus, in order to discuss the Kantian thesis fully, it was necessary not only to analyze the equation of existence, actuality, with absolute position but also correspondingly to analyze the equation of being with position generally; that is, it was necessary to show that position, positing, also has an intentional structure. We shall return to this point in the context of our discussion of the fourth thesis where we deal with being in the sense of the "is" of the copula, which Kant interprets as respectus logicus, that is, as the positing of being in general. Kant understands the being that he takes to be one with position generally as the "is" which is posited as the combining of subject and predicate in the proposition. For its analysis it is requisite that the structure of the positional character of the proposition be exhibited.

The provisional clarification of intentionality led us further to the difference in ontological constitution between the objective entity and the subjective entity, the Dasein, who exists. Plainly this distinction between the being that we ourselves are and the being that we are not—or, expressed in a formally Fichtean manner, between the ego and the non-ego—is not accidental but must somehow impress itself on the common consciousness, and philosophy is interested in it from the very beginning. We shall discuss it in the third thesis, so that the interconnection of the first thesis with the fourth and third already becomes clear.

In explicating the contents of the Kantian thesis we started from the concept of reality, thingness, from which existence was to be distinguished as a non-real character. Nevertheless, we should bear in mind that reality, too, is no more something real than existence is something existent, which is expressed in Kant by the fact that for him reality, like existence, is a category. Reality is an ontological characteristic that belongs to every being, whether it is actual or merely possible, insofar as each being is *something,* has a real content, a what-content. It is not enough to exclude existence as something non-real from the real determinations of a thing; it is equally necessary to determine the ontological sense of reality in general and to ask how the connection between reality and existence is to be conceived and how its possibility can be exhibited. This is a problem that lies virtually hidden in the Kantian thesis. It is none other than the content of the second thesis, to the discussion of which we shall now turn. We should keep in mind that the four theses are interconnected among themselves. The real content of any one of these problems includes within itself that of the others. The four theses formulate only externally and still covertly the systematic unity of the basic ontological problems, toward which we are groping by way of the preparatory discussion of the theses.

Chapter Two

The Thesis of Medieval Ontology Derived from Aristotle: To the Constitution of the Being of a Being There Belong Essence and Existence

§10. *The content of the thesis and its traditional discussion*

a) Preview of the traditional context of inquiry for the distinction between essentia and existentia

The discussion of the first thesis, being is not a real predicate, aimed at clarifying the sense of being, existence, and at determining Kant's interpretation of existence more radically in regard to its task. It was emphasized that existence differs from reality. Reality itself was not yet made a problem, nor was its possible relation to existence or even the distinction between the two. Since reality in the Kantian sense means nothing but essentia, the discussion of the second thesis, concerning essentia and existentia, includes all the questions about their relationship that were raised in earlier philosophy and that are not treated further by Kant but underlie his thinking as traditional notions to be taken for granted. In the course of discussion of the second thesis it will become still clearer how firmly the Kantian problem is rooted in the ancient and medieval tradition. Even though the second thesis is very closely associated with Kant's, the discussion of it is nevertheless not a repetition of the Kantian problem, for now, under the designation *essentia, reality* itself *becomes an ontological problem*. The problem accordingly becomes more acute. How do reality and existence belong to a being? How can the real have existence? How is the ontological interconnection of reality and existence to be defined? Not only do we now arrive at fundamentally new problems but, in the process, the Kantian problem grows more trenchant.

We can also characterize the new problem with reference to the *ontological difference*. This difference has to do with the distinction between beings and being. The ontological difference says: A being is always characterized by a specific constitution of being. Such being is not itself *a* being. But here what it is that belongs to the being of a being remains obscure. Following Kant's example, until now we have taken the expression "being" in the sense of existence, actuality, that is, as the *way* in which something actual or existent *is*. Now, however, it will appear that the constitution of the being of a being is not exhausted by the given way of being, if by this we mean actuality, extantness, existence. Rather, it will be made clear that it belongs to every being, in whatever manner it may be, that it is such and such. The character of the what, the what-character or, as Kant says, Sachheit /thingness, some-thingness/, reality, belongs to the ontological constitution of a being. Reality is no more something that *is*, something real, than are existence and being something that exists and *is*. Thus the distinction between reality and ex-istentia, or between essentia and existentia, does not coincide with the on-tological difference but belongs on the side of one member of the ontological difference. That is to say, *neither realitas nor existentia* is *a being*; rather, it is precisely the two of them that make up the structure of being. The distinction between realitas and existentia *articulates* being more particularly in its es-sential constitution.

Thus we see already that the ontological difference is not as simple in-trinsically as it appears in its plain formulation, but what ontology aims at, that which *differs* here, being itself, reveals an ever richer structure within itself. The second thesis will lead to the problem we discuss in Part Two under the heading of the basic articulation of being, namely, each single being's being determined in regard to its being by essentia and possible existence.

The *traditional discussion* of the second thesis, that essentia and existentia, or possible existence, belong to each being, lacks a solid foundation and a sure clue. The fact of this distinction between essentia and existentia has been well known since Aristotle and taken for granted as something self-evident. How this distinction between the two is to be defined is open to question in the tradition. In antiquity this question is not even raised. The problem of the distinction and the connection—of the distinctio and the compositio—between the what-character of a being and its way of being, essentia and existentia, first becomes urgent in the Middle Ages, not against the background of the basic question of the ontological difference, which was never seen as such, but rather within the same context of inquiry which we encountered in characterizing the Kantian thesis. To be sure, we are not now dealing so much with the question of the knowability and demonstrability of God's existence as with the still more original problem of the distinctness of the concept of God as an infinite being over against the being that is not God, the ens finitum. In the description of the Kantian thesis we were told that existence belongs to God's essence, to the essentia dei. This is a proposition that Kant, too, does not dispute. What he contests is solely that human beings are in a position to posit absolutely a being such that existence belongs to its essence, that is, to perceive it immediately, in the broadest sense to intuit it. God is a being who, by his essence, cannot not be. The finite being, however, can also not be. This means that existence does not necessarily belong to what the finite being is, its realitas. Now in case such a possible being (ens finitum) or its reality is actualized—in case this possible exists—then, viewed externally, possibility and actuality have manifestly come together in this being. The possible has become actual, the essentia is actual, it exists. Thus the question arises, How is the relationship of the what-character of an actual being to its actuality to be understood? We are now dealing not only with the Kantian problem, with actuality in general, but with the question of *how the actuality of a being relates to its reality*. We see that this ontological problem, too, which leads us back in Part Two to the basic problem of the articulation of being, is oriented in the tradition toward the problem of God, toward the concept of God as the ens perfectissimum. Aristotle's old identification of the prote philosophia, the first science, the science of being, with theologia receives renewed confirmation. We must now render this interconnection even more clear for ourselves in order to grasp the content of the second thesis in a correct way and to be in a position to extract what is philosophically decisive from the traditional discussion of this thesis in the Middle Ages. In elucidating the content of the thesis, we shall have to limit ourselves to essentials and give only an average characterization of the problem. We cannot give a full and detailed exposition of the historical course of discussion of this thesis of the relationship and distinction between essentia and existentia in Scholasticism (Thomas, the older Thomistic school, Duns Scotus, Suarez, the Spanish Scholastics in the age of the Counter-Reformation). Rather, by characterizing the chief doctrines—the views of *Thomas Aquinas, Duns Scotus,* and *Suarez*—we shall try to give an idea of how the Scholastics handled these problems and how at the same time the influence of ancient philosophy is manifest in this treatment of the problem itself, in its approach.

Suarez belongs to the so-called Late Scholasticism, which was revived in the Jesuit order in the age of the Counter-Reformation in Spain. Thomas was a member of the Dominican Order of Preachers, Duns Scotus of the

Franciscan Order of Friars Minor. Suarez is the thinker who had the strong-
est influence on modern philosophy. Descartes is directly dependent on
him, using his terminology almost everywhere. It is Suarez who for the first
time systematized medieval philosophy and above all ontology. Before him
the Middle Ages, including Thomas and Duns Scotus, treated ancient
thought only in commentaries, which deal with the texts seriatim. The basic
book of antiquity, Aristotle's *Metaphysics,* is not a coherent work, being
without a systematic structure. Suarez saw this and tried to make up for
this lack, as he regarded it, by putting the ontological problems into a
systematic form for the first time, a form which determined a classification
of metaphysics that lasted through the subsequent centuries down to Hegel.
In accordance with Suarez' scheme, distinctions were drawn between metaphysica generalis, general ontology, and metaphysica specialis, which included cosmologia rationalis, ontology of nature, psychologia rationalis,
ontology of mind, and theologia rationalis, ontology of God. This arrange-
ment of the central philosophical disciplines recurs in Kant's *Critique of Pure
Reason.* Transcendental logic corresponds in its foundations to general ontology. What Kant deals with in transcendental dialectic, the problems of
rational psychology, cosmology, and theology, corresponds to what modern
philosophy recognized as questions. Suarez, who gave an exposition of his
philosophy in the *Disputationes metaphysicae* (1597), not only exercised a
great influence on the further development of theology within Catholicism
but, with his order colleague Fonseca,* had a powerful effect on the shaping
of Protestant Scholasticism in the sixteenth and seventeenth centuries. His
thoroughness and philosophical level are higher by far than that which
Melanchthon, for example, attained in his commentaries on Aristotle.

This problem of the relationship between essentia and existentia has first
a theological significance that does not interest us in its narrow sense. It
concerns the problems of Christology and therefore is still discussed to the
present day in the schools of the theologians and most prominently in the
philosophical views of the individual orders. The controversy has not to
this day been settled. But since Thomas is taken before all others to be the
authoritative Scholastic as well as given ecclesiastical preference, the Jesuits,
who side in their doctrine with Suarez, who himself doubtless saw the
problem most acutely and correctly, have at the same time an interest in
associating their view with that of Thomas. As late as 1914 they requested
directly from the pope a decision as to whether it is necessary to conform
to Thomas in every respect in this matter. This question was decided
negatively in a decision that was not ex cathedra but was supposed to

---

*Heidegger apparently refers here to Petrus Fonseca (1528–1597), one of the leading
Spanish Neoscholastic writers, author of *Institutiones dialecticae* (Lisbon, 1564).

provide orientation in the area of theological and philosophical knowledge. These questions interest us here not directly but only retrospectively for understanding ancient philosophy and prospectively for the problems posed by Kant in the *Critique of Pure Reason* and by Hegel in his *Logic*. The history of the problem is very involved and not yet clear to this day.

To begin with, the problem can be traced back to Arabic philosophy, above all to Avicenna and his commentary on Aristotle. But Arabic Aristotelianism is influenced essentially by Neoplatonism and by a work that played a great role in the Middle Ages, the *Liber de causis*, the Book of Causes. The work was for a long time taken to be Aristotelian, though it is not. The distinction then occurs also in Plotinus, Proclus, Iamblichus and passed thence to Dionysius the Pseudo-Areopagite. They were all of special significance for medieval philosophy.

The problem must be understood in the philosophical context of the distinction between the concepts of the infinite being and the finite being. In Suarez this distinction is situated in a still wider context. In the *Disputationes metaphysicae*, which comprise in toto 54 disputations, the first part, disputations 1–27, deals with communis conceptus entis ejusque proprietatibus, being in general and its properties. The first part of metaphysics deals with being in general, where it is indifferent which particular being is taken into consideration. The second part, disputations 28–53, deals with the being of specific beings. Within the universe of beings, Suarez fixes the basic distinction between ens infinitum, deus, and ens finitum, creatura. The final disputation, 54, deals with ens rationis or, in the term preferred nowadays, ideal being. Suarez is the first one who—even if only timidly—tries to show, in opposition to the usual Scholastic opinion, that the ens rationis is also an object of metaphysics. Although the investigation of being represents in general an essential task of metaphysics, nevertheless deus as the primum and principium ens is at the same time id, quod et est totius metaphysicae primarium objectum, et primum significatum et analogatum totius significationis et habitudinis entis (*Opera omnia*. Paris, 1856–1861. vol. 26, disp. 31, prooem): God, as the first and principal being, is also the primary object of the whole of metaphysics, that is to say, of the whole of ontology, and the primum significatum, that which is signified first, that which constitutes the significance of all significances; the primum analogatum, that to which every assertion about beings and every understanding of being is traced back. The ancient conviction runs thus: Since every being that is actual comes from God, the understanding of the being of beings must ultimately be traced back to God. The prima divisio entis is that between ens infinitum and ens finitum. In disputation 28, Suarez reviews a series of formulations of this distinction, all of which already surfaced in earlier philosophy and were even explicitly fixed in terminology. Instead of being divided into infinite and finite, beings can also be divided into ens a se and ens ab alio: the being that is from itself and the being that is from another. Suarez traces this distinction back to Augustine; basically it is Neoplatonic. Consequently, reference is also made to God's aseity. Corresponding to this distinction there is a second one: ens necessarium and ens contingens, that which is necessarily and that which is only conditionally. Still another formulation of the distinction is between ens per essentiam and ens per participationem, the being that exists by reason of its essence and the being that exists only by participation in a being that exists on its own /eigentlich/. Here there appears a reflection of the ancient Platonic methexis. A further distinction is that between ens increatum and ens creatum, the uncreated being and the created, creaturely being. A final distinction runs: ens as actus purus and as ens potentiale, the being that is pure actuality and the being that is affected with possibility. For even that which is actual but is not God himself is always in the state of the possibility not to be. Even as something actual it is still a possible; that is, it is possible for it not to be or else to be other than it is, whereas by his essence God cannot not be. Suarez decides in favor of the first classification of the universe of beings into ens infinitum and ens finitum as the most fundamental, in connection with which he accords the other classifications their due. Descartes also uses this distinction in his *Meditations.* We shall see that for a more penetrating philosophical understanding of this distinction, quite apart from any theological orientation and therefore also from the question whether or not God actually exists, the division into ens increatum and creatum is decisive.

Starting from this distinction, which is tacitly present everywhere, even where it is not mentioned, we shall understand the Scholastic problem and at the same time the difficulties as well as the impossibility of making progress on this path. The ens infinitum is necessarium; it cannot not be; it is per essentiam, actuality belongs to its essence; it is actus purus, pure actuality without any possibility. Its essentia is its existentia. Existence and essence coincide in this being. God's essence is his existence. Because essentia and existentia coincide in this being, the problem of the difference between the two obviously cannot emerge here, whereas it must necessarily obtrude itself in reference to the ens finitum. For the ens per participationem only receives its actuality. Actuality occurs only to the possible, to that which can be something, that which is according to its what, to its essence.

After Suarez has discussed the ens infinitum, its concept and knowability, he proceeds, beginning in disputation 31 in the second part of his *Disputationes,* to the ontological investigation of the ens finitum. The first task is that of defining the communis ratio entis finiti seu creati, the general concept of the finite, or created, being. He discusses the general nature of the created being in disputation 31. It bears the characteristic title "De essentia entis finiti ut tale est, et de illius esse, eorumque distinctione," "On the essence of the finite being as such and on its being and their distinction." Suarez very often uses esse, like Thomas, in the sense of existentia.

b) Preliminary outline of esse (ens), essentia, and existentia in the horizon of the ancient and Scholastic understanding of them

The point now is to *outline the concepts* that are continually used in discussing the thesis—*essentia* and *existentia*— but only as far as the understanding of antiquity or of Scholasticism reaches. For our explication of the concepts of essentia and existentia we shall not choose the purely historical path but instead take our orientation on this matter from *Thomas,* who himself takes up the tradition and passes it on after giving it further determination. Thomas deals with essentia in a small but important youthful work which is entitled *De ente et essentia* or *De entis quidditate.*

Before we discuss the concept of essentia, let us introduce a brief orientation about the concepts esse and ens. They form the presupposition for all subsequent philosophy.

The concept of *ens,* as Scholasticism says, *conceptus entis,* must be taken in a twofold way, as conceptus formalis entis and as conceptus objectivus entis. In regard to the *conceptus formalis* the following is to be noted. Forma, morphe, is that which makes something into something actual. Forma, formalis, formale do not mean formal in the sense of formalistic, empty, having no real content; rather, conceptus formalis is the actual concept, conception in the sense of the actus concipiendi or conceptio. When Hegel treats the concept in his *Logic* he takes the term "Begriff," "concept" /usually translated "notion"/, contrary to the customary usage of his time, in the Scholastic sense as conceptus formalis. In Hegel, concept /Begriff/ means the conceiving and the conceived in one, because for him thinking and being are identical, that is to say, belong together. Conceptus formalis entis is the conceiving of a being; or, more generally and cautiously, it is the apprehending of a being. It is what *we* call, among other things, Seinsverständnis, the understanding of being, which we shall now be investigating more minutely. We say "understanding of being," "Seinsverständnis," because the explicit concept does not necessarily belong to this understanding of being.

But what does *conceptus objectivus* entis mean? The conceptus objectivus entis must be distinguished from the conceptus formalis entis, the understanding of being, the conceiving of being. The objectivum is that which, in apprehending and in grasping, is thrown over against, lies over against as the graspable, more exactly, as the grasped objectum, that which is conceived as such in the conceiving, the conceptual contents or, as is also said, the meaning. The expression conceptus objectivus is often equated in Scholasticism with the term ratio, ratio entis, corresponding again with the Greek. Conceptus, concipere, belongs to the logos ousias, the concept of being, the ratio, or intentio intellecta. Intentio would have to be taken here more exactly as intentum intellectum, that which is intended in the conceiving intention.

According to Suarez, in concurrence with Thomas, the object of general ontology is the conceptus objectivus entis, the objective concept of that which *is;* it is the universal in beings as such, the meaning of being in general with regard to being's complete abstraction, apart from all relation to any specific being. In the view of Scholasticism and of philosophy in general, this concept of being is the ratio abstractissima et simplicissima, the emptiest and simplest concept, the one that is most undetermined and simple, the immediate. Hegel defines being as the indeterminate immediate. To this there corresponds the ratio entis as abstractissima et simplicissima. No definition is possible of this most universal and empty concept; definiri non potest. For every definition must dispose what is to be defined in proper order under a higher determination. Table is a use-object; a use-object is something extant; something that is extant is a being; being belongs to beings. I cannot pass beyond being; I already presuppose it in every determination of a being; it is not a genus; it cannot be defined. Suarez says, however, that it is only possible declarare per descriptionem aliquam,[1] to make being clear by means of a certain description.

If we start from usage, ens means a being, something that is *[Seiendes]*. In linguistic form it is the participle of sum, existo, I am. According to this form it means ens quod sit aliquid actu existens;[1a] *that extantness, existence, actuality, belongs to a something.* In this significance the expression is sumptum participaliter, taken in the sense of the *participle.* Ens, being, can also be understood *nominaliter,* vi nominis, as a noun. Ens then means not so much that something exists; what is meant here is not something that has existence but rather id, quod sit habens essentiam realem est,[1b] that which exists having a determinate reality, the existent itself, the being, the *res.* It

1. [Francisco] Suarez, *Disputationes metaphysicae,* disp. 2, sec. 4, 1, in *Opera omnia,* vol. 25. [The *Disputationes* occupies volumes 25 and 26 in Charles Berton's edition of the works, *Opera omnia* (Paris: L. Vives, 1861). A reprint of the *Disputationes* in two volumes, from the Paris edition of 1866 by Charles Berton, is accessible (Hildesheim: G. Olms, 1965).]

1a. Ibid., disp. 2, sec. 4, 4.
1b. Ibid. [Actually, disp. 2, sec. 4, 5.]

belongs to each ens that it is res. Kant says reality, thingness *[Sachheit]*. We conjoin the twofold meaning of the expression ens, being. As a *participle* it states that a being is determined by a *way of being*. The participial meaning stresses the moment of *existentia*. In contrast, the *nominal meaning* emphasizes the moment of res, or of *essentia*.

Ens and res, being and thing, differ in what they mean and yet are convertible. Every being is ens and res: it has being and it has being as such and such. The res is more exactly understood as essentia realis or, concisely, essentia: essence with real content, whatness, thingness (realitas).

How does Thomas characterize the thingness (realitas) belonging to each being? This becomes clear from the different designations he puts together for thingness, Sachheit, all of which also go back to the corresponding basic ontological concepts in Greek.

We must formulate more exactly this concept of *reality* or, as Scholasticism says for the most part, *essentia*. Thingness is sometimes designated as *quidditas,* a formation derived from quid: quia est id, per quod respondemus ad quaestionem, *quid* sit res.[2] The quidditas is that to which we return, in the case of a being, when we answer the question raised about this being: *What* is it, ti estin? Aristotle formulates more exactly this what, which defines the ti estin, as to ti en einai. Scholasticism translates this as quod quid erat esse, that which each thing already was in its thingness, before it became actual. Any thing—a window, a table—*was* already what it is before it is actual, and it *must already have been* in order to become actual. It must *have been* with regard to its thingness, for it could become actualized only so far as it is thinkable as something possible to be actualized. That which each being, each actual being, has already been is designated in German as the *Wesen [*in English as the essence*]*. In this Wesen, to ti en, in the *was,* there is implied the moment of the past, the earlier. We reach back to the quidditas when we wish to circumscribe what a being primo, first of all, is, or when we settle upon what a being really and properly is, illud quod primo concipitur de re.[3] This first-of-all must not be taken in ordine originis, in the order of the genesis of our knowledge, of our attaining information (sic enim potius solemus conceptionem rei inchoare ab his quae sunt extra essentiam rei), sed ordine nobilitatis potius et primitatis objecti;[4] in the order of coming to know a thing we are accustomed rather to begin with determinations of the thing that lie outside its essence, accidental properties that come first to our attention. This first-of-all is not what the

---

2. Ibid., disp. 2, sec. 4, 6.
3. Ibid.
4. Ibid.

primo means; it is rather the primo in ratione nobilitatis, that which is first in rank in the res, that which the thing is in its realness, that which we define the thing as being in its thingness; and what does this defining is the horismos, in Latin, definitio. For this reason reality is understood not only as quidditas but also as *definitio*. This whatness that is circumscribable in the definition is what lends to each thing its determinateness and sure distinguishability from other things, constituting its delimitability, its figure. The definite circumscription, the certitudo (perfectio), is determined more exactly as *forma,* morphe. Forma, in this significance, is that which constitutes the figure of a being. Corresponding to it is how-the-thing-looks, the Greek eidos, that as which the thing is sighted. The third meaning of thingness, forma, the Greek morphe, goes back to eidos. That which constitutes the proper determinateness of a being is at the same time what is at its root, the radical, from which all of the thing's properties and activities are determined and prefigured. Hence what is thus rootlike in a being, its essence, is also designated as *natura,* the Aristotelian use of phusis. Today, too, we still speak of the "nature of the thing."

It is thus, finally, that the next term for thingness is also to be understood, the one that is most used: essentia. It is that which in the esse, in the being of an ens, of a being, if the being is conceived in its actuality, is properly thought with it, the Greek ousia in one of its meanings.

We shall see that these different names for Sachheit, or thingness— quidditas (whatness), quod quid erat esse (Wesen, essence), definitio (circumscription, definition), forma (shape, figure, aspect, look), natura (origin), names for what Kant calls reality and what Scholasticism, too, designates most frequently as essentia realis—are not accidental and are not based merely on the desire to introduce alternative names for the same thing. Rather, to all of them there correspond different aspects in which thingness can be regarded, specific basic conceptions of the interpretation of the essence, the thingness, and thus the being of a being in general. At the same time it becomes visible in the corresponding Greek terms that this interpretation of thingness goes back to the way Greek ontology posed its questions. Greek ontology becomes comprehensible in its fundamental orientation precisely thereby.

At first our concern was merely to see more clearly with the aid of these designations what the meaning is of *one of the members* of the distinction between essentia and existentia dealt with in the thesis. Now we must provisionally demarcate *the other member of the distinction,* existentia. It is striking that the concept *existentia* has for a long time not been as clearly comprehended and terminologically demarcated as that of essentia, although essentia and quidditas become intelligible exactly in terms of esse. Esse, existere, is basically more original. The opaqueness of the concept of existence and being is not an accident, because this concept is in part taken to be self-evident. In view of all the incompleteness of the interpretation of this concept in antiquity and Scholasticism and afterwards in modern times down to Kant, we must try to exhibit, precisely in connection with the phenomenological interpretation of the second thesis, the direction in which the pre-Kantian interpretation of the sense of being moves. But the difficulty of clearly formulating the concept in question is much greater than with the concept of essentia. In no case are we now permitted to inject into the discussion the Kantian concept of existence as tantamount to absolute position. In our characterization of the concept existentia, whether in Scholasticism or in antiquity, we must lay the Kantian interpretation wholly aside. It will appear later that the Kantian interpretation is not as far from the ancient one as might seem to be the case at first sight.

First we shall give in a merely general and provisional way the communis opinio of Scholasticism about the concept of existence. Ancient philosophy basically did not come to any settled view of it. Generally the term esse is used for existentia, existere. Thus Thomas says especially that esse [that is, existere] est actualitas omnis formae, vel naturae;[5] being is actualitas, literally the "Wirklichkeit," "actuality," of every essence and every nature, of every form and every nature. For the time being we need not be concerned about what this means more exactly. Being is actualitas. Something exists if it is actu, ergo, on the basis of an agere, a Wirken, a working, operating, or effecting (energein). Existence (existere) in this broadest sense—not as *we* take it, as the mode of being of the Dasein, but in the sense of extantness, the Kantian Dasein, actuality—means *Gewirktheit,* enactedness, effectedness, or again, the *Wirklichkeit,* actuality, that lies in enactedness (actualitas, energeia, entelecheia). Kant, too, uses this expression for existence. The German term "Wirklichkeit" is the translation of actualitas. The phenomenon of actualitas, under which heading we can have little to think at first, is the Greek energeia. By actualitas, says Scholasticism, res extra causas constituitur—by actuality a thing, that is, a mere possible, a specific what, is posited and placed outside the causes. This means: by actuality the enacted comes to stand on its own, it stands for itself, detached from causation and the causes. In this way a being, as actual, is a result that subsists for itself, detached, the ergon, the enacted or effected. If, by means of this en-actualizing, something is set standing on its own and is *actual* as this, it nevertheless also stands, as this actual being, outside the nothing. The expression "existence" as existentia is interpreted by Scholasticism as rei extra causas et nihilum sistentia, the thing's being-put or -placed outside the causes /German Ursachen, that is, Ur-Sachen, primary or original

---

5. Thomas Aquinas, *Summa theologiae* 1, qu. 3, art. 4.

things/ which actualize it and outside the nothing. We shall see later how this placedness in the sense of actualitas goes together with positedness in the sense of Kant's absolute position.

As essentia, or quidditas, whatness, gives the answer to the question *quid sit res*, ita actualitas respondit quaestioni *an sit*, so existence answers the question whether something is. We can also formulate the thesis in this way. Each being, as a being, can be questioned in a twofold way as to *what it is* and *whether it is*. To each being the what-question and the whether-question apply. At first we do not know why this is so. In the philosophical tradition it is taken as self-evident. Everyone has this insight. The res is actual on account of actualitas, existence. Looked at in the reverse direction, that is, from actuality, the res is the possible, that which is available for an actualization. Only in this reverse direction does the characteristic of what-ness, realitas, which plays a great role in Leibniz, arise from the idea of actuality: the determination of the essentia as the possible. In Leibniz what Kant calls realitas is conceived preponderantly as possibilitas, the Greek dunamei on. This designation is obviously suggested to Leibniz by going back directly to Aristotle.

We have thus roughly elucidated the constituents of the second thesis, essentia and existentia. To a being there belong a what (essentia) and a possible how (existentia, existence in the sense of extantness). We say "a possible" because it does not lie in the what of each and every being that this being exists.

c) The distinction between essentia and existentia in Scholasticism (Thomas Aquinas, Duns Scotus, Suarez)

In regard to the *relationship between essentia* and *existentia*, Scholasticism establishes two theses which clarify more exactly the thesis we have as our theme. The first thesis runs: In ente a se essentia et existentia sunt meta-physicae unum idemque sive esse actu est de essentia entis a se. In a being which is from itself, essence and existence [in Kant's language, Wesenheit and Dasein] are metaphysically [that is, ontologically] one and the same, or being actual belongs to the essence, derives from the essence, of a being which is in itself and is from its own self. Therefore, as was emphasized earlier, the ens a se is directly called actus purus, pure actuality, exclusive of every possibility. God has no possibilities in the sense that he might be something specific that he is not yet but could only come to be.

The second thesis runs: In omni ente ab alio inter essentiam et existen-tiam est distinctio et compositio metaphysica seu esse actu non est de essentia entis ab alio; in every being which is from another, that is, in every created being, there is an ontological distinction and composition between whatness and way-of-being, or being actual does not belong to the essence of the created being.

We must now specify more particularly this *distinctio* or this *compositio* that subsists between *essentia* and *existentia* in the case of the *ens finitum* and see how the distinctio is formulated, in order to obtain from this a clearer view of the sense of essence and existence and to see the problems that emerge here. Notice must be taken—we have already touched on this in our presentation of Kant—that the possible, res, quidditas, also has a certain being: *to be* possible is different from *to be* actual. If reality and possibile coincide, it is worthy of note that in Kant reality and possibility belong to different classes of categories, quality and modality. Realitas, too, is a specific mode of being of the real, just as actuality is that of the actual.

How are we to understand the mode of being or, as Scholasticism calls it, the entitas, of the res, namely, reality? In what way does reality, being-possible, become modified in actualization to actuality, when actuality accrues to it? What is this accruing actuality on account of which the possible becomes actual? Is it itself a res, so that in the actual being there exists a real difference, a distinctio realis, between essentia and existentia? Or is this difference to be taken otherwise? But how is it to be conceived? That there exists a difference between being possible and being actual is not disputed; being actual is something other than being possible. The question focuses on whether in the actualized possible, in the essentia actu existens, there exists a difference and, if so, what difference. It is a question now of the difference between essentia and existentia in the ens finitum, the ens creatum. In the ens increatum there is essentially no difference; there they are unum idemque.

With reference to the problem of the difference between essence and existence, or actuality, we distinguish *three different interpretative views* within Scholasticism: the *Thomistic*, the *Scotistic*, and that of *Suarez*. We use the name "Thomistic" intentionally. Here we mean at the same time the view advocated by the old school of Thomas Aquinas and also in part still advocated today, that the distinctio between essentia and existentia is a distinctio realis. How Thomas himself thought about this question has not been established clearly and consistently to the present day. Nevertheless, everything speaks in favor of his inclination to take the difference as a real one.

We can characterize these three views concisely. Thomas and his school conceive of the difference between essentia and existentia, this distinctio, as a distinctio *realis*. According to Scotus the distinctio is one of modality, distinctio *modalis* ex natura rei or, as the Scotists also say, distinctio *formalis*. By this name the Scotistic distinctio became famous. Suarez and his predecessors conceive of the difference between essence and existence as a distinctio *rationis*.

If these Scholastic views are taken merely superficially and passed off as scholastic in the usual sense, as merely subtle sophistical controversy, we would have to relinquish completely all claim to understanding the central problems of philosophy that lie at their basis. That Scholasticism attacked and discussed these questions only incompletely is no reason to dismiss the problem itself. The Scholastic way of posing the question is still to be regarded more highly than the unsurpassable ignorance about these problems in contemporary philosophy, which cannot posture enough metaphysically. We must try to press on toward the real, central content of the Scholastic problem and must not let ourselves be distracted by the controversies—often minute and toilsome—of the several Scholastic movements. In the exposition of these doctrinal views and controversies, we shall restrict ourselves to essentials. This will make evident how little clarification has been given to the problems of ancient ontology, to whose approach the Scholastic discussion ultimately reverts and with which modern philosophy, too, works as a foregone conclusion. We shall refrain from presenting and critically reviewing the individual arguments. A penetrating knowledge of this problem and of its rooting in Scholasticism is a presupposition for understanding medieval and Protestant theology. The mystical theology of the Middle Ages, for example, that of Meister Eckhart, is not even remotely accessible without comprehension of the doctrine of essentia and existentia.

It is the characteristic quality of *medieval mysticism* that it tries to lay hold of the being ontologically rated as the properly essential being, God, in his very essence. In this attempt mysticism arrives at a peculiar speculation, peculiar because it transforms the idea of essence in general, which is an ontological determination of a being, the essentia entis, into a being and makes the ontological ground of a being, its possibility, its essence, into what is properly actual. This remarkable alteration of essence into a being is the presupposition for the possibility of what is called mystical speculation. Therefore, Meister Eckhart speaks mostly of the "superessential essence"; that is to say, what interests him is not, strictly speaking, God— God is still a provisional object for him—but Godhead. When Meister Eckhart says "God" he means Godhead, not deus but deitas, not ens but essentia, not nature but what is above nature, the essence—the essence to which, as it were, every existential determination must still be refused, from which every additio existentiae must be kept at a distance. Hence he also says: "Spräche man von Gott er ist, das wäre hinzugelegt."[6] "If it were said of God that he is, that would be added on." Meister Eckhart's expression "das wäre hinzugelegt" is the German translation, using Thomas' phrase, of: it would be an additio entis. "So ist Gott im selben Sinne nicht und ist nicht dem Begriffe aller Kreaturen."[7] Thus God is for himself his "not"; that is to say, he is the most universal being, the purest indeterminate possibility of everything possible, pure nothing. He is the nothing over against the concept of every creature, over against every determinate possible and actualized being. Here, too, we find a remarkable parallel to the Hegelian determination of being and its identification with nothing. The mysticism of the Middle Ages or, more precisely, its mystical theology is not mystical in our sense and in the bad sense; rather, it can be conceived in a completely eminent sense.

α) The Thomistic doctrine of the distinctio realis between
essentia and existentia in ente creato

The problem of the relationship between essence and existence is resolved in the Thomistic school by saying that in an actual being the what of this being is a second res, something else for itself as over against the actuality; thus, in an actual being we have the combination or composition, compositio, of *two realities*, essentia and existentia. Therefore, the difference between essence and existence is a distinctio *realis*. Cum omne quod est praeter essentiam rei, dicatur accidens; esse quod pertinet ad quaestionem *an est*, est accidens;[8] since everything that [in the Kantian sense] is not a real predicate in a being is spoken of as something that befalls or is added to the being */accidens/*, to the what, therefore the actuality, or existence, that relates to the question *whether* a res with the totality of its realities exists, is an accidens. Actuality is something accessory to the what of a being. Accidens dicitur large omne quod non est pars essentiae; et sic est esse

---

6. *Meister Eckhart*, Predigten, Traktate, ed. Franz Pfeiffer (Leipzig, 1857), p. 659, lines 17–18. [*Deutsche Mystiker des Vierzehnten Jahrhunderts*, ed. Franz Pfeiffer, vol. 2, *Meister Eckhart* (Leipzig: G. J. Göschen, 1857). There is a 4th edition of volume 2 (Göttingen, 1924). A critical edition is in process: *Eckhart, Die deutschen Werke*, edited on behalf of the Deutsche Forschungsgemeinschaft by Josef Quint (Stuttgart: Kohlhammer, 1969–). For a translation see *The Works of Meister Eckhart* (Works edited by Franz Pfeiffer, volume 2), translated, with some omissions and additions, by C. de B. Evans (London: J. M. Watkins, 1924, 1956). In Pfeiffer, the passage quoted reads: "Sprêche man: er ist, daz wêre zuo geleit," "Liber positionum," §106. This is one of the omitted passages in the Evans translation.]

7. Ibid., p. 506, lines 30–31. [In Pfeiffer, this passage reads: "Sô ist got ime selben sîn niht und ist niht deme begriffe aller crêatûren." Treatise 11, "Von der Übervart der Gotheit," 2. In his translation of Pfeiffer's edition, Evans renders the sentence as: "But God is to himself his aught and naught to the mind of any creature." *The Works of Meister Eckhart*, vol. 1, p. 360.]

8. Thomas Aquinas, *Quaestiones Quodlibetales* 2, qu. 2, art. 3. [There is an edition of these *Quaestiones* by R. M. Spiazzi (Turin: Marietti, 1949).]

[that is, existere] in rebus creatis;[9] existence is not part of the reality but is added on to it. Quidquid est in aliquo, quod est praeter essentiam ejus, oportet esse causatum; everything that is outside the thing-content of a thing, everything that is not a real predicate of a res, must be caused, and indeed vel a principiis essentiae . . . vel ab aliquo exteriori,[10] either by reason of the essence itself or by another. In God, existence belongs to the res by reason of his essence. God's essence is his existence. In the created being, however, the causation of its actuality does not lie in that being itself. Si igitur ipsum esse [existere] rei sit aliud ab ejus essentia, necesse est quod esse illius rei vel sit causatum ab aliquo exteriori, vel a principiis essentialibus ejusdem rei; if therefore that which is, the existent, is something other than the whatness, it must necessarily be caused. Impossibile est autem, quod esse sit causatum tantum ex principiis essentialibus rei; quia nulla res sufficit, quod sit sibi causa essendi, si habeat esse causatum. Oportet ergo quod illud cujus esse est aliud ab essentia sua, habeat esse causatum ab alio;[11] it is impossible, however, that existing would be caused solely by the essential grounds of a thing [Thomas is speaking here only of created entities], since no thing suffices in its inherent content to be the cause of its own existence. This is reminiscent of a principle that Leibniz formulated as the law of sufficient reason, causa sufficiens entis, a law that in its traditional founding goes back to this problem of the relationship of essentia and existentia.

Existere is something other than essence; it has its being on the basis of being caused by another. Omne quod est directe in praedicamento substantiae, compositum est saltem ex esse et quod est;[12] each ens, therefore as ens creatum is a compositum ex esse et quod est, of existing and of whatness. This composition is what it is, compositio realis; that is to say, correspondingly: the distinctio between essentia and existentia is a distinctio realis. Esse, or existere, is conceived of also, in distinction from quod est or esse quod, as esse quo or ens quo. The actuality of an actual being is something else of such a sort that it itself amounts to a *res on its own account.*

If we compare it with the Kantian thesis, the Thomistic thesis says— indeed, in agreement with Kant—that existence, there-being, actuality, is not a real predicate; it does not belong to the res of a thing but is nevertheless a res that is added on to the essentia. By means of his interpretation, on the

---

9. *Quaestiones Quodlibetales* 12, qu. 5, art. 5.

10. Thomas Aquinas, *Summa theologiae* 1, qu. 3, art. 4.

11. Ibid.

12. Thomas Aquinas, *De veritate,* qu. 27, art. 1. [See *Truth,* "translated from the definitive Leonine text," 3 vols., translation of the *Quaestiones disputatae de veritate,* Library of Living Catholic Thought (Chicago: H. Regnery, 1952–1954). The passage quoted occurs on p. 312 of volume 3, translation by Robert W. Schmidt: "Consequently everything that is directly in the category of substance is composed at least of the act of being and the subject of being."]

other hand, Kant wishes to avoid conceiving of actuality, existence, itself as a res; he does this by interpreting existence as *relation* to the cognitive faculty, hence treating perception as position.

The most important disciples of Thomas who in the period of Late Scholasticism taught the distinction between essentia and existentia as distinctio realis include first of all Aegidius Romanus (d. 1316). He is known and worthy of esteem for a commentary on the *Sentences* of Peter Lombard. He belongs to the Augustinian Order of which Luther later was a member. Then there is Joannes Capreolus (d. 1444). He is most frequently called princeps Thomistarum, the prince of the Thomists. In Aegidius Romanus the motive which leads the Thomists to defend so stubbornly the real difference between essence and existence is already clearly expressed. It is nothing but the view that, if the difference were not held to be a real one, it would be impossible to speak at all about a createdness of things. This difference is the condition for the possibility that something can be created, that something as a possible can be conveyed over to actuality or, conversely, a finite being as such can also again cease to be. The Thomistic advocates of this doctrine surmise in the opposed interpretations the presence of a thesis that, because it denies that the difference is a real one, must at the same time deny the possibility of creation and thus the basic principle of this whole metaphysics.

β) The Scotistic doctrine of the distinctio modalis
(formalis) between essentia and existentia in ente creato

The second doctrinal position, that of Duns Scotus, has as its content a distinctio modalis or formalis. Esse creatum distinguitur ex natura rei ab essentia cujus est esse; the actuality of a created being is distinguished from its essence ex natura rei, by the essence of the thing itself, namely, as a created thing. Non est autem propria entitas; but the existence thus distinguished is not a proper being, omnino realiter distincta ab entitate essentiae, not a proper being that would be distinct simply realiter from the essence. Esse creatum, existere, is rather modus ejus, the essence's *mode*. This Scotistic distinctio formalis is in fact somewhat subtle. Duns Scotus describes it in more than one way. Dico autem aliquid esse in alio ex natura rei, quod non est in eo per actum intellectus percipientis, nec per actum voluntatis comparantis, et universaliter, quod est in alio non per actum alicujus potentiae comparantis;[13] I say something is in another ex natura rei, from the nature of the thing, quod non est in eo, which is not in it on account of an

---

13. Duns Scotus, *Reportata Parisiensia* 1, dist. 45, qu. 2, schol. 1. [In place of "percipientis" the *Grundprobleme* text has "negiciantis." But Heidegger himself replaces the latter with the former in restating what the passage says. The L. Wadding edition of the *Opera omnia* of Duns Scotus, originally published in 12 volumes (Lyon, 1639), has been reprinted in two editions (Paris: L. Vives, 1891–1895; Hildesheim: G. Olms, 1968–1969).]

actus intellectus percipientis, a comprehending activity of the understanding, and also not on account of an act of comparison. Something is in
another ex natura rei, which does not at all go back to any comparative and
determinative activity of apprehending but rather lies in the thing itself.
Dico esse formaliter in aliquo, in quo manet secundum suam rationem
formalem, et quidditativam;[14] I say it is in another formaliter, according to
its form, in which it remains on account of its quidditas. Applied to our
example this means that existence, actuality, belongs actually to the created
actual being; hence, in Kantian language, existence is not something due
to a relation of the res to the concept, to the apprehending understanding,
but according to Scotus existence actually belongs to the actual being and
yet, for all that, existence is not a res. Where something is present, presence
is there; it lies in the being that is present and can be distinguished from
it as belonging to it, but nevertheless in such a way that this difference and
this distinguishing cannot supply a thing-content that somehow *is* on its
own for itself, a res on its own with its own reality.

γ) Suarez' doctrine of the distinctio sola rationis between
essentia and existentia in ente creato

The third interpretation is that of Suarez, the distinctio rationis. The
difference between essence and existence in the created being is solely
conceptual. Suarez' discussions aim chiefly at showing that his own view
really agrees with that of Scotus, more precisely, that it is not at all necessary
to introduce this distinction of a distinctio modalis, as Scotus does, but that
this modal distinction is nothing other than what he, Suarez, calls distinctio
rationis.

Suarez says: Tertia opinio affirmat essentiam et existentiam creaturae
. . . non distingui realiter, aut ex natura rei tanquam duo extrema realia, sed
distingui tantum ratione.[15] He thus draws the line between his view and
the other two doctrines. His interpretation fixes more clearly the point of
comparison of the distinction in question: comparatio fiat inter actualem
existentiam, quam vocant esse in actu exercito, et actualem essentiam existentem.[16] He stresses that the problem relative to the distinction between
essence and existence consists in the question whether and how the actualized what, the what of an actual being, differs from this being's actuality.

---

14. Ibid.

15. Suarez, *Disputationes metaphysicae,* disp. 31, sec. 1, 12. [In *Opera omnia,* ed. Berton,
vol. 26. "This third view asserts that the essence and existence of creatures . . . are not really
different, as if they were two real opposites by the nature of things, but that they are
rationally or conceptually different." My translation.]

16. Ibid., disp. 31, sec. 1, 13. ["The comparison should be made between actual existence,
which is said to be actually exercised, and the actually existent essence." My translation.]

It is not the problem of how the pure possibility, the essentia as something which is purely possible and then actualized, differs from the actuality; the question rather is, Can the actuality and the thing-content of the actual be distinguished really in the actual being itself? Suarez says: essentia et existentia non distinguunter *in re* ipsa, licet essentia, abstracte et praecise concepta, ut est in potentia [possibile], distinguatur ab existentia actuali, tanquam non ens ab ente;[17] in the actual being itself I cannot distinguish realiter essence and actuality, although I can think abstractly the essence as pure possibility and then fix the difference between a non-being, nonexistent, and an existent. He goes on to say: Et hanc sententiam sic explicatam existimo esse omnino veram;[18] I am of the opinion that this view is altogether true. Ejusque fundamentum breviter est, quia non potest res aliqua intrinsece ac formaliter constitui in ratione entis realis et actualis, per aliud distinctum ab ipsa, quia, hoc ipso quod distinguitur unum ab alio, tanquam ens ab ente, utrumque habet quod sit ens, ut condistinctum ab alio, et consequenter non per illud formaliter et intrinsece.[19] The foundation of this third interpretation is solely this, that something like existence, actuality—which intrinsece et formaliter, most inwardly and in accordance with the essence, constitutes something like the actual—cannot be distinguished as a being on its own account from what is thus constituted. For if existence, actuality, were itself a res, in Kantian terms a real predicate, then both res, both things, essence and existence, would have a being. The question would then arise how the two can be taken together in a single *unity* which itself *is*. It is impossible to take existence as something existent.

To gain access to this problem, which is discussed along different lines in the three doctrines, let us first briefly mention Scholasticism's way of conceiving the distinctio in general. If we disregard the Scotistic view, Scholasticism differentiates between a distinctio realis and a distinctio rationis. Distinctio realis habetur inter partes alicujus actu (indivisi) entis quarum entitas in se seu independenter a mentis abstractione, una non est altera; a *real distinction* obtains when of those that are distinguished, in conformity with their what-contents, the one is not the other, and indeed in itself, without regard to any apprehension by means of thinking.

The *distinctio rationis* is that qua mens unam eandemque entitatem diversis conceptibus repraesentat, that distinction by which the understanding

---

17. Ibid.
18. Ibid.
19. Ibid. ["And the reason for that, briefly, is that something cannot intrinsically and formally be constituted as a real and actual being by something different from itself, because, by the very fact that one is different from the other as a being from a being, each has what it takes to be and to be condistinct from the other and consequently [cannot be] formally and intrinsically through the other." My translation.]

represents to itself by different concepts not two different res but one and the same thing. Scholasticism further divides the distinctio rationis into (1) a *distinctio rationis pura* or also *ratiocinantis* and (2) a *distinctio rationis ratiocinata*. The former is the distinction that can be exemplified in the difference between homo and animal rationale, human being and rational animal. By this I distinguish something, to be sure, but what I distinguish is one and the same res. A difference exists only in the manner of apprehending this res; in the one case what is meant, homo, is thought unexpressly, implicite, in the other case explicite, the moments of the essence being brought out. In both cases of this distinctio rationis pura, the res is one and the same realiter. This distinctio has its origin and motive solely in the ratiocinari itself, in the conceptual act of distinguishing. It is a distinction that is accomplished only from my standpoint. To be distinguished from this distinctio rationis is the distinctio rationis ratiocinata, or distinctio rationis cum fundamento in re. The latter is the familiar expression. It refers not simply to the mode of apprehension and the degree of its clarity but is present quandocumque et quocumque modo ratio diversae considerationis ad rem relatam oritur, when the distinction arises as not in some sort motivated by the apprehending in its active operation but ratiocinata, by that which is objicitur, cast over against, in the ratiocinari itself, hence ratiocinata. The essential point is that for the second distinctio rationis there is a motive having to do with the thing-content in the distinguished thing itself. By this, the second distinctio rationis, which is motivated not only by the apprehending intellect but by the apprehended thing itself, receives a position in between the purely logical distinctio, as the distinctio pura is also called, and the distinctio realis. For this reason it coincides with the distinctio modalis or formalis of Duns Scotus, and therefore Suarez is correct in saying that in terms of real content he agrees with Scotus except that he regards the introduction of this further distinction as superfluous. There are theological reasons why the Scotists doggedly championed their distinctio modalis.

The problem of the distinction between essentia and existentia that occupies us first of all in the framework of the Scholastic interpretation should become clearer in its real content and in reference to its rootedness in ancient philosophy. But to this end we must still pursue Suarez' doctrine in some further detail so as to reach the true nub of the question. For his and his predecessors' view is the one most appropriate for working out the phenomenological exposition of the problem. Suarez argues for his thesis not merely by saying, in the manner already mentioned, that it is impossible to comprehend existence as something that itself exists, because then the question would arise anew how these two beings are supposed once again to constitute an existent unity; he argues for it also by an appeal to Aristotle.

In order to make this appeal legitimate he has to amplify the Aristotelian interpretation. Suarez says: Probari igitur potest conclusio sic exposita ex Aristotele, qui ubique ait; ens adjunctum rebus nihil eis addere; nam idem est ens homo, quod homo; hoc autem, cum eadem proportione, verum est de re in potentia et in actu; ens ergo actu, quod est proprie ens, idemque quod existens, nihil addit rei seu essentiae actuali.[20] Aristotle says that the expression "being," if it is adjoined to any thing, adds nothing to it, and that it is the same whether I say "man," homo, or ens homo, "existent man." The passage in Aristotle runs: tauto gar heis anthropos kai on anthropos kai anthropos, kai ouch heteron ti deloi;[21] it is the same to say "one man" or "an existent man." Aristotle here intends merely to say: Even when I think a res, a mere what, I must already think it in some sense as being; for possibility and thought-ness are also being possible and being thought. When I say "man," I am also thinking being along with this, in this being which is in some way thought of as being. Suarez now carries over to existence this Aristotelian suggestion that in everything thought of, whether it be thought of as actual or as possible, being is thought along with it. He says: the same thing (namely, that being adds nothing to res) holds also precisely of proprie ens, being proper, that is, existing. Existence adds nothing. This is exactly the Kantian thesis. Existentia nihil addit rei seu essentiae actuali. Existence adds nothing to the actual what.

To make this clear Suarez must enter into a characterization of the mode of being of the possible in general, that is, into the mode of being of the Sache, the thing, the essentia priusquam a deo producatur,[22] before it has been created by God himself. Suarez says, the essences or possibilities of things before their actualization have no being of their own. They are not realities sed omnino nihil,[23] but nothing at all. To that which, like the pure possibilities, is in this sense nothing with regard to its being, nothing can be added in its actualization as well. The nature of actualization consists, rather, precisely in the fact that the essence first of all receives a being or, to speak more accurately, comes into being, and in such a way indeed that later, as it were, as viewed from the actualized thing, its possibility can also be apprehended in a certain sense as being. Suarez calls this pure possibility the potentia objectiva and allows this possibility to be only in ordine ad

---

20. Ibid., disp. 31, sec. 6, 1. ["The conclusion, as explained, can therefore be proved by the authority of Aristotle where he says that adding being to a thing does not add anything to it, for existent man is the same as man, and this is proportionally true of the thing both in potency and in act; therefore being in act, which is being proper and the same thing as existing, adds nothing to the thing or to the actual essence." My translation.]

21. Aristotle, *Metaphysica*, book Gamma, 2.1003^{b}26 f.

22. Suarez, *Disputationes metaphysicae*, disp. 31, sec. 2. [The phrase comes from the title of section 2.]

23. Ibid., disp. 31, sec. 2, 1.

alterius potentiam,[24] in relation to another being that has the possibility of thinking such things. But this possible as, say, God thinks it, non dicere statum aut modum positivum entis, does not signify a special positive way of being of a being; rather, this possible must precisely be apprehended negatively, as something which nondum actu prodierit, does not yet actually exist.[25] When in creation this possible goes over into actuality, this transition is to be understood, not in the sense that the possible relinquishes a way of being, but rather in the sense that it first of all receives a being. The essentia now is not only, non tantum in illa, in that potency, namely, of being thought by God, but it is only now properly actual, ab illa, et in seipsa, the being is only now first created by God and, as this created being, it at the same time stands on its own in its own self.[26]

The difficulty of the problem of making the distinction intelligible at all depends on how in general actualization is thought of as the transition of a possible to its actuality. Expressed more exactly, the problem of the distinction between essentia and existentia in ente creato depends on whether in general the interpretation of being in the sense of existence is oriented toward actualization, toward creation and production. If the question of existence and the question of essence are oriented toward actualization in the sense of creation and production, then perhaps this whole context of questions, as it comes to the fore in the three doctrinal views, cannot indeed be avoided. The fundamental question, however, is whether the problem of actuality and of existence must be oriented as it was in Scholasticism or in antiquity.

Before answering this question, we must make clear to ourselves *that* the question about the sense of existence and actuality in pre-Kantian philosophy is oriented toward the phenomenon of actualization, of *production,* and also *why.* In closing, let us once more compare the third and first views. Suarez' distinctio rationis says that actuality does not belong to the realitas, the thingness [Sachheit], of the created being insofar as this reality is thought of for itself; but, on the other hand, it maintains that the actual cannot be thought without actuality, without it therefore being said that the actuality is itself an actual being. Suarez holds that these theses are compatible—that, for one thing, actuality does not belong realiter to the possible, the essentia, but that, on the other hand, the actuality nevertheless in itself lies enclosed in the actual being and is not merely a relation of the actual being to a subject. In contrast, the first view holds a compatibility of these two propositions to be impossible. Only if existence does *not* belong to the

---

24. Ibid., disp. 31, sec. 3, 4.
25. Ibid.
26. Ibid.

essentia is anything like a creation at all possible. For in creation existence is added to the actual and can at any time be taken away from it. It is easily seen that in this controversy, especially on closer consideration, the real point of the question constantly shifts: essentia is understood first as pure possibility, the purely thought essence, but then secondly as the actualized essence in the actuality itself. The first and third interpretations also differ in starting-point as determined by their methods. The first view proceeds in a purely deductive way. It tries to demonstrate its thesis from the idea of the created being. If a created being is to be possible as created, actuality must be added on to the possibility, that is to say, the two must differ realiter. From the principle "creation of the world must be possible," the necessity of the real distinction between essentia and existentia is inferred. The third view does not start from the necessity of a possible creation but attempts to solve the problem of the relationship between the what and the way of being in the actually given being itself. It makes this attempt but never actually gets into the clear with it. The actually given being is taken as the primary court of appeal. With this in view the actuality can in no way be exhibited as itself something actual and bound up actually as an ens with the essentia.

In the actual being, actuality cannot be read off as a special res on its own account but can only be expressly thought of. It must be thought of as something that belongs to the actual being in conformity with the actual being's essence—the actualized essence but not the thought-of essence as such. However, the outcome is this. Suarez agrees in a certain way with Kant when he says that existence, actuality, is not a real predicate. But he differs from Kant in positive interpretation, inasmuch as he conceives of actuality as something which, even if not real, nevertheless belongs to the actual being itself, while Kant interprets actuality as a relation of the thing to the cognitive faculty.

§11. Phenomenological clarification of the problem underlying the second thesis

The account of the discussion of the distinction between essence and existence made it clear that a distinction was in dispute here without the terms to be distinguished having been sufficiently explained—without even the attempt having been made to give beforehand an adequate explanation of what was to be distinguished or even to come to an understanding about the path and the requirements necessary for such an explanation. To be sure, it should not be naively imagined that this omission of a prior interpretation of essence and existence was merely a mistake or a matter of indolence. Rather, these concepts are, for one thing, held to be self-evident. That beings must be understood as created by God is adhered to as an unshakable conviction. By this ontical declaration a putting of the ontological question is condemned from the start to impossibility. But, above all, there is no available way of interpreting these concepts. The horizon for putting the question is lacking. In Kantian language, there is no possible way of establishing the birth certificate of these concepts and proving it to be genuine. The concepts employed in the traditional discussion must originate in a common interpretation which offers itself for this purpose to begin with and constantly. We now ask from an objective historical viewpoint, Whence do the concepts get the meaning they have as they are used in the above-mentioned discussion? We must try to obtain a clue to the *origin* of these *concepts* of *essentia* and *existentia*. We shall ask what their birth certificate is and whether it is genuine or whether the genealogy of these basic ontological concepts takes a different course, so that at bottom their distinction and their connection have a different basis. If we succeed either in discovering the genealogy of these basic concepts or in first finding the direction of the path along which we can push forward or backward to their derivation, then this thesis—a what and a possible how of being belong to each being—must also receive an enhanced clarification and an adequate foundation.

a) The question of the origin of essentia and existentia

Let us forget for the time being the controversies about essence and existence and their distinction. We shall attempt to trace the origin of the concepts essentia and existentia or to define and understand the task of such an interpretation by way of the origin. We shall not forget that the interpretation of these concepts or of the phenomena lying at their ground has not advanced today any further than in the Middle Ages and antiquity despite the initiatives given by Kant. These Kantian initiatives have for a long time been taken up only negatively. To be sure, there was for a half century and still is a Neo-Kantianism, which, especially as concerns the Marburg School, has its special merit. Now that the revival of Kant has begun to go out of fashion the attempt is being made to replace it by a revival of Hegel. These revivals even flatter themselves on being the caretakers of respect for the past. But at bottom such revivals are the greatest disrespect the past can suffer, because it is degraded into a tool and servant of a fashion. The basic presupposition for being able to take the past seriously lies in willing not to make one's own labor easier than did those who are supposed to be revived. This means that we first have to press forward to the real issues of the problems they laid hold of, not in order to stand pat with them and bedeck them with modern ornaments, but in order to make progress on the problems thus grasped. We wish to revive neither Aristotle nor the ontology of the Middle Ages, neither Kant nor Hegel, but only ourselves; that is to say, we wish to emancipate ourselves from the phraseologies and conveniences of the present, which reels from one fickle fashion to the next.

However, let us also forget the Kantian solution of the problem and ask now, Why is existence conceived of as actualization and actuality? Why does the interpretation of existence go back to agere, agens, energein, ergazesthai? Apparently we are returning to the issue of the first thesis. But only apparently, for the problem now also includes the question of the origin of reality, the origin of the ontological structure of what Kant does not even make problematic in explaining his thesis. When he says that existence is not a real predicate, he presupposes that it is already clear what reality is. But we are now asking at the same time about the ontological origin of the concept of essentia—in Kantian terms the concept of reality—and moreover not only about the origin of these two concepts but about the origin of their possible interconnection.

The following discussions differ from the earlier ones carried on within the framework of the Kantian thesis in that, in pursuing the origin of the existence concept, we come upon a different horizon for the interpretation of existence as actuality than in Kant or, more accurately, upon a *different direction of vision within the same horizon,* a horizon that was even less unmistakably fixed and developed in the Middle Ages and antiquity than in Kant and his successors. To exhibit the origin of essentia and existentia now means to bring to light the horizon of the understanding and inter- pretation of what is denominated in these concepts. Only later shall we have to inquire how far the horizons of the ancient and Kantian interpre- tation of the concepts of being coincide at bottom and why it is just they that dominate the formulation of ontological questions and still dominate it even today. But first of all we must try to lay hold of this horizon of ancient and medieval ontology.

The verbal definition of existentia already made clear that *actualitas* refers back to an *acting* on the part of some indefinite subject or, if we start from our own terminology, that the extant /das Vorhandene/ is somehow referred by its sense to something for which, as it were, it *comes to be before the hand,* at hand, to be handled. The apparently objective interpretation of being as actualitas also at bottom refers back to the subject, not, however, as with Kant, to the apprehending subject in the sense of the relation of the res to the cognitive faculties, but in the sense of a relation to our Dasein as an acting Dasein or, to speak more precisely, as a creative, *productive* Dasein. The question is whether this horizon for the interpretation of existence as actualitas is derived merely from the literal meaning of the word itself—so that we simply infer from the designation for existence, "actualitas," to an agere—or whether it can be made clear from the *sense* of actuality as it was conceived in ancient thought and Scholasticism that actuality is understood *by going back to the productive behavior of the Dasein.* If this latter is the case, then it should also be possible to show that the concept of reality and of essentia, and consequently all the concepts we have enumerated for essentia (quidditas, natura, definitio, forma), must be made intelligible from this horizon of productive behavior. The next question then is, How do the two traditional interpretations of existence and actuality—the Kantian, which has recourse to apprehending, perceptual behavior, and the ancient-medieval, which goes back to productive behavior—go together? Why are both really necessary, and how is it that until now both of them, in this one-sidedness and uniqueness, could so decisively dominate the ontological problem of the question about being in general?

We ask, What was it that loomed before the understanding and interpretation of beings in the development of the concepts essentia and existentia? How did beings have to be understood with regard to their being so that these concepts could grow out of the ontological interpretation? We shall first investigate the origin of the existence concept.

We said at first, quite crudely, that *existentia* is conceived as actualitas, actuality, and hence with regard to actus, agere. Actuality, Wirklichkeit, is at first intelligible to everyone without having a concept at his disposal. Let us orient ourselves briefly as to how this natural understanding looks in medieval philosophy, an understanding that in a certain sense coincides with the natural conception of existence.

We saw that the adherents of the third doctrinal view try to look toward the given and to find and determine actuality in the actual. These interpretations are only very meager and rough. In antiquity they consist only of quite scattered, occasional remarks (Aristotle, *Metaphysics,* book 9). The medieval period shows no new approaches. Suarez attempts a detailed circumscription of the concept but, of course, wholly within the framework of the traditional ontology. We shall start out from his discussion of the existence concept and, while doing so, tacitly bear in mind the Kantian interpretation.

Res existens, ut existens, non collocatur in aliquo praedicamento;[1] an actual thing as actual is not placed under any predicate having real content. This is also the Kantian thesis. Quia series praedicamentorum abstrahunt ab actuali existentia; nam in praedicamento solum collocantur res secundum

---

1. Suarez, *Disputationes metaphysicae,* disp. 31, sec. 7, 4.

ea praedicata, quae necessario seu essentialiter eis conveniunt;[2] for the series of basic predicates with real content disregards whether the being of which they are asserted is actual or not. Existentia rei absolute non est respectus, sed absolutum quid;[3] the actuality of a thing is not a relation to something else but something absolute in its own self. This implies that actuality belongs to the actual and is just what makes the actual actual, without itself being something actual. This is the standing riddle. To be sure, according to the Christian view, a being's actualization is accomplished by God, but the actualized being, as actualized, nevertheless exists absolutely for itself, is something that is for itself. On this path, however, we shall discover nothing about actuality as such but only something about the actualizing of the actual. Actualitas is a determination of the actum of an agens. Aegidius Romanus says in his commentary on the sentences: Nam agens non facit quod potentia sit potentia. . . . Nec facit agens ut actus sit actus, quia cum hoc competat actui sec. se; quod actus esset actus non indiget aliqua factione. Hoc ergo facit agens, ut actus sit in potentia et potentia sit sub actu.[4] Esse nihil est aliud quam quaedam actualitas impressa omnibus entibus ab ipso Deo vel a primo ente. Nulla enim essentia creaturae est tantae actualitatis, quod possit actu existere, nisi ei imprimatur actualitas quaedam a primo ente.[5] There is exhibited here a naive idea according to which actuality is something that is, as it were, impressed upon things. Even the defenders of the distinctio realis resist conceiving of existentia as an ens. Capreolus says: esse actualis existentiae non est res proprie loquendo . . . non est proprie ens, secundum quod ens significat actum essendi, cum non sit quod existit. . . . Dicitur tamen [existentiae] entis, vel rei.[6] Actuality is not a thing in the strict sense of the word; properly speaking, it is not a

---

2. Ibid.

3. Ibid., disp. 31, sec. 6, 18.

4. Aegidius Romanus, *In secundum librum Sententiarum quaestiones,* Sent. 2, dist. 3, qu. 1, art. 1. ["For the agent does not cause the potency to be potency. . . . Nor does the agent cause the act to be act, because this belongs to act as such; no cause is needed for the act to be act. What the agent does therefore is this: that the act should be in the potency and that the potency should be actualized." My translation. Aegidius Romanus was also known as Egidio Colonna and as Giles of Rome. For a recent reprint of the 1581 edition of the above work, see *In secundum librum Sententiarum* (Frankfurt: Minerva GmbH, Wissenschaftlicher Verlag und Buchhandlung, 1968).]

5. Ibid., citing Joannes Capreolus [*Quaestiones in quattuor libros Sententiarum*], Sent. 1, dist. 8, qu. 1, art. 1 (fifth conclusion). ["Being is nothing else but a certain actuality impressed on all beings by God or the first being. For no essence of a created being is of such actuality that it can exist actually unless a certain actuality is impressed on it by the first being." My translation. A recent reprint of the Tours 1899–1908 edition is *Joannis Capreoli Defensiones theologiae divi Thomae Aquinatis,* ed. C. Paban and Th. Pegues, 7 vols. (Frankfurt: Minerva GmbH, Wissenschaftlicher Verlag und Buchhandlung, 1966–1967).]

6. Capreolus, Sent. 1, dist. 8, art. 2 (Solutiones, 4).

being; it itself is not something that exists; it is not a being but something that is in or of a being (quid entis), something that belongs to a being. The following passage makes this clearer: esse creaturae . . . non subsistit; et ideo, nec illi debetur proprie esse, nec fieri, nec creari, ac per hoc nec dicitur proprie creatura, sed quid concreatum . . . Nec valet si dicatur: esse creatum est extra nihil; igitur est proprie ens. Quia extra nihil non solum est quod est; immo etiam dispositiones entis, quae non dicuntur proprie et formaliter entia, sed entis; et in hoc differunt a penitus nihilo.[7] The actualness of the created is not itself actual; it is not itself in need of a coming-to-be or a being-created. Therefore, it may not be said that actuality is something created. It is rather quid concreatum, *con*created with the creation of a created thing. Certainly actuality belongs to the actual, though actuality itself is not something actual but rather quid entis and as such concreatum quid, or instead a dispositio entis, a state of a being.

In summary we can say: Actuality is not a res, but it is not on that account nothing. It is explained, not by reference to the experiencing subject, as in Kant, but rather by reference to the creator. Here the interpretation runs into a blind alley, in which no further progress is possible.

What do we learn from this description of actuality with respect to the question of the direction of interpretation? If we compare this interpretation with Kant's, we see that Kant has recourse to the relation to the cognitive faculty (perception) and tries to interpret actuality with respect to cognition and apprehension. In Scholasticism, by contrast, the actual is interpreted with respect to actualization, that is to say, not in the direction in which what is already extant is conceived of as actual, but in the direction in which the extant *[Vorhandenes]* comes to hand and first can be *at hand* at all, as something that it is possible subsequently to apprehend or lay hold of, in general as something at hand. Thus here, too, there appears, even though still indefinitely, a relation to the "subject," to the Dasein: to have at hand the at-hand as something pro-duced by a pro-duction, as the actual of an actualizing. This corresponds to the meaning of actualitas and energeia, that is, to the tradition of the concept. In the modern period it is customary to interpret the concept of actuality and the actual in another way. It is taken in the sense of that which influences, that is, acts or works inwards upon the subject or as that which acts or works on another, stands with another in an interconnection of efficacious action. The actuality of things consists in their exercising the action of forces on each other.

The two meanings of actuality and the actual, that which acts inwards on the subject or which acts outwards on something else, presuppose the first meaning, which is ontologically prior, that is, actuality understood with

---

7. Ibid., dist. 8, qu. 1, art. 2 (Solutiones, 1).

reference to actualization and being enacted. That which acts inwards upon the subject must itself already be actual in the first sense of the word, and interconnections of efficacious action are possible only if the actual is extant. It is ontologically incorrect and impossible to interpret actuality and its ontological sense in terms of these two meanings just mentioned. Rather, actuality, as the traditional concept actualitas implies, must be understood with reference to actualization. It is completely obscure, however, how actuality should be understood in this way. We shall try to shed some light on this obscurity, to explain the origin of the concepts essentia and existentia, and to show how far the two concepts are derived from an *understanding of being* that comprehends beings with respect to an *actualizing* or, as we say generally, to a *productive comportment of the Dasein.* The two concepts essentia and existentia are an outgrowth from an interpretation of beings with regard to productive comportment, and indeed with regard to a productive comportment that is not expressly and explicitly conceived in this interpretation. How is this to be more particularly understood? Before answering this question, we must show that the horizon of understanding that has just been pointed to—the Dasein as productive—has not been merely fixed by us on the basis of the relation of* the being of a being to the subject and to God as producer of things, but that the basic ontological determinations of a being grow universally out of this horizon. We shall attempt this proof in reference to the interpretation of thingness, *realitas,* by which the common origin of essentia and existentia becomes clear.

We shall not at first characterize particularly the Dasein's productive mode of behavior. We shall attempt solely to show that the determinations adduced for Sachheit /thingness, reality/, essentia—forma, natura, quod quid erat esse, definitio—are obtained with regard to the producing of something. Production stands in the guiding horizon of this interpretation of whatness. For this proof we cannot keep to the medieval terms, because they are not original but translations of ancient concepts. It is only by turning to the latter that we shall be able to make visible their true origin. In doing so, we must stay clear of all modern interpretations and revisions of these ancient concepts. We can only outline the proof that the chief ancient determinations for the thingness or reality of a being originate in productive activity, the comprehension of being by way of production. What would be required would be an investigation of the individual stages of development of ancient ontology up to Aristotle and an account of the subsequent development of the individual fundamental concepts.

---

*The text reads "the relation for the being of a being," which is awkward and possibly represents a typographical error.

b) Return to the productive comportment of the Dasein toward beings as implicit horizon of understanding for essentia and existentia

Among the concepts that are characteristic for essentia, we mentioned morphe, eidos (forma), to ti en einai (that which a being already was, the essence) or the genos, and, in addition, phusis (nature), horos, horismos (definitio), and ousia (essentia). We begin by considering the morphe concept. What determines the thingness, Sachheit, in a being is its figure [Gestalt]. Something takes this or that shape, it becomes such and such. The expression is drawn from the sphere of sensory intuition. Here we first think of spatial figure. But the term should be freed from this restriction. What is intended is not just spatial figure but the whole characteristic form impressed on a being from which we read off what it is. We gather from the shape and impressed form of a thing what the case may be with it. Forming and shaping lend its own peculiar look to what is to be produced and has been produced. Look is the ontological sense of the Greek expression eidos or idea. In the look of a thing we are able to see what it is, its thingness, the peculiar character impressed on it. If we take a being as encountered in perception, then we have to say that the look of something is based on its characteristic form. It is the figure that gives the thing its look. With regard to the Greek concepts, the eidos, the look, is founded, grounded, in the morphe, the form.

For *Greek ontology,* however, the founding connection between eidos and morphe, look and form, is exactly the reverse. The look is not grounded in the form but the form, the morphe, is grounded in the look. This founding relationship can be explained only by the fact that the two determinations for thingness, the look and the form of a thing, are not understood in antiquity primarily in the order of the perception of something. In the order of apprehension I penetrate through the look of a thing to its form. The latter is essentially the first in the order of perception. But, if the relationship between the look and the form is reversed in ancient thought, the guiding clue for their interpretation cannot be the order of perception and perception itself. We must rather interpret them *with a view to production.* What is formed is, as we can also say, a shaped product. The potter forms a vase out of clay. All forming of shaped products is effected by using an image, in the sense of a model, as guide and standard. The thing is produced by looking to the anticipated look of what is to be produced by shaping, forming. It is this anticipated look of the thing, sighted beforehand, that the Greeks mean ontologically by eidos, idea. The shaped product, which is shaped in conformity with the model, is as such the exact likeness of the model.

If the shaped product, the form (morphe), is founded in the eidos, then this means that both concepts are understood by reference to the process of shaping, forming, producing. The order and connection of these two concepts is established by the performance of the process of forming and shaping and the necessary precedence in that process of the look of what is to be formed. The anticipated look, the proto-typical image, shows the thing as what it is before the production and how it is supposed to look as a product. The anticipated look has not yet been externalized as something formed, actual, but is the image of imag-ination, of fantasy, phantasia, as the Greeks say—that which forming first brings freely to sight, that which is sighted. It is no accident that Kant, for whom the concepts of form and matter, morphe and hule, play a fundamental epistemological role, con-jointly assigns to imagination a distinctive function in explaining the objec-tivity of knowledge. The eidos as the look, anticipated in imagination, of what is to be formed gives the thing with regard to what this thing already was and is before all actualization. Therefore the anticipated look, the eidos, is also called to ti en einai, that which a being already was. What a being already was before actualization, the look from which production takes the measure for its product, is at the same time that whence what is formed properly derives. The eidos, that which a thing already was beforehand, gives the kind of the thing, its kin and descent, its genos. Therefore thing-ness /or reality, Sachheit/ is also identical with genos, which should be translated as stock, family, generation. That is the ontological sense of this expression and not, say, the usual sense of the German Gattung /genus in the sense of a group or sort/. The logical meaning is founded on the former. When he deals with the highest what-determinations of a being, Plato most frequently speaks of the gene ton onton, the races, stocks, generations, of beings. Here, too, thingness is interpreted by looking to that from which the being derives in becoming formed.

The determination phusis also points toward the same direction of inter-pretation of the what. Phuein means to let grow, procreate, engender, pro-duce, primarily to produce its own self. What makes products or the produced product possible (producible) is again the look of what the product is supposed to become and be. The actual thing arises out of phusis, the nature of the thing. Everything earlier than what is actualized is still free from the imperfection, one-sidedness, and sensibilization given necessarily with all actualization. The what that precedes all actualization, the look that provides the standard, is not yet subject to change like the actual, to coming-to-be and passing-away. It is also earlier than the mutable thing; and as being *always* earlier, that is, as what a being—always conceived of as pro-ducible and produced—was already beforehand, it is what is true in and of the being of a being. The Greeks at the same time interpret what is thus veritable in the being of a being as that which itself truly is, so that the ideas, as constituting the actuality of the actual, are for Plato himself the properly and truly actual.

The look, eidos, and the form, morphe, each encloses within itself that which belongs to a thing. As enclosing, it constitutes the limiting boundary of what determines the thing as finished, complete. The look, as enclosing the belongingness of all the real determinations, is also conceived of as constituting the finishedness, the completedness, of a being. Scholasticism says perfectio; in Greek it is the teleion. This boundedness of the thing, which is distinctively characterized by its finishedness, is at the same time the possible object for an expressly embracing delimitation of the thing, for the horismos, the definition, the concept that comprehends the boundaries containing the reality of what has been formed.

In summary, the result relative to the characteristics of realitas is that they all develop with regard to what is configured in configuring, formed in forming, shaped in shaping, and made in making. Shaping, forming, making all signify a letting-come-here, letting-derive-from. We can characterize all these modes of action by a *basic comportment of the Dasein* which we can concisely call *producing [Herstellen]*. The characters of thingness (realitas) mentioned above, which were fixed for the first time in Greek ontology and later faded out and became formalized, that is, became part of the tradition and are now handled like well-worn coins, determine that which belongs in one way or another to the producibility of something produced. But to *pro*-duce, to place-*here*, *Her*-stellen, means at the same time to bring into the narrower or wider circuit of the accessible, here, to this place, to the Da, so that the produced being *stands for itself* on its own account and remains able to be found there and to *lie-before there [vorliegen]* as *something established stably for itself.* This is the source of the Greek term hupokeimenon, that which lies-before. That which first of all and constantly lies-before in the closest circle of human activity and accordingly is constantly disposable is the whole of all *things of use,* with which we constantly have to do, the whole of all those existent things which are themselves meant to be used on one another, *the implement that is employed* and the constantly used products of nature: house and yard, forest and field, sun, light and heat. What is thus tangibly present for dealing with *[vor-handen]* is reckoned by everyday experience as that which *is,* as a being, in the primary sense. Disposable possessions and goods, property, are beings; they are quite simply that which is, the Greek ousia. In Aristotle's time, when it already had a firm terminological meaning philosophically and theoretically, this expression ousia was still synonymous with property, possessions, means, wealth. The pre-philosophical proper meaning of ousia carried through to the end. Accordingly *a being* is synonymous with *an at-hand [extant] disposable.* Essentia is only the literal translation of ousia. This expression essentia, which was employed for whatness, reality, expresses at the same time the specific mode of being of a being, its disposability or, as we can also say, its at-handness, which belongs to it due to its having been produced.

The characteristics of essentia developed in reference to what is produced in producing or else to what belongs to producing as producing. The basic concept of ousia, in contrast, lays more stress on the producedness of the produced in the sense of things disposably present at hand. What is meant here primarily is what is present at hand, house and yard, the Anwesen, as the German has it—property as the present premises—the extant as what is present in that way. The verb einai, esse, existere, must be interpreted by way of the meaning of ousia as the disposably present-at-hand and that which is present *[as property and premises are present]*. Being, being-actual, or existing, in the traditional sense, means presence-at-hand. But producing is not the only horizon for the interpretation of existentia. With regard to its presence at hand, the extant is conceived of ontologically not so much by referring to the disposability for use or by reverting to the productive and in general the practical mode of activity as, rather, by reverting to our *finding present* *[finding there before us, Vorfinden]* what is thus disposable. But this comportment, too, the finding present of the produced and present-at-hand, belongs to producing itself. All producing is, as we say, fore-sighted *[vor-sichtig]* and circum-sighted *[um-sichtig]*. It really has its *sight;* it is sighted, and only because it is so can it sometimes set about things blindly. Sight is not an appendage to productive behavior but belongs positively to it and to its structure, and it guides the action. Therefore it is not surprising if this seeing, in the sense of the circumspective seeing that belongs to the ontological constitution of producing, becomes prominent also where ontology interprets the what which is to be produced. All shaping and forming has from the first an out-look upon the look (eidos) of that which is to be produced. Here it may already be seen that the phenomenon of sight which pertains to producing comes forward in characterizing the whatness of a thing as eidos. In the process of producing, that which the thing was is already sighted beforehand. Hence the pre-eminence of all these expressions in Greek ontology: idea, eidos, theorein. Plato and Aristotle speak of omma tes psuches, the soul's eye, which sees being. This looking toward the produced or the to-be-produced does not yet need to be theoretical contemplation in the narrower sense but is at first simply looking-toward in the sense of circumspective self-orientation.

Nevertheless, for reasons which we need not further touch on here, the Greeks define the mode of access to the extant primarily as an *intuitive finding present* *[das anschauende Vorfinden]*, a beholding perception, noein, or even theorein. This activity is also called aisthesis, aesthetic beholding in the proper sense, just as Kant still employs the expression "aesthetics," purely contemplative perception of the extant. In this purely intuitive activity, which is only a modification of seeing in the sense of circumspection, of productive behavior, the actuality of the actual is manifested. Parmenides, the true founder of ancient ontology, says: to gar auto noein estin te kai einai; noein, perceiving, simple apprehension, intuiting, and being, actuality, are the same. When Kant says that actuality is perception, his thesis is literally anticipated in the proposition of Parmenides.

We now see more clearly that the interpretation of essentia, and also exactly the interpretation of the basic concept for essentia, ousia, refer back to productive comportment toward beings, while pure beholding is fixed as the proper access to a being in its being-in-itself. We may observe incidentally that this interpretation of the basic ontological concepts of ancient philosophy does not by any means exhaust everything that would have to be said here. Above all, the Greek concept of the world, which could be set forth only by way of an interpretation of Greek existence, has been completely disregarded here.

For us there follows the task of showing that essentia and existentia have a common origin in the interpretative resort to productive comportment. In ancient ontology itself we discover nothing explicit about this recourse. *Ancient ontology performs in a virtually naive way its interpretation of beings and its elaboration of the concepts mentioned.* We do not discover anything about how to conceive the connection and the difference between the two and how to prove that they are necessarily valid for every being. But—it might be said—is this a defect and not rather an advantage? Is not naive inquiry superior in the certainty and importance of its results to all inquiry that is reflective and all too conscious? This can be affirmed but it must at the same time be taken as understood that naive ontology, too, if it is ontology at all, must already always, because necessarily, be reflective— reflective in the genuine sense that *it seeks to conceive beings with respect to their being by having regard to the Dasein* (psuche, nous, logos). Reference to the comportments of the Dasein in the matter of ontological interpretation can occur in such a way that what is referred to, the Dasein and its comportments, does not expressly become a problem but rather the naive ontological interpretation goes back to the Dasein's comportments in the same way in which it is acquainted with the Dasein's everyday and natural self-understanding. Ontology is naive, then, not because it does not look back at all to the Dasein, not because it does no reflecting at all—this is excluded—but because this necessary looking back toward the Dasein does not get beyond a common conception of the Dasein and its comportments and thus—because they belong to the Dasein's general everydayness—does not expressly emphasize them. Reflection here remains within the rut of pre-philosophical knowledge.

If reference to the Dasein and its comportments belongs to the essential nature of ontological inquiry and interpretation, then the ontological problematic of antiquity can be brought to itself and conceived in its possibility only if and when the necessity of this return to the Dasein is taken seriously. This return is at bottom no return at all, since the Dasein, corresponding to the nature of its existence, is always already consciously with its own self, is disclosed for itself, and as such always understands something like the being of a being. The Dasein does not first need to go back to itself. This talk of a return is justified only by the fact that the Dasein has apparently been forgotten in naive ancient ontology. Not only is *the explicit elaboration of the basis of ancient ontology* possible in principle for a possible philosophical understanding, but it is factually demanded by the incompleteness and indeterminateness of ancient ontology itself. Apart from the fact that the basic concepts are not themselves given an express and explicit foundation but are simply there, one knows not how, it remains before all else obscure whether what the second thesis says is valid and why it is valid: that essentia and existentia belong to every being. It is in no way proved and immediately evident that this thesis holds good of *every* being. This question becomes decidable only if it is established beforehand that every being is actual—that the realm of beings actually extant coincides with that of beings generally, that being coincides with actuality, and that every being is constituted by means of a whatness. If the attempted proof of the correctness of the thesis fails, that is, if being does not coincide with existentia in the ancient sense of actuality, extantness, then the thesis all the more requires an express foundation in its *restricted validity for all beings in the sense of the extant [at-hand]*. The question then has to be asked again whether what is intended in the thesis retains its universal validity if the essential content of the thesis is sufficiently extended and fundamentally conceived in regard to all possible modes of being. We not only wish to but must understand the Greeks better than they understood themselves. Only thus shall we actually be in possession of our heritage. Only then is our phenomenological investigation no mere patchwork or contingent alteration and improvement or impairment. It is always a sign of the greatness of a productive achievement when it can let issue from itself the demand that it should be understood better than it understands itself. Matters of no importance need no higher intelligibility. Ancient ontology, however, is fundamentally not unimportant and can never be overcome, because it represents the first necessary step that any philosophy in essence has to take, so that this step must always be repeated by every actual philosophy. Only a self-complacent modernity lapsed into barbarism can wish to make us believe that Plato, as it is tastelessly expressed, is done for. To be sure, antiquity will not be better understood by shifting our station to a further stage of the development of philosophy and taking it up, say, with Kant or with Hegel so as to interpret ancient thought with the aid of a Neo-Kantianism or a Neo-Hegelianism. All these revivals are already antiquated before they see the light. The point is to note that both Kant and Hegel still stand fundamentally on the soil of antiquity—that they, too, do not make up for the omission, due to neglect, that remained hidden as a necessity in the entire development of Western philosophy. The thesis that essentia and existentia belong to every being requires not only the clarification of the origin of these concepts but a universal foundation in general.

For us the concrete question arises, What are the problems to which our attempt to really understand the second thesis leads us? We may enlighten ourselves about this matter by way of proving the inadequate foundation of the traditional way of dealing with the problem.

§12. Proof of the inadequate foundation of the traditional treatment of the problem

a) Intentional structure and the understanding of being in productive comportment

The inadequacy of traditional thought becomes visible in the necessary *positive task*. The basic ontological concepts of thingness /Sachheit/, essentia, and of actuality, existentia, arise with a view to what is produced in productive activity or, again, with a view to the producible as such and the producedness of the produced, which is met with directly in intuition and perception as something already finished. The way might thus well be prescribed for a *more original* interpretation of essentia and existentia. In the discussion of the Kantian thesis, the task arose of investigating the intentional structure of perception in order to get clear of the ambiguity of the Kantian interpretation. Likewise, there is now suggested the path of providing an ontological foundation for the concepts essentia and existentia by going back to the *intentional structure of the productive mode of comportment*. We shall say in analogy to what was said in opposition to Kant: Actuality (existere, esse) is obviously not identical with producing and the produced any more than with perceiving and the perceived. However, actuality is also not identical with perceivedness, for to be perceived is only a characteristic of a being that has to do with its being apprehended; it is not the determination of the being's being-in-itself. But perhaps in producedness we find a character that defines the being-in-itself of a being? For a thing's being produced is after all the presupposition for its capacity to be apprehended in perception. When we have in mind the apprehendability of a being, we understand this being necessarily in relation to the apprehending subject, the Dasein generally speaking, but not the being of the being in itself, before all else and without its being in any way apprehended. But does not the same state of affairs obtain here, too, in regard to producedness as in relation to perceptual apprehension? Is there not implicit also in productive comportment a relation of the subject to what is produced, so that the character of producedness expresses no less a subjective reference than does the character of perceivedness? Here, however, foresight and mistrust are required in regard to all so-called acuteness that argues only with so-called rigorous concepts but is stricken with blindness when it comes to what the concepts really are supposed to mean, the phenomena.

The sense of direction and apprehension peculiar to productive comportment toward something involves taking that to which the productive activity relates as something which, in and through the producing, is supposed to be extant as finished *in its own self*. We described the directional sense that at any given time belongs to intentional comportment as the *understanding of being* belonging to intentionality. In productive comportment toward something, the being of that toward which I act in a productive manner is understood in a specific way in the sense of the productive intention. Indeed, it is understood in such a way that the productive activity, corresponding to its own peculiar sense, absolves what is to be produced from relation to the producer. Not *contrary* to its intention but in *conformity* with it, it releases from this relation the being that is to be produced and that which has been produced. Productive comportment's understanding of the being of the being toward which it is behaving takes this being beforehand as one that is to be released for its own self so as to stand independently on its own account. The *being [Sein]* that is *understood in productive comportment* is exactly the *being-in-itself of the product*.

To be sure, in its ontological nature as comportment of the Dasein toward something, productive comportment always and necessarily remains a relationship to beings; but it is an attitude and behavior of such a peculiar sort that the Dasein, keeping itself in the productive process, says to itself exactly, whether explicitly or not: The whereto of my action, conformable to its own peculiar mode of being, is not tied to this relation but rather is supposed to become, precisely by means of this action, something that stands on its own as finished. Not only is it, as finished, factually no longer bound to the productive relation but also, even as something still to be produced, it is understood beforehand as intended to be released from this relation.

Accordingly, in the specific intentional structure of production, that is, in its understanding of being, there is present a peculiar *character of discharge and release* as concerns that to which this behavior comports itself. Correspondingly, producedness (actuality as effectedness) includes within itself, to be sure, a reference to the producing Dasein; but this reference, corresponding to its own ontological sense, understands the product as released for its own self and thus as being in itself. Something like this intentionality of producing and the type of understanding of being peculiar to it should be seen simply with a vision that has not been dazzled and made squint-eyed by some current theory of knowledge. No matter how logically rigorous concepts may be, if they are blind then they are worthless. To see something like such an intentional structure of production and interpret it in one's analysis without prepossession, to make it accessible and keep hold of it and adapt one's concept to what is thus held fast and seen—this is the sober sense of the much ventilated so-called phenomenological Wesens-schau. Anyone who gets his information about phenomenology from newspapers and weekly reviews must let himself be talked into the notion that phenomenology is something like a mysticism, something like the "logic of the Indian contemplating his navel." This is not just a matter to be laughed at; it is actually current among people who wish to be taken in scientific earnest.

The thing to see is this. In the intentional structure of production there is implicit reference to something, by which this something is understood as not bound to or dependent on the subject but, inversely, as released and independent. In terms of fundamental principle, we encounter here an extremely peculiar transcendence of the Dasein, which we shall consider later in more detail and which, as will appear, is possible only on the basis of temporality.

This noteworthy character of the release of the thing to be produced in productive comportment has not, however, been interpreted completely by what has been said. The thing to be produced is not understood in productive action as something which, as product in general, is supposed to be extant /at hand/ in itself. Rather, in accordance with the productive intention implicit in it, it is already apprehended as something that, qua finished, is available at any time for *use*. It is intended in productive action not simply as something somehow put aside but as something put *here, here in the Dasein's sphere,* which does not necessarily have to coincide with the producer's own sphere. It can be the sphere of the user, which itself stands in an inner essential connection with that of the producer.

What we are trying to bring to light here by means of phenomenological analysis in regard to the intentional structure of production is not contrived and fabricated but already present in the everyday, pre-philosophical productive behavior of the Dasein. In producing, the Dasein lives in such an understanding of being without conceiving it or grasping it as such. There is immediately present in productive comportment toward something the understanding of the being-in-itself of that to which the comportment relates. Therefore it is no accident that ancient ontology, in its specific naivete—in the good sense of that term—oriented itself, even though only implicitly, in accordance with this everyday and familiar behavior of the Dasein, for in productive behavior there is obviously suggested of itself, for the Dasein, an attitude toward beings within which a being's being in-itself is immediately understood. But, after all, does not the interpretation of the being of a being as a product contain within itself an intolerable one-sidedness? Can every being be taken as a product and can the concepts of being be attained and fixed by having regard to productive comportment? Surely not everything of which we say that it *is* is brought into being by the Dasein as producer. That very being which the Greeks especially made the starting point and theme of their ontological investigations, that which is as nature and cosmos, is surely not produced by the Dasein as producer. How is Greek ontology, which was oriented primarily to the cosmos, supposed to have understood the being of the cosmos in terms of production, especially when it is precisely ancient thought which is not in the least familiar with anything like a creation and production of the world but rather is convinced of the world's eternity? For it, the world is the aei on, the always already extant, agenetos, anolethros, unoriginated and imperishable. In the face of this being, the cosmos, what is the point of looking toward production? Does not our interpretation of ousia, einai, existere, as presence-at-hand and producedness run aground here? Is it not in any case un-Greek, even if it may otherwise be valid? If we were to concede to being impressed by such arguments and to grant that productive comportment cannot be the guiding horizon for ancient ontology, then we would betray by this admission that, despite the analysis of the intentionality of production that has just been carried out, we have not yet seen this intentionality in a sufficiently phenomenological way. In the understanding of being that belongs to productive comportment, this comportment, as relating itself to something, releases just that to which it relates itself. It seems as though only a being that is produced could be understood in this sense. However, it only seems so.

If we bring to mind productive comportment in its full structure we see that it always makes use of what we call *material,* for instance, material for building a house. On its part this material is in the end not in turn produced but *is already there*. It is met with as a being that does not need to be produced. In production and its understanding of being, I thus comport myself toward a being that is not in need of being produced. I comport myself toward such a being not by accident but corresponding to the sense and essential nature of production, so far as this production is always the producing of something *from* something. What is not in need of being produced can really be understood and discovered only within the understanding of being that goes with production. In other words, it is first of all in the understanding of being that belongs to productive comportment and thus in the understanding of what does not need to be produced that there can grow the understanding of a being which is extant in itself *before* all production and *for* all further production. It is this understanding of what does not need to be produced, possible only in production, which understands the being of what already lies at the ground of and precedes everything to be produced and thus is all the more already extant in itself. The understanding of being in production is so far from merely understanding beings as produced that it rather opens up precisely the understanding of the being of that which is already simply extant. In production, therefore, we come up against just what does not need to be produced. In the course of producing and using beings we come up against the actuality of what is already there before all producing, products, and producibles, or of what offers resistance to the formative process that produces things. The concepts of matter and material have their origin in an understanding of being that is oriented to production. Otherwise, the idea of material as that *from which* something is produced would remain hidden. The concepts of matter and material, hule, that is, the counter-concepts to morphe, form, play a fundamental role in ancient philosophy not because the Greeks were materialists but because matter is a basic ontological concept that arises necessarily when a being—whether it is produced or is not in need of being produced—is interpreted in the horizon of the understanding of being which lies as such in productive comportment.

Productive comportment is not limited just to the producible and produced but harbors within itself a remarkable breadth of possibility for understanding the being of beings, which is at the same time the basis for the universal significance assignable to the fundamental concepts of ancient ontology.

But this still does not explain *why* ancient ontology interprets beings from exactly this direction. This is not self-evident and it cannot be an accident. From this question, why it was precisely production that served as horizon for the ontological interpretation of beings, arises the need to work out this horizon and give explicit reasons for its ontological necessity. For the mere fact that ancient ontology moves in this horizon is not yet the ontological foundation of its legitimacy and necessity. Only when the founding argument is given is a legitimate birth certificate issued for the concepts of essentia and existentia which grew out of this way of posing ontological problems. The argument for the legitimacy of the horizon described above for the interpretation of beings with regard to their essentia and existentia can be carried out only by making intelligible from the most distinctive *constitution of the Dasein's being* why the Dasein primarily and for the most part has to understand the being of beings in the horizon of productive-intuitive comportment. We must ask, What function does the action of producing and using in the broadest sense have within the Dasein itself? The answer is possible only if the constitution of the Dasein's being is first brought to light in its general basic features, that is, if the ontology of the Dasein is made secure. Then it can be asked whether from the Dasein's mode of being, from its way of existing, it can be made intelligible why ontology is oriented at first naively in conformity with this productive or perceptual-intuitive comportment. However, we are not yet prepared for the more penetrating analysis of the Dasein's mode of being. What we have to see for the present is only that ancient ontology interprets a being in its being by way either of production or perception and that, since Kant also interprets actuality with reference to perception, there is manifest here an undeviating continuity of tradition.

b) The inner connection between ancient (medieval) and Kantian ontology

Thus the attempt to get to the roots of the problem fixed in the second thesis leads us anew to the same task as did the original interpretation of the Kantian thesis. The Kantian interpretation of actuality by recourse to perception and intuition generally lies in the same direction as the Greek interpretation of being by reference to noein and theorein. But with Kant, and already long before him, the stock of ontological categories handed down from antiquity had become routine, deracinated and deprived of its native soil, its origin no longer understood.

If an inner connection exists in this way between ancient and Kantian ontology then—on the basis of the interpretation of ancient ontology, hence of productive comportment and its understanding of being—we must also be able to make clear to ourselves what Kant's interpretation of actuality as absolute position really means. Obviously, absolute positing does not mean for Kant that the subject posits the actual outside itself in the sense that it freely and arbitrarily first deposits something of the kind there and subjectively assumes something to be actual, for some reason or other judges that something is actual. Rather, *absolute positing* understood properly—even if Kant does not interpret it explicitly—means positing as the *letting something stand of its own self* and indeed absolutely, as detached, set free as "an und vor sich selbst," in and for its own self, as Kant says. If phenomenological interpretation is pushed far enough, we can also see in the Kantian interpretation of actuality as perception or as absolute position that here, too, use is made of the character of release and setting free that proffered itself to us particularly in the intentional structure of production. In other words, the specific sense of the direction of perception and of the understanding of being that belongs to intuition also has the character of a setting free of the at-hand to let it be encountered. It is no accident that as early as ancient ontology it is precisely perception, noein in the broadest sense, that functions as the activity which serves as the clue for ontologically defining a being that is encountered in it. For pure intuition and perception, if its intentional sense is understood, has the character of setting-free much more purely than production, because in intuition, in pure beholding, Dasein comports itself in such a way that it even desists from all commerce *with* the being, from occupation with it. Even more, in mere intuition every reference to the subject is pushed into the background and beings are understood not only as things to be set free, to be produced, but as themselves already extant, being encountered of themselves, on their own account. Hence, from antiquity to Kant and Hegel, intuition is the ideal of knowledge, the ideal of the apprehending of beings in general, and the concept of truth in knowledge is oriented to intuition. As regards Kant it is still to be noticed that, in conformity with the traditional theological founding of ontology, he measures knowledge by the idea of creative knowing, which, as knowing, first posits the known, brings it to being and thus first of all lets it be (intellectus archetypus). Truth in the proper sense is truth of beholding, intuitive apprehension.

With regard to the origin of ancient ontology from the productive and intuitive comportments toward beings, one further matter, which we may touch on briefly, becomes intelligible. In itself it is not simply a matter of course that ancient philosophy should have been adopted by Christian theology in the Middle Ages. In fact, it was only after arduous struggles and controversies that even Aristotle, who from the thirteenth century onward served as the standard for determining Christian and not only Catholic theology, was installed in the authoritative position that he still occupies. The reason this could happen, however, is the fact that for the Christian interpretation of the world, in conformity with the creation story of Genesis, every being that is not God himself is created. This presupposition is simply taken for granted. And even if creation out of nothing is not identical with producing something out of a material that is found already on hand, nevertheless, this creating of the creation has the general ontological character of producing. Creation is also interpreted in some sense with regard to production. Despite its different origins, it was as if ancient ontology in its foundations and basic concepts were cut to fit the Christian world-view and interpretation of that which *is* as ens creatum.

God as the ens increatum is the being which is absolutely without need of being produced and the causa prima of every other being. Of course, ancient ontology experienced an essential deviation by its reception in the Middle Ages so that the specifically ancient formulation of the problems was lost, a matter which we shall not now further pursue. But in this remodeling by the Middle Ages ancient ontology entered into the modern age through Suarez. Even where, as in Leibniz and Wolff, modern philosophy makes an independent return to antiquity, it occurs in terms of the understanding of the ancient basic concepts for which Scholasticism had already prepared the way.

Thus it has become clear that we should not and need not be satisfied with a common understanding of the basic concepts essentia and existentia, that there exists the possibility of exhibiting their origin. Only a radical interpretation of essentia and existentia can provide the basis on which the problem of their distinction can first of all be posed. The distinction must spring of itself from the roots they have in common.

Hence the question arises here whether the thesis that essentia and existentia belong to every being remains valid in this form—whether it can be made to hold in its purportedly universal ontological validity for every being in general. If sought, such a proof turns out to be impossible. In other words, the thesis cannot be maintained in the sense that has been described. Beings present at hand can certainly be interpreted ontologically in the horizon of production. It can certainly be shown that in every instance a whatness having the characteristics mentioned belongs to being-at-hand. Nevertheless, the question remains whether the *whole universe* of beings is exhausted by the at-hand. Does the realm of the extant, the at-hand, coincide with the realm of beings in general? Or is there any being that, precisely due to the sense of its being, cannot be conceived as being at hand? In point of fact, the being that can least of all be conceived as extant, at hand, the Dasein that in each instance we ourselves are, is just that to which all understanding of being-at-hand, actuality, must be traced back. The sense of this retracing has to be explained.

c) Necessity for restricting and modifying the second thesis. Basic articulation of being and ontological difference

If the Dasein exhibits an ontological constitution completely different from that of the extant at-hand, and if to exist, in our terminological usage, means something other than existere and existentia (einai), then it also becomes a question whether anything like Sachheit, thingness, whatness, reality, essentia, ousia, can belong to the ontological constitution of the Dasein. Sachheit, thingness, whatness, reality, realitas, or quidditas, is that which answers the question *Quid* est res, *what* is the thing? Even a rough consideration shows that the being that we ourselves are, the Dasein, cannot at all be *interrogated* as such by the question *What* is this? We gain access to this being only if we ask: *Who* is it? The Dasein is not constituted by whatness but—if we may coin the expression—by *whoness.* The answer does not give a thing but an I, you, we. But on the other hand we still ask: *What* is this *who* and this whoness of the Dasein—what is the who in distinction from the aforementioned what in the narrower sense of the reality of the extant at-hand? No doubt we do ask such a question. But this only shows that this what, with which we also ask about the nature of the who, obviously cannot coincide with the what in the sense of whatness. In other words, the basic concept of essentia, whatness, first becomes really problematic in the face of the being we call the Dasein. The inadequate founding of the thesis as a universally ontological one becomes evident. If it is to have an ontological significance at all, then it is in need of a *restriction* and *modification*. It must be shown positively in which sense each being can be interrogated regarding its what but also in which sense a being must be queried by the who-question. Only from here on does the problem of the distinctio between essentia and existentia become complicated. It is not only the question of the relationship of *whatness* and *extantness* but at the same time the question of the relationship of *whoness* and *existence [Existenz]*—existence understood in our sense as the mode of being of the being that we ourselves are. Formulated more generally, the thesis that essentia and existentia belong to each being merely points to the general problem of the articulation of each being into a being *that* it is and the *how* of its being.

We have already pointed earlier to the connection between the *basic articulation of being* and the *ontological difference*. The problem of the articulation of being into essentia and existentia, formulated in Scholastic terms, is only a more special question touching on the ontological difference generally, the difference between *a* being and being. It now appears that the ontological difference is becoming more complicated, however formal this difference sounds and looks. More complicated because under the heading "being" we now have *not only essentia* and *existentia* but *also whoness* and *existence* in our sense. The articulation of being varies each time with the way of being of a being. This way of being cannot be restricted to at-hand extantness and actuality in the traditional sense. The question of the possible *multiplicity of being* and therewith at the same time that of the *unity of the concept of being in general* becomes urgent. Simultaneously, the empty formula for the ontological difference grows ever richer in the problems it contains.

First, however, one problem makes its claim on our attention: besides the extant (at-hand extantness) there are beings in the sense of the Dasein, who exists. But this being which we ourselves are—was this not always already known, in philosophy and even in pre-philosophical knowledge? Can one make such a fuss about stressing expressly the fact that besides the extant at-hand there is also this being that we ourselves are? After all, every Dasein, insofar as it is, always already knows about itself and knows that it differs from other beings. We ourselves said that for all its being oriented primarily to the extant at-hand, ancient ontology nevertheless is familiar with psuche, nous, logos, zoe, bios, soul, reason, life in the broadest sense. Of course. But it should be borne in mind that the ontical, factual familiarity of a being does not after all guarantee a suitable interpretation of its being. The Dasein is indeed already aware that it is not just another being which it experiences. At least the Dasein can be aware of it. Not every Dasein has this awareness; for example, mythical and magical thinking identifies things with itself. But even when the Dasein does take cognizance that it itself is not another being, this does not include the explicit knowledge that its mode of being is different from that of the being which it itself is not. Rather, as we see in the example of antiquity, the Dasein can ontologically interpret itself and its mode of being with regard to the extant at-hand and its way of being. The specific question about the ontological constitution of the Dasein gets blocked and confused by many preconceptions which are grounded in the Dasein's own existence. That this is so will be made clear to us, among other things, by the discussion of the third thesis. It will aim above all at making generally plainer to us the problem of the multiplicity of ways of being extending beyond the uniqueness of mere at-hand extantness.

Chapter Three

The Thesis of Modern Ontology: The Basic Ways of Being Are the Being of Nature (Res Extensa) and the Being of Mind (Res Cogitans)

§13. Characterization of the ontological distinction between res extensa and res cogitans with the aid of the Kantian formulation of the problem

The discussion of the first two theses led us in each case to turn the question of the meaning of actuality, or of thingness and actuality, back to the Dasein's comportments. Using as a clue the intentional structure of these comportments and the understanding of being immanent in each comportment, we were thus enabled to ask to what each comportment relates: the perceived of perception in its perceivedness, the product (producible) of production in its producedness. The two comportments at the same time revealed an interconnection. All producing is oriented by visual awareness; it is perceptual in the broadest sense.

The necessity of such a reversion to the Dasein's comportments is generally an indication that the Dasein itself has a distinctive function for making possible an adequately founded ontological inquiry in general. This implies that the investigation of the Dasein's specific mode of being and ontological constitution is unavoidable. Furthermore, we stressed repeatedly that all ontology, even the most primitive, necessarily looks back to the Dasein. Wherever philosophy awakens, this entity already stands in the sphere of vision, even if with a different clarity and with varying insight into its function for fundamental ontology. In antiquity and the Middle

Ages the use made of this return to the Dasein was by a virtually necessary constraint. In Kant we see a conscious reversion to the ego. To be sure, this reversion to the subject has other motives for him. It does not spring directly from insight into the fundamental-ontological function of the Dasein. This return in the specifically Kantian view is rather a result of the orientation of philosophical problems already predominant in him, an orientation toward the subject. This orientation itself is the one that determines the philosophical tradition and, beginning with Descartes, starts from the ego, the subject. The motive of this primary orientation toward the subject in modern philosophy is the opinion that this being which we ourselves are is given to the knower first and as the only certain thing, that the subject is accessible immediately and with absolute certainty, that it is better known than all objects. In comparison, objects are accessible only by way of a mediation. In this form, this view is untenable, as we shall later see.

a) The modern orientation toward the subject; its motive as not fundamental-ontological; and its dependence on traditional ontology

In the ensuing discussion of the *third thesis,* we are not interested in the pre-eminent role claimed by subjectivity in modern philosophy. We are even less interested in the motives that led to this pre-eminence of the subject or the consequences that resulted for the development of modern philosophy. Rather, we are taking aim at a problem of principle. We have so far seen that ancient philosophy interprets and understands the being of beings, the actuality of the actual, as being extant /in the sense of being at hand/. The ontologically exemplary entity, the being from which being and its meaning are gathered, is nature in the broadest sense, including natural products and equipment made from them, things disposable or available in the widest sense or, in the language customary since Kant, objects. Modern philosophy made a total turnabout of philosophical inquiry and started out from the subject, the ego. It will be surmised and expected that, in conformity with this fundamental diversion of inquiry to the ego, the being now standing at the center would become decisive in its specific mode of being. It will be expected that ontology now takes the subject as exemplary entity and interprets the concept of being by looking to the mode of being of the subject—that henceforth the subject's *way of being* becomes an ontological problem. But that is precisely what does not happen. The motives for modern philosophy's primary orientation to the subject are not fundamental-ontological. The motive is not to know precisely *that* and *how* being and being's structure can be clarified in terms of the Dasein itself.

Descartes, who carried through the turn to the subject that was already prepared for in different ways, not only does not pose the question of the being of the subject but even interprets the subject's being under the guidance of the concept of being and its pertinent categories as developed by ancient and medieval philosophy. Descartes' basic ontological concepts are drawn directly from Suarez, Duns Scotus, and Thomas Aquinas. The Neo-Kantianism of recent decades introduced the historical construction that with Descartes a completely new epoch of philosophy begins. Everything before him back to Plato, who was himself interpreted by Kantian categories, was supposed to be mere darkness. In opposition to this notion, it is rightly stressed today that modern philosophy since Descartes still continues to work with the ancient metaphysical problems and thus, along with everything new, still remains within the tradition. But this correction of the Neo-Kantian interpretation of the history of thought does not yet touch the decisive point for a philosophical understanding of modern philosophy. It implies not only that the old metaphysical problems continued to be treated along with the new problems but also that precisely the newly posed problems were posed and treated on the foundation of the old—that therefore the philosophical revolution of modern philosophy, seen fundamentally in ontological terms, was not a revolution at all. On the contrary, by this turnabout, by this allegedly critical new beginning of philosophy in Descartes, the traditional ontology was taken over. By this allegedly critical new beginning ancient metaphysics became dogmatism, which it had not earlier been in this style; it became a mode of thought that with the aid of traditional metaphysical concepts seeks to gain a positively ontical knowledge of God, the soul, and nature.

Although in modern philosophy everything in principle remained as it was, the marking out and accentuating of the subject had to result in shifting the distinction between subject and object in some way to the center and, associated with that, in conceiving with greater penetration the peculiar nature of subjectivity.

We must first of all see in what way modern philosophy conceives this distinction between subject and object or, more precisely, how subjectivity is characterized. This distinction between subject and object pervades all the problems of modern philosophy and even extends into the development of contemporary phenomenology. In his *Ideas,* Husserl says: "The theory of categories must begin absolutely from this most radical of all distinctions of being—being *as consciousness* [res cogitans] and being as being that *'manifests'* itself in consciousness, 'transcendent' being [res extensa]."[1] "Be-

---

1. Husserl, *Ideen,* vol. 1, p. 174. [Edmund Husserl, *Ideen zur reinen Phänomenologie und phänomenologische Philosophie,* first published in *Jahrbuch für Philosophie und phänomenologische Forschung,* vol. 1, edited by Husserl (Halle: Max Niemeyer, 1913, 1922, 1928), trans. W. R. Boyce-Gibson, *Ideas* (London: Macmillan, 1931). The quoted passage is on p. 212. There are

tween consciousness [res cogitans] and reality [res extensa] there yawns a veritable abyss of meaning."[2] Husserl continually refers to this distinction and precisely in the form in which Descartes expressed it: res cogitans— res extensa.

How is this distinction more exactly defined? How is the being of the subject or ego conceived as compared with reality, which here means actuality, extantness? The fact that this distinction is asserted does not yet imply that the differing ways of being of these entities are also expressly conceived. But, if the being of the subject should reveal itself as other than extantness, then a fundamental limit would be set to the hitherto prevailing equation of being with actuality, or extantness, and thus to ancient ontology. The question of the unity of the concept of being becomes all the more pressing in the face of these two diversities of being which first come to view.

In what respect are subject and object distinguished ontologically? To answer this question we could conveniently turn to Descartes' formulation. He moved this distinction for the first time explicitly to the center. Or we could seek for particulars at the decisive terminus of the development of modern philosophy, in Hegel, who formulates the difference as that between nature and spirit or between substance and subject. We choose neither the beginning nor the end of the development of this problem but instead the decisive intermediate station between Descartes and Hegel, the *Kantian version of the problem,* which was influenced by Descartes and in its turn influenced Fichte, Schelling, and Hegel.

b) Kant's conception of ego and nature (subject and object) and his definition of the subject's subjectivity

How does Kant conceive the distinction between ego and nature, subject and object? How does he characterize the ego—what does the *essential nature of egohood* consist in?

α) Personalitas transcendentalis

Basically Kant here retains Descartes' conception. However essential Kant's own investigations have become and will always remain for the

---

two recent German editions of *Ideen,* vol. 1, the first edited by Walter Biemel as a "new edition based on the handwritten additions of the author" (The Hague: Martinus Nijhoff, 1950), and the second edited by Karl Schuhmann, which contains "the text reproduced as it was in Husserl's lifetime, 1913, 1922, 1928, 'three almost completely identical editions,' " and "all of Husserl's manuscript additions in the second half-volume" (The Hague: Martinus Nijhoff, 1976). Both these later editions appear in the series: *Husserliana: Edmund Husserl, Gesammelte Werke.*]

2. *Ideen,* p. 117. [*Ideas,* p. 153.]

ontological interpretation of subjectivity, the I, the ego, is for him, as it was for Descartes, res cogitans, *res, something,* that thinks, namely, something that represents, perceives, judges, agrees, disagrees, but also loves, hates, strives, and the like. Descartes calls all these modes of behavior cogitationes. But according to Descartes cogitare is always cogito *me* cogitare. Every act of representing is an *"I* represent," each judging an *"I* judge," each willing an *"I* will." The "I-think," "me-cogitare," is always co-represented even though it is not held in mind expressly and explicitly.

Kant adopts this definition of the ego as res cogitans in the sense of cogito me cogitare except that he formulates it in a more fundamental ontological way. He says the ego is that whose determinations are representations in the full sense of repraesentatio. We know that "determination" /Bestimmung/ is not an arbitrary concept or term for Kant but the translation of the term determinatio or realitas. The ego is a res, whose realities are representations, cogitationes. As *having* these determinations the ego is res cogitans. Res must be taken to mean only what is meant by the rigorous ontological concept, namely, "something." However, in traditional ontology—we may recall Baumgarten's *Metaphysics* §36—these determinations, determinationes or realitates, are the notae or praedicata, the predicates of things. Representations are determinations of the ego, its predicates. In grammar and general logic, that which has predicates is called the subject. As res cogitans, the ego is a subject in the grammatical-logical sense; it has predicates. Subjectum is to be taken here as a formal-apophantic category. A category is called apophantic if it belongs to the structure of that which is the formal structure of the assertive content of an assertion in general. That about which the assertion is made, the about-which, is the subjectum, that which lies at the basis of the assertion. The asserted what is the predicate. The ego which has the determinations is, like every other something, a subjectum that has predicates. But *how* does this subject, as an ego, have its predicates, the representations? This res est cogitans; this something thinks, which means according to Descartes cogitat se cogitare. The thinker's being-thinking is co-thought in the thinking. The *having* of the determinations, the predicates, is a *knowing* of them. The ego as subject—taken throughout in the grammatically formal-apophantical sense—has its predicates in a cognizing way. In thinking, I know this thinking as my thinking. As this peculiar subject, I know about the predicates I have. *I know myself.* Because of this distinctive having of its predicates, this subject is a distinctive subject, that is to say, the ego is the subject kat' exochen. The ego is a subject in the sense of self-consciousness. This subject not only is *distinct* from its predicates but also *has* them as known by it, which means as *objects.* This res cogitans, the something that thinks, is a subject of predicates and as such it is a subject *for* objects.

The subject concept in the sense of subjectivity, of egohood, is connected in the most intimate way ontologically with the formal-apophantic category of the subjectum, the hupokeimenon, in which at first nothing at all of egohood is present. On the contrary, the hupokeimenon is the extant, the disposable. It is because the ego is the subject proper or, in Greek, the substance proper, hupokeimenon, for the first time explicitly in Kant, even though already prefigured in Descartes and above all in Leibniz, that Hegel can say that the true substance is the subject or the true meaning of substantiality is subjectivity. This principle of the Hegelian philosophy lies in the direct line of development of the problems of modern thought.

What is the most general structure of the ego, or what constitutes egohood? Answer: self-consciousness. All thinking is "I am thinking." The ego is not simply any arbitrary isolated point; it is "I-*think*." However, it does not perceive itself as a being that would have other determinations beside this one, that it just thinks. Rather the ego knows itself as the *ground* of its determinations, its comportments, as the ground of its own unity in the multiplicity of these comportments, as the ground of the selfness of its own self. All the determinations and comportments of the ego are ego-based. I perceive, I judge, I act. The "I-think," says Kant, must be able to accompany all my representations, that is, every cogitare of cogitata. This statement is not to be taken, however, as though the idea of the ego is present along with every comportment, with every thinking in the broadest sense. Instead, I am conscious of the linkage of all comportments with my ego; that is to say, I am conscious of them in their multiplicity as *of my* unity, which has its ground as such in my egohood (as subjectum). It is only on the basis of the "*I*-think" that any manifold can be given to me. In a summary way, Kant interprets the ego as the "original synthetic unity of apperception." What does this mean? The ego is the original *ground* of the *unity* of the manifold of its determinations in this sense, that as ego I have them all together with regard to myself, I keep them together, combine them, from the outset—synthesis. The original ground of unity *is* what it is, it is this ground as *unifying*, as synthetic. The combining of the manifold of representations and of what is represented in them must always be thought along with them. The combining is of such a sort that in thinking I am also thinking *myself*. I do not simply apprehend what is thought and represented, I do not just perceive it, but in all thinking I think myself along with it. I do not perceive but *ap*perceive the ego. The *original synthetic unity of apperception* is the *ontological characteristic* of the distinctive *subject*.

From what has been said it becomes clear that with this concept of egohood the formal structure of personality or, as Kant says, *personalitas transcendentalis* has been gained. What does this term "transcendental" signify? Kant says: "I call transcendental all knowledge which is occupied not so much with objects as with our mode of knowing objects insofar as this knowledge is supposed to be possible a priori."[3] Transcendental knowledge relates not to objects, not to beings, but to the concepts that determine the being of beings. "A system of such concepts would be called transcendental philosophy."[4] Transcendental philosophy denotes nothing but ontology. That this interpretation does not do violence to Kant's meaning is attested by the following sentence that Kant wrote about a decade after the second edition of the *Critique of Pure Reason,* in the essay that was published immediately after his death, *On the Prize Question proposed for the year 1791 by the Royal Academy of Sciences at Berlin,* "*What Real Progress has Metaphysics made in Germany since the Times of Leibniz and Wolff?*" "Ontology (as a branch of metaphysics) is the science that consists of a system of all concepts and principles of the understanding, but only so far as they are directed at objects which can be given to the senses and therefore can be verified by experience."[5] Ontology "is called transcendental philosophy because it contains the conditions and first elements of all our *knowledge* a priori."[6] Kant always stresses here that as transcendental philosophy ontology has to do with the *knowledge* of objects. This does not mean, as Neo-Kantianism interpreted it, epistemology. Instead, since ontology treats of the being of beings and, as we know, Kant's conviction is that being, actuality, equals perceivedness, being-known, it follows that ontology as science of being must be the science of the being-known of objects and of their possibility. It is for this reason that ontology is transcendental philosophy. The interpretation of Kant's *Critique of Pure Reason* as epistemology completely misses the true meaning.

From our previous considerations we know that for Kant being equals perceivedness. The basic conditions of the being of beings, or of perceivedness, are therefore the basic conditions of the being-known of things. However, the basic condition of knowing as knowing is the ego as "I-think." Hence Kant continually inculcates that the ego is not a representation, that it is not a represented object, not a being in the sense of an object, but rather the ground of the possibility of all representing, all perceiving, hence of all the perceivedness of beings and thus the ground of all being. As original synthetic unity of apperception, the ego is the fundamental ontological condition of all being. The basic determinations of the being of

---

3. Kant, *Critique of Pure Reason,* B25.
4. Ibid.
5. Kant, *Werke* (Cassirer), vol. 8, p. 238. [Kant did not submit the essay in the competition. On the title page in Cassirer it is called *Fortschritte der Metaphysik.* Heidegger later refers to it as *On the Progress of Metaphysics.*]
6. Ibid.

beings are the categories. The ego is not one among the categories of beings but the condition of the possibility of categories in general. Therefore, the ego does not itself belong among the root concepts of the understanding, as Kant calls the categories; instead, as Kant expresses it, the ego is "the vehicle of all concepts of the understanding." It first of all makes possible the basic a priori ontological concepts. For the ego is not something isolated, not a mere point, but always "I-think," that is, "I-combine." And Kant interprets the categories as that which, in every combining by the understanding, has already been seen and understood beforehand as what provides the corresponding unity of the combined for each combining to be accomplished. The categories are the possible forms of unity of the possible modes of the thinking ego, the "I-combine." Combinability and, corresponding to it, its own form, its respective unity, are grounded in the "I-combine." Thus the ego is the fundamental ontological condition, the transcendental that lies at the basis of every particular a priori. We now understand that the ego as the I-think is the formal structure of personality as personalitas transcendentalis.

β) Personalitas psychologica

This, however, does not exhaustively define the concept of subjectivity in Kant. To be sure, this concept of the transcendental ego remains the model for the further interpretation of egohood, personality in the formal sense. But personalitas transcendentalis does not coincide with the complete concept of personality. From the personalitas transcendentalis, the ontological concept of egohood in general, Kant distinguishes the *personalitas psychologica*. By this he means the factual faculty, grounded in the personalitas transcendentalis, in the "I think," to become conscious of its empirical states, of its representations as occurrences that exist and are always varying. Kant makes a distinction between pure self-consciousness and empirical self-consciousness or, as he also puts it, between the ego of apperception and the *ego of apprehension*. Apprehension means perception, the experience of the extant, namely, the experience of extant psychical processes by means of the so-called inner sense. The pure ego, the ego of self-consciousness, of transcendental apperception, is not a fact of experience; in all empirical experiencing, I am already conscious of this ego as "I experience," the ontological ground of the possibility of all experiencing. The empirical ego as soul can likewise be thought theoretically as an idea and then it coincides with the concept of soul, where soul is conceived as the ground of animality or, as Kant says, of animateness, of life in general. The ego as personalitas transcendentalis is the ego that is essentially always only subject, the subject-ego. The ego as personalitas psychologica is the ego that is always only an object, something encountered as extant, the object-ego, or as Kant explicitly says, "this object-ego, the empirical ego, is a thing *[Sache]*." All psychology is therefore positive science of extant entities. In the essay *On the Progress of Metaphysics,* Kant says: "For human intelligence, psychology is nothing more and also can become nothing more than anthropology, knowledge of man, but restricted to this condition: so far as he knows himself as an object of inner sense. He is also, however, conscious of himself as an object of his external senses: he has a body, connected with which is the object of inner sense called man's soul."[7] From this psychological ego Kant distinguishes the ego of apperception as the logical ego. The term "logical ego" needs a more detailed interpretation because Neo-Kantianism has completely misunderstood this concept along with many other essentials in Kant. By the designation "logical ego" Kant does not intend to say, as Rickert thinks, that this ego is a logical abstraction, something universal, nameless, and unreal. "The ego is a logical ego" does not mean for Kant, as it does for Rickert, an ego that is logically conceived. It means instead that the ego is subject of the logos, hence of thinking; the ego is the ego as the "I combine" which lies at the basis of all thinking. At the same place where he is speaking of the logical ego Kant says in full profusion: "it is, as it were, like the substance [that is, like the hupokeimenon] which remains over when I have abstracted all the accidents inhering in it."[8] This egohood is the same in all factual subjects. This cannot mean that the logical ego is something universal, nameless; it is precisely by its essential nature always mine. It pertains to egohood that the ego is always mine. A nameless ego is an absurdity. When I say "I think" or "I think of myself," the first ego is not some other ego as though, say, a universal, unreal ego were speaking in the first ego. Rather it is quite the same as the ego being thought or, as Kant says, the determinable ego. The ego of apperception is identical with the determinable ego, the ego of apprehension, except that what I am as a determinate empirical ego does not have to be thought simultaneously in the concept of the determinant ego. Fichte applied these concepts of the determinant and determinable ego as fundamental for his *Wissenschaftslehre.* The determinant ego of apperception *is.* Kant says that we cannot assert anything more about this being and its being than *that it is.* Only because this ego is as this I myself, this ego itself, can it encounter itself as an empirical ego.

" 'I am conscious of myself' is a thought that already contains a twofold ego, the ego as subject and the ego as object. Although it is an indubitable

7. Ibid., p. 294.
8. Ibid., p. 249.

fact, it is simply impossible to explain how it is possible that I who am thinking myself can be my own object (of intuition) and thus can differentiate myself from myself. However it points to a faculty elevated so far above all sense intuitions that, as the ground of possibility of an understanding, it has as its consequence our complete separation from every beast, to which we have no reason to ascribe the capacity to say 'I' to itself, and it looks beyond to an infinity of self-made representations and concepts [the ontological ones]. What is intended by this, however, is not a double personality; only I who think and intuit am the person, whereas the ego of the object that is intuited by me is, like other objects outside me, the thing [Sache]."[9] That the ego of transcendental apperception is logical, the subject of the "I combine," does not signify that it is a different ego compared with the actual, existent psychical ego; it does not even mean that it is not anything that *is*. Only this much is asserted, that the being of this ego is problematic; according to Kant it is in general indeterminable, and in any case in principle not capable of determination by means of psychology. The personalitas psychologica presupposes the personalitas transcendentalis.

γ) Personalitas moralis

But the true and central characterization of the ego, of subjectivity, in Kant is not yet gained by describing the ego as personalitas transcendentalis and personalitas psychologica, subject-ego and object-ego. It lies in the concept of *personalitas moralis*. According to Kant, man's personality, the constitution of his being a person, is exhausted neither by the personalitas psychologica, which is the ground of animality, nor by the personalitas transcendentalis, which characterizes man's rationality in general, nor by both together. This is indicated by a passage from Kant's work *Religion Within the Limits of Reason Alone*. In book 1, section 1, entitled "Concerning the Original Predisposition to Good in Human Nature," Kant enumerates three elements of man's determination: animateness, humanity, and personality.[10] The first determination, animateness, distinguishes man as a living being in general; the second determination, humanity, as a living and at the same time a rational being; the third determination, personality, as a rational being and at the same time a responsible, accountable being. When he speaks of personality as the third element in distinction from humanity as the second, it is apparent that personality is meant here in a narrower sense contrasted with personalitas transcendentalis, which is iden-

---

9. Ibid., pp. 248–249.

10. Kant, *Werke* (Cassirer), vol. 6, p. 164. [*Die Religion innerhalb der Grenzen der blossen Vernunft*, trans. Theodore M. Greene and Hoyt H. Hudson, *Religion Within the Limits of Reason Alone* (New York, Evanston and London: Harper and Row, 1960), pp. 21–23.]

tical with humanity. To the complete concept of personalitas belongs not only rationality but also responsibility. Consequently, personality has a two-fold meaning for Kant: first, the broad formal concept of egohood in general in the sense of self-consciousness, whether the transcendental I-think or the empirical object-ego; and, secondly, the narrower and proper concept which in a certain way includes the other two meanings, or what they mean, but has its center in the determination we now have to consider. *Personality proper* is *personalitas moralis.* If the formal structure of personality in general lies in self-consciousness, then the personalitas moralis must express a specific *modification of self-consciousness* and thus it must represent a peculiar kind of self-consciousness. It is this moral personality that really characterizes the person in regard to what that personality *is.* How does Kant elucidate moral self-consciousness? What does the human being know himself to be insofar as he understands himself morally, as an acting being? What does he then understand himself to be and of what nature is this moral self-knowledge? Obviously, moral self-knowledge cannot coincide with the types of self-consciousness discussed previously, either empirical or transcendental. Above all, moral self-consciousness cannot be the empirical knowledge and experience of a factual state simply extant; it cannot be an empirical—which always means for Kant a sensible—self-consciousness, one mediated by inner or outer sense. Moral self-consciousness, especially if it concerns personalitas in the strict and proper sense, will be man's true being as a mental being /Geistigkeit/ and will not be mediated by sense-experience. According to Kant there pertains to sensibility in the broader sense not only the faculty of sensation but also the faculty he commonly designates as the feeling of pleasure and unpleasure, or delight in the agreeable, or the reverse. Pleasure in the widest sense is not only desire *for* something and pleasure *in* something but always also, as we may say, *enjoyment;* this is a way in which the human being, turning with pleasure toward something, *experiences himself as enjoying*—he is joyous.

We must elucidate this state of affairs phenomenologically. It pertains in general to the essential nature of feeling not only that it is feeling *for* something but also that this feeling for something at the same time makes feelable the feeler himself and his state, his being in the broadest sense. Conceived in formally universal terms, feeling expresses for Kant a peculiar mode of revelation of the ego. In having a feeling *for* something there is always present at the same time a *self*-feeling, and in this *self*-feeling a mode of becoming revealed to oneself. The manner in which I become manifest to myself in feeling is determined in part by that for which I have a feeling in this feeling. Thus it appears that feeling is not a simple reflection upon oneself but rather a feeling of *self* in having a feeling *for* something. This is a structure already somewhat complex but intrinsically unitary. The essential feature in what Kant designates as feeling is not the one we customarily have in mind in our everyday understanding—feeling, contrasted with conceptually theoretical apprehension and self-knowledge, as indefinite, vague, a momentary presentiment, and the like. What is phenomenologically decisive in the phenomenon of feeling is that it directly uncovers and makes accessible that which is felt, and it does this not, to be sure, in the manner of intuition but in the sense of a direct having-of-oneself. Both moments of the structure of feeling must be kept in mind: feeling as feeling-for and simultaneously the self-feeling in this having-feeling-for.

It should be noted that for Kant not every feeling is sensible, that is, determined by pleasure, and hence sensibility. If the moral self-consciousness is not to make manifest an accidental momentary state of the empirical subject, if it cannot be sensibly empirical, this does not exclude it from being like a feeling in the well-defined Kantian sense. The moral self-consciousness *must* be a feeling if it is to be distinguished from theoretical knowledge in the sense of the theoretical "I think myself." Kant therefore speaks of "moral feeling" or of the "feeling of my existence." This is not an accidental empirical experience of myself, but neither is it a theoretical knowing and thinking of the ego as subject of thinking; it is instead a making manifest of the ego in its non-sensible character, a revealing of itself as an acting being.

What is this moral feeling? What does it reveal? How does Kant, starting from what is itself revealed by moral feeling, define the ontological structure of the moral person? For him the moral feeling is *respect, Achtung.* In this feeling of respect the moral self-consciousness, personalitas moralis, man's true personality, must reveal itself. We shall first try to take a closer look at the Kantian analysis of this phenomenon of respect. Kant calls it a feeling. The essential structure of feeling discussed above must be able to be exhibited in respect, so that, first, it is the having of a feeling for something, and, secondly, as this having-feeling-for, it is a revelation of that which feels its own self. Kant gives the analysis of respect in the *Critique of Practical Reason,* chapter 3, "On the Motives of Pure Practical Reason." Given the limited purposes of our description of Kant's analysis, we cannot enter into all the particulars and fine details, and still less can we represent all the concepts of morality basically necessary for understanding it, like duty, action, law, maxims, freedom. Kant's interpretation of the phenomenon of respect is probably the most brilliant phenomenological analysis of the phenomenon of morality that we have from him.

He says: "The essential thing in all determinations of the will by the moral law is that as a free will it should be determined solely by the law and, moreover, not merely without the co-operation of sensuous impulses but even with the repulsion of all such impulses and with the breaking off of all inclinations so far as they go counter to that law."[11] This statement gives only a negative definition of the effect of the moral law as a motive of moral action. The law brings about a breaking off that is practiced on the inclinations, or sensible feelings. But this negative effect of feeling, the rupturing of sensible feelings, the repelling of them, "is itself a feeling."[12] This recalls the well-known statement of Spinoza in his *Ethics* that an emotion can be overcome only by an emotion. If a repulsion of sensible feelings is present, then a positive feeling which performs the repulsion must admit of being exhibited in it. Therefore Kant says: "Consequently, we can see a priori [from the phenomenon of the repudiation of sensible feelings] that the moral law, as a determining ground of the will, in thwarting all our inclinations [the sensible feelings] must [itself] produce a feeling."[13] From the negative phenomenon of repulsion the force that performs and grounds the repelling must become visible a priori and positively. All the sensible inclinations subjected to the break are inclinations in the sense of self-love and self-conceit. The moral law strikes down self-conceit. "But, after all, this law is intrinsically positive, namely, the form of an intellectual [not sensible] causality, the causality of freedom; therefore, in *weakening* self-conceit by acting against subjective opposition, namely, the inclinations in us, it is at the same time an object of *respect;* and since it even *strikes down* self-conceit, humiliates it, it is an object of the greatest respect and moreover the ground of a positive feeling which does not have an empirical origin and can be known a priori. Respect for the moral law is therefore a feeling that is produced by an intellectual ground, and this feeling is the only one we can know completely a priori and whose necessity we can comprehend."[14] This feeling of respect for the law can "be called a moral feeling."[15] "This feeling (under the title of the moral) is also produced solely by reason [not by sensibility]. It serves not for judging actions nor even for substantiating the objective ethical law itself but merely as a motive in order to make the ethical law itself into a maxim [into the subjective determining ground of the will]. But what name could be more fitly applied to this singular feeling which cannot be drawn into comparison with any pathological feeling [that is, with any feeling conditioned by bodily circumstances]? It is of such a peculiar kind that it seems to stand at the command solely of reason and indeed of practical pure reason."[16]

Since the analysis is somewhat difficult in these formulations, let us try

---

11. Kant, *Werke* (Cassirer), vol. 5, p. 80.
12. Ibid., p. 81.
13. Ibid.
14. Ibid., pp. 81–82.
15. Ibid., p. 83.
16. Ibid., p. 84.

to make it clearer for ourselves. What can we gather from these statements? Respect is respect for the law as determining ground of moral action. As this respect-*for*—namely, for the law—responsibility is determined by something positive, the law, which itself is not empirical. This feeling of respect for the law is produced by reason itself; it is not a feeling patholog-ically induced by sensibility. Kant says that it does not serve for judging actions; moral feeling does not present itself after the event, following upon the ethical deed, as the manner in which I assume an attitude toward the already accomplished action. Instead, respect for the law, as a motive, first really constitutes the possibility of the action. It is the way in which the law first becomes accessible to me as law. This means at the same time that this feeling of respect for the law also does not serve, as Kant puts it, for substantiating the law; the law is not what it is *because* I have respect for it, but just the reverse: my having a feeling of respect for the law and with it this specific mode of revelation of the law is the only way in which the moral law is able to approach me.

Feeling is having-feeling-for, and so much so that in it the feeling ego at the same time feels its own self. Applied to respect, this means that in respect for the law the respectful ego must simultaneously become manifest to itself in a specific way. This must occur not subsequently and not merely occasionally; instead, respect for the law—this specific type of revelation of law as the determining ground of action—is as such conjointly a specific revelation of my own self as the agent. What the respect is for, or that for which this feeling is the having of a feeling, Kant entitles the moral law. Reason, as free, gives this law to itself. Respect for the law is the active ego's respect for itself as the self which is not understood by means of self-conceit and self-love. Respect as respect for the law relates in its specific revelation to the person. "Respect always goes to persons alone, never to things."[17] In respect for the law, I submit myself to the law. The specific having of a feeling for the law which is present in respect is a self-subjection. I subject myself in respect for the law to my own self as the free self. In this subjection of myself I am manifest to myself; I am as I myself. The question is, As what or, more precisely, as *whom*?

In subjecting myself to the law, I subject myself to myself as pure reason; but that is to say that in this subjection to myself I raise myself to myself as the free, self-determining being. This submissive self-elevation of myself to myself reveals, discloses as such, me to myself in my *dignity*. Speaking negatively, in the respect for the law that I give to myself as a free being I cannot have disrespect for myself. Respect is the mode of the ego's being-with-itself [Bei-sich-selbst-sein] according to which it does not disparage

_____

17. Ibid.

the hero in its soul. The moral feeling, as respect for the law, is nothing but the self's being responsible to itself and for itself. This moral feeling is a distinctive way in which the ego understands itself as ego directly, purely, and free of all sensuous determination.

This self-consciousness in the sense of respect constitutes the personalitas moralis. It is important to see that in respect, as a feeling, there is present, for one thing, having a feeling for the law in the sense of self-subjection. This self-subjection, in conformity with the content of that to which I subject myself and *for which* I have a feeling in my respect, is at the same time a self-elevation as a becoming self-manifest in my ownmost dignity. Kant sees clearly this curiously counterstriving double tendency in the intentional structure of respect as a self-subjecting self-elevation. In a note to the *Foundations of the Metaphysics of Morals,* in a passage in which he is taking precautions against the possible charge that he is seeking "behind the word 'respect' merely a flight to an obscure feeling," he says that respect has "something analogous at once" to inclination and fear.[18] To understand this remark we may briefly recall that ancient philosophy characterized practical behavior in the broadest sense, orexis, by dioxis and phuge. Dioxis signifies following in the manner of pursuit, a striving toward something. Phuge signifies a yielding, fleeing, retreat from, striving away from. For dioxis, striving toward, Kant says inclination for; and for phuge, giving way before, he takes fear as a shrinking standing in fear of. He says that the feeling of respect has something analogous, something corresponding to the two phenomena, inclination and fear, striving toward and striving away from. He speaks of analogy because these two modifications of orexis, feeling, are sensibly determined, whereas respect is a striving toward and simultaneously a striving away from of a purely mental kind. To what extent does respect have something analogous to inclination and fear? Self-subjection to the law is in a certain way a standing in fear of, a yielding to it as to a demand. On the other hand, however, this self-subordination to the law as phuge is at the same time a dioxis, a striving inclination toward, in the sense that, in the respect for the law which reason, as free, gives itself, reason raises itself to itself, strives toward itself. This analogizing of respect to inclination and fear makes evident how clearly Kant saw this phenomenon of respect. The basic structure of respect and its significance for the Kantian interpretation of morality has been overlooked in phenomenology, in consequence of which Scheler's criticism of the Kantian ethics in *Formalism in Ethics and Material Ethics of Value* missed the point completely.

---

18. Kant, *Werke* (Cassirer), vol. 4, pp. 257–258. [The quotation is from the *Grundlegung zur Metaphysik der Sitten,* First Section, Kant's footnote 2. This work has been translated under different titles more or less approximating *Foundations of the Metaphysics of Morals* in many editions.]

By this analysis of respect, we have made clear to ourselves that there is present here a phenomenon which in Kant's sense is not just any indiscriminate feeling which happens also to appear among other states transpiring in the empirical subject; rather, this feeling of respect is the true mode in which man's existence becomes manifest, not in the sense of a pure ascertainment or taking cognizance of, but in the sense that in respect I myself *am*—am *acting.* Respect for the law means eo ipso action. The manner of self-consciousness in the sense of respect already makes manifest a mode of the type of being of the person proper. Although Kant does not press directly in this direction, nevertheless the possibility is present in reality. For an understanding of this matter the basic formal structure of feeling in general must be recalled: having-feeling-for, self-feeling, and this self-feeling as a mode of becoming-self-manifest. Respect reveals the dignity before which and for which the self knows itself to be responsible. Only in responsibility does the self first reveal itself—the self not in a general sense as knowledge of an ego in general but as in each case mine, the ego as in each case the individual factical ego.

c) Kant's ontological disjunction of person and thing *[Sache].* The ontological constitution of the person as an end-in-itself

Although Kant does not raise his question in the way in which we do, we shall nevertheless formulate the question thus: Given that in the above-described way the self is revealed *ontically* in the moral feeling of respect as being an ego, how is that self to be defined *ontologically?* Respect is the ontical access to itself of the factically existent ego proper. In this revelation of itself as a factically existent entity, the possibility must be given for determining the constitution itself of the being of this entity thus manifest. In other words, what is the ontological concept of the personalitas moralis, the moral person who is thus revealed in respect?

Although Kant does not explicitly pose this question, he in fact gives the answer to it in his *Metaphysics of Morals.* Metaphysics means ontology. Metaphysics of morals signifies the ontology of human existence. That Kant gives the answer in the ontology of human existence, or the metaphysics of morals, shows that he has an unclouded understanding of the methodological sense of the analysis of the person and thus also of the metaphysical question What is man?

Let us once more make clear to ourselves what is inherent in moral feeling: man's dignity, which exalts him insofar as he serves. In this dignity in unity with service, man is at once master and servant of himself. In respect, in acting ethically, man makes himself, as Kant declares in one place.[19] What is the *ontological meaning of the person thus made manifest in respect?* Kant says: "Now I maintain that man and every rational being in general exists as an end in himself, not merely as a means to be used arbitrarily by this or that will; instead in all his actions, whether they are addressed to himself or to other rational beings, he must always be considered at the same time as an end."[20] Man exists as an end in himself; he is never a means, not even a means for God; before God, too, he is his own end. From this, from the ontological characterization of the being that is not only viewed by others as an end and taken as an end but exists objectively—actually—as an end, the proper ontological meaning of the moral person becomes clear. The moral person exists as its own end; it *is* itself an end.

Only thus is the *basis* gained for distinguishing *ontologically* between *beings that are egos* and *beings that are not egos,* between *subject* and *object, res cogitans* and *res extensa.* "The beings whose existence rests indeed not on our will but on nature [on nature in the sense of physical organization] have nevertheless, if they are beings lacking reason, only a relative value as means and are therefore called *things [Sachen];* in contrast, rational beings are called *persons* because their nature [nature here is synonymous with phusis as equivalent to essentia] singles them out already as ends in themselves, as something which may not be used merely as a means, and hence to this degree limits all arbitrary choice (and is an object of respect)."[21] What constitutes the nature of the person, its essentia, and limits all choice, which means that it is determined as freedom, is an object of respect. Conversely, that which is objective in respect, what is revealed in it, makes manifest the personality of the person. The ontological concept of the person is briefly this: persons are "objective ends, that is, things *[Dinge]* [res in the broadest sense] whose existence is an end in itself."[22]

This interpretation of the personalitas moralis first makes clear what man is and defines his quidditas, man's essential nature, the rigorous concept of *Menschheit,* humanity. Kant does not use this last expression to denote the sum of all humans; it is instead an ontological concept and means the *ontological constitution of man.* As actuality is the ontological constitution of

---

19. Kant, *Kritik der praktischen Vernunft,* in *Werke* (Cassirer), vol. 5, p. 107. [The passage is from the section on the "Critical Examination of the Analytic of Pure Practical Reason." See p. 203 in *Kant's Critique of Practical Reason and Other Writings in Moral Philosophy,* trans. and ed. with an introduction by Lewis White Beck (Chicago: University of Chicago Press, 1949).]

20. Kant, *Werke* (Cassirer), vol. 4, *Grundlegung zur Metaphysik der Sitten,* p. 286. [Second Section.]

21. Ibid., pp. 286–287.

22. Ibid., p. 287.

the actual, so humanity is the essence of the human, equity the essence of the equitable. Kant is consequently able to formulate the basic principle of morality, the categorical imperative, in the following way. "Act so that you use humanity in your own person as well as in the person of everyone else never merely as a means but always at the same time as an end."[23] This principle marks the proper ought-to-be of man. It prescribes what man can be as defined by the essential nature of his existence. The imperative is categorical, not hypothetical. It is not subject to an if-then. The principle of ethical action does not say: *If* you want to attain this or that, this specific end or that one, *then* you must behave thus and so. It does not give any *if* and any hypothesis here, because the acting subject, which is the only topic under discussion here, is of its own nature itself an end, the end of and for its own self, not conditioned by or subordinated to another. Because there is no hypothesis present here, no *if-then,* this imperative is categorical, if-free. As a moral agent, as existent end of his own self, man is in the kingdom of ends. End, purpose, must be understood here always in the objective sense as existent end, person. The *realm of ends* is the *being-with-one-another,* the *commercium of persons* as such, and therefore the realm of freedom. It is the realm of existing persons among themselves and not, say, some system of values to which any active ego relates and in which, as something human, ends are founded in their interconnection as gradients of intentions toward something. "Realm of ends" must be taken in an ontical sense. An end is an existing person; the realm of ends is the with-one-another of the existing persons themselves.

We must adhere to the disjunction that Kant fixed on the basis of the analysis of the moral ego, the *separation* between *person* and *thing [Sache].* According to Kant both person and thing are res, things *[Dinge]* in the broadest sense, things that have existence, that exist. Kant uses the terms for existence—Dasein and Existieren—in the sense of Vorhandensein, being extant. Although he uses this indifferent expression "Dasein" in the sense of extantness for the type of being of person and of things, we must nevertheless take note that he makes a sharp ontological distinction between person and thing as *two basic kinds of beings.* Correspondingly, two different ontologies, two kinds of metaphysics, are also correlated with the two basic kinds of beings. In the *Foundations of the Metaphysics of Morals*, Kant says: "In this way there arises the idea of a twofold metaphysics, a metaphysics of nature and a metaphysics of morals,"[24] which is to say, an ontology of res extensa and an ontology of res cogitans. The metaphysics of morals, the ontology of the person in the narrower sense, is defined by Kant thus:

---

23. Ibid.
24. Ibid., p. 244. [Preface.]

it "is to investigate the idea and the principles of a possible pure will and not the actions and conditions of the human will in general, which in large part are obtained from psychology."[25]

With this we have gained an insight, crude but nevertheless central, into the way in which Kant conceives the distinction in ontological principle between res cogitans and res extensa as that between person and nature (thing, Sache) and into the way he assigns different ontologies to the different ways of being. There comes to light here a wholly different level of inquiry than is present in Descartes. But it seems that we have gained even more. Have we not thus fixed the true distinction between subject and object, so that it appears not only superfluous but even impossible to think of finding here still more, not to say more fundamental, problems? But it is with this latter intention that we discuss the third thesis. We are not in search of problems for problems' sake, however; it is because we want by means of them to attain the knowledge of what is continually alleged to us to be knowable: the knowledge of the ontological constitution of the being that we ourselves are. We are not striving for criticism at any price simply in order to produce criticism; instead, criticism and problems must arise from confrontation with the things themselves. However unequivocal the Kantian interpretation may be of the distinction between res cogitans and res extensa, there are nevertheless problems concealed in it which we must now make clearer for ourselves by making this Kantian interpretation itself doubtful. We must try to make clear what is problematic in the Kantian interpretation of personality.

§14. Phenomenological critique of the Kantian solution and demonstration of the need to pose the question in fundamental principle

The problem before us is to determine the being of the being which we humans each ourselves are. We must ask in particular, Did Kant adequately define man's being by his interpretation of personalitas transcendentalis, personalitas psychologica, and personalitas moralis?

a) Critical examination of Kant's interpretation of personalitas moralis. Adumbration of the ontological determinations of the moral person but avoidance of the basic problem of its mode of being

We begin the critical examination with reference to Kant's interpretation of the *personalitas moralis*. The person is a thing, res, something, that exists

---

25. Ibid., p. 247. [Preface.]

as its own end. To this being belongs purposiveness, more precisely, self-purposiveness. Its way of being is to be the end or purpose of its own self. This determination, to be the end of its own self, belongs indisputably to the ontological constitution of the human Dasein. But does this clarify the Dasein's way of being? Has the attempt even been made to show how the Dasein's mode of being is determined with regard to its being constituted by purposiveness? We seek in vain for an elucidation of this question in Kant, and indeed even for the question itself. On the contrary, the quotations adduced show that Kant talks about man's existence and about the existence of things as ends; but the terms for existence—Existieren and Dasein—signify for him merely extantness. He talks in the same way about the Dasein of nature, the Dasein of the thing *[Sache]*. He never says that the concept of existence *[Existenz and Dasein]* has a different sense as applied to man. Kant shows only that the essentia of man as an end is determined otherwise than the essentia of things *[whether taken in the broad sense or in the particular sense of things of nature]*. But although he does not talk explicitly about the specific mode of being of the moral person, perhaps he nonetheless has it in mind de facto?

A being that exists as its own end has itself in the way of respect. Respect means responsibility toward oneself and this in turn means being free. Being free is not a property of man but is synonymous with behaving ethically. But behaving is acting. Thus the specific mode of being of the moral person would lie in free action. Kant says in one place: "That is intellectual whose concept is an action."[1] This terse observation means that a mental being is one which *is* in the manner of action. The ego is an "I act" and as such it is intellectual. This peculiar usage of Kant's should be held firmly in mind. The ego as "I act" is intellectual, purely mental. Therefore he also often calls the ego an intelligence. Intelligence, again, signifies, not a being that *has* intelligence, understanding, and reason, but a being that exists as intelligence. Persons are existing ends; they are intelligences. The realm of ends, the being-with-one-another of persons as free, is the intelligible realm of freedom. In another place Kant says that the moral person is humanity. Being human is determined altogether intellectually, as intelligence. Intelligences, moral persons, are subjects whose being is acting. Acting is an existing in the sense of being extant. The being of intelligible substances as moral persons is indeed characterized in this way but Kant *does not comprehend ontologically* and make into an express problem *what*

---

1. *Reflexionen Kants zur Kritik der reinen Vernunft*, ed. Benno Erdmann (Leipzig, 1884), Reflection No. 968. [The reference is to volume 2 of *Reflexionen Kants zur kritischen Philosophie*, edited by Benno Erdmann from Kant's manuscript notes, vol. 1: *Reflexionen Kants zur Anthropologie* (1882); vol. 2: *Reflexionen Kants zur Kritik der reinen Vernunft* (1884) (Leipzig: R. Reisland).]

sort of way of existing, of being extant, this acting represents. The ego is not a thing but a person. We can see that Fichte begins his inquiry at this point. Starting out from Kant, he tries to express more radically the tendency of modern philosophy, which grows stronger in Kant, to concentrate its problems around the ego. If the ego is determined by the mode of being of acting and hence is not a thing, then the beginning for philosophy, which starts with the ego, is not an active thing but an active deed.

The question remains, How is this acting itself to be interpreted as a way of being? In reference to Kant the question becomes, Does he not after all fall back again into conceiving this active ego as an end in the sense of one extant being among other extant beings? *The interpretation of the ego as a moral person provides us with no really informative disclosure about the mode of being of the ego.* Perhaps, however, we may more readily gain such information about the subject's mode of being if we ask how Kant defines the I of the "I think" or, as we can say inexactly, the theoretical as over against the practical subject, the personalitas transcendentalis. For with regard to the personalitas psychologica we shall expect no answer from the start, since Kant flatly calls the object-ego, the ego of apprehension, of empirical self-consciousness, a thing and thus expressly assigns to it the mode of being of nature, of the extant—although it is questionable whether this move is correct.

b) Critical examination of Kant's interpretation of personalitas transcendentalis. His negative demonstration of the impossibility of an ontological interpretation of the I-think

Did Kant determine the ego's way of being in his interpretation of the "I think", the transcendental ego? *In the Kantian interpretation of the personalitas transcendentalis too we seek in vain for an answer to this question,* not only because Kant in fact simply does not make an attempt to interpret the mode of being of the ego as "I think," but also because he tries to show quite explicitly *that* and *why* the ego's existence, its mode of being, cannot be elucidated. He furnishes this proof of the impossibility of the interpretation of the being of the I as the "I think" in the *Critique of Pure Reason,* the transcendental dialectic, book 2, chapter 1, "The Paralogisms of Pure Reason."[2] The treatment in the first edition (A) is fuller.

Viewed historically, Kant's doctrine of the paralogisms of pure reason is a critique of psychologia rationalis, the traditional metaphysics of the soul

---

2. Kant, *Critique of Pure Reason,* B399 ff.

as a dogmatic metaphysics, for which he substitutes in fact the metaphysics of morals. It is characteristic of psychologia rationalis that with the aid of purely ontological concepts which it applies to the ego as "I think" it tries to achieve some knowledge about this ego as a being, as soul. In the "Paralogisms of Pure Reason," Kant points out that these arguments of metaphysical psychology drawn from ontological concepts and their application to the "I think" are fallacious. He calls the basic ontological concepts by the name "categories." These he divided into four classes: the categories of quantity, quality, relation, and modality.[3] With these four classes, which he believed to be the sole possible categories, Kant correlates the basic ontological concepts employed by rational psychology for knowledge of the soul as such.

Considered under the category of relation, with regard to the relation of an accident to a substance in general, the soul is substance—so says the old metaphysical psychology. In quality the soul is simple; in quantity it is one, numerically identical, one and the same at different times; and in modality it is existent in relation to possible objects in space. From the application of these four basic concepts from among the four classes of categories—the concepts of substance, simplicity, selfsameness, and existence—proceed the four basic determinations of the soul, as metaphysical psychology maintains in the following four inferences.

First. As substance, as something extant, the soul is given in inner sense. It is therefore the opposite of what is given in outer sense, which is determined as matter and body; the soul, as substance given in inner sense, is immaterial.

Second. As simple substance the soul is something indissoluble. As simple it cannot be decomposed into parts. Consequently it is imperishable, incorruptible.

Third. As one and always the same in various changing states at different times, the soul is in this sense a person; it is something that lies absolutely at the ground, that persists (personality of the soul).

Kant also combines the first three determinations—immateriality, incorruptibility, and personality—as the determinations of spirituality, in the concept of spirit that belongs to metaphysical psychology. This concept of spirituality must be distinguished fundamentally and in principle from Kant's concept of mind as intelligence in the sense of the morally acting person as an end.

In terms of the fourth category, modality, the immaterial, incorruptible person is determined as existing in reciprocity with a body. Consequently, this spiritual thing animates a body. We call such a ground of life in matter

---

3. Ibid., B106.

the soul in the strict sense. But if this ground of animality, that is, of animateness, as was demonstrated for the first category, is simple, incorruptible, and self-subsistent, then the soul is immortal. The immortality of the soul follows from its spirituality.

We have already observed that Kant showed for the first time that in no sense can anything be asserted about the ego as spiritual substance by means of an application of the categories to the ego as "I think." Why are these inferences fallacious? Why are these categories, as categories of nature, of the extant, of things, not applicable to the ego? Why is it impossible to gain ontical knowledge of the soul and the ego from these categorial determinations? These inferences fail because they rest on a fundamental error. They apply categories to the ego as "I think," to the personalitas transcendentalis, and derive from the assertion of such categories about the ego ontical propositions regarding the ego as soul. But why should this not be possible? What are the categories?

The ego is "I think," which in every thinking is thought along with it as the conditioning ground of the unifying I-combine. The categories are the forms of possible combination which thinking can accomplish as combining. As ground of possibility of the "I think," the ego is at the same time the ground and the condition of possibility of the forms of combination, the categories. Since these categories are conditioned by the ego, they cannot be applied in turn again to the ego in order to apprehend it. That which conditions absolutely, the ego as the original synthetic unity of apperception, cannot be determined with the aid of what is conditioned by it.

This is one reason for the impossibility of applying the categories to the ego. The other reason, connected with it, is that the ego is not established merely by experience but lies at the basis of all experience as something absolutely non-manifold that makes it possible. The categories grounded in the ego and its unity, as forms of unity for a synthesis, are applicable only where a combinable is given. Every combining, every judgmental determining of a combinable, requires something which is advanced for combination, for synthesis. But something is advanced and given to us always only by means of affection, by our being approached and acted on by something other than our own self. In order to have something combinable for judging, we must be determined by the faculty of receptivity. The ego as "I think," however, is not affection, being acted upon, but pure spontaneity or, as Kant also says, function, functioning, doing, acting. If I wish to make assertions about my Dasein, something determinable has to be given to me from my Dasein itself. But anything determinable is given to me only by means of receptivity or on the basis of the forms of receptivity, space and time. Space and time are forms of sensibility, of sense-experience. So far as I determine my Dasein and combine it by following the guidance of the categories, I take my ego as a sensibly empirical thinking. In contrast, the ego of apperception is inaccessible for any determining. If it happens, then I am thinking the ego in the categories of the extant as a natural thing. This results in a subreptio apperceptionis substantiae, a surreptitious substitution of the ego conceived as extant for the pure ego. The pure ego itself is never given to me as a determinable for determination, for applying the categories. For that reason an ontical knowledge of the ego and, consequently, an ontological determination of it is impossible. The only thing that can be said is that the ego is an "I-am-acting." This shows a certain interconnection between the ego of transcendental apperception and the personalitas moralis. Kant summarizes his thought as follows: "The 'I think' expresses the act of determining my existence [my extantness]. The existence is thereby already given but the manner in which I am to determine it, the way in which I am to posit in myself the manifold pertaining to it, is not yet thereby given. To it [the giving itself] there belongs a self-intuition which has lying at its basis an a priori given form, time, which is sensible and belongs to the receptivity of the determinable. Now if I do not have still another self-intuition which gives that which *does the determining* in me—of whose spontaneity alone I am conscious—before the act of *determining*, as *time* [does in the case of] the determinable, then I cannot determine my existence as that of a self-active being; instead, I represent to myself only the spontaneity of my thinking, of the determining, and my existence remains determinable only sensibly, as the existence of an appearance. But it is owing to this spontaneity that I call myself an *intelligence*."[4] Put briefly, this means that we have no self-*intuition* of our self, but all intuition, all immediate giving of something, moves within the forms of space and time. However, on Kant's view, which adheres to the tradition, time is the form of sensibility. Thus no possible basis is given for the application of the categories to the knowledge of the ego. Kant is wholly right when he declares the categories, as fundamental concepts of nature, unsuitable for determining the ego. But in that way he has only shown negatively that the categories, which were tailored to fit nature, break down here. He has not shown that the "I act" itself cannot be interpreted in the way in which it gives itself, in this self-manifesting ontological constitution. Perhaps it is precisely time which is the a priori of the ego—time, to be sure, in a more original sense than Kant was able to conceive it. He assigned it to sensibility and consequently from the beginning, conforming with tradition, he had in view natural time alone.

It does *not* follow from the inadequacy of the categories of nature that every ontological interpretation whatever of the ego is impossible. That

---

4. Ibid., B158 n.

follows only on the presupposition that the same type of knowledge which is valid for nature is taken as the sole possible basis for knowledge of the ego. From the impropriety of applying the categories to the pure ego there follows the necessity *to inquire beforehand into the possibility of a suitable ontological interpretation of the subject, one that is free from the entire tradition.* This inquiry suggests itself all the more obviously because in his metaphysics of morals, or ontology of the person, in opposition to his theory in the paralogisms of pure reason, Kant himself attempts an ontological interpretation of the ego as an end, an intelligence. To be sure, he doesn't exactly raise the fundamental question about the way of being of an end, an intelligence. He carries out a certain ontological interpretation of the practical ego; he even holds a "practical dogmatic metaphysics" to be possible, one which can determine the human self and its relationship to immortality and God by way of practical self-consciousness.

Thus there is unveiled an essential *flaw in the ego-problem in Kant.* We are confronted by a peculiar discordance within the Kantian doctrine of the ego. With regard to the theoretical ego, its determination appears to be impossible. With regard to the practical ego, there exists the attempt at an ontological definition. But there is not only this discordance of attitude toward the theoretical and practical ego. Present in Kant is a peculiar omission: he fails to determine originally the unity of the theoretical and practical ego. Is this unity and wholeness of the two subsequent or is it original, prior to both? Do the two originally belong together or are they only combined externally afterward? How is the being of the ego to be conceived in general? But the ontological structure of this whole theoretical-practical person is indeterminate not merely in its wholeness; even less determinate is the relation of the theoretical-practical person to the empirical ego, to the soul, and beyond that the relation of the soul to the body. Mind, soul, and body are indeed ontologically determined or undetermined for themselves, and each in a different way, but the whole of the being that we ourselves are, body, soul, and mind, the mode of being of their original wholeness, remains ontologically in the dark.

We may now summarize provisionally the *Kantian position on the problem of the interpretation of subjectivity:*

First. In reference to the personalitas moralis, Kant factually gives ontological determinations (which, as we shall later see, are valid) without posing the basic question of the mode of being of the moral person as end.

Second. In reference to the personalitas transcendentalis, the "I think," Kant shows negatively the non-applicability of the categories of nature for the ontical cognition of the ego. However, he does not show the impossibility of any other kind of ontological interpretation of the ego.

Third. Given this divergent position of Kant's on the ontology of the ego, it is not surprising that neither the ontological interconnection between the personalitas moralis and the personalitas transcendentalis nor that between these two in their unity on the one hand and the personalitas psychologica on the other, not to say the original wholeness of these three person-determinations, is made an ontological problem.

Fourth. The free "I act" of the being that exists as an end, the spontaneity of intelligence, is fixed as the specific character of the ego. Kant employs the expression "intelligence" as well as "end"; he says: "There exist ends" and "There are intelligences." Intelligence is not a mode of behavior and a property of the subject but the subject itself, which *is* as intelligence.

Fifth. Intelligences, persons, are distinguished as mental substances from natural things as bodily substances, things *[Sachen]*.

This then would be our view on Kant's interpretation of the distinction between res cogitans and res extensa. Kant sees clearly the impossibility of conceiving the ego as something extant. In reference to the personalitas moralis he even gives positive ontological determinations of egoity, but without pressing on toward the fundamental question of the mode of being of the person. We could formulate our view of Kant in this way, but in so doing we would be doing away with our own central understanding of the problem, because the view thus expressed does not yet contain the final critical word.

c) Being in the sense of being-produced as horizon of understanding for the person as finite mental substance

One thing remains striking. Kant speaks of the *existence [Dasein] of the person* as he does of the *existence of a thing [Ding]*. He says that the person exists as an end in itself. He uses "exist" in the sense of extantness. Precisely where he touches on the structure proper to the personalitas moralis, that of being autotelic, he assigns to this being the ontological mode of extantness. This does not happen by chance. In the concept of the thing-in-itself, whether or not it is knowable in its whatness, the traditional ontology of extantness is already implicitly contained. Even more, the central positive interpretation that Kant gives of egoity as spontaneous intelligence moves wholly within the horizon of the ontology transmitted from antiquity and the Middle Ages. The analysis of respect and of the moral person remains but an attempt, even though immensely successful, to shake off unconsciously the burden of the traditional ontology.

But how can we claim that even in the determination of the ego as spontaneity and intelligence the traditional ontology of the extant is still working itself out as it did in Descartes, undiminished in every particular?

When we first began our consideration of the Kantian analysis of the ego, we saw that he defines the ego as subjectum in the sense of the hupokeimenon, that which lies present there for determinations. In conformity with the ancient view of being, beings are understood fundamentally as being extant. Ousia, that which *is* in the strict and proper sense, is what is in its own self available, pro-duced, present constantly for itself, lying present there, the hupokeimenon, subjectum, substance. Corporeal things and mental things are substances (ousiai).

We have also emphasized a number of times that for ancient and medieval metaphysics one particular being stands out as the prototype of all being, God. This continues to hold also for modern philosophy from Descartes to Hegel. Although Kant holds that a theoretical proof of God's existence is impossible, and a theoretical-speculative knowledge of God as well, nevertheless God remains for him, as ens realissimum, the ontological prototype, the prototypon transcendentale, the ontological model, in conformity with which the idea of original being is conceived and the determinations of all derivative beings are normalized. God, however, is the ens infinitum, as we saw in Suarez and Descartes, whereas the non-divine being is an ens finitum. God is the true substance. The res cogitans and res extensa are finite substances (substantiae finitae). Kant presupposes these basic ontological theses of Descartes without further ado. According to Kant non-divine beings—things, corporeal things and mental things, persons, intelligences—are finite beings. They make up the universe of extant entities. We must now show that the person is also viewed by Kant as at bottom an extant entity—that here, too, he does not get beyond the ontology of the extant.

If this is to be proved, then we are obliged to show that the ancient interpretative horizon for beings—reference to production—sets the standard also for the interpretation of the person, the finite mental substance. It should be noted that finite substances, things *[Sachen]* as well as persons, are not simply extant in any arbitrary way, but exist in reciprocity, in a commercium. This reciprocal action is founded on causality, which Kant takes to be the faculty of producing effects. In correspondence with the basic ontological distinction between things and persons he distinguishes a double causality: causality of nature and causality of freedom. Ends, purposes, form a commercium of free beings. The reciprocal action of substances is a central problem of modern metaphysics since Descartes. It is sufficient simply to mention the names of the various solutions to this problem of the reciprocal action of substances and their relation to God: mechanism, occasionalism, harmonia praestabilita. Kant rejects all these solutions. It is a basic principle of Kantian metaphysics that we know "everything in the world" only "as cause in the cause [only in its capacity to operate as cause], or only the causality of the production of effects, hence only the effect, and thus not the thing itself and the determinations by means of which it produces the effects" and by which they are produced.[5] "The substantial [the substance] is the thing in itself and is unknown."[6] Only the accidents, the effects of things on one another, are manifested and therefore perceptible. Persons are finite substances and as intelligences they are characterized by spontaneity. The question arises, In what does the finitude of the person and of substance generally consist? Chiefly in this, that each substance from the outset has its limit in the next, strikes against it as if against a being which is in each case already given to the substance and given specifically in such a way that this being shows itself solely in its effects. The effects that are thus manifested by one substance for another must be able to be received by the second substance if it is at all to be able to come to know something about a being that it itself is not and knowingly comport itself toward this being, that is, if any commercium at all is to come about between the substances. For intelligence this means that the substance, because it is not the other being, must have a capacity to be affected, as it were, by this being. The finite substance, therefore, cannot be only spontaneity but must be determined in equally original fashion as receptivity, as a capacity of being susceptible to effects and receptive of the effects of other substances. A commercium between finite mental substances is possible only if these substances are determined not only by spontaneity, by a capacity to operate outward from themselves, but also by receptivity. Kant designates by the term "affection" the effects of other substances so far as they relate to the susceptibility of a substance. Hence he can also say that in the sense of intelligence substance is not only function, cognition, but also affection. Finite substances apprehend of another being only what that being turns as its own effect toward the perceiver. Only the outside, not the inside, is always accessible and perceptible, if we may for once use this terminology that Kant also employs, even though it is misleading. The finiteness of intelligences lies in their being necessarily relegated to receptivity. There must be between them an influxus realis, a reciprocal influence on one another of their reality, of their predicates, their accidents. A direct commercium of substances is impossible.

What is the ontological foundation of this interpretation of the finitude of mental substances? Why cannot the finite substance apprehend the substantial component, the true being of another substance? Kant asserts this

---

5. Kant, Reflection No. 1171.
6. Reflection No. 704.

impossibility unmistakably in one of his reflections: "but finite substances cannot of themselves know other things, because they are not their creator."[7] In a lecture on metaphysics he says: "No being except the creator alone can cognitively grasp the substance of another thing."[7a] If we take these two fundamental propositions together, they assert that a genuine cognitive grasp of a being in its being is available only to that being's creator. The primary and direct reference to the being of a being lies in the *production* of it. And this implies that *being of a being* means nothing but *producedness*. The advance to the true and proper being of beings is blocked to finite substances because finite intelligences do not and have not themselves produced the beings to be apprehended. Being of a being must be understood here as being-produced, if indeed the producer, the originator, alone is supposed to be able to apprehend the substance, that which constitutes the being of the being. Only the creator is capable of a true and proper cognition of being; we finite beings get to know only what we ourselves make and only to the extent that we make it. But we ourselves are beings who do not simply by our own resources produce our own selves. Instead, we are ourselves produced and, therefore, as Kant says, we are creators only in part.[8] The reason for the unknowability of the being of substances, of things extant in their proper being, is that they are produced. The being of finite entities, whether things or persons, is from the beginning conceived in the horizon of production as producedness, and certainly in a direction that does not directly coincide with that of ancient ontology but nevertheless belongs to it and descends from it.

We shall try to get clear on the point that ultimately the foundation of the Kantian interpretation of the moral person also lies in ancient-medieval ontology. To understand this it is necessary to comprehend the general definition of the *person* as *finite substance* and to determine what finitude means. *Finitude is being referred necessarily to receptivity, that is, the impossibility of being oneself the creator and producer of another being.* Only the creator of a being knows this being in its proper being. The being of things is understood as being-produced. In Kant this is present basically as a self-evident matter of course, but it does not receive explicit expression. The Kantian interpretation of finite substances and their interconnection also

---

7. Reflection No. 929.

7a. Kant, *Vorlesungen über die Metaphysik*, ed. Pölitz (Erfurt, 1821), p. 97. [The reference here is to the original publication: *Immanuel Kant's Vorlesungen über die Metaphysik*, "prepared for the press by the editor of Kant's *Vorlesungen über die philosophische Religionslehre*" (i.e., Karl H. L. Pölitz), with an introduction (Erfurt, Keysersche Buchhandlung, 1821). There is a second edition, following the 1821 edition, edited by K. H. Schmidt (Roswein: Pflugbeil, 1925).]

8. Reflection No. 1117.

traces back to the same ontological horizon that we encountered in the interpretation of ousia and of all the determinations that were given of the essential nature of beings. To be sure, production functions here in a different sense, which connects up with the function mentioned.

Earlier we said that the production of something involves a peculiar character of discharge and release on the basis of which the product is apprehended from the beginning as having been put there for itself and being present there independently and of itself. It is apprehended in this way in the producing itself, not only after the producing, but already in the consciousness of the project. In the function of production now under discussion, its function for the interpretation of the possibility of knowing the being of a being, a different structural moment of production comes into question, one that we also touched on earlier. All production takes place in conformity with an original and prototypical image as model. The antecedent imagining of such a model is part of the producing. We heard earlier that the concept of eidos also had grown from the horizon of production. In the antecedent imagining and projecting of the prototypical image, there is already a direct grasp of what the product-to-be really is. What is at first thought of as the original, prototypical model is apprehended directly in the imagining. What constitutes the being of the being is already anticipated in the eidos. That which says how the thing will look or, as we also say, how it will turn out—if and when, of course, it *has* turned out— is already anticipated and circumscribed in the eidos. The anticipation of the prototypical pattern which takes place in production is the true knowledge of what the product is. It is for this reason that only the producer of something, its originator, perceives a being in the light of what it is. Because the creator and producer imagines the model beforehand, he is therefore also the one who really knows the product. As self-producer, he is also the authentic being.

By reason of this connection, the concept ousia already has a twofold meaning in Greek ontology. For one thing ousia signifies the produced extant entity itself or also its producedness. But at the same time ousia also signifies much the same thing as eidos in the sense of the prototypical pattern which is merely thought of or imagined—what the being already really is as produced, its appearance, what outlines it, the way in which it will show up and look, how it will turn out.

God is regarded as a sculptor and specifically as the prototypical modeller of all things who needs nothing given to him beforehand and therefore also is not determined by receptivity. By reason of his absolute spontaneity, as actus purus, he is the first giver of everything that is, and not just that but even more, of everything possible. The finitude of things and persons is due to the producedness of things in general. The ens finitum is finite because it is ens creatum. But this implies that esse, ens, beingness, means producedness—to be a being is to be a product. Thus the ontological question of the reason for the finitude of persons or subjects leads us to recognize their being (existence) also as producedness and to see not alone that in his *basic ontological orientation Kant* is still moving *along the path of ancient and medieval ontology*, but further, that only in this way does the line of questioning taken in the *Critique of Pure Reason* become intelligible.[9]

From what has been said something essential results for our fundamental question about the character of the ontological constitution of the subject (person) in Kant. The subject as person is a distinctive subjectum inasmuch as *knowledge* of its predicates, thus of itself, belongs to it. The subjectivity of the subject is therefore synonymous with self-consciousness. Self-consciousness constitutes the actuality, the being of this being. Hence it comes about that, in an extreme version of Kant's or Descartes' thought, German idealism (Fichte, Schelling, Hegel) saw the true actuality of the subject in self-consciousness. From there, following upon the start made by Descartes, the whole problematic of philosophy was developed. Hegel says: "The most important point for the nature of mind is not only the relationship of what it is *in itself* to what it is *actually* but also of what it *knows itself as* to what it actually is; because spirit [is] essentially consciousness, this self-knowing is a basic determination of its *actuality*."[10] This is the reason why German idealism is at pains to get, as it were, behind the mode of being of the subject and of mind by way of this peculiar dialectic of self-consciousness. But in this interpretation of the subject starting from self-consciousness, which was prefigured in Descartes and for the first time rigorously thought in Kant, the primary determination of the subject in the sense of the hupokeimenon, that which lies present there, is suppressed, or else this determination is dialectically sublated in self-consciousness, in self-conceiving. In

9. In a valuable article, Heinz Heimsoeth has compiled the material that illuminates these ontological foundations of the Kantian philosophy: "Metaphysische Motive in der Ausbildung des Kantischen Idealismus," *Kant-Studien* 29 (1924), p. 121 ff. To be sure, fundamental ontological questions and a corresponding interpretation of the material are completely lacking in Heimsoeth. But compared with the uncertain and, basically, purely fictional Kant-interpretations of the Neo-Kantianism of the last century, it is in any case a step forward on the way to an adequate Kant-interpretation. In the middle of the nineteenth century, before the emergence of Neo-Kantianism, the Hegelian school saw these connections much more clearly (Johann Eduard Erdmann above all). Among contemporaries, Hans Pichler for the first time made reference again to the ontological foundations of the Kantian philosophy in his *Über Christian Wolffs Ontologie* [Leipzig: (Dürr) F. Meiner, 1910], particularly in the final section, "Ontologie und transzendentale Logik" (p. 73 ff.).

10. Hegel, preface to the second edition of the *Logik* (F. Meiner), vol. 1, p. 16. [The reference is to Hegel's *Wissenschaft der Logik,* edited by Georg Lasson and published in the *Sämtliche Werke* as volume 3, parts 1 and 2 (Leipzig and Hamburg: F. Meiner, 1923, 1975). "Vol. 1" in the note thus refers to part 1. Trans. Arnold V. Miller, *Hegel's Science of Logic* (London: George Allen and Unwin; New York: The Humanities Press, 1969), p. 37.]

Kant it was already no longer a specific ontological problem but was among things taken for granted as evident. In Hegel this determination of the subject as hupokeimenon undergoes sublation into the interpretation of the subject as self-consciousness—as self-conceiving, as concept or notion /Begriff/. For him the essential nature of substance lies in its being the concept of its own self. The possibility of a fundamental ontological interpretation of the beings we ourselves are was retarded even more than earlier by this development of the interpretation of subjectivity by way of self-consciousness. Even if it may be inadequate to define our existence by the fact that we ourselves are also extant in a certain way and have not and do not produce ourselves, still there is a problem of a fundamental kind in this moment of the fully conceived subject concept as hupokeimenon and as self-consciousness. Perhaps the question about the subject as hupokeimenon is falsely posed in this form; nevertheless, it must be acknowledged equally that the being of the subject does not consist merely in self-knowing—not to mention that the mode of being of this self-knowing remains undetermined—but rather that the being of the Dasein is at the same time determined by its being in some sense— employing the expression with suitable caution—extant and in fact in such a way that it has not brought itself into existence by its own power. Although Kant advances further than others before him into the ontological structure of personality, he is still unable, as we have now seen in all the different directions of the problem, to reach the point of explicitly posing the question about the mode of being of the person. It is not just that the mode of being of the whole being—the unity of personalitas psychologica, transcendentalis, and moralis, as which the human being after all in fact exists—remains ontologically undetermined; the question of the being of the Dasein as such is simply not raised. The subject remains with the indifferent characterization of being an extant entity. And defining the subject as self-consciousness states nothing about the mode of being of the ego. Even the most extreme dialectic of self-consciousness, as it is worked out in different forms in Fichte, Schelling, and Hegel, is unable to solve the problem of the existence of the Dasein because the question is not at all asked. However, if we contemplate the energy of thought and interpretation that Kant bestows precisely on the elucidation of subjectivity, despite which he did not advance to the specific ontological constitution of the Dasein, as we are at first alone maintaining, then this clearly indicates that the interpretation of this being which we ourselves are is the least obviously evident and the most subject to the danger of being located in the wrong horizon. Therefore, there is need for explicit reflection on the path on which the Dasein itself can be determined in an ontologically suitable way.

For us the question arises, What positive problems grow out of this problematic situation in which the subject is primarily determined by means of subjectivity, self-knowing, so that the question of its ontological constitution still remains fundamentally neglected?

§15. The fundamental problem of the multiplicity of ways of being and of the unity of the concept of being in general

From Descartes onward the distinction between res cogitans and res extensa does indeed get particular emphasis and is made the guiding clue to the problems of philosophy. But there is no success in exhibiting the various modes of being of the beings thus labeled, taken particularly and in their diversity, and still less success in subordinating this diversity of being as *a multiplicity of ways of being* to *an original idea of being in general.* There is no success, or rather, to speak more precisely, the attempt was not even undertaken at all. Instead, res cogitans and res extensa are comprehended uniformly, following the lead of an *average concept of being* in the sense of *being-produced.* We know, however, that this interpretation of being was developed *with a view toward the extant, toward the being that the Dasein is not.* Consequently, the question becomes more urgent: How must we determine the being of the being that we ourselves are, mark it off from all being of beings not of the type of Dasein, but yet understand it by way of the unity of an original concept of being? We designated the being of the Dasein by the term "existence." *What does existence mean?* What are the *essential moments* of existing?

a) Initial preview of the existential constitution of the Dasein. Commencement with the subject-object relation (res cogitans — res extensa) as a mistaking of the existential constitution of the being of those beings who understand being

If we undertake to elucidate the existence of the Dasein, we are fulfilling a twofold task—not only that of ontologically distinguishing one being of a peculiar sort from other beings but also that of exhibiting the being of *that* being to whose being (existence) *an understanding of being belongs* and *to the interpretation of which all the problems of ontology generally return.* We must not of course think that the essential nature of existence can be caught and completely explicated in a proposition. We are concerned now only to characterize the *direction of the line of questioning* and to give a *first preview of the constitution of the Dasein's existence.* This is done with a view to making clearer how far the possibility of ontology in general depends on how and to what extent the ontological constitution of the Dasein is laid open. We are thus repeating afresh that in the active stress upon the subject in philosophy since Descartes there is no doubt a genuine impulse toward philosophical inquiry which only sharpens what the ancients sought; on the other hand, it is equally necessary not to start simply from the subject alone but to ask whether and how the *being* of the subject must be determined as an entrance into the problems of philosophy, and in fact in such a way that orientation toward it is *not one-sidedly subjectivistic.* Philosophy must perhaps start from the "subject" and return to the "subject" in its ultimate questions, and yet for all that it may not pose its questions in a one-sidedly subjectivistic manner.

The account and critical discussion of Kant's analysis of personality aimed precisely at making clear that it is by no means a matter of course to come upon the ontological constitution of the subject or even to inquire about it in a correct way. Viewed ontically, we are closest of all to the being that we ourselves are and that we call the Dasein; for we are this being itself. Nevertheless, what is thus nearest to us ontically is exactly farthest from us ontologically. Descartes entitles the second of his meditations on metaphysics "De natura mentis humanae: quod ipsa sit *notior* quam corpus," "On the nature of the human mind, that it is *better known* than the body" *[*Heidegger's emphasis*]*. Despite or precisely because of this allegedly superior familiarity of the subject, *its mode of being is misunderstood and leaped over* everywhere in the period following him, so that no dialectic of mind can once more reverse the effect of this neglect. Admittedly, the sharp division between res cogitans and res extensa seems to guarantee that in this way precisely the peculiar nature of the subject will be encountered. But we know from our earlier reflections during the course of the discussion of the first thesis that the Dasein's comportments have an *intentional character* and that on the basis of this intentionality the subject already stands in relation to things that it itself is not.

If we apply this to the Kantian formulation of the subject-object concept, it will then signify that the ego is a subjectum having knowledge about its predicates, which are representations, cogitationes in the widest sense, and which as such are intentionally directed toward something. This implies that, in the cognitive possession of its predicates as intentional comportments, the ego also already comports itself to the beings toward which the comportments are directed. Since such beings toward which comportments are directed are always designated in a certain way as objects, it can be said formally that to the subject always belongs an object, that one cannot be thought without the other.

Given this determination, the one-sided subjectivistic formulation of the concept of the subject certainly *seems* already to have been overcome. Natorp says: "Accordingly, there would be in all three moments which are intimately bound together in one in the expression 'consciousness' [res cogitans] but still should be kept apart by abstraction: 1. the something of which one of them is conscious; 2. that which is conscious of this something; 3. the relation between the two such that someone is conscious of something. Solely for brevity of reference I call the first [that of which there is consciousness] the *content,* the second the *ego,* and the third *conscioushood [die Bewusstheit]."*[1] By this last term, "conscioushood," Natorp seems to mean the same thing that phenomenology designates as intentionality. Formally it is certainly correct. But closer examination could show that for Natorp this conscioushood is, as he says, "an irreducible ultimate"[2] and that further it can undergo no modification whatever. According to Natorp, there are no different modes of conscioushood of something, but instead all difference of consciousness is a difference in the content, that of which there is consciousness. The res cogitans is by its concept an ego related by conscioushood to a content of which it is conscious. The relation to the object belongs to the ego, and, conversely, to the object belongs the relation to the subject. The relation is a correlation.

The subject-object relation is conceived even more formally, perhaps, by Rickert. He says: "The concepts of subject and object require each other just as other concepts do, for example, those of form and content or of identity and otherness."[3] It must, however, be asked here why these concepts, subject and object, "require" each other. Plainly, of course, only because what they mean does the requiring. But does an object require a subject? Of course. For something standing-over-against always stands-over-against *for* a perceiver. Certainly. However, is every being necessarily an object? Must natural events be objects for a subject in order to be what they are? Plainly not. To begin with, a being is taken to be an object. The deduction can then be made from this that a subject belongs to it. For in characterizing the being as an object I have already tacitly co-posited the subject. However, by this characterization of beings as objects, and in that sense as entities that stand over *against [Gegen*stände*]*, I now no longer have as a problem the being in its own self in regard to the peculiar mode of being belonging to it, but instead the being as *standing-opposite, as standing-*

---

1. Paul Natorp, *Allgemeine Psychologie nach kritischer Methode* (Tübingen, 1912), p. 24. [This volume carries a subheading identifying it as "Book 1: Object and Method of Psychology." The publisher was J. C. B. Mohr.]

2. Ibid., p. 27.

3. H. Rickert, *Der Gegenstand der Erkenntnis,* 3rd ed., p. 3. [Heinrich Rickert, *Der Gegenstand der Erkenntnis: Einführung in die Transzendentalphilosophie,* 3rd ed., completely revised and expanded (Tübingen: J. C. B. Mohr, 1915); 1st ed., with different subtitle (Freiburg i. Br.: Mohr, 1892); 2nd ed., improved (Tübingen: Mohr, 1904). There are 4th, 5th, and 6th editions (Tübingen: Mohr, 1921, 1928).]

over-against. In this presumptively pure Kantian interpretation, being then means the same as objectiveness.

Clearly, then, if an object is counterposed to the subject, the question still doesn't reach the dimension of asking about the specific mode of being of the being that has become an object in this being's relationship to the mode of being of a subject. Conversely, to a subject, taken as apprehender, there belongs an apprehended. But *must* the subject necessarily apprehend? Does the possibility of a subject's being depend on something being given as an object for it to apprehend? Not at all. In any case, the question cannot be decided straight away. It seems at first sight as if in beginning with the subject-object relation a more appropriate point of departure for inquiry has been gained and a less biased way of taking the problem than the one-sided start from the subject. Scrutinized more closely, however, this beginning with a subject-object relation obstructs access to the real ontological question regarding the mode of being of the subject as well as the mode of being of the entity that may possibly but does not necessarily have to become an object.

But even if we grant the legitimacy of starting not with an isolated subject but with the subject-object relation it must then be asked: Why does a subject "require" an object, and conversely? For an extant entity does not of itself become an object so as then to require a subject; rather, it becomes an object only in being objectified *by* a subject. A being is without a subject, but objects exist only for a subject that does the objectifying. Hence the existence of the subject-object relation depends on the mode of existence of the subject. But why? Is such a relation always posited with the existence of the Dasein? The subject could surely forgo the relation to objects. Or is it unable to? If not, then it is not the object's concern that there exists a relation of a subject to it, but instead *the relating belongs to the ontological constitution of the subject* itself. To relate itself is implicit in the concept of the subject. In its own self the subject is a being that relates-itself-to. It is then necessary to pose the question about the being of the subject in such a way that this essential determination of relating-itself-to, *intentionality,* is thought as a constituent in the concept of the subject, so that the relation to an object is not something occasionally joined to the subject on the basis of a contingent presence at hand of an object. Intentionality belongs to the existence of the Dasein. For the Dasein, with its existence, there is always a being and an interconnection with a being already somehow unveiled, without its being expressly made into an object. *To exist* then means, among other things, *to be as comporting with beings [sich verhaltendes Sein bei Seiendem].* It belongs to the nature of the Dasein to exist in such a way that it is always already with other beings.

b) The Dasein directs itself toward beings in a manner that understands being, and in this self-direction the self is concomitantly unveiled. The Dasein's factical everyday understanding of itself as reflection from the things with which it is concerned

But what have we thus gained for elucidating the Dasein's existence? We stood at this place earlier during the discussion of the first thesis when we brought out the intentionality in the phenomenon of perception. We characterized intentionality there by means of intentio and intentum and also by the fact that to every intentional comportment belongs an understanding of the being of the being to which this comportment relates. But with this we leave open the question *how* the understanding of being "belongs" to intentional behavior. We did not inquire further about this after the first characterization of intentionality but said only that it is mysterious.

Now, however, in the context of the question about the interpretation of the subject's being, the question forces itself upon us: How does the *ego* determine itself through the intentionality of every comportment? We left the ego aside in the earlier determinations of intentionality. If intentionality means *self-direction-toward*, then it is obviously the ego that is directed. But then what about this ego? Is it a point or a center or, as is also said in phenomenology, a pole that radiates ego-acts? The decisive question arises once again: *What mode of being does this ego-pole "have"?* May we ask about an ego-pole at all? May we infer from the formal concept of intentionality, self-direction toward something, an ego as bearer of this act? Or must we not ask phenomenologically in what way its ego, its self, is given to the Dasein itself? *In what way is the Dasein, in existing, itself,* its own, or by strict literalness "ownly" or authentic? The self which the Dasein is, is there somehow in and along with all intentional comportments. To intentionality belongs, not only a self-directing-toward and not only an understanding of the being of the being toward which it is directed, but also *the associated unveiling of the self* which is comporting itself here. Intentional direction-toward is not simply an act-ray issuing from an ego-center, which would have to be related to the ego only afterward, in such a way that in a second act this ego would turn back to the first one, the first self-directing-toward. Rather, the co-disclosure of the self belongs to intentionality. But the question remains, *In what way is the self given?* Not—as might be thought in adherence to Kant—in such a way that an "I think" accompanies all representations and goes along with the acts directed at extant beings, which thus would be a reflective act directed at the first act. Formally, it is unassailable to speak of the ego as consciousness-*of*-something that is at the same time conscious of *itself,* and the description of res cogitans as cogito me cogitare, or self-consciousness, is correct. But these formal determinations, which provide the framework for idealism's dialectic of consciousness, are nevertheless very far from an interpretation of the phenomenal circumstances of the Dasein, from *how* this being shows itself to itself in its factual existence, if violence is not practised on the Dasein by preconceived notions of ego and subject drawn from the theory of knowledge.

We must first of all see this one thing clearly: the Dasein, as existing, is there for itself, even when the ego does not direct itself to itself in the manner of its own peculiar turning around and turning back, which in phenomenology is called inner perception as contrasted with outer. The self is there for the Dasein itself without reflection and without inner perception, *before* all reflection. Reflection, in the sense of a turning back, is only a mode of self-*apprehension*, but not the mode of primary self-disclosure. The way in which the self is unveiled to itself in the factical Dasein can nevertheless be fittingly called reflection, except that we must not take this expression to mean what is commonly meant by it—the ego bent around backward and staring at itself—but an interconnection such as is manifested in the optical meaning of the term. To reflect means, in the optical context, to break at something, to radiate back from there, to show itself in a reflection from something. In Hegel—who saw and was able to see in philosophy so much more than had ever been seen before, because he had an uncommon power over language and wrested concealed things from their hiding-places—this optical significance of the term resounds, even if in a different context and with a different intention. We say that the Dasein does not first need to turn backward to itself as though, keeping itself behind its own back, it were at first standing in front of things and staring rigidly at them. Instead, it never finds itself otherwise than in the things themselves, and in fact in those things that daily surround it. It *finds itself* primarily and constantly *in things* because, tending them, distressed by them, it always in some way or other rests in things. Each one of us is what he pursues and cares for. In everyday terms, we understand ourselves and our existence by way of the activities we pursue and the things we take care of. We understand ourselves by starting from them because the Dasein finds itself primarily in things. The Dasein does not need a special kind of observation, nor does it need to conduct a sort of espionage on the ego in order to have the self; rather, as the Dasein gives itself over immediately and passionately to the world, its own self is reflected to it from things. This is not mysticism and does not presuppose the assigning of souls to things. It is only a reference to an elementary phenomenological fact of existence, which must be seen prior to all talk, no matter how acute, about the subject-object relation. In the face of such talk we have to have the freedom to adapt our concepts to this fact and, conversely, not shut ourselves off from the phenomena by a framework of concepts. It is surely a remarkable fact that we encounter ourselves, primarily and daily, for the most part by way of things and are disclosed to ourselves in this manner in our own self. Ordinary understanding will rebel against this fact. As blind as it is nimble, it will say: That is simply not true and cannot be true; this can be clearly demonstrated. Let us take a quite simple example—the craftsman in his workshop, given over to his tools, materials, works to be produced, in short to that with which he concerns himself. Here it is quite clear, isn't it, that the shoemaker is not the shoe, not the hammer, not the leather and not the thread, not the awl and not the nail. How should he find himself in and among these things? How should he understand *himself*, starting out from them? Certainly the shoemaker is not the shoe, and nevertheless he understands *himself* from his things, *himself*, his own self. The question arises, How must we conceive phenomenologically of this self, which is understood so naturally and in such a commonplace way?

What does this self-understanding in which the factical Dasein moves look like? When we say the factical Dasein understands itself, its own self, from the things with which it is daily concerned, we should not rest this on some fabricated concept of soul, person, and ego but must see in what self-understanding the factical Dasein moves in its everyday existence. The first thing is to fix the general sense in which the self is experienced and understood here. First and mostly, we take ourselves much as daily life prompts; we do not dissect and rack our brains about some soul-life. We understand ourselves in an everyday way or, as we can formulate it terminologically, *not authentically* in the strict sense of the word, not with constancy from the most proper and most extreme possibilities of our own existence, but *inauthentically*, our self indeed but as we are *not our own*, as we have lost our self in things and humans while we exist in the everyday. "Not authentically" means: not as we at bottom are *able* to be own to ourselves. Being lost, however, does not have a negative, depreciative significance but means something positive belonging to the Dasein itself. The Dasein's average understanding of itself takes the self as in-authentic. This in-authentic self-understanding of the Dasein's by no means signifies an ungenuine self-understanding. On the contrary, this everyday having of self within our factical, existent, passionate merging into things can surely be genuine, whereas all extravagant grubbing about in one's soul can be in the highest degree counterfeit or even pathologically eccentric. The Dasein's inauthentic understanding of itself via things is neither ungenuine nor illusory, as though what is understood by it is not the self but something else, and the self only allegedly. Inauthentic self-understanding experiences the authentic Dasein as such precisely in its peculiar "actuality," if we may so say, and in a genuine way. The genuine, actual, though inauthentic understanding of the self takes place in such a way that this self, the self of our thoughtlessly random, common, everyday existence, "reflects" itself to itself from out of that to which it has given itself over.

c) More radical interpretation of intentionality for elucidating everyday self-understanding. Being-in-the-world as foundation of intentionality

But the question refuses to be dismissed: *How are we to make philosophically comprehensible this mysterious reflection of the self from things?* One thing is certain. We can succeed in finding this interpretation only if we adhere to the phenomenon and do not, by premature explanations, cause it to disappear at the moment when it first seems as if we cannot have done with an actual phenomenon, so that we would feel compelled to search for a way out.

The self that is reflected to us from things is not "in" the things in the sense that it would be extant among them as a portion of them or in them as an appendage or a layer deposited on them. If we are to encounter the self as coming to us from things then the Dasein must in some way be with them. The Dasein's mode of being, its existence, must make comprehensible that and in what way the asserted reflection of the inauthentic self from things is possible. The Dasein must be *with* things. We have also already heard that the Dasein's comportments, in which it exists, are intentionally directed-toward. The directedness of these comportments expresses a being-*with* that *with which* we have to do, a dwelling-*with,* a going-along-*with* the givens. Certainly, but intentionality as thus conceived still doesn't make comprehensible how we rediscover ourselves in things. The Dasein surely doesn't "transport" itself over into the place of things and surely doesn't put itself as a being of *their* type into their company so as later to discover itself as being present there. Of course not. Yet it is only on the basis of an *antecedent* "transposition" that we can, after all, come back to ourselves from the direction of things. The question is only how to understand this "transposition" and how the ontological constitution of the Dasein makes it possible.

One thing is certain. The appeal to the intentionality of comportments toward things does not make comprehensible the phenomenon occupying us, or, speaking more cautiously, *the sole characterization of intentionality hitherto customary in phenomenology proves to be inadequate and external.* On the other hand, however, the Dasein does not "transport" itself to the things by leaping out of a presumably subjective sphere over into a sphere of objects. But perhaps we have before us a "transposition" of a peculiar sort, so that we can bring to view its peculiarity exactly when we do not let disappear from the phenomenological field of vision this phenomenon that we have been discussing, inauthentic self-understanding. How does this apply to the "transposition" we are affirming?

We have a twofold task: (1) *to conceive intentionality itself more radically,* and then (2) to elucidate its consequences for what we have called the "transposition" of the Dasein over to things. In other words, what are we to understand by what is customarily called *transcendence* in philosophy? It is commonly taught in philosophy that what is transcendent is things, objects. But what is originally transcendent, what *does the transcending,* is not things as over against the Dasein; rather, it is the Dasein itself which is transcendent in the strict sense. *Transcendence* is a *fundamental determination of the ontological structure of the Dasein.* It belongs to the existentiality of existence. Transcendence is an existential concept. It will turn out that intentionality is founded in the Dasein's transcendence and is possible solely for this reason—that transcendence cannot conversely be explained in terms of intentionality. The task of bringing to light the Dasein's existential constitution leads first of all to the twofold task, intrinsically one, of *interpreting more radically the phenomena of intentionality and transcendence.* With this task—of bringing to view, along with the more original conception of intentionality and transcendence, a basic determination of the Dasein's whole existence—we also run up against a central problem that has remained unknown to all previous philosophy and has involved it in remarkable, insoluble aporiai. We may not hope to solve the central problem in a single attempt or indeed even to make it sufficiently transparent as a problem.

α) Equipment, equipmental contexture, and world. Being-in-the-world and intraworldliness

For the present we need only to realize clearly that the ontological distinction between res cogitans and res extensa, between ego and non-ego, to speak formally, cannot in any way be conceived directly and simply, as for instance in the form that Fichte uses to initiate the problem when he says, "Gentlemen, think the wall, and then think the one who thinks the wall." There is already a constructive violation of the facts, an unphenomenological onset, in the request "Think the wall." For in our natural comportment toward things we never think a *single* thing, and whenever we seize upon it expressly for itself we are taking it *out* of a contexture to which it belongs in its real content: wall, room, surroundings. The request "Think the wall," understood as the beginning of a return to the one who is thinking the wall, as the beginning of the philosophical interpretation of the subject, is saying: Make yourselves blind to what is already given to you in the very first place and for all apprehending that is explicitly thinking. But what is thus antecedently given? How do the beings with which we dwell show themselves to us primarily and for the most part? Sitting here in the auditorium, we do not in fact apprehend walls—not unless we are getting bored. Nevertheless, the walls are already present even before we think them as objects. Much else also gives itself to us before any determining of it by thought. Much else—but how? Not as a jumbled heap of things but as an environs, a surroundings, which contains within itself a closed, intelligible contexture. What does this mean? One thing with these properties here, another with those properties there, a whole juxtaposition of things alongside, above, and through one another, so that, as it were, we grope forward from one to the next, progressively taking the single things together, in order finally to establish a coherent interconnection of them? That would be quite an ingenious construction. What is primarily given instead—even if not in explicit and express consciousness—is a thing-*contexture* *[ein Dingzusammenhang]*.

In order to see this we must formulate more clearly what *thing* means in this context and what ontological character the things have that are the initial beings here. The *nearest things* that surround us we call *equipment*. There is always already a manifold of equipment: equipment for working, for traveling, for measuring, and in general things with which we have to do. What is given to us primarily is the unity of an *equipmental whole,* a unity that constantly varies in range, expanding or contracting, and that is expressly visible to us for the most part only in excerpts. The *equipmental contexture* of things, for example, the contexture of things as they surround us here, stands in view, but not for the contemplator as though we were sitting here in order to describe the things, not even in the sense of a contemplation that dwells with them. The equipmental contexture *can* confront us in both ways and in still others, but it doesn't have to. The view in which the equipmental contexture stands at first, completely unobtrusive and unthought, is the view and sight of practical *circumspection,* of our practical everyday orientation. "Unthought" means that it is not thematically apprehended for deliberate thinking about things; instead, in circumspection, we find our bearings in regard to them. Circumspection uncovers and understands beings primarily as equipment. When we enter here through the door, we do not apprehend the seats, and the same holds for the doorknob. Nevertheless, they are there in this peculiar way: we go by them circumspectly, avoid them circumspectly, stumble against them, and the like. Stairs, corridors, windows, chair and bench, blackboard, and much more are not given thematically. We say that an equipmental contexture environs us. Each individual piece of equipment is by its own nature *equipment-for*—for traveling, for writing, for flying. Each one has its immanent reference to that *for which* it is what it is. It is always something *for,* pointing to a *for-which.* The specific structure of equipment is constituted by a *contexture of the what-for, in-order-to.* Each particular equipmental thing has as such a specific reference to another particular equipmental thing. We can formulate this reference even more clearly. Every entity that we uncover as equipment has with it a specific *functionality, Bewandtnis* [an in-order-to-ness, a way of being functionally deployed]. The contexture of the what-for or in-order-to is a whole of functionality relations. This functionality which each entity carries with it within the whole functionality complex is not a property adhering to the thing, and it is also not a relation which the thing has only on account of the extant presence of another entity. Rather, the functionality that goes with chair, table, window is exactly that which makes the thing what it is. The *functionality contexture* is not a relational whole in the sense of a product that emerges only from the conjoint occurrence of a number of things. The functionality whole, narrower or broader—room, house, neighborhood, town, city—is the prius, within which specific beings, as beings of this or that character, are as they are and exhibit themselves correspondingly. If we are actually thinking the wall, what is already given beforehand, even if not apprehended thematically, is living room, drawing room, house. A specific functionality whole is *pre*-understood. What we here explicitly and firstly attend to or even apprehend and observe in the equipmental contexture which in the given instance surrounds us most closely is not determinable but always optional and variable within certain limits. Existing in an environment, we dwell in such an intelligible functionality whole. We make our way throughout it. As we exist factically we are always already in an *environing world [Umwelt,* milieu]. The being that we ourselves are is not *also* present in the lecture hall here, say, like the seats, desks, and blackboards, merely with the difference that the being that we ourselves are knows about the relation it has to other things, say, to the window and the bench. The difference is not just that things like the chair and bench are juxtaposed to each other, whereas in contrast the Dasein, in being juxtaposed with the wall, also knows about its juxtaposition. This distinction between knowing and not knowing is inadequate to fix in a clear, unequivocal ontological manner the essentially different way in which extant things are extant together and in which a Dasein comports itself toward things extant. The Dasein is not also extant among things with the difference merely that it apprehends them. Instead, the Dasein exists in the manner of *being-in-the-world,* and this *basic determination of its existence* is the *pre-supposition for being able to apprehend anything at all.* By hyphenating the term we mean to indicate that this structure is a unitary one.

But what are surrounding world and *world?* The surrounding world is different in a certain way for each of us, and notwithstanding that we move about in a common world. But not much has been said in making this observation on the concept of world. Elucidation of the world-concept is one of the most central tasks of philosophy. The concept of world, or the phenomenon thus designated, is what has hitherto not yet been recognized in philosophy. You will think that this is a bold and presumptuous assertion. You will raise these objections: How can it be that the world has not hitherto been seen in philosophy? Didn't the very beginnings of ancient philosophy lie in asking about nature? And as for the present, do we not seek today more than ever to re-establish this problem? Have we not repeatedly attached great importance, in our discussions so far, to showing that traditional ontology grew out of its primary and one-sided orientation to the extant, to nature? How then can we maintain that hitherto the phenomenon of the world has been overlooked?

Nevertheless—the world is not nature and it is certainly not the extant, any more than the whole of all the things surrounding us, the contexture of equipment, is the environing world, the Umwelt. Nature—even if we take it in the sense of the whole cosmos as that which we also call, in ordinary discourse, the universe, the whole world—all these entities taken together, animals, plants, and humans, too, are not the world, viewed philosophically. What we call the universe is, like everything that may be important or not important, not the world. Rather, the universe of beings is—or, to speak more carefully, can be—the *intraworldly,* what is *within the world.* And the world? Is it the sum of what is within the world? By no means. Our calling nature, as well as the things that surround us most closely, the intraworldly and our understanding them in that way already presuppose that we understand world. World is not something subsequent that we calculate as a result from the sum of all beings. The world comes not afterward but beforehand, in the strict sense of the word. Beforehand: that which is unveiled and understood already in advance in every existent Dasein before any apprehending of this or that being. The world as already unveiled in advance is such that we do not in fact specifically occupy ourselves with it, or apprehend it, but instead it is so self-evident, so much a matter of course, that we are completely oblivious of it. World is that which is already previously unveiled and from which we return to the beings with which we have to do and among which we dwell. We are able to come up against intraworldly beings solely because, as existing beings, we are always already in a world. We always already understand world in holding ourselves in a contexture of functionality. We understand such matters as the in-order-to, the contexture of in-order-to or being-for, which we call the contexture of *significance [Bedeutsamkeit].* Without entering into an investigation of the very difficult phenomenon of the world in its different possible aspects, we must strictly distinguish the phenomenological concept of world from the ordinary pre-philosophical concept of world, according to which world means that which *is,* itself—nature, things, and the universe of beings.

What this pre-philosophical concept of world designates we call, in philosophical language, the totality of intraworldly beings, which on its part presupposes world in the phenomenological sense that has yet to be defined. Being-in-the-world belongs to the Dasein's existence. A chair does not have being-in-the-world's mode of being; instead it occurs within the intraworldly extant. The chair does not *have* a world from which it might understand itself and in which it could exist as the being that it is, but rather it is extant. The question arises once again, What is this mystery, the world, and above all, *how* is it? If the world is not identical with nature and the universe of beings, and if also it is not their result, then in what way *is* it? Is it a mere fiction, a hypothesis? How shall we give a definitive characterization of the world's own mode of being?

We shall now attempt to define the Dasein in its ontological structure by drawing the moments of the definition itself from the actual phenomenal evidence pertaining to this being. In doing so, we shall be setting out in a certain way, roughly speaking, from the object in order to get to the "subject." We shall see, however, that it is necessary to ponder this mode of departure and that it depends on whether we include within it everything that in any way belongs to it. We have already seen that a being which is given to us is not just a thing that we might or might not think—that in thinking some extant thing we do not really have something that just might possibly stand over against the Dasein. It is also not just a contexture of things that we have. Rather, we say that before the experiencing of beings as extant, world is already understood; that is, we, the Dasein, in apprehending beings, are always already in a world. Being-in-the-world itself belongs to the determination of our own being. In raising the question how the world accosted in being-in-the-world *is,* we are standing in a position which, like others, carries particular danger for philosophy and in regard to which we could easily evade the real problem in order to procure for ourselves some convenient and initially acceptable solution. The world is not the sum total of extant entities. It is, quite generally, not extant at all. It is a determination of being-in-the-world, a moment in the structure of the Dasein's mode of being. The world is, so to speak, Dasein-ish. It is not extant like things but it is *da,* there-here, like the *Dasein,* the being-*da* [das Da-sein] which we ourselves are: that is to say, it exists. We call the mode of being of the being that we ourselves are, of the Dasein, by the name of existence. This implies as a pure matter of terminology that the world is not extant but rather it exists, it has the Dasein's mode of being.

At this place another obstacle that is characteristic for all philosophizing again stands in our way. Our inquiry comes up against phenomena that are not familiar to the common understanding and therefore are for it without being, for which reason this understanding is compelled to set them aside by arguments. We shall follow one such plausible argument, taking note of what it is saying. If the world belongs to the being that I myself in each instance am, to the Dasein, then it is something subjective. If it is subjective and nature and the universe of beings as intraworldly are objective, then these latter beings—nature and the cosmos—are really subjective. With our assertion that the world is not extant but instead exists, has a being of like kind as the Dasein's, we have thus taken the stand of a most extreme subjective idealism. The foregoing interpretation of the world is untenable.

First of all, in fundamental opposition to this argument, we must say that even if the definition of the world as being subjective led to idealism, that would not yet have decided and proved that this interpretation is untenable. For to this very day I am unaware of any infallible decision according to which idealism is false, just as little as I am aware of one that makes realism true. We may not make into the criterion of truth what is the fashion and bias of the time, a solution belonging to some faction or other. Instead, we have to ask what this idealism—which today is feared almost like the foul fiend incarnate—really is searching for. It is not an already settled matter whether idealism does not in the end pose the problems of philosophy more radically than any realism ever can. But perhaps also it is not tenable in the form in which it has obtained up to now, whereas of realism it cannot even be said that it is untenable, because it has not yet even pressed forward at all into the dimension of philosophical problems, the level where tenability and untenability are decidable. To declare something to be idealism may, in contemporary philosophy, be a very dexterous partisan political stroke in outlawing it, but it is not a real ground of proof. Viewed with minute exactitude, the anxiety that prevails today in the face of idealism is an anxiety in the face of philosophy—and this does not mean that we wish to equate philosophy straightway with idealism. Anxiety in the face of philosophy is at the same time a failure to recognize the problem that must be posed and decided first of all so as to judge whether idealism or realism is tenable.

We described in the following way the argument of ordinary understanding in regard to the concept of world which was expounded. If the world is not something extant but belongs to the Dasein's being, if the world *is* in the Dasein's way of being, then it is something subjective. This seems to be very logical and acutely thought. But the principal problem whose discussion led us to the phenomenon of the world is, after all, to determine exactly what and how the subject is—what belongs to the subjectivity of the subject. Until the ontology of the Dasein is made secure in its fundamental elements, it remains a blind philosophical demagoguery to charge something with the heresy of subjectivism. In the end it is precisely the phenomenon of the world that forces us to a more radical formulation of the subject concept. We shall learn to understand that that is how matters stand. But we shall also not conceal from ourselves the fact that for this purpose it is less acuteness that is required than freedom from bias.

The world is something "subjective," presupposing that we correspondingly define subjectivity with regard to this phenomenon of world. To say that the world is subjective is to say that it belongs to the Dasein so far as this being is in the mode of being-in-the-world. The world is something which the "subject" "projects outward," as it were, from within itself. But are we permitted to speak here of an inner and an outer? What can this projection mean? Obviously not that the world is a piece of myself in the sense of some other thing present in me as in a thing and that I throw the world out of this subject-thing in order to catch hold of the other things with it. Instead, the Dasein itself is as such already projected. So far as the Dasein exists a world is cast-forth with the Dasein's being. To exist means, among other things, to cast-forth a world,* and in fact in such a way that with the thrownness of this projection, with the factical existence of a Dasein, extant entities are always already uncovered. With the projection, with the forth-cast world, that is unveiled from which alone an intraworldly extant entity is uncoverable. Two things are to be established: (1) being-in-the-world belongs to the concept of existence; (2) factically existent Dasein, factical being-in-the-world, is always already being-with intraworldly beings. To factical being-in-the-world there always belongs a being-with intraworldly beings. Being with things extant in the broader sense, for example, circumspective commerce with things in the more confined and the broader environment, is founded in being-in-the-world.

It is important for the first understanding of these phenomena that we should make clear to ourselves the essential difference between the two structures, the difference between being-in-the-world as a determination of the Dasein and intraworldliness, being within the world, as a *possible* determination of things extant. Let us try to characterize once more, by contrasting the two structures, this difference between being-in-the-world as a determination of the Dasein's ontological constitution and intraworldliness or being within the world as a possible but not necessary determination of extant entities.

An example of an intraworldly entity is nature. It is indifferent in this connection how far nature is or is not scientifically uncovered, indifferent whether we think this being in a theoretical, physico-chemical way or think of it in the sense in which we speak of "nature out there," hill, woods,

---

*The phrase Heidegger uses, sich Welt vorher-werfen, also suggests that the world is thrown beforehand, in advance, and not merely "forth"; it is pre-thrown, pre-cast; it is an a priori of the Dasein.

meadow, brook, the field of wheat, the call of the birds. This being is intraworldly. But for all that, intraworldliness does not belong to nature's being. Rather, in commerce with this being, nature in the broadest sense, we understand that this being *is* as something extant, as a being that we come up against, to which we are delivered over, which on its own part already always is. It is, even if we do not uncover it, without our encountering it within our world. Being within the world *devolves upon* this being, nature, solely when it is *uncovered* as a being. Being within the world does not *have* to devolve upon nature as a determination, since no reason can be adduced that makes it evident that a Dasein necessarily exists. But if and when a being that we ourselves are exists, when there is a being-in-the-world, then eo ipso beings as intraworldly are also factually uncovered in greater or lesser measure. Intraworldliness belongs to the being of the extant, nature, *not* as a determination of its being, but as a *possible* determination, and one that is necessary for the possibility of the uncoverability of nature. Of nature *uncovered*—of that which is, so far as we comport toward it as an unveiled being—it is true that it is always already in a world; but being within the world does not belong to the *being* of nature. In contrast, what belongs to the being of the Dasein is not being within the world but being-in-the-world. Intraworldliness cannot even devolve upon the Dasein, at any rate not as it does upon nature. On the other hand, being-in-the-world does not devolve upon the Dasein as a possible determination, as intraworldliness does upon nature; rather, so far as the Dasein *is,* it is in a world. It "is" not in some way without and before its being-in-the-world, because it is just this latter that constitutes its being. To exist means to be in a world. Being-in-the-world is an essential structure of the Dasein's being; intraworldliness, being within the world, is not an ontological structure or, more carefully expressed, it does not belong to nature's being. We say "more carefully" because we have to reckon here with a restriction, so far as there is a being which *is* only insofar as it is intraworldly. There are beings, however, to whose being intraworldliness belongs in a certain way. Such beings are all those we call *historical* entities—historical in the broader sense of world-historical, all the things that the human being, who is historical and exists historically in the strict and proper sense, creates, shapes, cultivates: all his culture and works. Beings of this kind *are* only or, more exactly, arise only and come into being only *as* intraworldly. Culture *is* not in the way that nature is. On the other hand, we must say that once works of culture, even the most primitive tool, have come into the world, they are still capable of being when no historical Dasein any longer exists. There is a remarkable relationship here, which we can only briefly indicate, in that every historical being, in the sense of world history—works of culture—stands with regard to its coming-to-be under quite different ontological conditions than with regard to its decay and possible perishing. These are relationships which belong to the ontology of history and which we are merely pointing to in order to make clear the restriction under which we are saying that being within the world does not belong to the being of things extant.

World is only, if, and as long as a Dasein exists. Nature can also be when no Dasein exists. The structure of being-in-the-world makes manifest the essential peculiarity of the Dasein, that it projects a world for itself, and it does this not subsequently and occasionally but, rather, the projecting of the world belongs to the Dasein's being. In this projection the Dasein has always already *stepped out beyond itself*, ex-sistere, it *is in* a world. Consequently, it is never anything like a subjective inner sphere. The reason why we reserve the concept "existence" for the Dasein's being lies in the fact that being-in-the-world belongs to this its being.

β) The for-the-sake-of-which. Mineness as basis for inauthentic and authentic self-understanding

From this determination of being-in-the-world, which we cannot yet realize for ourselves in a truly phenomenological manner, we shall indicate two further moments of the existential structure of the Dasein which are important for understanding what follows. The Dasein exists in the manner of being-in-the-world and as such *it is for the sake of its own self*. It is not the case that this being just simply is; instead, so far as it is, it is occupied with its own capacity to be. That it is for its own sake belongs to the concept of this existent being, just like the concept of being-in-the-world. The Dasein exists; that is to say, it is for the sake of its own capacity-to-be-in-the-world. Here there comes to view the structural moment that motivated Kant to define the person ontologically as an end, without inquiring into the specific structure of purposiveness and the question of its ontological possibility.

And furthermore, this being that we ourselves are and that exists for the sake of its own self is, as this being, *in each case mine*. The Dasein is not only, like every being in general, identical with itself in a formal-ontological sense—every thing is identical with itself—and it is also not merely, in distinction from a natural thing, conscious of this selfsameness. Instead, the Dasein has a peculiar selfsameness with itself in the sense of selfhood. It *is* in such a way that it is in a certain way *its own*, it *has itself*, and only on that account can it *lose* itself. Because selfhood belongs to existence, as in some manner "being-one's-own," the existent Dasein can *choose itself on purpose* and determine its existence primarily and chiefly starting from that choice; that is, it can exist authentically. However, it can also let itself be determined in its being by others and thus exist *inauthentically* by existing primarily in forgetfulness of its own self. With equal originality, the Dasein is at the same time determined in its possibilities by the beings to which it relates as to intraworldly beings. The Dasein understands itself first by way of these beings: it is at first unveiled to itself in its inauthentic selfhood. We have already said that inauthentic existence does not mean an apparent existence or an ungenuine existence. What is more, inauthenticity belongs to the essential nature of factical Dasein. Authenticity is only a modification but not a total obliteration of inauthenticity. We further emphasized that the Dasein's everyday self-understanding maintains itself in inauthenticity and in fact in such a way that the Dasein knows about itself without explicit reflection in the sense of an inner perception bent back on itself but in the manner of finding itself in things. We have tried to explain, by the interpretation of existence just given, how something like this should be possible on the basis of the ontological constitution of the Dasein.

To what extent has the possibility of everyday self-understanding by way of things become more visible as a result of the analysis of *some of the essential structures of the Dasein's existence?* We have seen that, in order to understand in the contexture of their functionality the beings that are closest to us and all the things we encounter and their equipmental contexture, we need an antecedent understanding of functionality-whole, significance-contexture, that is, world in general. We return from this world thus antecedently understood to beings within the world. Because as existents we already understand world beforehand we are able to understand and encounter ourselves constantly in a specific way by way of the beings which we encounter as intraworldly. The shoemaker is not the shoe; but shoe-gear, belonging to the equipmental contexture of his environing world, is intelligible as the piece of equipment that it is only by way of the particular world that belongs to the existential constitution of the Dasein as being-in-the-world. In understanding itself by way of *things,* the Dasein understands itself as being-in-the-world by way of its world. The shoemaker is not the shoe but, existing, he is his world, a world that first and alone makes it possible to uncover an equipmental contexture as intraworldly and to dwell with it. It is primarily things, not as such, taken in isolation, but as intraworldly, in and from which we encounter ourselves. That is why this self-understanding depends not so much on the extent and penetration of our knowledge of things as such as on the immediacy and originality of being-in-the-world. Even what we encounter only fragmentarily, even what is only primitively understood in a Dasein, the child's world, is, as intraworldly, laden, charged as it were, with world. What is important is only whether the existent Dasein, in conformity with its existential possibility, is original enough still to *see* on its own the world that is always already unveiled with its existence, to verbalize it, and thereby to make it expressly visible for others.

Poetry, creative literature, is nothing but the elementary emergence into words, the becoming-uncovered, of existence as being-in-the-world. For the others who before it were blind, the world first becomes visible by what is thus spoken. We may listen to a quotation from Rainer Maria Rilke's *The Notebooks of Malte Laurids Brigge* as testimony on this point.

Will anyone believe that there are such houses? No, they will say that I'm falsifying. But this time it's the truth, nothing left out and naturally also nothing added. Where should I get it from? It's well known that I'm poor. Everyone knows. Houses? But, to be precise, they were houses that no longer existed. Houses that were torn down from top to bottom. What was there was the other houses, the ones that had stood alongside them, tall neighboring houses. They were obviously in danger of collapsing after everything next to them had been removed, for a whole framework of long tarred poles was rammed aslant between the ground of the rubble-strewn lot and the exposed wall. I don't know whether I've already said that I mean this wall. But it was, so to speak, not the first wall of the present houses (which nevertheless had to be assumed) but the last one of the earlier ones. You could see their inner side. You could see the walls of rooms on the different storeys, to which the wallpaper was still attached, and here and there the place where the floor or ceiling began. Along the whole wall, next to the walls of the rooms, there still remained a dirty-white area, and the open rust-stained furrow of the toilet pipe crept through it in unspeakably nauseating movements, soft, like those of a digesting worm. Of the paths taken by the illuminating gas, gray dusty traces were left at the edges of the ceilings, and here and there, quite unexpectedly, they bent round about and came running into the colored wall and into a black hole that had been ruthlessly ripped out. But most unforgettable were the walls themselves. The tenacious life of these rooms refused to let itself be trampled down. It was still there; it clung to the nails that had remained; it stood on the handsbreadth remnant of the floor; it had crept together there among the onsets of the corners where there was still a tiny bit of interior space. You could see that it was in the paint, which it had changed slowly year by year: from blue to an unpleasant green, from green to gray, and from yellow to an old decayed white that was now rotting away. But it was also in the fresher places that had been preserved behind mirrors, pictures, and cupboards; for it had drawn and redrawn their contours and had also been in these hidden places, with the spiders and the dust, which now lay bare. It was in every streak that had been trashed off; it was in the moist blisters at the lower edge of the wall-hangings; it tossed in the torn-off tatters, and it sweated out of all the ugly stains that had been made so long ago. And from these walls, once blue, green, and yellow, which were framed by the tracks of the fractures of the intervening walls that had been destroyed, the breath of this life stood out, the tough, sluggish, musty breath which no wind had yet dispersed. There stood the noondays and the illnesses, and the expirings and the smoke of years and the sweat that breaks out under the armpits and makes the clothes heavy, and the stale breath of the mouths and the fusel-oil smell of fermenting feet. There stood the pungency of urine and the burning of soot and the gray reek of potatoes and the strong oily stench of decaying grease. The sweet lingering aroma of neglected suckling infants was there and the anguished odor of children going to school and the sultriness from the beds of pubescent boys. And much had joined this company, coming from below, evaporating upward from the abyss of the streets, and much else had seeped down with the rain, unclean above the towns. And the domestic winds, weak and grown tame, which stay always in the same street, had brought much along with them, and there was much more too coming from no one knows where. But I've said, haven't I, that all the walls had been broken off, up to this last one? Well, I've been talking all along about this wall. You'll say that I stood in front of it for a long time; but I'll take an oath that I began to run as soon as I recognized the wall. For that's what's terrible—that I recognized it. I recognize all of it here, and that's why it goes right into me: it's at home in me.[4]

Notice here in how elemental a way the world, being-in-the-world—Rilke calls it life—leaps toward us from the things. What Rilke reads here in his sentences from the exposed wall is not imagined into the wall, but, quite to the contrary, the description is possible only as an interpretation and elucidation of what is "actually" in this wall, which leaps forth from it in our natural comportmental relationship to it. Not only is the writer able to see this original world, even though it has been unconsidered and not at all theoretically discovered, but Rilke also understands the philosophical content of the concept of life, which Dilthey had already surmised and which we have formulated with the aid of the concept of existence as being-in-the-world.

d) Result of the analysis in regard to the principal problem of the multiplicity of ways of being and the unity of the concept of being

In conclusion, we shall try to *summarize* what we have first of all critically discussed in the third chapter, *in regard to the principal problem of the question*

---

4. R. M. Rilke, *Werke*, a selection in two vols. (Leipzig, 1953), vol. 2, pp. 39–41. [The date of this edition makes it impossible that Heidegger referred to it in 1927. Thomas Sheehan ("Caveat Lector: The New Heidegger," *The New York Review of Books*, December 4, 1980, p. 40, n. 5) identifies the edition Heidegger used as that of 1927, vol. 1, pp. 64–67. The original publication was: Rainer Maria Rilke, *Die Aufzeichnungen des Malte Laurids Brigge*, 2 vols. (Leipzig: Insel Verlag, 1910). The authoritative edition of Rilke is now *Sämtliche Werke*, edited by the Rilke Archive in association with Ruth Sieber-Rilke and supervised by Ernst Zinn, 6 vols. (Frankfurt: Insel Verlag, 1955–). Volume 6 contains *Malte Laurids Brigge* and other prose, 1906–1926. *The Notebooks of Malte Laurids Brigge*, trans. M. D. Herter Norton (New York: Norton, 1949). The quoted passage occurs on pp. 46 ff.]

about the multiplicity of ways of being and the unity of the concept of being. We have brought before our eyes the fundamental problems resulting from the fact that since Descartes and above all in German idealism the ontological constitution of the person, the ego, the subject, is determined by way of self-consciousness. It is not sufficient to take the concept of self-consciousness in the formal sense of reflection on the ego. Rather, it is necessary to exhibit diverse forms of the Dasein's self-understanding. This leads to the insight that self-understanding is always determined by way of the Dasein's mode of being, by way of the authenticity and inauthenticity of existence. From this emerges the need for putting the question in the reverse direction. We cannot define the Dasein's ontological constitution with the aid of self-consciousness, but, to the contrary, we have to clarify the diverse possibilities of self-understanding by way of an adequately clarified structure of existence.

In order to mark out the path of such an examination, let us give more particular consideration to reflection in the sense of self-understanding by way of the things themselves. This reflection in the sense of a mirroring-back of the self from things, which was at first so puzzling, became clearer for us when we asked: In what sense are the things of the environing world to be grasped? What ontological character do they have and what is presupposed for their apprehension? They have the character of functionality /the mode of deployment of the in-order-to/. They stand in a functionality-totality, which is understandable only if and when something like world is unveiled for us. This led us to the concept of the world. We tried to make clear that world is nothing that occurs within the realm of the extant but belongs to the "subject," is something "subjective" in the well-understood sense, so that the mode of being of the Dasein is at the same time determined by way of the phenomenon of the world. We fixed being-in-the-world as the basic determination of existence. This structure has to be differentiated from being within the world, intraworldliness, which is a possible determination of nature. It is not necessary, however, that nature be uncovered, that it should occur within the world of a Dasein.

The constitution of the Dasein's existence as being-in-the-world emerged as a peculiar transposition of the subject which makes up the phenomenon which we shall yet more particularly define as the Dasein's transcendence.

With his monadological interpretation of beings, Leibniz already had in view, in a certain sense, this peculiar phenomenon of the world, but without fixing it as such. He says that every being, in its possibility, reflects the universe of beings in conformity with the various degrees of wakefulness of its representing. Each monad, each individual being for itself, is characterized by representation, the possibility of mirroring the whole of the world. However great may be the difficulties of his monadology—principally because he embedded his genuine intuition in traditional ontology—nevertheless in this idea of the monads' representation something positive must be seen that has hitherto hardly been worked out in philosophy.

We have achieved several results:

First. Self-understanding should not be equated formally with a reflected ego-experience but varies in each case with the mode of being of the Dasein and in fact in the basic forms of authenticity and inauthenticity.

Second. Being-in-the-world belongs to the Dasein's ontological constitution; it is a structure that must be sharply distinguished from the intraworldliness, being within the world, of extant entities, since intraworldliness does not belong to the being of the extant, or in particular to that of nature, but only devolves upon it. Nature can also be without there being a world, without a Dasein existing.

Third. The being of beings which are not a Dasein has a richer and more complex structure and therefore goes beyond the usual characterization of the extant as a contexture of things.

Fourth. It emerges from a correctly conceived self-understanding of the Dasein that the analysis of self-consciousness presupposes the elucidation of the constitution of existence. Only with the aid of a radical interpretation of the subject can an ungenuine subjectivism be avoided and equally a blind realism, which would like to be more realistic than things themselves are because it misconstrues the phenomenon of the world.

Fifth. The characterization of being-in-the-world as a basic structure of the Dasein makes it clear that all comportment of the self toward intraworldly beings, or what we previously called intentional comportment toward beings, is grounded on the basic constitution of being-in-the-world. Intentionality presupposes the Dasein's specific transcendence, but this transcendence cannot be explicated by means of the concept of intentionality as it has hitherto been usually conceived.

Sixth. To intentionality, as comportment toward *beings,* there always belongs an *understanding of the being* of those beings to which the intentio refers. Henceforth it will be clear that this understanding of the being of beings is connected with the *understanding of world,* which is the presupposition for the experience of an intraworldly being. But, now, since world-understanding is at the same time an *understanding of itself by the Dasein*—for being-in-the-world constitutes a determination of the Dasein—the understanding of being that belongs to intentionality *embraces* the Dasein's being as well as the being of intraworldly beings which are not Daseins. This means that

Seventh. This understanding of being, which embraces all beings in a certain way, is, to begin with, *indifferent*—we commonly say of everything that in any way is encountered as a being, that it *is*, without differentiating in regard to specific ways of being. Our understanding of being is indifferent but it is at any time *differentiable*.

Eighth. Whereas the apparently unequivocal separation of beings into res cogitans and res extensa is effected under the guidance of an overarching concept of being—being equals extantness—our present analysis showed that there are radical differences of ontological constitution between these two beings. The ontological difference between the constitution of the Dasein's being and that of nature proves to be so disparate that it seems at first as though the two ways of being are incomparable and cannot be determined by way of a uniform concept of being in general. *Existence* and *extantness* are more disparate than, say, the determinations of God's being and man's being in traditional ontology. For these two latter beings are still always conceived as extant. Thus the question becomes more acute. Given this radical distinction of ways of being in general, can there still be found any single unifying concept of being in general that would justify calling these different ways of being ways of *being*? How can we conceive the unity of the concept of being in reference to a possible multiplicity of ways of being? How is the indifference of being, as it is unveiled in our everyday understanding of beings, related at the same time to the unity of an original concept of being?

The question of the indifference of being and its initially universal validity brings us to the problem of the fourth chapter.

Chapter Four

The Thesis of Logic:
Every Being, Regardless of Its
Particular Way of Being, Can Be
Addressed and Talked About by Means
of the "Is." The Being of the Copula

In our account of the *fourth thesis* we meet with a very central problem, one that is recurrently discussed in philosophy but only in a limited horizon—the question of being in the sense of the "is," the copula in assertion, in the logos. The "is" has received this designation "copula" because of its combinatory position in the proposition intermediate between subject and predicate: S is P. Corresponding to the fundamental position in which the "is" occurs in the logos or assertion, and in conformity with the progress of the problem's development in ancient ontology, this "is" as copula was dealt with in the science of the logos, logic. Thus it came about that a very central and by no means arbitrary problem of being *was forced aside into logic.* We say "forced aside" because logic itself developed into a separate discipline within philosophy and because it became the discipline that most of all succumbed to induration and separation from the central problems of philosophy. It was Kant who first gave logic a central philosophical function again, though in part at the cost of ontology and above all without trying to rescue so-called academic logic from its philosophically alienated superficiality and vacuity. Even Hegel's more advanced attempt to conceive of logic as philosophy once again was more an elaboration of the traditional problems and stock of knowledge than a radical formulation of the problem of logic as such. The nineteenth century is not at all able to maintain itself at the level of Hegel's approach to the question but relapses into academic logic and, in fact, in such a way that questions of an epistemological and psychological nature get confused with specifically logical problems. Among the most significant treatments of logic in the nineteenth century, we may cite those of John Stuart Mill, Lotze, Sigwart, and Schuppe. Schuppe's epistemological logic receives much too little attention nowadays.* It is characteristic of the status of logic within the philosophy of the second half of the nineteenth century that, for example, a man of Dilthey's stature was satisfied throughout his lifetime in expounding in his lectures the most tedious academic logic warmed up a bit with psychology. In his *Logical Investigations* (1900−1901) Husserl was the first to bring light again to logic and its problems. But he, too, did not succeed in conceiving logic philosophically; he even intensified the tendency to develop logic into a separate science, as a formal discipline detached from philosophy. Logic itself, from whose area of inquiry the first phenomenological investigations grew, was not able to keep step with the development of phenomenology. From the more recent period there are two works, self-willed and betraying a philosophical impulse, that are noteworthy—Emil Lask's *Die Logik der Philosophie* (1911) and *Die Lehre vom Urteil* (1912). If Lask, too, treats things for the most part formalistically and in the conceptual schemata of Neo-Kantianism, he nevertheless consciously pushes on toward a philosophical understanding of logic and in doing so is compelled under pressure from the subject matter itself to return to the ontological problems. Still, Lask was unable to free himself from the conviction of his contemporaries that Neo-Kantianism had the vocation to renovate philosophy.

This crude sketch of the fate of logic is intended to indicate that *because* the problem of the copula, the "is," is treated in logic, it necessarily gets detached from the truly relevant problems of philosophy as the science of being. The problem will make no further progress as long as logic itself has not been taken back again into ontology, as long as Hegel—who, in contrast, dissolved ontology into logic—is not comprehended. And this means always that Hegel must be overcome by radicalizing the way in which the problem is put; and at the same time he must be appropriated. This overcoming of Hegel is the intrinsically necessary step in the development of Western philosophy which must be made for it to remain at all alive. Whether logic can successfully be made into philosophy again we do not know; philosophy should not prophesy, but then again it should not remain asleep.

---

*Christoph Sigwart (1830−1904) was a dominant figure in the field of logic in the nineteenth century in Germany. In his view, logic was to be understood and developed as a normative and methodological doctrine. His basic work in the area was *Logik*, 2 vols. (Tübingen, 1873−1878; 4th ed., 1911; trans., London, 1895). Wilhelm Schuppe (1836−1913) was the chief representative of the philosophy of immanence, an anti-metaphysical position allied to empiriocriticism and positivism. He wrote mainly on ethics, philosophy of right, and logic. The two fullest treatments of logic among his writings were *Erkenntnistheoretische Logik* (Bonn, 1878) and *Grundriss der Erkenntnistheorie und Logik* (Berlin, 1894; 2nd ed., 1910).

Our *problem* is to answer the *question of the connection between the "is" as copula and the basic ontological problems.* To this end it would be necessary to begin by describing with sufficient concreteness the problem of the copula in the tradition. This would require that we run through the main stages in the history of logic. But the economy of the lecture format forbids this. We shall choose an alternative route and orient ourselves about some characteristic treatments of the problem of the copula as they have emerged in the history of logic. We shall first follow the rise of the problem in *Aristotle,* who is customarily called the father of logic. Then we shall portray an altogether extreme interpretation of the copula and assertion, that of *Thomas Hobbes.* In connection with this view we shall take note of the definition of the copula in *John Stuart Mill,* whose logic was of decisive significance for the nineteenth century. Finally we shall fix the problems that cluster around the copula as *Lotze* presented them in his logic. In this way we shall see how this apparently simple problem of the "is" has a many-sided complexity, so that the question arises for us, how the different attempts at a solution, at an interpretation of the "is," can be understood originally by way of the simple unity of the ontological setting of the problem.

§16. *Delineation of the ontological problem of the copula with reference to some characteristic arguments in the course of the history of logic*

We have already repeatedly met with being in the sense of the copula, being as the "is," in our discussions. We referred to it once when it was necessary to point to the fact that in our everyday existence, without actually conceiving being at all, we nevertheless always already understand something like being, since we always use the expression "is," as well as verbal expressions with various inflexions in general, with a certain understanding. Then again, when we were discussing the first thesis and had occasion there to consider Kant's interpretation of actuality as absolute position, we saw that Kant is acquainted with a still more general concept of being. He says: "Now something can be thought as posited merely relatively, or, better, we can think merely the relation (respectus logicus) of something as a mark to a thing, and then being, that is, the position of this relation, is nothing but the combining concept in a judgment."[1] In accordance with what was discussed earlier, we must say that being is here equivalent in meaning to the

---

1. Kant, *Beweisgrund,* p. 77. [In *Werke* (Cassirer), vol. 2.]

positedness of the subject-predicate relation, positedness of the combination posited in the formal "I combine" which belongs to judgment.

a) Being in the sense of the "is" of assertion in combinatory thinking in Aristotle

Aristotle had already come up against this meaning of being as subject-predicate relation or combination in his treatise *Peri hermeneias, De interpretatione,* "On assertion" or, better, "On interpretation." This treatise takes as its theme the logos or, more precisely, the logos apophantikos, that discourse and form of discourse whose function it is to exhibit that which is, as it is. Aristotle distinguishes between logos in general—discourse that has meaning and has some form, which can be a prayer, demand, or complaint—and logos apophantikos, discourse that has the specific function of showing, exhibiting, displaying, which in English is called assertion, statement, proposition, and in German Aussage, Satz or, in a misleading way, judgment, Urteil.

Aristotle first defines the logos apophantikos as a phone semantike, hes ton meron ti semantikon esti kechorismenon,[2] an articulate sound in words which is capable of signifying something and in such a way that each part of this verbal complex, each single word, already signifies something for itself, the subject concept and the predicate concept. Not every logos or discourse is exhibitive discourse. Although all discourse is semantikos, or signifies something, nevertheless not all discourse has the function of exhibiting that which is, as it is. Only discourse en ho to aletheuein e pseudesthai huparchei,[3] in which trueness and falseness occur, is exhibitive. Trueness, being-true, is a specific being (Sein). In the logos as assertion there is present, for one thing, in conformity with its form S is P, the "is," being as copula. For another, each logos as assertion is either *true* or *false.* Its being-true or being-false is connected in a certain way with the "is," being either identical with it or different from it. The question arises, How is being-true related to the being that is also present in the assertion in the sense of the "is" as copula? How must the problem be posed so as really to see this *connection between truth and copula* and to interpret it *ontologically?*

Let us first talk about how Aristotle sees the being of the copula. He says: Auta men oun kath' hauta legomena ta rhemata onomata esti kai semainei ti,—histesi gar ho legon ten dianoian, kai ho akousas eremesen,—all' ei estin e me oupo semainei · ou gar to einai e me einai semeion esti tou

---

2. Aristotle, *De interpretatione,* 4.16ᵇ26 f.
3. Ibid., 17ᵃ2f.

pragmatos, oud' ean to on eipes psilon. Auto men gar ouden estin, prossemainei de sunthesin tina, hen aneu ton sugkeimenon ouk esti noesai.[4] In
this passage Aristotle is speaking of verbs, which—as he says—carry with
them the signification of time, for which reason we are accustomed in
German to call them Zeitworte, time-words. We shall give an elucidative
translation of the passage cited from the text. If we utter verbs for themselves, for example, going, making, striking, then they are nouns and signify
something: the going, the making. For he who utters such words histesi
ten dianoian, arrests his thinking: he dwells on something, he means something specific by them. And, correspondingly, he who hears such words as
going, standing, lying comes to rest: he stops with something, with what
is understood by these words. All these verbs *mean something* but they do
not say whether what they mean *is* or *is not*. If I say "to go," "to stand,"
"going," "standing," then I haven't said whether anyone is *actually* going or
standing. Being, not-being, to be, not to be, do not signify a thing—we
would say they do not in general signify something which itself *is*. Not even
if we utter the word "being," to on, quite nakedly for itself, for the determination being, in the sense of to-be, in the expression "being" *is nothing;*
being is not itself *a* being. But the expression certainly *con*signifies something—signifies something *along with* its principal meaning, prossemainei—and indeed a certain sunthesis, a certain combining, which cannot be
thought unless what is already combined or combinable has been or is being
thought. Only in thinking of the combined, of the combinable, can sunthesis, combinedness, be thought. So far as being means this combinedness
in the proposition S is P, being has a meaning only in our thinking of the
combined. Being has no independent meaning but prossemainei, it implies,
it signifies in-addition, besides, namely, the additional signifying and meaningful thinking of such items as are related to each other. In doing this,
being expresses the relation itself. The einai prossemainei sunthesin tina
expresses a certain combining. Kant, too, says that being is a *combining-*
concept.

We cannot enter into further detail in regard to the passage here cited
any more than in regard to the whole treatise *De interpretatione*. It offers

---

4. Ibid., 16^b19–25. ["Verbs in and by themselves are substantival and have significance,
for he who uses such expressions arrests the hearer's mind, and fixes his attention; but they
do not, as they stand, express any judgment, either positive or negative. For neither are 'to
be' and 'not to be' and the participle 'being' significant of any fact, unless something is
added; for they do not themselves indicate anything, but imply a copulation, of which we
cannot form a conception apart from the things coupled." Trans. E. M. Edghill, in *The
Works of Aristotle*, ed. W. D. Ross (Oxford: Clarendon, 1908 –). *De interpretatione* is included
in vol. 1.]

immense difficulties for exegesis. The ancient commentators on Aristotle, Alexander of Aphrodisias and Porphyry, each interpreted this passage in a different way. Thomas views it still differently. This is a sign, not of a defective transmission of the text, but of the real difficulty of the problem itself.

For the present we have only to keep in mind the realization that the "is" signifies the being of a being and is not itself like an existent thing. In the statement "The board is black," both the subject, board, and the predicate, black, mean something existent—the thing that is the board and this thing as blackened, the black that is present in it. The "is," in contrast, does not signify something which would be existent like the board itself and the black in it. About this "is" Aristotle says: ou gar esti to pseudos kai to alethes en tois pragmasin, hoion to men agathon alethes to de kakon euthus pseudos, all' en dianoia;[5] what this "is" means is not a being occurring among things, something present like them, but en dianoia, in thinking. This "is" is synthesis and in fact, as Aristotle says, it is sunthesis noematon,[6] the being-combined of what is thought in thinking. Aristotle is here speaking of the synthesis of the S and P. In the passage cited, however, he says at the same time endechetai de kai diairesin phanai panta,[7] but all of this—the combining of the S and P in a proposition, which combination is expressed by the "is"—can be taken as diairesis. S = P is not only a combination but also at the same time a separation. This observation by Aristotle is essential for understanding the structure of the proposition, which we have yet to investigate. In a corresponding passage Aristotle says that this "is" means a synthesis and is accordingly en sumploke dianoias kai pathos en taute,[8] it is in the coupling that the intellect produces as combining intellect, and this "is" means something that does not occur among things; it means a being, but a being that is, as it were, a state of thought. It is not an exo on, not a being outside thought, and not a choriston, not something that stands for itself independently. But what sort of a being this "is" means is obscure. This "is" is supposed to mean the being of a being which does not occur among the extant entities and yet it is surely something in the intellect or,

---

5. Aristotle, *Metaphysica*, book Epsilon, 4.1027^{b}25ff. ["For falsity and truth are not in things—it is not as if the good were true and the bad were in itself false—but in thought." Trans. W. D. Ross, in *The Works of Aristotle* (Ross), vol. 8.]

6. Aristotle, *De anima*, 3.6.430^{a}28.

7. Ibid., 430^{b}3f.

8. Aristotle, *Metaphysica*, book Kappa, 8.1065^{a}22–23. [The context reads: "As to that which 'is' in the sense of being true, . . . [it] depends on a combination in thought and is an affection of thought (which is the reason why it is the principles, not of that which 'is' in this sense, but of that which is outside and can exist apart, that are sought)." Trans. Ross, in *The Works of Aristotle* (Ross), vol. 8.]

crudely speaking, in the subject, subjective. We can make a correct decision between these determinations, that the being designated by "is" and "to be" is not among things but nevertheless is in the intellect, only if we are clear about what intellect and subject mean here and how the basic relation of the subject to extant entities must be defined, that is, only if we can elucidate what being-true means and how it stands in regard to the Dasein. In whatever way we may be able to set about taking hold of these central but difficult problems, we can see at first the intrinsic affinity of Aristotle's and Kant's views. Being in the sense of the copula is, according to Kant, respectus logicus, and, according to Aristotle, it is synthesis in the logos. Because for Aristotle this being, this ens, is not en pragmasin, does not occur among things, but en dianoia, it signifies not an ens reale but an ens rationis, as Scholasticism puts it. But this is merely the translation of on en dianoia.

b) The being of the copula in the horizon of whatness (essentia) in Thomas Hobbes

The *interpretation* of *copula* and *proposition* advanced by *Hobbes* is also subject to the influence of the Aristotelian-Scholastic tradition. His view of logic is usually described as an example of the most extreme nominalism. Nominalism is the view of logical problems which, in the interpretation of thought and knowledge, starts from the thinking expressed in assertion and indeed from assertion as it manifests itself as a spoken verbal complex, words and names—hence nominalism. All the problems that arise regarding the proposition, and thus also the problem of truth and the question of the copula, are oriented by nominalism toward the context of words. We saw that from early on among the Greeks the question of the proposition and knowledge was oriented toward the logos, and therefore thinking about knowledge became logic. There remains only the question in which direction the logos is made thematic, in which respect it is regarded. In ancient logic at the time of Plato and Aristotle, one form of nominalism was already widespread, that of the Sophists, and later in the Middle Ages different varieties of this tendency of thought were revived, above all in the school of the English Franciscans. The most extreme representative of late Scholasticism is Ockham, whose nominalistic attitude was of significance for his theological problems but also for Luther's formulation of theological questions and the immanent difficulties associated with it. It is no accident that Hobbes elaborated an extreme nominalism. He gives his discussion of the copula in connection with his discussion of the proposition, the propositio, in his "Logica," the first part of his treatise *On Body.*[9] We shall purposely treat Hobbes' concept of copula and assertion in somewhat more detail, not just because it is less well known but because this extreme nominalistic formulation of the problem is carried through here with unsurpassable clarity in which—quite apart from the question of its tenability—philosophical power is always manifest.

The "is" is a simple constituent of a proposition, S is P. Accordingly, that "is" receives its more particular determination from the concept of the proposition, or assertion. How does Hobbes define the propositio? In obvious adherence to Aristotle, he starts with the delineation of possible forms of speech, logos, oratio. He enumerates precationes, prayers, promissiones, promises, optiones, wishes, iussiones, commands, lamentationes, complaints, and says of all these forms of speech that they are affectuum indicia, signs of mental feelings. The characteristic interpretation is already evident from this. He starts out from the *verbal character* of these forms of speech: they are *signs* for something psychical. But he does not interpret these forms of speech more precisely in their structure, and in fact this is always, down to the present, the source of a fundamental difficulty of interpretation. Of the form of speech that is alone decisive for logic, the propositio, he says: Est autem Propositio oratio constans ex duobus nominibus copulatis qua significat is qui loquitur, concipere se nomen posterius ejusdem rei nomen esse, cujus est nomen prius; sive (quod idem est) nomen prius a posteriore contineri, exempli causa, oratio haec homo est animal, in qua duo nomina copulantur per verbum Est, propositio est; propterea quod qui sic dicit, significat putare se nomen posterius animal nomen esse rei ejusdem cujus nomen est homo, sive nomen prius homo contineri in nomine posteriore animal.[10] The proposition, however, is a discourse consisting of two coupled names, by which the speaker signifies he understands that the second name,

---

9. Thomas Hobbes, *Elementorum philosophiae:* section 1, "De corpore," part 1, "Computatio sive Logica," chap. 3, "De propositione," ff. [The German text's note erroneously omits the term "Computatio" from the title of this section on logic. The original publication was *Elementorum philosophiae: Sectio prima, De corpore* (London, 1655). Part 1 is entitled "Computatio sive Logica." Reprinted in Sir William Molesworth's 5-volume edition, *Opera philosophica, quae latine scripsit omnia* (London: J. Bohn, 1839–1845; reprinted, Aalen: Scientia, 1962). See vol. 1. The original English version was contained in *Elements of Philosophy: The First Section, Concerning Body,* "written in Latin by Thomas Hobbes of Malmesbury, and now translated into English" (London: Andrew Crooke, 1656). The corresponding Part 1 here is entitled "Computation or Logic." Reprinted in Molesworth's 11-volume edition, *The English Works of Thomas Hobbes of Malmesbury* (London: J. Bohn, 1839–1845; reprinted, Aalen: Scientia, 1962), vol. 1. The passages cited by Heidegger in the Latin may thus be compared with their original translation in *Elements of Philosophy* or *The English Works.*]

10. Thomas Hobbes, "Logica," chap. 3, 2, in *Opera philosophica, quae latine scripsit, omnia,* ed. Molesworth (1839–45), vol. 1. [In *The English Works,* vol. 1, p. 30.]

or predicate, is the name of the same thing as is named also by the first; or, what is the same, he understands that the first name, the subject, is contained in the second. For example, this utterance "Man is an animal," in which two names are coupled by the verb "is." This speech states a proposition. It should be observed that in this definition Hobbes takes the subject and predicate from the beginning as two names and views the proposition in a wholly external way: two names, S is P. P is the second name, S the first, while the "is" is the coupling of the first and the second. In this portrayal he views assertion as a sequence of words, words emerging successively, and the whole of this verbal sequence is a sign (significat) that the one who employs these words understands that the two names in the proposition refer to the same thing. Animal means the same thing as man. Corresponding to this, the est or "is" is a signum, a sign.

Taken purely externally, there is present the same initial approach to the problem of interpretation of the propositio as in Aristotle. Aristotle begins the discussion in his treatise *De interpretatione* with the general characterization: Esti men oun ta en te phone ton en te psuche pathematon sumbola, kai ta graphomena ton en te phone.[11] "The verbal articulation, however, is a sumbolon, a symbol, a distinguishing sign of a psychical state, and, likewise, what is written is a symbol, a sign of the utterance." For Aristotle, too, there is a connection between what is written, spoken, and thought: script, word, thought. And of course this connection is conceived by him only with the guidance of the wholly formal and unexplicated concept of the sumbolon, the sign. In Hobbes this sign-relation is even more externalized. Only in recent times has this problem been pursued in an actual investigation. In the first of his logical investigations, "Expression and Meaning," Husserl gives the essential determinations concerning sign [Zeichen], mark or symptom [Anzeichen], and designation [Bezeichnung], taking all of them together in distinction from Bedeuten [the verbal noun for meaning or signifying, whose participial substantive form, Bedeutung, is then to be read as significance or meaning]. The sign-function of the written form with reference to the spoken form is altogether different from the sign-function of the written form with reference to what is meant in the speech, and conversely from that of the written form, the script, with reference to what is meant by it. A multiplicity of symbol-relations appears here which are very hard to grasp in their elementary structure and require extensive investigations. Some inquiries of this kind are to be found, as supplements to Husserl's investigation, in *Being and Time* (§17, "Reference and Signs"), the orientation there being toward principles. Today the symbol

---

11. Aristotle, *De interpretatione*, 4.16ª3f.

has become a favorite formula, but those who use it either dispense with any investigation as to what is generally meant by it or else have no suspicion of the difficulties that are concealed in this verbal slogan.

Subjectum is the prior name in the proposition, praedicatum is the posterior name, and the "is" is the coupling. How can the "is" as combining-concept be determined more precisely in its sign-function? The coupling, says Hobbes, does not necessarily have to be expressed by the *est,* the "is," nam et ille ipse ordo nominum, connexionem suam satis indicare potest,[12] for the very order of the names itself can indicate the connection sufficiently. The sign of the coupling itself, if expressed, the copula or an inflexion form of the verb, has on its part a specific indicative function. Et nomina [namely, the nomina copulata] quidem in animo excitant cogitationem unius et ejusdem rei, the names, subject and predicate, arouse the thought of one and the same thing. Copulatio autem cogitationem inducit causae propter quam ea nomina illi rei imponuntur;[13] the coupling itself, however, or its sign, the copula, likewise induces a thought, in which we think the reason why the two successive names are assigned to one and the same thing. The copula is not simply the sign of a combination, a combining-concept, but the index of *that on which the combination is grounded,* causa.

How does Hobbes elucidate this view of the copula, which must be startling within his extreme nominalistic orientation? Let us take an example: corpus est mobile,[14] "body is movable." By corpus and mobile we think rem ipsam, the thing itself, utroque nomine designatam,[15] designated by the two names. But with these two names set down twice, one after the other, we do not simply think the same thing, body-movable; non tamen ibi acquiescit animus, our mind here does not just set itself at rest but goes on to ask: What is this being-body or being-movable, sed quaerit ulterius, quid sit illud esse corpus vel esse mobile?[16] Hobbes traces the indicative function of the copula back to the indication of the entity meant in the nomina copulata, back to the question of what it is *in the thing named* that makes the difference on the basis of which it is named precisely that way and not otherwise as compared with other things. In asking about the esse aliquid we are asking about the quidditas, about the whatness of a being. It now first becomes clear what functional sense Hobbes assigns to the copula. As indication of the thought of the *ground* of the coupling of the names, the copula is the *index of this,* that *in the propositio,* in the assertion, we think the *quidditas,* the whatness of things. The propositio is the answer

12. Thomas Hobbes, "Logica," chap. 3, 2.
13. Ibid., chap. 3, 3.
14. Ibid.
15. Ibid.
16. Ibid.

to the question *What is* the thing? From the nominalist viewpoint this means: What is the reason for the assignment of two different names to the same thing? To utter the "is" in the proposition, to think the copula, means to think the ground of the possible and necessary identical relatedness of subject and predicate to the same thing. What is thought in the "is," the ground or cause, is whatness (realitas). Accordingly, the "is" announces the essentia or the quidditas of the res which is asserted about in the assertion.

According to Hobbes, from the structure of the propositio as thus conceived a fundamental division of names into nomina concreta and abstracta becomes intelligible. It is an ancient conviction of logic that concepts develop out of the judgment and are determined by means of judgment. Concretum autem est quod rei alicujus quae existere supponitur nomen est, ideoque quandoque suppositum, quandoque subjectum Graece hupokeimenon appellatur,[17] the concretum is the name for something that is thought of as existent. Therefore, suppositum and subjectum (hupokeimenon) are also employed for the expression concretum. Examples of such names are body (corpus), movable (mobile), or like (simile). Abstractum est, quod in re supposita existentem nominis concreti causam denotat,[18] the abstract name designates the cause, present in the underlying thing, of the concrete name. Examples of abstract names are corporeity (esse corpus), movability (esse mobile), or likeness (esse simile).[19] Nomina autem abstracta causam nominis concreti denotant, non ipsam rem,[20] abstract names designate the cause of the concrete name, not the thing itself. Quoniam igitur rem ita conceptam voluimus appellari corpus, causa ejus nominis est, esse eam rem extensam sive extensio vel corporeitas,[21] but that we nevertheless wish to call a given concrete body, for example, by that name is due to its being extended, that is, determined by corporeity. Described as they occur in the proposition, concrete names come first, abstract names second. For, says Hobbes, abstract names, which express whatness, quidditas, could not be without the "is" of the copula. According to Hobbes they *arise out of the copula.*

We must keep in mind this characterization of the copula. It points to the ground of the possible identical relatedness of subject and predicate to the same thing. What is meant by this indication of the ground, or cause, is the whatness of the thing, and accordingly the copula, the "is," expresses whatness. Hobbes denies that the "is" expresses in any sense "exists," "is

---

17. Ibid.
18. Ibid.
19. Ibid.
20. Ibid.
21. Ibid.

present," or the like. This confronts us with a question. Given that the copula expresses whatness, what then is the relation of its expressive function to the phenomenon or to the expression of extantness, existence?

The copula indicates the *cause* of the assignment of different names to the same thing. This determination must be retained. The "is" says that there subsists a cause for this identifying relatedness of the subject-name and the predicate-name to a single thing. This has still further consequences for the more specific determination of the propositio. We have already indicated that a being-true or being-false lies in the assertive statement and that some sort of connection subsists between being in the sense of the "is" and being-true. The question arises, How does Hobbes conceive of the veritas or falsitas, truth or falsehood, belonging to the propositio? His view of this connection becomes evident in the following sentence: Quoniam omnis propositio vera est . . . , in quo copulantur duo nomina ejusdem rei, falsa autem in qua nomina copulata diversarum rerum sunt,[22] every proposition is true in which the coupling of the names, subject and predicate, relates to the same thing; but it is false if the coupled names mean different things. Hobbes sees the truth of the proposition as lying in a correct identifying reference of the propositional terms to the same thing as the *unifying* reason for their being combined. He defines the copula in the same sense as truth. As copula, the "is" is at the same time the expression of being-true in the proposition. We shall not enter into the affinity of this definition of truth with Aristotle's, despite essential differences. In accordance with this definition of truth, Hobbes can say: Voces autem hae verum, veritas, vera propositio, idem valent,[23] these words "true," "truth," "true proposition" signify the same thing. Hobbes says without qualification: Truth is always a true proposition. Veritas enim in dicto, non in re consistit,[24] truth has its subsistence in the said as such, but not in things. This reminds us of the Aristotelian statement: Aletheuein, being-true, is not en pragmasin, in things, but en dianoia, in thought. In line with his extreme nominalistic tendency, Hobbes says in contrast that truth lies in *articulated* thinking, in the proposition.

Hobbes' attempt to demonstrate this thesis is characteristic. Nam etsi verum opponatur aliquando apparenti, vel ficto, id tamen ad veritatem propositionis referendum est,[25] for even if at times the true is opposed to the apparent and the imaginary, nevertheless this concept of "true" must be referred back to truth in the strict and proper sense, the truth of the

---

22. Ibid., chap. 5, 2.
23. Ibid., chap. 3, 7.
24. Ibid.
25. Ibid.

proposition. Hobbes recalls that, in a usage familiar in the tradition, we also speak, for example, of a "true" man. Here we mean an "actual" man as over against one who is painted, portrayed, or reflected in a mirror. This "true" in the sense of "actual" or "real," says Hobbes, does not have a primary significance, but traces back to the *veritas in the propositio*—a thesis basically advocated also by Thomas Aquinas, even if he takes a different position from that of Hobbes regarding this truth of things. Hobbes stresses in a completely one-sided way that being-true is a determination of the proposition and that we speak of true *things* merely figuratively. *Nam ideo simulachrum hominis in speculo, vel spectrum, negatur esse verus homo, propterea quod haec propositio, spectrum est homo, vera non est; nam ut spectrum non sit verum spectrum, negari non potest. Neque ergo veritas, rei affectio est, sed propositionis.*[26] For it is denied that the image of the man in the mirror (spectrum), the mirror-image, eidolon, is a true man, because this *assertion* "The mirror-image is a man" is not true as an assertion. For it cannot be denied that the image is not a true man. We call a *thing* true only because the *assertion* about it is true. The ascription of truth to things is a secondary mode of speech. We *call* a being true, for example, a *true* man, in distinction from one which is apparent, because the assertion about it is true. Hobbes believes he can clear up the meaning of the term "truth" by means of this thesis. But the question immediately arises, Why is the assertion about this being true? Obviously, because that *about* which we are making the assertion is not an illusion but a real, true man. We may not go so far as to claim that a so-called circle obtains here—for in the one case it is a matter of *elucidating* the meaning "truth" by means of judgmental truth; the other case has to do with the question of a genuine *confirmation* of something *true* as a judgment. Nevertheless, a puzzling connection shows up here between the *actuality* of a being and the *truth of the assertion* about this actual being—a connection that impressed us in the interpretation of the Kantian view of being: being equals perceivedness, positedness.

To this discussion, in which he reduces the truth of things to the truth of propositions about things, Hobbes appends the characteristic remark: *Quod autem a metaphysicis dici solet ens unum et verum idem sunt, nugatorium et puerile est; quis enim nescit, hominem, et unum hominem et vere hominem idem sonare.*[27] But what is customarily said by the metaphysicians, that to be, to be one, and to be true are the same, is idle, childish babble, for who does not know that man and one man and an actual man mean the same thing. Hobbes is here thinking of the Scholastic doctrine of the transcendentals, which goes back to Aristotle—those determinations

---

26. Ibid.
27. Ibid.

that belong to every something in general as something, according to which each something in some sense *is*, is an ens, each something is *one*, unum, and each something, simply qua being, that is, as thought in some way by God, is a *true* something, verum. Nevertheless, Scholasticism does not say, as Hobbes imputes to it, that ens, unum, verum, the transcendentals, *idem sunt*, mean the same thing. It merely says that these determinations are convertible; one can be substituted for the others, because all of them together belong with equal originality to each something as something. But we cannot discuss further in this place the reasons why Hobbes necessarily has to be blind to the fundamental significance of the transcendentals, which even Scholasticism did not properly realize. It is necessary to see only how drastically he denies every truth of things and assigns the determination of truth solely to assertion.

Hobbes' view, which is of particular significance for the understanding of contemporary logic because the latter also adheres to this thesis, will become still clearer as a result of the following discussions, which bring into closest proximity genuine vision and one-sided interpretation. Intelligitur hinc veritati et falsitati locum non esse, nisi in iis animantibus qui oratione utuntur,[28] from this it becomes intelligible that the place of truth and falsity is only in such living beings as make use of speech. Because assertion is speech, a contexture of words, and the place of truth lies in assertion, there is truth only where there are living beings making use of assertion. Etsi enim animalia orationis expertia, hominis simulachrum in speculo aspicientia similiter affecta esse possint, ac si ipsum hominem vidissent, et ob eam causam frustra eum metuerent, vel abblandirentur, rem tamen non apprehendunt tanquam veram aut falsam, sed tantum ut similem, neque in eo falluntur,[29] and even if the living creatures which do not share in language, the animals, can be affected on seeing the human image in the mirror just as though they had caught sight of the man himself and therefore can fear him or fawn upon him with gestures, nevertheless they do not apprehend what is thus given *as* true or false but solely as similar, and in this they are not subject to error. We may remark incidentally that a great difficulty presents itself here, which is how to make out what is given to animals as living beings and how the given is unveiled for them. Hobbes says that the given is not given to them as true or false because they cannot speak and make assertions about what is given to them. But he must surely say that the mirror-image is given to them *as* similar. The question would already obtrude here as to how far, in general, something can be given *as* something to animals. We also come here to the further question whether,

---

28. Ibid., chap. 3, 8.
29. Ibid.

in general, anything is given *as a being* to animals. It is as yet a problem to establish ontically how something is given to animals. On closer consideration we see that, speaking cautiously, since we ourselves are not mere animals, we basically do not have an understanding of the "world" of the animals. But since we nevertheless also live as existents—which is itself a special problem—the possibility is available to us, by going back from what is given to us as existents, to make out reductively what could be given to an animal that merely lives but does not exist. All of biology necessarily makes use of this methodological continuity, but it is still far from being clarified. We have indeed reached the point today where these fundamental questions of biology regarding the basic determinations of a living being and its world have become fluid. This indicates that the biological sciences have once again uncovered the philosophy necessarily immanent in them. Hobbes contents himself on this score with saying that animals have no language, and thus the given is not given to them as true or false, even though it is given *as* similar. Quemadmodum igitur orationi bene intellectae debent homines, quicquid recte ratiocinantur; ita eidem quoque male intellectae debent errores suos; et ut philosophiae decus, ita etiam absurdorum dogmatum turpitudo solis competit hominibus,[30] just as for men [and with this he sharpens the fundamental distinguishing characteristic of language] it is to well-understood speech that they owe everything they know rationally, so they are indebted to the same speech and language, when badly understood, for their errors. Just as the ornament of philosophy belongs solely to man, so also does the ugliness of meaningless assertions. Habet enim oratio (quod dictum olim est de Solonis legibus) simile aliquid telae aranearum; nam haerent in verbis et illaqueantur ingenia tenera et fastidiosa, fortia autem perrumpunt,[31] language and speech are like the webs of spiders, which was also said of Solon's laws. Tender and squeamish minds stick to the words and get ensnared in them, but strong minds break through them. Deduci hinc quoque potest, veritates omnium primas, ortas esse ab arbitrio eorum qui nomina rebus primi imposuerunt, vel ab aliis posita acceperunt. Nam exempli causa verum est hominem esse animal, ideo quia eidem rei duo illa nomina imponi placuit,[32] it can be inferred from this that the first *truths* sprang from the free judgment of those who first imposed names on things or received them from others as already imposed. For, to take an example, the proposition "Man is a living being" is true because they were pleased to impose the two names on the *same* thing.

So much for Hobbes' view regarding assertion, the copula, truth, and

---

30. Ibid.
31. Ibid.
32. Ibid.

language in general. It has become clear from what was just said about language that Hobbes takes the assertion as a pure sequence of words. But we also saw from the earlier citations that his nominalism cannot be carried through successfully. For Hobbes cannot persist in holding the assertion to be merely a sequence of words. He is necessarily compelled to relate this verbal sequence to some res, but without interpreting in further detail this specific reference of names to things and the condition for the possibility of this capacity for reference, the *significative* character of names. Despite his whole nominalistic attack on the problem, the "is" means, for Hobbes, too, more than a mere phenomenon of sound or script which is somehow inserted between others. The copula as a coupling of words is the index of the thought of the cause for the identical referability of two names to the same thing. The "is" means the whatness of the thing about which the assertion is made. Thus beyond the pure verbal sequence there emerges a manifold which belongs to assertion in general: identifying reference of names to a thing, apprehension of the whatness of the thing in this identifying reference, the thought of the cause for the identifying referability. Subjected to the constraint of the phenomena involved in the interpretation of the assertion as a sequence of words, Hobbes more and more surrenders his own initial approach. This is characteristic of all nominalism.

c) The being of the copula in the horizon of whatness (essentia) and actualness (existentia) in John Stuart Mill

Let us now attempt to delineate *John Stuart Mill's* theory of assertion and copula. In it a new problem regarding the copula greets us, so that the leading question about the interconnection between being and being-true becomes even more complicated. John Stuart Mill (1806–1873) developed his theory of assertion and copula in his chief work, *A System of Logic*. The main sections relevant for our problem are to be found in volume 1, book 1, chapter 4, "On Propositions," and chapter 5, "On the Content of Propositions." John Stuart Mill was influenced philosophically by British empiricism, Locke and Hume, and further by Kant, but principally by the work of his father, James Mill (1773–1836), *The Analysis of the Phenomena of the Human Mind*. Mill's *Logic* attained great significance in the first and second halves of the nineteenth century. It essentially affected all logical work, in France as well as among us in Germany.

In its design as a whole, Mill's logic is not at all balanced with respect to its basic conviction, which is supposed to be nominalistic though not the extreme nominalism of Hobbes. Whereas we may indeed recognize a nominalism in Mill in the first book, which develops the theory of nominalism, nevertheless a view of things that is opposed to his theory and hence is non-nominalistic comes to dominate the fourth book, where he works out his theoretical convictions in his interpretation of the methods of the sciences, so that he finally turns quite sharply against all nominalism as well as against Hobbes. Mill begins his investigation of propositions with a general description of this form of speech. "A proposition . . . is a portion of discourse in which a predicate is affirmed or denied of a subject. A predicate and a subject are all that is necessarily required to make up a proposition: but as we cannot conclude from merely seeing two names put together, that they are a predicate and a subject, that one of them is intended to be affirmed or denied of the other, it is necessary that there should be some mode or form of indicating that such is the intention; some sign to distinguish a predication from any other kind of discourse."[33] Here once more appears the approach according to which subject and predicate are put together as names. But a sign is needed that this juxtaposition of words is a predication.

This is sometimes done by a slight alteration of one of the words, called an *inflection;* as when we say, Fire burns; the change of the second word from *burn* to *burns* showing that we mean to affirm the predicate burn of the subject fire. But this function [of indicating predication] is more commonly fulfilled by the word *is,* when an affirmation is intended, *is not,* when a negation; or by some other part of the verb *to be.* The word which thus serves the purpose of a sign of predication is called, as we formerly observed, the *copula.* It is important that there should be no indistinctness in our conception of the nature and office of the copula; for confused notions respecting it are among

---

33. John Stuart Mill, *System der deduktiven und induktiven Logik,* trans. Theodor Gomperz, 2nd ed. (Leipzig, 1884), vol. 1, pp. 85–86. [The German translation cited is *System der deduktiven und induktiven Logik: Eine Darlegung der Grundsätze der Beweislehre und der Methoden wissenschaftlicher Forschung.* It was included in the edition of Mill's collected works, *John Stuart Mills gesammelte Werke,* translated by various hands under the general editorship of Gomperz (Leipzig: Fues, 1868–). In its second edition, to which the *Grundprobleme* text refers, the *System der Logik* constituted volumes 3 and 4 of the set (Leipzig: Fues, 1884). There is a new printing of the *Gesammelte Werke,* "from the last German edition," in twelve volumes (Aalen: Scientia, 1968); the *Logik* is contained in volumes 2, 3, and 4. Gomperz's translation was done "with the collaboration of the author." Mill's English title is *A System of Logic, Ratiocinative and Inductive, Being a Connected View of the Principles of Evidence and the Methods of Scientific Investigation.* The original publication was in two volumes (London: J. W. Parker, 1843). There have been numerous editions and reprints of this work. The 8th edition was published in the year before Mill's death, the 9th two years afterward. The German translation cited above was made from the 8th edition (London: Longmans, 1872). A critical edition is included, under the above title, in *Collected Works of John Stuart Mill,* vol. 7, books 1–3; vol. 8, books 4–6 and appendices; ed. J. M. Robson, with an introduction by R. F. McRae. In this text, "the 8th edition, the last in Mill's lifetime, is printed with the substantial textual changes found in a complete collation of the eight editions and the Press-copy Manuscript" (vol. 7, p. ci). Since so many editions and printings are distributed among readers, it will henceforth be most convenient to identify references, not by the page numbers given in the German edition, but by the original book, chapter, and section numbers, e.g., 1.4.1 for the present reference. Instead of attempting a re-translation from Gomperz's German, I have used Mill's actual language.]

the causes which have spread mysticism over the field of logic, and perverted its speculations into logomachies.

It is apt to be supposed that the copula is something more than a mere sign of predication; that it also signifies existence [extantness]. In the proposition, Socrates is just, it may seem to be implied not only that the quality *just* can be affirmed of Socrates, but moreover that Socrates *is*, that is to say, exists. This, however, only shows that there is an ambiguity in the word *is*; a word which not only performs the function of the copula in affirmations, but also has a meaning of its own, in virtue of which it may itself be made the predicate of a proposition. That the employment of it as a copula does not necessarily include the affirmation of existence, appears from such a proposition as this: A centaur is a fiction of the poets; where it cannot possibly be implied that a centaur exists, since the proposition itself expressly asserts that the thing has no real existence.

Many volumes might be filled with the frivolous speculations concerning the nature of Being (to on, ousia, Ens, Entitas, Essentia, and the like,) which have arisen from overlooking the double meaning of the word *to be;* from supposing that when it signifies *to exist,* and when it signifies to *be* some specified thing, as to *be* a man, to *be* Socrates, to *be* seen or spoken of, to *be* a phantom, even to *be* a nonentity, it must still, at bottom, answer to the same idea; and that a meaning must be found for it which shall suit all these cases. The fog which rose from this narrow spot diffused itself at an early period over the whole surface of metaphysics. Yet it becomes us not to triumph over the great intellects of Plato and Aristotle because we are now able to preserve ourselves from many errors into which they, perhaps inevitably, fell.[34]

Here, too, the sober Englishman's misreading of history appears quite clearly. We see from the quotation that Mill first approaches the problem in the same direction as nominalism in general. The proposition is a verbal sequence which needs a sign in order to be recognizable as predication. The further factor that already foretellingly characterizes Mill's view of the copula lies in his belief that there is an ambiguity in the copula, in the "is," since on the one hand it has the *function of combination,* or the function of being a sign, but at the same time signifies *existence.* Mill emphasizes that the attempt to bring together these two meanings of the copula, its combinatory function, or sign-character, and its signification as an expression of existence, drove philosophy to mysticism. In the course of our discussion we shall see what the situation is regarding this question as to whether and how the copula is equivocal and perhaps even more ambiguous than that. But it is precisely for this reason that the problem of inquiring into the *unitary ground* of this *ambiguity* necessarily emerges. For an ambiguity of the same word is never accidental.

Mill's opening makes it appear as if he were attempting to sever the

---

34. Mill, *Logic,* 1.4.1.

assertion as a verbal sequence from the things themselves about which it is asserted or, as is common in British empiricism, to take the assertion not so much as a complex of words but more as a complex of representations which are linked solely in the subject. However, Mill turns very sharply against this conception of the judgment as a combination of representations or even of mere words. He says: "It is, of course, true that in any case of judgment, as for instance when we judge that gold is yellow, a process takes place in our minds. . . . We must have the idea of gold and the idea of yellow, and these two ideas must be brought together in our mind"[35] Mill admits this empiricistic interpretation of thinking in a certain sense—some sort of putting together of ideas in the soul. "But in the first place, it is evident that this is only a part of what takes place [in judgment]";[36] "but my belief [that is, assensus, as Descartes says, the assent that is present in the judgment] has not reference to the ideas, it has reference to the things. What I believe [that to which I assent, to which I say yes in the judgment], is a fact."[37] It must be inferred from this, however, that the "is" in the proposition expresses the factuality of the thing, its existence, and is not just a sign of a combination of names. On the one hand, this means that the proposition refers to facts, but, on the other hand, it is said that the "is" is a sign of the coupling of names. How is this equivocity of the copula to be eliminated?

Mill tries to do this by introducing a general classification of all possible propositions. He distinguishes between *essential* and *accidental* propositions. What he intends here emerges from the further characteristics he assigns to this classification of propositions. He also calls the essential propositions *verbal* propositions and designates the accidental ones as *real* propositions. He has still another distinction in which he adheres to tradition and, as he believes, to Kant. The essential, or verbal, propositions are *analytic,* and the real, accidental propositions are *synthetic.* Kant made this distinction of judgments the guide for his main problem, which took the shape of the question as to how synthetic propositions a priori are possible. Unspoken within this is the question of how ontology is possible as a science. Mill's classification does not agree with Kant's, although that is indifferent here. An essential judgment is always verbal; this means that the essential judgment only explicates verbal meaning. It does not refer to facts but to the meaning of names. Now since the meanings of names are wholly arbitrary, verbal propositions or, more precisely, propositions which explicate words, are strictly speaking neither true nor false. They have no criterion in things but depend only on agreement with linguistic usage. *Definitions* fall among

---

35. Ibid., 1.5.1.
36. Ibid.
37. Ibid.

verbal or essential propositions. According to Mill the simplest and most important notion of a definition is that of a proposition which declares the meaning of a word, "namely, either the meaning which it bears in common acceptation, or that which the speaker or writer, for the particular purposes of his discourse, intends to annex to it."[38] Definition is nominal definition, explanation of *words*. Mill's theory of proposition and definition does not agree with what he develops practically in book 4. This latter is better than his theory. "The definition of a name . . . is the sum total of all the *essential* propositions which can be framed with that name for their subject. All propositions the truth of which [Mill really didn't have the right to say this] is implied in the name, all those which we are made aware of by merely hearing the name, are included in the definition, if complete."[39] All definitions are of names, but—and now the theory is actually breached—"in some definitions it is clearly apparent that nothing is intended except to explain the meaning of the word, while in the others, *besides* explaining the meaning of the word, it is intended to be implied that *there exists a thing* corresponding to the word. Whether this [the expression of the existence of that about which the assertion is made] be or be not implied in any given case cannot be collected from the mere form of the expression."[40] Here we can see Mill breaking through the nominalistic approach. He must return, beyond the verbal sequence, to the context of what is meant in that sequence.

"'A centaur is an animal with the upper parts of a man and the lower parts of a horse,' and 'A triangle is a rectilineal figure with three sides,' are, in form, expressions precisely similar; although in the former it is not implied that any *thing,* comformable to the term, really exists [instead, what is said is only what the word "centaur" means], while in the latter it is."[41] Mill says that the test of the difference between two such propositions which seem to have the same character consists in the fact that the expression "means" can be substituted for "is" in the first proposition.[42] In the case of the first proposition I can say "A centaur means an animal, etc.," and I can say this without the sense of the proposition being altered. In the second case, however, "A triangle is a rectilineal figure with three sides," I cannot

---

38. Ibid., 1.8.1.
39. Ibid.
40. Ibid., 1.8.5. [Italics have been added in the *Grundprobleme* text. This passage and several others succeeding it were originally written by Mill in a review of Archbishop Whately's *Logic,* published in the *Westminster Review* (January 1828). Mill declared that, although that review contained "some opinions which I no longer entertain, I find [that with] the following observations . . . my present view of that question is still sufficiently in accordance." The question had to do with the validity of the distinction between nominal and real definitions.]
41. Mill, *Logic,* 1.8.5.
42. Ibid.

substitute "means" for "is." For then it would be impossible to deduce any of the truths of geometry from this definition, which is no mere verbal definition, and yet such deductions are made. In this second proposition, about the triangle, the "is" does not signify merely "means" but conceals within itself an assertion of *existence*. Lurking in the background here is a very difficult problem—what is to be meant by mathematical existence and how this existence can be established axiomatically. In various places Mill utilizes this possibility of replacing "is" by "means" as a criterion for distinguishing between pure definitions as verbal explanations and propositions asserting existence. It appears from this that in so-called verbal propositions or essential assertions he attempts to interpret "is" in the sense of "it means." These propositions have the subject-*word* as their subject. The subject-word is what is to be defined as a word, for which reason he calls these propositions *verbal* propositions. But those propositions which assert "is" in the sense of "exists" are *real* propositions, because they intend reality, or actuality as equivalent to existence, as in Kant.

By means of this alteration of the expression in the case of analytic, that is, essential or verbal propositions, Mill tries to avoid the ambiguity of the copula and thus to settle the question of the different meanings of being in the "is." But it is easily seen that even when "is" is replaced in essential propositions by "it means," the copula nevertheless is still present, and in fact in the inflected form of the verb "to mean" which is now introduced. It is also easily shown that in every *meaning* of a name some *reference to things* is implied, so that Mill's allegedly verbal propositions cannot be completely severed from the beings they intend. Names, words in the broadest sense, have no a priori fixed measure of their significative content. Names, or again their meanings, change with transformations in our knowledge of things, and the meanings of names and words always change according to the predominance of a specific line of vision toward the thing somehow named by the name. All significations, including those that are apparently mere verbal meanings, arise from reference to things. Every terminology presupposes some knowledge of things.

With regard to Mill's division between verbal propositions and real propositions, the following therefore has to be said. Real assertions, assertions about beings, are constantly enriching and modifying the verbal propositions. The distinction that is really operative in Mill's mind is that between the view of beings that makes itself manifest in common meaning and understanding, as it is already laid down in every language, and the explicit apprehension and investigation of beings, whether in practice or in scientific inquiry.

The separation between verbal and real propositions is not feasible in this sense. All verbal propositions are only abbreviations of *real* propositions. Mill himself has to speak against his distinction, and in his more precise explanation of definition he already has to recur to the point that all verbal assertions are also referred to the experience of things. "How to define a name, may not only be an inquiry of considerable difficulty and intricacy, but may involve considerations going deep into the nature of the things which are denoted by the name."[43] "The only adequate definition of a name is . . . one which declares the facts, and the whole of the facts, which the name involves in its signification."[44] Here Mill is saying unmistakably that verbal propositions, too, are referred back to the facts. But furthermore, the "means" which Mill substitutes for "is" in verbal propositions also brings to expression an assertion about being; this can easily be seen from the term Mill employs for verbal propositions when he calls them essential propositions: they are called this because they express the essentia of a thing—the what-it-*is*. Hobbes resolved all propositions into propositions about whatness.

The ambiguity of the copula has thus become heightened. Hobbes says that all propositions express whatness, a mode of being. Mill says that apart from verbal propositions, which strictly speaking are not intended to be assertions about beings, the proposition, as real proposition, expresses something about existing things. For Hobbes the "is" and the est are synonymous with *essentia,* for Mill with *existentia.* In discussing the second thesis we saw that these two concepts of being somehow go together and determine every being. We thus see how an ontological theory about being works itself out into the various possible logical theories about the "is."

We need not here enter further into real propositions and the way in which Mill interprets them, particularly since he conceives of them by means of the concept of existence, of reality, in an indifferent sense and does not pursue this further as a problem. We need only take note that he recognizes three different categories, three fields of the real: first, feelings or states of consciousness; second, substances of a corporeal and mental kind; and third, attributes. Also, we cannot here go into the way Mill's propositional theory influences his theory of induction and inference.

We may say, then, that in Mill's theory there emerges a particular emphasis on the meaning of "is" in the sense of "exists."

d) The being of the copula and the theory of double judgment in Hermann Lotze

Let us turn in conclusion to *Lotze's* view of the copula. Lotze was early on occupied with the problems of logic. We have two treatments by him,

---

43. Ibid., 1.8.7.
44. Ibid., 1.8.3.

the small *Logic* and the large *Logic,* which he worked out almost simultaneously with a small and large *Metaphysics.* The small *Logic* (1843) grew out of an attempt to come to terms with Hegel, but it is still very much influenced by Hegel. The large *Logic* (1874; 2nd edition, 1880) is a far more extensive and independent exposition. It is oriented toward theories of science, particularly under the strong influence of Mill.

In the small *Logic* Lotze speaks of the "copula, which combines as well as separates."[45] He once more brings to bear here the thought that Aristotle had already stressed, that assertion is *sunthesis* as well as *diairesis.* He calls the copula an essential judgmental figure. How firmly Lotze takes the "is" as copula—sees in it the function of combination and understands it as Kant does, as a combinatory concept—becomes evident in a remark about the negative judgment, S is not P, which has been a basic difficulty for logic and ontology since Plato's *Sophist.* The copula here has the character of the "is not," being as it were a negative copula. Lotze says that "a negative copula is impossible,"[46] since a separation (negation) is not a mode of combination. It is Lotze's opinion that, if I say "S is not P" and deny the P of the S, then this cannot mean that I am combining P with S. This thought brings him to a theory essential for the later large *Logic:* in negative judgment, the negation is only a new, second judgment about the truth of the first, which latter properly has to be thought always as positive. The second judgment is a judgment about the truth or falsehood of the first. This leads Lotze to say that every judgment is, as it were, a double judgment. "S equals P" means: S is P, yes, that is true. "S does not equal P" means: no, it is not true, namely, the S equals P which is always there as the underlying positive judgment.

Without entering upon a criticism, we must first face up to Lotze and ask whether negation is simply to be taken as equal to separation. What does separation imply here when Lotze declares a negative copula, a separative combining, to be impossible? We must ask further, Is the primary sense of the copula, then, combination? Doubtless that is what the name says. But the question remains whether we are permitted without further ado to orient the problem of the "is" and its ontological meaning to the designation of the "is" as copula, whether in taking the "is" as copula, as combination, I have not already committed myself to a pre-judged interpretation of the "is," which perhaps does not at all allow of forging ahead to the center of the problem.

As we have already emphasized, Lotze developed still further this theory of the doubling of judgment and of all assertion. He calls this doubling also a doubling into the principal thought and the subsidiary thought. S's being

---

45. Hermann Lotze, *Logik* (1843), p. 87. [Leipzig: Weidmann'sche Buchhandlung.]
46. Ibid., p. 88.

P is the principal thought; it expresses the propositional content. The "yes, it is so," "yes, it is true," that supervenes is the subsidiary thought. We see here again how, in this dissociation of principal and subsidiary thoughts in judgment, what Aristotle had already stressed recurs once again: on the one hand the "is" signifies *combination* and on the other it means *being-true*. In his large *Logic* Lotze says: "It is already clear by now that only so many essentially distinct forms of judgment will be possible for us as there are essentially distinct significations of the *copula*, different subsidiary thoughts which we form about the way subject and predicate are linked and express more or less completely in the syntactical form of the proposition."[47] Regarding the categorical assertion, which serves most frequently as exemplar in logic, Lotze observes: "There is hardly anything to explain about this form, whose construction seems to be completely transparent and simple; we have only to show that this apparent clarity is completely puzzling and that the obscurity which hovers over the meaning of the copula in the categorical judgment will for a long time to come constitute the impelling motive to the subsequent transformations of logical investigation."[48] Lotze indeed saw more here than those who followed him. It was just this problem of the copula, whose history we have only hinted at in a few places, which could not receive adequate recognition in the course of the development of Lotze's work. On the contrary, the result of a peculiar interweaving of Lotzean ideas with the epistemological revival of the Kantian philosophy was that, since about 1870, the problem of the copula was even further excluded from the area of ontological inquiry.

We saw that Aristotle defined the assertion, the logos, as that which can be true or false. The judgment is the vehicle of truth. It is knowledge, however, which has the distinctive characteristic of being true. Hence the basic form of knowledge is the judgment, that which is true not only primarily but solely. Hobbes' thesis that knowledge is judgment became the creed of modern logic and theory of knowledge. That toward which knowledge is directed is its object—the Objekt, the Gegenstand, that which

---

47. Lotze, *Logik* (1874) (Leipzig: Felix Meiner, 1912), p. 59. [The original publication was *Logik: Drei Bücher vom Denken, vom Untersuchen, und vom Erkennen*. It was part 1 of the *System der Philosophie*, the second part of which was a volume on metaphysics (Leipzig: S. Hirzel, 1874; 2nd ed., 1880). The edition cited in the *Grundprobleme* text has the same title. It includes also a translation into German of Lotze's autobiographical essay in English, "Philosophy in the last forty years." This edition was edited and introduced by Georg Misch, Philosophische Bibliothek, vol. 141 (Leipzig: F. Meiner, 1912; 2nd ed., 1928). The translation into English is: *System of Philosophy: Part 1, Logic in three books: of thought, of investigation, and of knowledge*, ed. Bernard Bosanquet (Oxford: Clarendon Press, 1884; 2nd ed., 1887, 1888). I have translated the citations directly from the *Grundprobleme* text, so as to correspond with Heidegger's treatment of Lotze's language.]

48. Ibid., p.72.

stands-over-against. According to Kant's so-called Copernican Revolution, knowledge is not to be adapted to its objects, but just the reverse, the objects are to conform to knowledge. The necessary consequence is that cognitive truth, truth of judgment, thereupon becomes the standard for the object or, more precisely, for objectivity. But the copula shows that, in judgment, *being* of some kind is always expressed. True judgment is knowledge of the object. True being-judged defines the *objectivity* of known objects. Objectivity is what knowledge attains to when taken in the sense of judgment about something concerning beings. The *being* of beings becomes *identical with objectivity,* and objectivity means nothing but *true being-judged.*

It was first of all Husserl who showed, in the *Logical Investigations,* that in regard to judgment a distinction has to be made between the making of the judgment and the factual content being judged. This latter, the judged content which is intended in making the judgment, or the propositional content, the propositional sense, or simply the sense, is what is *valid.* Sense *[Sinn]* designates that which is judged as such in a true judgment. It is this, the sense, that is *true,* and what is true is constituted by nothing but objectivity. The *being-judged* of a true assertion equals *objectivity* equals *sense.* This conception of knowledge, which is oriented toward the judgment, the logos, and which therefore became the *logic* of knowledge (the title of the chief work by Hermann Cohen, founder of the Marburg School), and this orientation of truth and being toward the *logic* of the proposition is a principal criterion of Neo-Kantianism. The view that knowledge equals judgment, truth equals judgedness equals objectivity equals valid sense, became so dominant that even phenomenology was infected by this untenable conception of knowledge, as appears in the further investigation of Husserl's works, above all in the *Ideas toward a Pure Phenomenology and Phenomenological Philosophy* (1913). Nevertheless, Husserl's interpretation should not be straightway identified with the Neo-Kantian interpretation, even though Natorp in a detailed criticism believed he was entitled to identify Husserl's position with his own. The more recent representatives of Neo-Kantianism, particularly *[Richard]* Hönigswald, one of the most acute representatives of this group, are influenced by the logical interpretation of knowledge in the Marburg School and by the analysis of judgment in Husserl's *Logical Investigations.*

e) The different interpretations of the being of the copula and the want of radical inquiry

From this survey of interpretations of the "is," which is called the copula, we have seen that a whole series of determinations becomes intertwined with this phenomenon. Being means whatness on the one hand (Hobbes), existence on the other (Mill). The "is" is that which is judged in the subsidiary thought of the judgment, in which the being-true of the judgment is fixed (Lotze); as Aristotle said, this being also signifies being-true, and in addition this "is" has the function of combination. The characteristic determinations for the copula are:

1. The "is," or its being, equals whatness, essentia.
2. The "is" equals existence, existentia.
3. The "is" equals truth or, as it is also called today, validity.
4. Being is a function of combination and thus an index of predication.

We must now ask whether all these differing interpretations of the "is" are accidental or whether they arise from a specific necessity. And why have these different interpretations failed not only to be bound together and simplified but also to be comprehended as necessary by the raising of radical questions about them?

Let us make a summary review of the course of our historical presentation of a few characteristic treatments of the problem of the copula. We saw that *Hobbes* attempts an extreme nominalistic interpretation of the proposition or assertion, while *Mill* limits nominalism in theory to those propositions alone which he calls essential or verbal propositions, definitions. In these propositions "is" is synonymous with "the subject-term means." According to him the "is" signifies being only in the propositions he calls accidental or real assertions, those which assert something about beings. But for us it turned out that verbal propositions, too, those which explicate meanings, are necessarily related to a knowledge of fact and thus to a relationship to beings. The separation that Mill first embarks on cannot be carried through; he himself is led beyond his nominalism in the course of his reflections. This is important as a fact relating not only to Mill's theory but to nominalism in general. It provides evidence that nominalism is not tenable as a theory. *Lotze's* copula theory is characterized by his attempt to integrate the meaning implied in the "is" into the propositional structure by saying that each judgment is really a double judgment consisting of principal and subsidiary thoughts. The principal thought is fixed as the judgment's content, and the subsidiary thought is a second judgment about the first, in which the first judgment is asserted to be either true or false. From Lotze's theory of judgment, intertwined with the Neo-Kantian conception of knowledge as judgment, there arises a specific conception of the objectivity of objects and with it the conception of the being of beings as being-judged in a true judgment. This being-judged is identified with that to which the judgment refers, the object standing-over-against in knowing.

Being-judged is equal to objectivity as standing-over-against-ness, and objectivity, true judgment, and sense /Sinn/ are identified.

To test our understanding of this entire contexture we can provide ourselves with a control by taking a few propositions as examples and interpreting them according to the different theories. The test should be made with particular regard to the phenomenological discussions we shall be pursuing in the subsequent paragraphs. To this end we may choose quite trivial propositions.

"The sky is blue." *Hobbes* interprets this proposition in conformity with his theory by taking the two words "sky" and "blue" to be referring to one and the same res. The cause of combinability of these words is expressed by the res. The cause of combinability is expressed because in this something, to which subject and predicate terms are identically related, the *whatness* gets expressed. "The sky is blue" must necessarily be interpreted by Hobbes in such a way that in this proposition the whatness of an object is asserted.

In contrast, *Mill* would stress that this proposition not only asserts whatness in the sense of a factually real determination of the subject but at the same time asserts that the sky *is* blue—the thing which *is at hand,* if we may so say, the sky, exists in such and such a manner. *Not only* is *whatness,* or essentia, asserted but also, together with it, esse in the sense of existentia, being as being extant.

Applying his theory, Hobbes is simply unable to interpret our second example, "The sun is," whereas Mill would approach this proposition as the basic example for propositions asserting existence, esse, existentia. "The sun is" means that the sun is at hand, it is extant, it exists /in the sense of being extant/.

In accordance with his theory, Hobbes must in principle interpret the proposition "Body is extended" as expressing whatness. But Mill, too, will have to see in it an essential proposition which says nothing about existence, about the being extant of a body, but only declares that extension belongs to the essence, to the idea of body. If Mill were to take this essential proposition to be also a verbal one, as signifying merely that the word "body" means extension, we should immediately have to ask how and why this meaning "means" any such thing. What is the reason for it? Is it merely an arbitrary convention in which I fix a meaning and say that it is to have this or that content? Or does this verbal proposition, according to Mill, say something about a real content, but in such a way that it remains indifferent whether this content does or does not exist? "Body is extended" is in a certain sense an analytic judgment, but it is not verbal. It is an analytic judgment which provides a real determination concerning the reality of body, or, in the Kantian sense, about its realitas. Here "is" has the meaning of esse in the sense of esse essentiae, but it certainly does not have merely the function that Mill intends when he equates "is" and "means."

A fourth example, taken from Mill, reads "The centaur is a fiction of the poets." According to Mill this sentence is purely verbal. It is for him an example of the existence of propositions which do not assert being in the sense of existence but are explanations of words. If we examine this proposition more closely, it indeed appears that something is asserted in it, namely, what the centaur is. But this whatness which is asserted of the centaur expresses, precisely, a way of the centaur's being. Its intended meaning is that things like centaurs exist only in an imaginary way. This proposition is an assertion about existence. If this proposition is to be understood at all in its restrictive form and signification, existence in the broadest sense must in a certain way be thought in thinking it. Its intended meaning is: Centaurs do not exist actually but *are* only inventions of the poets. This proposition is, again, not a verbal judgment; the "is" also does not signify existence in the sense of being extant, but it nevertheless expresses a certain mode of being.

All these propositions we have mentioned contain still another meaning in their "is," for in all propositions as uttered their *being-true* is implicitly intended. This is the reason why *Lotze* lights upon the theory of the subsidiary thought. How is this being-true connected with the "is" itself? How are these differing meanings of "is" concentrated in the unity of an assertion? The answers must be given by the positive analysis of the proposition, so far as we can accomplish it at this stage of our considerations.

We may now offer this brief outline of all the different interpretations of the copula:

First. Being in the sense of the "is" has no independent signification. This is the ancient Aristotelian thesis: prossemainei sunthesin tina—it signifies only something in a combinatory thinking.

Second. According to Hobbes, this being signifies being-the-cause of the combinability of subject and predicate.

Third. Being means whatness, esse essentiae.

Fourth. In so-called verbal propositions, being is either identical with signifying or else synonymous with existence in the sense of being extant, esse existentiae (Mill).

Fifth. Being signifies the being-true or being-false that is asserted in the subsidiary thought of every judgment.

Sixth. Being-true—and with this we return to Aristotle—is the expression of an entity that is only in thought but not in things.

In summary we may say that the following are implied in the "is": (1) *being-something [Etwas-sein]* (accidental), (2) *whatness* or *being-what [Was-*

sein] (necessary), (3) *being-how* or *howness [Wie-sein]*, and (4) *being-true, trueness [Wahr-sein]*. The *being of beings* means *whatness, howness, truth.* Because every being is determined by the what and the how and is *unveiled* as a being *in its whatness and howness,* its being-what and being-how, the copula is necessarily ambiguous. However, this ambiguity is not a "defect" but only the expression of the *intrinsically manifold structure of the being of a being*—and consequently *of the overall understanding of being.*

The question of being as copula, pursuant to the expositions we have given of assertion and truth of assertion, is more precisely oriented toward the phenomenon of the combination of words. The characterization of the "is" as copula is not an accidental imposition of a name but the expression of the fact that the interpretation of this "is" which is designated as the copula is oriented to assertion as *spoken,* as an uttered sequence of words.

We have to ask whether this delineation of the "is" as copula really hits the mark with regard to the *ontological sense* of being expressed by "is." Can the approach made by the traditional type of inquiry relating to the "is" be maintained, or does not the confusion of the problem of the copula reside precisely in the fact that this "is" is characterized beforehand and then all further research into the problem is channeled in that direction?

§17. *Being as copula and the phenomenological problem of assertion*

a) Inadequate assurance and definition of the phenomenon of assertion

The problem of the copula is difficult and intricate not because inquiry into it takes its start in general from the logos but because this phenomenon of the logos as a whole has been inadequately assured and circumscribed. The logos is simply snatched up as it first forces itself upon the common experience of things. Regarded naively, an assertion offers itself as an extant complex of spoken words that are themselves extant. Just as there are trees, houses, and people, so also there are words, arranged in sequences, in which some words come before other words, as we can see clearly in Hobbes. If such a complex of extant words is given, the question arises, What is the bond that establishes the unity of this interconnection? The question of a combination, a copula, arises. We have already pointed out that a limitation of the problem to assertion as pure verbal sequence cannot in fact be maintained. At bottom something that the nominalistic theory would not wish to grant as valid is already implied in every assertion, even when it is taken as a pure sequence of words.

In the propositions with which *Aristotle* prefaced his treatise on the logos it was already manifest that many determinations belong to assertion and that it is not merely a verbal articulation and sequence. This entails that the logos is not merely a phone or phonetic whole but is also related by the words to meanings which are thought in a thinking that at the same time thinks things that *are*. The complete constitution of the logos includes from the very beginning word, signification, thinking, that which is thought, that which *is*. What we here enumerate as belonging to the logos is not simply ranged in mere sequence and juxtaposition in such a way that, given the conjoint presence of words, meanings, thought processes, thought objects, and existent things, certain relations among them result. It is insufficient to formally characterize these relations between words, meanings, thinking, things thought, and beings as the relation between sign and signified. Even the relationship of word-sound to word-meaning must not be viewed as a sign-relation. The verbal sound is not a sign for a meaning as a road sign is the sign for the direction of the road. Whatever this relation between word and meaning may be, the relation between the meaning and what is thought in the meaning is again different from the relation between word and what is thought; and the relation between what is thought in the meaning and the being that is meant in what is thus thought is again different from the relationship between either the verbal sound or the meaning and what is thought. There is no way in which we can manage to get on with a general formal description of the complex of word, signification, thinking, object thought, beings. We saw in Hobbes and particularly in Mill that the nominalistic theory of the proposition, which is oriented primarily toward verbal sequences, is driven beyond itself to the phenomena of *what is thought* and of the *beings that are thought,* so that at root the nominalistic theory also takes into consideration matters going beyond verbal sound.

However, the decisive question remains, *how that which belongs necessarily to the logos beyond the verbal sequence can be apprehended in a primary way.* It could be that starting with the logos as a verbal sequence leads directly to misinterpretation of the remaining constituents of the logos. In fact this can even be demonstrated. If the proposition is a verbal sequence which requires a combination, then corresponding to the sequence of the words there will be a sequence of ideas for which a combination will also be needed. This sequence of ideas corresponding to the verbal sequence is something psychical, present in thinking. And, given that in the assertion something is asserted about beings, it follows that some thing or some complex of physical things must correspond to this complex of ideas present in thinking. We then have corresponding to the verbal complex an idea-tional complex *in the mind,* and this ideational complex is supposed to refer to a complex of beings *outside* the mind. The problem arises, How can the ideational complex in the mind *agree with* the external things? This is customarily formulated as the problem of truth or objectivity. But this *fundamentally wrongheaded approach to the question* is motivated by the fact that assertion is taken first as verbal sequence. The Greeks, too, conceived the logos in this way, even though not exclusively so. This manner of starting passed into the traditional approach of logic and has to this day not been overcome.

It becomes clear from what has been said that we not only require a general delineation of what pertains to the complete concept of the logos— that it is not enough to say, in going beyond nominalism, that signification, what is thought, and what *is* belong to the logos—but that the essential thing is the portrayal of the specific *contextural interconnection* of these phenomena which belong essentially to the whole of the logos. This contexture must not merely come about after the fact by a process of composition under the constraint of things. Instead, this relational whole of word, signification, thinking, what is thought, what *is* must be determined in a primary way beforehand. We must ask: In what way can the ground-plan of this whole be sketched so that the specific structure of the logos can then be drawn in? When we raise this question, we free ourselves from the start from the isolated and isolating orientation toward the complex of spoken words of the problem of assertion. Spoken articulation *can* belong to the logos, but it does not have to. If a proposition is spoken, this is possible only because it is primarily something other than a verbal sequence somehow coupled together.

b) Phenomenological display of several essential structures of assertion. The intentional comportment of assertion and its foundation in being-in-the-world

What is the *logos* when taken *as assertion?* We cannot expect to condense the whole of this structure into a few propositions. We can only try to bring to view the essential structures. Have the considerations thus far undertaken prepared us in any way for this? In what direction must we look in making the logos as a whole our problem? Assertion has the characteristic double signification that it means both *asserting* and *asserted*. Asserting is *one of the Dasein's intentional comportments*. In essence it is an asserting *about* something and thus is intrinsically referred to *some being or beings*. Even if that about which an assertion is made should turn out not to be, an empty illusion, this in no way gainsays the intentionality of the structure of assertion but only demonstrates it. For when I judge *about* an appearance I am still related to beings. Today this sounds almost self-evident to us. But it required centuries of development of ancient philosophy before Plato discovered this self-evident fact and saw that the false and the apparent is also a being. To be sure, the apparent or false is a being which is not as it is supposed to be—it lacks something, it is a me on. The apparent and false is not nothing, not an ouk on, but a me on, a being, yes, but affected with a defect. In the *Sophist* Plato arrives at the knowledge that every logos is as such logos tinos, every assertion an assertion *about* something. This is seemingly trivial and yet it is a puzzle.

We heard earlier that *every intentional relation has within itself a specific understanding of the being of the being* to which the intentional comportment as such relates. In order for something to be a possible about-which for an assertion, it must *already* be somehow given for the assertion *as unveiled* and accessible. Assertion does not as such primarily unveil; instead, it is always, in its sense, already related to something antecedently given as unveiled. This implies that assertion as such is not knowledge in the strict sense. Some being must be antecedently given as unveiled in order to serve as the possible about-which of an assertion. But so far as a being is antecedently given as *uncovered* for a Dasein it has, as we showed earlier, the character of *being within the world. Intentional comportment* in the sense of *assertion* about something is *founded* in its *ontological structure* in the basic constitution of the Dasein which we described as *being-in-the-world.* Only because the Dasein exists in the manner of being-in-the-world is some being unveiled along *with* the Dasein's existence in such a way that what is thus unveiled can become the possible object of an assertion. So far as it exists, the Dasein is always already dwelling with some being or other, which is uncovered in some way or other and in some degree or other. And not only is this being with which the Dasein dwells uncovered, but that being which is the Dasein itself is also at the same time unveiled.

Assertion can but need not be uttered in articulate verbal fashion. Language is at the Dasein's free disposal. Hobbes is so far in the right when he refers to the fundamental significance of language for the essential definition of man. But he does not get beyond externals because he does not inquire how this entity must be to whose mode of being language belongs. Languages are not themselves extant like things. Language is not identical with the sum total of all the words printed in a dictionary; instead, because language is as the Dasein is, because it exists, it is historical. In speaking about something, the Dasein *speaks itself out, expresses itself, as existent being-in-the-world, dwelling with* and *occupying itself with beings.* Only a being that exists, that *is* in the manner of being-in-the-world, understands that which is, beings. Insofar as what is is understood, something of the nature of significance-contextures is articulated by means of this understanding. These contextures are potentially expressible in words. It is not the case that first there are the words, which are coined as signs for meanings, but just the reverse—it is from the Dasein which understands itself and the world, from a significance-contexture already unveiled, that these meanings accrue, each to its own word. If words are grasped in terms of what they mean by their essential nature, they can never be taken as free-floating things. If we took them as such, we could not ask what connections they might have. This mode of inquiry will always remain unsatisfactory, if it aims to interpret assertion and thereby knowledge and truth.

We have thus only very roughly outlined the plan within which we shall find the structure of assertion. We have fixed our guiding vision on the whole, which we have to see beforehand in order to obtain a survey of the relational interconnection between words, meanings, things thought, and beings. This whole, which has to be antecedently in view, is nothing but the existent Dasein itself.

The primary character of assertion is apophansis, a determination that Aristotle, and in principle Plato, too, already saw. Translated literally, it means the exhibiting of something from its own self, apo, letting it be seen as it is in itself, phainesthai. The basic structure of assertion is the exhibition of that about which it asserts. That about which the assertion asserts, that which is primarily intended in it, is the being itself. When I say "The board is black," I am making an assertion not about ideas but about what itself is meant. All further structural moments of assertion are determined by way of this basic function, its character of display. All the moments of assertion are determined by its *apophantic structure*.

Assertion is for the most part taken in the sense of predication, the attribution of a predicate to a subject or, taken altogether externally, the relation of a second word to a first or else, going beyond verbal orientation, the relation of one idea to another. However, the primary character of assertion as display must be maintained. It is only from this display character that the *predicative structure* of assertion can be determined. Accordingly, predication is primarily a disparting of what is given for assertion, and in fact an *exhibitive disparting*. This disparting does not have the sense of a factual taking apart of the given thing into thing-pieces but is apophantic: it dis-plays the belonging-together of the manifold determinations of the being which is asserted about. In this disparting, that being is at the same time made visible, exhibited, in the unity of the belonging-together of its self-exhibitive determinations. This exhibition in the sense of assertion both disparts and displays, and as such it is *determinant*. Disparting and *determination* belong together with equal originality to the sense of predication, which on its part is apophantic. What Aristotle is familiar with as sunthesis and diairesis must not be interpreted externally as it was in antiquity and continued to be later on, as though ideas are first taken apart from one another and then once more combined. Instead, this synthetic and diairetic comportment of assertion, of the logos, is intrinsically display.

As display, however, this determinative disparting always relates to some being that has already been unveiled. What thus becomes accessible in determinative display can be *communicated* in assertion as uttered. Assertion is the exhibition of the particular structure of determinative disparting, and this can be *communication.* Assertion as uttered is communication. And the character of communication must likewise be conceived apophantically. Communicating does not mean the handing over of words, let alone ideas, from one subject to another, as if it were an interchange between the psychical events of different subjects. To say that one Dasein communicates by its utterances with another means that by articulating something in display it shares with the second Dasein the same understanding comportment toward the being about which the assertion is being made. In communication and through it, one Dasein enters with the other, the addressee, into the same being-relationship to that about which the assertion is made, that which is spoken of. Communications are not a store of heaped up propositions but should be seen as possibilities by which one Dasein enters with the other into the same fundamental comportment toward the entity asserted about, which is unveiled in the same way.

It becomes clear from all this that assertion has not a primary cognitive function but only a secondary one. Some being must already be unveiled if an assertion about it is to be possible. Of course, not all discourse is a sequence of assertions and their corresponding communication. In an ideal sense, that would be the form of a scientific discussion. But philosophical conversation already has a different character, since it not only presupposes some optional basic attitude toward beings but requires still more original determinations of existence, into which we shall not here enter. In dealing with assertion here we have as our theme only a quite distinctive phenomenon, which cannot be used to interpret every arbitrarily chosen linguistic statement. We have to take into consideration that most statements in language, even if they have the character of assertion when taken literally, nevertheless also show a different structure, which is correspondingly modified as compared with the structure of assertion in the narrower sense of exhibition. We can define assertion as *communicatively determinant exhibition.* The primary moment of the structure of assertion is fixed by exhibition.

c) Assertion as communicatively determinant exhibition and the "is" of the copula. Unveiledness of beings in their being and differentiation of the understanding of being as ontological presupposition for the indifferent "is" of assertion

But where then does the copula remain? What have we gained for an understanding of the copula by our delineation of the structure of assertion?

To begin with, this one thing, that we shall not allow ourselves to be misled by the term "copula" so far as the name of this "is" already tends to push us toward a specific view of it. We shall now be asking about the "is" in the proposition, still without regard to the copulative character it presents externally as it appears in the verbal sequence.

The "is" behaves as if it were an expression of being. In its role as belonging to assertion, to which being can and must it relate? How and to what extent does assertion, to which the "is" belongs, relate to beings? Can we understand from that why this "is," externally extracted from the verbal sequence of the proposition, turns out to be ambiguous, which means indifferent in its signification? Must this indifference of meaning of the "is," or its ambiguity, be regarded as a defect, or does this ambiguity or indifference of the "is" correspond to its specific expressive character with reference to assertion? We saw that the dispartively determinant display of whatever being is spoken about in assertion already presupposes the unveiledness of this entity. Prior to the assertion and for the sake of making it, the asserter already comports himself toward the relevant entity and understands it in its being. In an assertion about something, that *understanding of being* must necessarily *achieve expression* in which the Dasein which is doing the asserting, that is, doing the displaying, already exists as such, since as existent it always already comports itself to beings, understanding them. But because the primary unveiling of the entity which can be the possible object of dispartive assertion is not accomplished by the assertion but is already carried out in the original showing of the unveiling, the asserter already understands the *mode of being* of the entity about which he is speaking, even before making his assertion. This understanding of the being of what is being spoken about does not first develop because of the assertion; rather, the assertion expresses it. The "is" can be indifferent in its signification because the different mode of being is already fixed in the primary understanding of beings.

Because being-in-the-world belongs essentially to the Dasein and the Dasein is itself unveiled in unity with it, every factically existing Dasein—every Dasein that speaks and expresses itself—already understands many different kinds of beings in their being. The indifference of the copula is not a defect; it is merely characteristic of the secondary nature of all assertion. The "is" in the proposition can, as it were, achieve this indeterminacy of its meaning because, as uttered, it arises from the Dasein which is uttering *itself* and which already understands in one sense or another the being intended in the "is." *Before* being uttered in the proposition, the "is" has already received its differentiation in factual understanding. And so far as in communication the entity spoken of is antecedently fixed, the understanding of the being of this entity is therewith also already given antecedently and the meaning of the "is" is fixed, so that this meaning need not necessarily obtrude for itself, whether in the "is" or in the inflexion. In the understanding of beings that occurs before assertion, what is always already latently understood is (1) the *whatness* of the entity to be unveiled and (2) this entity in a *specific mode of its being,* for example, extantness, being on hand. If, on the contrary, the procedure is reversed and the beginning is made from the proposition as uttered, then it is hopeless ever to understand the character of the "is," its specific indifference, positively by way of its origin and in its necessity and possibility. The differentiation of signification of the "is" which is already accomplished in the display function of the logos can remain indeterminate in assertion as communication, because *display* itself *presupposes the unveiledness of beings* and thus the *differentiation of the understanding of being.* If the start is made from the verbal sequence, then the only remaining possibility is to characterize the "is" as a combinatory word.

But it will be said that, although the character of the "is" as a combinatory word may be taken externally, this copulatory character of the "is" nevertheless cannot remain so completely accidental. Perhaps prior to any linkage of words or ideas this "is" signifies a linkage in the being itself about which the assertion is made. Even we ourselves said that sunthesis and diairesis, taking-together and laying-asunder, in the sense of determining belong to the display structure of assertion. If sunthesis and diairesis have the function of *displaying* some being, then obviously this being must, as a being, with respect to its being, be of such a sort that, roughly speaking, it demands such a combining as the display function appropriate to it. Dispartively determinant assertion aims at making accessible in its unity the organized manifoldness of the given entity. Thus the determinations of the entity itself, of that about which the assertion is made, have a character of *being together* which, taken externally, is a character of being combined. But then, insofar as the assertion is asserted about some being, the "is" will necessarily signify such a togetherness. The "is" will necessarily express a synthesis, quite apart from whether in its form as a word within the spoken sentence it does or does not function as copula. The "is" then would not be a combinatory concept because it functions as copula in the proposition, but just the reverse, it is a copula, a combinatory word in the proposition, only because its meaning in the expressing of a being means this being and the being of this being is essentially determined by togetherness and combination. In the idea of being, as we shall see, there is thus present something like combination, taken quite externally, and it is no accident that the "is" gets the character of the copula. Except that then the characterization of the "is" as copula is neither phonetic nor verbal but purely ontological, understood by way of that about which assertion asserts.

The closer we get to this "is," the more puzzling it becomes. We must not believe that the "is" has been clarified by what has so far been said. But one thing should now be clear, namely, that determination of the "is" by way of the uttered proposition does not lead to the sphere of the appropriate ontological inquiry. Indifferent in its linguistic form, the "is" always has a different meaning in living discourse. Assertion, however, is not primarily revelatory but presupposes the unveiledness of some being. Assertion, dispartive and displaying, hence *does not signify a being just in general or as such but, instead, signifies a being in its unveiledness.* Thus the question arises whether this determining of that which is spoken about in assertion—a being in its unveiledness—enters into the signification of the "is" by which the being of the assertion's object is exhibited. If so, not only would there be present each time in the "is" a meaning of being already differentiated prior to the assertion, being as extantness, as esse existentiae, or as esse essentiae or both together, or a meaning of being in some other mode of being, but also there would simultaneously belong to the signification of the "is" the *unveiledness* of that which is asserted about. In uttering assertions we are accustomed often to stress the "is." For example, we say "The board *is* black." This stress expresses the way in which the speaker himself understands his assertion and intends for it to be understood. The stressed "is" permits him to be saying: the board is in fact black, is in truth black; the entity about which I am making the assertion is just *as* I assert it to be. The stressed "is" expresses the *being-true* of the assertion uttered. To speak more precisely, in this emphasis that sometimes occurs, we see simply that at bottom in every uttered assertion the being-true of the assertion is itself co-intended. It is not an accident that in setting out from this phenomenon Lotze arrived at his theory of the subsidiary thought. The question is whether our attitude to this theory must be positive—that is, whether it is necessary to resolve every assertion into a double judgment, or whether, in contrast, this additional signification of the "is," this being-true, cannot be conceived immediately from the idea of being.

In order to clarify this as a problem we must first ask what this being-true of the assertion, which at times also gets expressed in the stressed "is" by the way the assertion is uttered, means. What is the relationship of this being-true of the assertion to the being of the entity about which the assertion is made, which being *[Sein]* the "is" in the sense of the copula means primarily?

§18. *Assertional truth, the idea of truth in general, and its relation to the concept of being*

a) The being-true of assertion as unveiling. Uncovering and disclosing as ways of unveiling

We have already taken note of Aristotle's striking thesis about the being-true of the logos, assertion, one that has been maintained in the tradition since his time. According to it the being-true of assertion is ouk en prag-masin, not in things, but en dianoia, in the understanding, in intellectu, as Scholasticism puts it. We shall be able to decide whether this thesis of Aristotle's is correct and in what sense it is tenable only if we first attain a satisfactory concept of truth. It could then be shown how truth is not itself a being that appears among other extant things. But if truth does not appear among the extant as something itself extant, that does not yet decide whether it may not nevertheless constitute a determination of the being of the extant, of extantness. As long as this question is not cleared up, Aris-totle's proposition "truth is not 'in' things" will remain ambiguous. But the positive part of his thesis, according to which truth is supposed to be in the intellect, will remain equally ambiguous. Here, too, we have to ask, What does "truth *is* in the understanding" mean? Is it supposed to be saying that truth is something which occurs like a psychical process? In what sense is truth supposed to be in the understanding? In what way *is* the understanding itself? We see that here we come back again to the question about the mode of being of the understanding, of the act of understanding as a comportment of the Dasein's, the question about the existential determination of the Dasein itself. Without this we shall not be able to answer the question in what sense truth *is* if it is in the understanding, which /understanding/ belongs to the Dasein's being.

Both components of the Aristotelian thesis are ambiguous, so that the question arises in what sense the thesis is tenable. We shall see that neither its negative part nor its positive part can be maintained in the form it assumes in the naive and customary interpretation. But this means that, while truth belongs in a certain way to things, it is not present among things themselves as another extant entity like them. And on the opposite side, truth is not in the understanding if understanding is thought of as a process within an extant psychical subject. It thus will emerge that truth neither is present among things nor does it occur in a subject but lies—taken almost literally—in the middle "between" things and the Dasein.

If Aristotle's thesis is taken in a purely external manner, as it is usually taken, it leads to impossible problems. For it is said: truth is not in things; it therefore is not in the objects but in the subject. This then leads to the statement that truth is in some sense a determination of the mind, some-thing inside it, immanent in consciousness. The problem then arises, How can something immanent in consciousness refer to something transcendent out there in the objects? Inquiry here gets irretrievably pushed into a hope-less situation; since the question is itself put the wrong way, an answer can never be attained. The consequences of this impossible predicament of inquiry appear in the theory's being driven to every possible device—for instance, it sees that truth is not in objects, but also not in subjects, and so it comes up with a third realm of meaning, an invention that is no less doubtful than medieval speculation about angels. If this impossible situation is to be avoided, the sole possibility lies in reflecting on what would be the subject "inside" which something like being-true is supposed to have its own existence.

We shall first ask what it means to say that an assertion is true. To find the answer it is necessary to go back to the determination of assertion that was given, that it is communicative-determinative exhibition. The last-mentioned character, exhibition, is primary. It means that an assertion lets that which is talked about in it be seen in the way of determinative predication; assertion makes that which is talked about accessible. This predicative exhibition of a being has the general character of unveiling letting-be-encountered. In understanding the communicated assertion, the hearer is not directed toward words or meanings or the psychical processes of the communicator. Instead, so far as the assertion is on its own part in keeping with the thing, the hearer is directed from the very beginning in his understanding of it toward the entity talked about, which should then come to meet him in its specific being /So-sein/. Exhibition has the character of *unveiling*, and it can be determination and communication only because it unveils. This unveiling, which is the *basic function of assertion*, constitutes the character traditionally designated as *being-true*.

The *way of unveiling* correlative to the entity about which an assertion is made varies with the *intrinsic content* and the *mode of being* of the assertion's object. We shall call the unveiling of an extant being—for example, nature in the broadest sense—*uncovering*. The unveiling of the being that we ourselves are, the Dasein, and that has existence as its mode of being, we shall call not uncovering but *disclosure, opening up*. Within certain limits terminology is always arbitrary. But the definition of being-true as unveiling, making manifest, is not an arbitrary, private invention of mine; it only gives expression to the understanding of the phenomenon of truth, as the Greeks already understood it in pre-scientific as well as philosophical understanding, even if not in every respect in an originally explicit way. Plato says explicitly that the function of logos, of assertion, is deloun, making plain, or, as Aristotle says more exactly with regard to the Greek expression of truth: aletheuein. Lanthanein means to be concealed; a- is the privative, so that a-letheuein is equivalent to: to pluck something out of its concealment, to make manifest or reveal. For the Greeks truth means: to take out of concealment, uncovering, unveiling. To be sure the Greeks' interpretation of this phenomenon was not successful in every respect. Therefore the essential initial approaches made by this understanding of truth could not be followed through favorably but—for reasons we cannot here consider more closely—fell victim to misunderstanding, so that today in the tradition the original sense of the Greek understanding of truth is completely hidden.

We shall attempt to investigate in further detail the understanding of the truth phenomenon. Being-true means unveiling. We include in this the mode of uncovering as well as that of disclosure, the unveiling of the being whose being is not that of the Dasein and the unveiling of the being that we ourselves are. We take *being-true* in this wholly *formal sense* as *unveiling,* in which it is not yet cut to fit a specific being and its mode of being. *Being-true as unveiling* yields itself as a *way of being of the Dasein* itself, of the Dasein's *existence.* So far as it exists—and this means, in conformity with our earlier results, so far as it is in such a way that it is in a world—the Dasein is true; that is to say, with the unveiled world there are always already beings unveiled, disclosed, uncovered, for it. The uncovering of extant beings is founded on the circumstance that the Dasein, as existent, in each case already comports itself to a world which is disclosed. In existing, the Dasein thus understands something like its world, and *with the disclosure of its world* the Dasein is at the same time *unveiled to its own self for itself.* We have already heard that this self-disclosure of the Dasein, its self-understanding, at first gained factically, is appropriated on the path of self-understanding by way of things that are in some sense uncovered and with which the Dasein dwells as itself existing. Because this disclosure of itself, and in unity with it the uncoveredness of intraworldly beings, belongs to the essential nature of the Dasein, we can say that the Dasein exists *in truth,* that is, *in the unveiledness of itself* and *of the beings* to which it comports itself. Only because as existing it is *essentially* already in truth can it err as such, and only for that same reason is there concealment, pretense, and taciturn reserve.

Being-true is unveiling, unveiling is a comportment of the ego, and therefore, it is said, being-true is something subjective. We reply, "subjective" no doubt, but in the sense of the well-understood concept of the "subject" as existing Dasein, the Dasein as being in the world. We can now understand in what way the Aristotelian thesis that being-true does not occur in things but en dianoia, in the understanding, is valid. But we can also see in what way it is invalid. If understanding and thinking are taken as a psychical understanding of an extant mind, then the presumed meaning of the assertion that truth occurs in the sphere of the subject remains unintelligible. But if, on the contrary, dianoia, intellect, understanding, is taken in the way this phenomenon must be taken, in its apophantic structure, as the unveiling exhibiting of something, then it becomes clear that understanding as unveiling exhibiting of something is determined intrinsically in its structure by being-true as unveiling. Thinking, as a free comportment of the human being, is situated in the possibility, as unveiling, to meet suitably or to miss the entity that is given to it. The being-true of assertion lies in its structure, because assertion is intrinsically a comportment of the Dasein, and the Dasein, as existing, is determined by being-true.

b) The intentional structure of unveiling. The existential mode of being of truth. Unveiledness as determination of the being of a being

Since the Dasein exists as being-in-the-world, it is always already dwelling with some being. "With some being" we say—that is, this being is unveiled in some sense or other. To the Dasein as *unveiling* there belongs essentially *something unveiled* in its *unveiledness,* some entity to which the unveiling relates in conformity with its intentional structure. There belongs to unveiling, as to every other intentional comportment, an *understanding of the being* of that to which this comportment relates as such. In unveiling assertion the Dasein is directed toward something which it understands beforehand in that entity's unveiledness. The intentum of the intentio of unveiling assertion has the character of unveiledness. If we equate being-true with unveiling, aletheuein with deloun, and if unveiling is essentially, not accidentally, related in its intrinsic intentionality to something to be unveiled, then there belong to the concept of truth the moment of unveiling and the unveiledness to which, by its structure, this unveiling relates. But there is unveiledness only *so far* as there is an unveiling, so far as the Dasein exists. *Truth* and *being-true* as unveiledness and unveiling have *the Dasein's mode of being.* By its very nature, truth is never extant like a thing but exists. Thus Aristotle's thesis, when properly understood, becomes valid again in its negative part. Being-true, says Aristotle, is not something in things; it is not something extant. Nevertheless, the Aristotelian thesis requires supplementation and more precise determination. For just because truth is only so far as it exists, having the Dasein's mode of being, and because there belongs to it at the same time the unveiledness of that to which it relates, it is admittedly not anything extant; but, *as the unveiledness* of that to which assertion refers, it is *a possible determination of the being of the extant.* It is a determination of the being of the extant so far as the extant is, for example, unveiled in an unveiling assertion.

When we say that being-true does not mean something that is extant among things, this mode of speech still suffers from an ambiguity. For being-true, as the unveiling of something, *means* precisely, each time, this entity to which it relates; it means this extant entity in its unveiledness.

Unveiledness is indeed not an *extant* determination of something extant, not a property of it, but belongs to existence qua unveiling. Nevertheless, as a determination of that about which assertion is made, unveiledness is a determination of the being of the extant.

With reference to the Aristotelian thesis, the result emerges that truth is *not* in the understanding, if the understanding is taken to be an extant subject. Truth is in things, so far as things are taken as uncovered, the uncovered *objects* of the assertion that is made about them. Being-true is *extant* neither in things nor in a mind. On the other hand, however, truth as unveiling is in the Dasein as a determination of its intentional comportment, and it is also a determinateness of some being, something extant, with regard to its being as an unveiled entity. It follows from this that being-true is something that "lies between" the subject and the object, if these two terms are taken in their ordinary external signification. The phenomenon of truth is interconnected with the basic structure of the Dasein, its *transcendence.*

c) Unveiledness of whatness and actualness in the "is" of assertion. The existential mode of being of truth and the prevention of subjectivistic misinterpretations

We are now in a position to focus more sharply on the problem of the "is" in the proposition. Here the *"is"* can mean (1) the *extantness* of a being, existentia, (2) the *whatness* of something extant, essentia, or (3) both together. In the proposition "A is," "is" asserts being, for example, being extant. "A is B" can mean that B is predicated of A as a determination of A's being-such *[So-sein]*, where it remains undetermined whether A is or is not actually extant. But "A is B" can also signify that A is extant and B is a determination extant in A, so that existentia and essentia of a being can be intended simultaneously in the proposition "A is B." In addition, "is" signifies *being-true.* Assertion as unveiling intends the extant entity in its *unveiled,* its *true* being-such. It is not necessary to have recourse to a so-called subsidiary thought and a second judgment within assertion. So far as the "is" in assertion is understood and spoken, it already signifies intrinsically the *being* of a being which is asserted about *as unveiled.* In the uttering of the assertion, that is to say, in the uttering of exhibition, this exhibition, as intentionally unveiling comportment, expresses itself about that to which it refers. By its essential nature, that which is referred to is unveiled. So far as this unveiling comportment expresses itself *about* the entity it refers to and determines this being in its being, the unveiledness of that which is spoken of is eo ipso co-intended. The moment of unveiledness is implied in the concept of the being of the entity which is meant in the assertion. When I say "A is B," I mean not only the being-B of A but also the being-B of A as unveiled. It is understood as implied in the uttered "is," so that I do not afterward make another special judgment whose content is that the first judgment is true. This theory of Lotze's stems from a concept of truth that is turned upside down; consequently, it is not seen that being-true already lies in assertive comportment itself, in the first judgment, in conformity with its structure. The extant entity itself is in a certain way true, not as intrinsically extant, but as uncovered in the assertion. Uncoveredness is not itself extant in the extant entity, but instead the extant entity is encountered within the world of a Dasein, which world is disclosed for the existent Dasein. Viewed more closely, assertion, as communicative-determinative exhibition, is a mode in which the Dasein *appropriates* for itself the uncovered being as uncovered. This appropriation of a being in true assertion about it is not an ontical absorption of the extant entity into a subject, as though things were transported into the ego. But it is just as little a merely subjectivistic apprehending and investing of things with determinations which we cull from the subject and assign to the things. All these interpretations invert the basic structure of the comportment of as-sertion itself, its apophantic, exhibitive nature. Assertion is exhibitive letting-be-seen of beings. In the exhibitive appropriation of a being just as it is qua uncovered, and according to the sense of that appropriation, the uncovered entity's real determinativeness which is then under consideration is explicitly appropriated *to* it. We have here once again the peculiar cir-cumstance that the unveiling appropriation of the extant in its being-such is precisely not a subjectivizing but just the reverse, an appropriating of the uncovered determinations *to* the extant entity as it is in itself.

As unveiling and in one with the unveiledness pertinent to what is unveiled, truth belongs to the Dasein; truth exists. Truth possesses the mode of being of the Dasein, and the Dasein is by its essential nature transcendent; therefore, truth is also a possible determination of beings encountered within the world. Such a being, for example, nature, does not depend in its being—that and whether it is a being or not—on whether it is true, whether or not it is unveiled and encountered as unveiled for a Dasein. There is truth—unveiling and unveiledness—only when and as long as Dasein exists. If and when there are no "subjects," taken in fact in the well-understood sense of the existent Dasein, then there is neither truth nor falsehood. But does not truth then become dependent on the "subject"? Does it not thus become subjectivized, while we nevertheless know that it is something "objective," exempt from the inclinations of any subjects? Is all objective truth denied when we say "Truth exists and it is only so far as

Dasein exists"? If truth is only so far as Dasein exists, does not all truth then fall victim to the inclination and caprice of the ego? If, by its consequences, this interpretation of truth—as unveiling that belongs to the Dasein's existence, as something that stands and falls with the existence or the non-existence of the Dasein—makes all binding and obligating objective decision impossible and declares all objective knowledge to be by the grace of the subject, must it not be characterized from the very outset as untenable? To avoid these fatal consequences, must we not from the very outset presuppose for all science and all philosophical knowledge that there is a truth which subsists in itself, which, as it is said, is timeless?

Such arguments are in fact offered generally or everywhere. Common sense is surreptitiously called to aid, arguments are employed that do not provide objective reasons, surreptitious appeal is made to the consensus of ordinary understanding, for which it would be unbearable if there were no eternal truths. But in the first place it must be said that philosophical knowledge and scientific knowledge in general do not trouble themselves about the consequences, no matter how uncomfortable they may be to the philistine understanding. What is at stake is the sober, unmitigated clarity of the concept and the recognition of the results of investigation. All other consequences and sentiments are irrelevant.

Truth belongs to the ontological constitution of the Dasein itself. When it is said that truth is something intrinsically timeless, the following problem arises: To what extent does not our interpretation explain truth subjectively, level all truth relativistically, and relinquish theory to skepticism? After all, 2 times 2 equals 4 is true not just since the day before yesterday and not just until the day after tomorrow. Surely this truth does not depend on any subject. What does this imply then about the statement that truth is only if and as long as there is Dasein which unveils, is true, exists in truth? Newton's laws, which are often used in arguments having to do with the interpretation of truth, have not existed from all eternity, and they were not true before they were discovered by Newton. They became true only in and with their uncoveredness, because this uncoveredness is their truth. It follows from this neither that, if they first became true with their uncovering, they were false before the uncovering nor that they will become false when their uncoveredness and their unveiledness become impossible, when no Dasein any longer exists. Before being discovered the Newtonian laws were neither true nor false. This cannot mean that the entity which is uncovered with the unveiled laws was not previously in the way in which it showed itself after the uncovering and now is as thus showing itself. Uncoveredness, truth, unveils an entity precisely as that which it already was beforehand regardless of its uncoveredness and non-uncoveredness. As an uncovered being it becomes intelligible as that which is just how it is and will be, regardless of every possible uncoveredness of itself. For nature to be as it is, it does not need truth, unveiledness. The content intended in the true proposition "2 times 2 = 4" can subsist through all eternity without there existing any truth about it. So far as there is a truth about it, this truth understands precisely that nothing in what it means depends on it for being what it is. But that there may be eternal truths will remain an arbitrary assumption and affirmation just so long as it is not demonstrated with absolute evidence that from all eternity and for all eternity something like a human Dasein exists, which can by its own ontological constitution unveil beings and appropriate them to itself as unveiled. The proposition "2 times 2 = 4" as a true assertion is true only as long as Dasein exists. If in principle no Dasein any longer exists, then the proposition is no longer valid, not because the proposition is invalid as such, not because it would have become false and 2 times 2 = 4 would have changed into 2 times 2 = 5, but because the uncoveredness of something as truth can only co-exist with the existing Dasein that does the uncovering. There is not a single valid reason for presupposing eternal truths. It is even more superfluous if we were to presuppose that there were such a thing as truth. A favorite theory of knowledge today believes that, in response to skepticism about all science and knowledge, we have to make the presupposition that there is truth. This presupposition is superfluous, for so far as we exist we are in truth, we are unveiled for ourselves and the intraworldly beings which we are not are at the same time unveiled for us in some way or other. The extent and limit of unveiledness is a matter of indifference in this case. It is not *we* who need to presuppose that somewhere there is "in itself" a truth in the form of a transcendent value or valid meaning floating somewhere. Instead, truth itself, the basic constitution of the Dasein, presupposes *us,* is the presupposition for our own existence. Being-true, unveiledness, is the fundamental condition for our being able to be in the way in which we exist as Dasein. Truth is the presupposition for our being able to presuppose anything at all. For presupposing is in every case an unveiling establishment of something as being. Presupposition everywhere presupposes truth. We do not first have to presuppose truth in order to arrive at knowledge. But that an entity which by its essential nature exists in truth is necessary, not to say eternal, can never be proved. It may be believed on the basis of certain religious or other reasons—but we are not talking about a knowledge which in its demonstrative sense would only be quite far from suitable as a foundation for scientific knowledge. Has any factually existing Dasein, has any one of us as such, decided freely of himself and will any existing Dasein ever be able to decide of itself whether it will or will not enter into existence? Never. The establishment of eternal truths remains a fanciful assertion, just as it remains a naive misunderstanding to believe that truth, if it exists only and as long as Dasein exists, is delivered over to relativism and skepticism. On the contrary, the theories of relativism and skepticism spring from a partially justified opposition to an absurd absolutism and dogmatism of the concept of truth, a dogmatism that has its ground in the circumstance that the phenomenon of truth is taken externally as a determination of the subject or of the object or, if neither of these notions works, as some third realm of meaning. If we do not impose on ourselves or surreptitiously permit hidden convictions of one sort or another to play a role in our investigation, then this insight emerges: unveiling and unveiledness—which is just to say, truth—are grounded in *the Dasein's transcendence;* they exist only so far as Dasein itself exists.

d) The existential mode of being of truth and the basic ontological question of the meaning of being in general

But one more step is needed. Truth is not something extant, but it is indeed a possible determination of the being of the extant so far as the extant entity is uncovered. How can the being of a being, and especially the being of the extant, which in its essential nature is independent of the existence of a Dasein, be determined by uncoveredness? If the being of an extant entity is to be determinable by uncoveredness, then the being of a being or, more precisely, the mode of being of each being must have the ontological character of truth. However, can we say then that being itself has a mode of being? A being, something that *is,* is and has a being; but being itself is surely not *a* being. Yet in the proposition "Being is not a being" we are already asserting the "is" about being. What does the "is" here mean when I say that being *is* this or that? What sense does the copula have in all assertions about being, which is not a being?[1] What meaning does the copula have in all ontological propositions? This question is the central mystery which Kant investigates in his *Critique of Pure Reason,* even if it is not readily visible from the outside. Something like being must in some sense be, if we validly speak of it and if we comport toward beings as beings, that is, if we understand them in their being. In what way "is there" being? *[In what way is being "given"?]* Is there being only if and when truth exists, when the Dasein exists? Does it depend on the existence of the Dasein whether there is or is not being? If so, then this does not again affirm that whether there are or are not beings, for example nature, depends on the existence of the Dasein. The manner in which being is and can only

---

1. Cf. Aristotle, *Metaphysica,* book Gamma, 2.1003ᵇ10: dio kai to me on einai me on phamen. ["It is for this reason that we say even of non-being that it *is* non-being." Trans. Ross, in *The Works of Aristotle* (Ross), vol. 8.]

be given does not prejudice the case regarding whether and how beings are qua beings.

The problem becomes concentrated into the question, How is the existence of truth related to being and to the manner in which there is being? Are being and truth essentially related to each other? Does the existence of being stand and fall with the existence of truth? Is it the case that a being, so far as it is, is independent of the truth about it, but that truth exists only when the Dasein exists, and, conversely, if we may for once speak in an abbreviated way, that being exists?

By our critical discussion of the "is" and its *ambiguity,* and above all in regard to its *interconnection with being-true,* we are driven back once more to the *fundamental ontological question.* In the fourth thesis, too, we see what in each instance emerged from the discussion of the three previous theses: the concept of being is in no way simple and just as little is it self-evident. The *meaning of being* is most intricate and the ground of being is obscure. What is needed is a disentangling of the entanglements and an illuminating of the obscurity. Have we set about this task so well that the light and the clue for carrying it through are at our disposal? Not only have the considerations of the first part of our lectures, now concluded, brought closer to us the ambiguity and difficulty of apparently trivial questions, but also the different ontological problems, because of their own contents, have forced our inquiry again and again back to the question about the being that we ourselves are. This being that we ourselves are, the Dasein, thus has its own distinction within the field of ontological inquiry. We shall, therefore, speak of the *ontological priority of the Dasein.* In the course of our considerations, we saw that throughout philosophy, even where it is apparently primarily and solely the ontology of nature, there occurs a movement back to the nous, mind, psuche, soul, logos, reason, the res cogitans, consciousness, the ego, the spirit—that all elucidation of being, in any sense, is oriented toward this entity.

We have already roughly characterized the reason for this ontological precedence of the Dasein. It lies in the circumstance that this being is so uniquely constituted in its very makeup that the *understanding of being* belongs to its existence, an understanding on the basis of which alone all comportment toward beings, toward extant things as well as toward its own self, becomes possible. If, now, we take hold of the *basic problem of philosophy* and ask the question about the meaning and ground of being, then, if we do not wish to work merely imaginatively, we must keep a firm hold methodically on what makes something like being accessible to us: the understanding of being that belongs to the Dasein. So far as understanding of being belongs to the Dasein's existence, this understanding and the being that is understood and meant in it become all the more suitably and originally accessible, the more originally and comprehensively the *constitution of the Dasein's being* itself and the *possibility of the understanding of being* are brought to light. If the Dasein has a priority in all the problems of ontology, because of the understanding of being that belongs to it, then it is requisite that the Dasein be subjected to a *preparatory ontological investigation* which would provide the foundation for all further inquiry, which includes the question of the being of beings and the being of the different regions of being. We therefore call the preparatory ontological analytic of the Dasein *fundamental ontology*. It is *preparatory* because it *alone first leads to the illumination of the meaning of being* and of *the horizon of the understanding of being*. It can only be preparatory because it aims only to establish the foundation for a radical ontology. Therefore, after the exposition of the meaning of being and the horizon of ontology, it has to be repeated at a higher level. Why no circle is implicit in this path or, better, why the circle and the circularity of all philosophical interpretation is not the monster it is most often feared to be we cannot here discuss in further detail. By means of fundamental ontology, which has the Dasein as its ontological theme, the being that we ourselves are moves over to the center of philosophical inquiry. This can be called an anthropocentric or subjectivistic-idealistic philosophy. But these signboards of the philosophical trade are without any meaning; they simply become either an insubstantial commendation of some standpoint or an equally insubstantial demagogical accusation of it. That the Dasein becomes the theme of fundamental ontology is not a whim of ours but springs on the contrary from necessity and from the essential content of the idea of being in general.

The task of the fundamental ontological interpretation of the Dasein is thus clear in its main lines. But to carry it out is by no means simple. After all, we should not succumb to the illusion that the task can be finished with a wave of the hand. The more unambiguously the problem of being is posed, the more impenetrable become the difficulties, particularly in a lecture course, which cannot presuppose an already complete mastery of method and a satisfactorily comprehensive view of the whole problem. Here our aim can only be that of providing some orientation in regard to the basic problem of ontology. This is certainly unavoidable if we wish to provide an adequate conception of philosophy as it has been vitally active in our history since Parmenides.

PART TWO

The Fundamental Ontological Question of the Meaning of Being in General

•

The Basic Structures and Basic Ways of Being

The discussion of the four theses in Part One was intended in each case to make an ontological problem accessible to us. This was to be done in such a way that the four groups of problems thus arising would show themselves to be intrinsically a unit, the problems constituting the whole of the basic problems of ontology. The following emerged as the *four basic ontological problems:* first, the problem of the *ontological difference,* the distinction between being and beings; secondly, the problem of the *basic articulation of being,* the essential content of a being and its mode of being; thirdly, the problem of the *possible modifications of being* and of the *unity of the concept of being* in its ambiguity; fourthly, the problem of the *truth-character of being*.

We shall assign the *four chapters* of this *second part* each to one of these four basic problems.

Chapter One

The Problem of the
Ontological Difference

It is not without reason that the problem of the distinction between being in general and beings occurs here in first place. For the purpose of the discussion of this difference is to make it possible first of all to get to see thematically and put into investigation, in a clear and methodically secure way, the like of being in distinction from beings. The possibility of ontology, of philosophy as a science, stands and falls with the possibility of a sufficiently clear accomplishment of this differentiation between being and beings and accordingly with the possibility of negotiating the passage from the ontical consideration of beings to the ontological thematization of being. The discussions in this chapter will therefore claim our preponderant interest. Being and its distinction from beings can be fixed only if we get a proper hold on the understanding of being as such. But to comprehend the understanding of being means first and foremost to understand *that* being to whose ontological constitution the understanding of being belongs, the Dasein. Exposition of the basic constitution of the Dasein, its existential constitution, is the task of the preparatory ontological analytic of the Dasein's existential constitution. We call it the existential analytic of the Dasein. It must aim at bringing to light the ground of the basic structures of the Dasein in their unity and wholeness. To be sure, in the first part we occasionally gave *individual portions* of such an existential analytic, so far as the positively critical discussions provisionally required. But we have neither run through them in their systematic order nor given an express exposition of the Dasein's basic constitution. Before we discuss the basic ontological problem, the existential analytic of the Dasein needs to be developed. This, however, is impossible within the present course, if we wish to pose the basic ontological problem at all. Therefore, we have to choose an alternative and presuppose the essential result of the existential analytic of the Dasein as a result already established. In my treatise on *Being and Time,* I set forth what the existential analytic encompasses in its essential results. The outcome of the existential analytic, the exposition of the ontological constitution of the Dasein in its ground, is this: *the constitution of the Dasein's being is grounded in temporality [Zeitlichkeit]*. If we presuppose this result, it does not mean that we may permit ourselves to be satisfied just to hear the word "temporality." Without explicitly adducing here the proof that the Dasein's basic constitution is grounded in temporality, we must nevertheless attempt in some way to gain an understanding of what temporality means. To this end we choose the following path. We shall *take as our starting point the common concept of time* and learn to see how what is commonly known as time and was for a long time the only concept of time made into a problem in philosophy, *itself presupposes temporality.* The point is to see that and how time in its common sense belongs to and springs from temporality. By means of this reflection we shall work our way toward the phenomenon of temporality itself and its basic structure. What shall we gain by doing this? Nothing less than *insight into the original constitution of the Dasein's being. But then, if indeed the understanding of being belongs to the Dasein's existence, this understanding too must be based in temporality. The ontological condition of the possibility of the understanding of being is temporality itself. Therefore we must be able to cull from it that by way of which we understand the like of being. Temporality* takes over the enabling of the understanding of being and thus the *enabling of the thematic interpretation of being and of its articulation and manifold ways;* it thus makes ontology possible. From this arises a whole set of specific problems related to temporality. We call this entire problematic *Temporality [Temporalität]*. The term "Temporality" *[*Temporalität*]* does not wholly coincide with the term "temporality" *[*Zeitlichkeit*]*, despite the fact that, in German, Temporalität is merely the translation of Zeitlichkeit. It means temporality insofar as temporality itself is made into a theme as the condition of the possibility of the understanding of being and of ontology as such. The term "Temporality" is intended to indicate that temporality, in existential analytic, represents the horizon from which we understand being. What we are inquiring into in existential analytic, existence, proves to be temporality, which on its part constitutes the horizon for the understanding of being that belongs essentially to the Dasein.

The main point is to see being in its Temporal determination and to unveil its problematics. But if being becomes phenomenologically visible in its Temporal determination, we thereby put ourselves in a position to grasp the distinction between being and beings more clearly as well, and to fix the ground of the ontological difference. This gives us the design for the first chapter of Part Two, which is to deal with the problem of the ontological difference:

§19. Time and temporality
§20. Temporality *[Zeitlichkeit]* and Temporality *[Temporalität]*
§21. Temporality *[Temporalität]* and being
§22. Being and beings

§19. *Time and temporality*

The aim now is to press forward through the common understanding of time toward temporality, in which the Dasein's ontological constitution is rooted and to which time as commonly understood belongs. The first step is to make certain of the common understanding of time. What do we mean by time in natural experience and understanding? Although we constantly reckon with time or take account of it without explicitly measuring it by the clock and are abandoned to it as to the most commonplace thing, whether we are lost in it or pressed by it—although time is as familiar to us as only something in our Dasein can be, nevertheless, it becomes strange and puzzling when we try to make it clear to ourselves even if only within the limits of everyday intelligibility. Augustine's remark about this fact is well known. Quid est enim "tempus"? Quis hoc facile breviterque explicaverit? Quis hoc ad verbum de illo proferendum vel cogitatione conprehenderit? Quid autem familiarius et notius in loquendo conmemoramus quam "tempus"? Et intellegimus utique, cum id loquimur, intellegimus etiam, cum alio loquente id audimus.— Quid est ergo "tempus"? Si nemo ex me quaerat, scio; si quaerenti explicare velim, nescio; fidenter tamen dico scire me, quod, si nihil praeteriret, non esset praeteritum tempus, et si nihil adveniret, non esset futurum tempus, et si nihil esset, non esset praesens tempus.[1] "What then is time; who can explain it easily and briefly? Who has comprehended it in thought so as to speak of it? But what is there that we mention in our discourse more familiar and better known than time? And we always understand it whenever we speak of it, and we understand it too when we hear someone else speak of it.—What then is time? If no one asks me, I know; if I am supposed to explain it to one who asks, I do not know; yet I say confidently that I know: if nothing were to pass away there would be no past time, and if nothing were coming there would be no time to come, and if nothing were to exist there would be no present time." Simplicius the Neoplatonist says: ti de depote estin ho chronos, erotetheis mogis

---

1. Augustine, *Confessiones,* 11.14.

an ho sophotatos apokrinaito;[2] "as to what time may be, then, to this question hardly the wisest would be able to find an answer." Further evidence for the difficulty of apprehending and interpreting time is superfluous. Every attempt we ourselves make to elucidate what we mean by time in our natural understanding of it, every attempt to lay out unveiled and in its purity what is to be understood by time, convinces us of this. At first we are without any orientation at all. We do not know where to look, where to seek and find the like of time. But there is a way that begins to help us out of this perplexity. The common understanding of time very early reached conceptual expression in philosophy. Accordingly, in the explicit concepts of time, we have at our disposal a portrayal of the time phenomenon. This phenomenon need no longer give us the slip completely if we hold on to a conceptual characterization of it. However, even if time becomes more manageable when we comprehend these time concepts, we should not be led by this gain to surrender all methodical foresight and criticism. For, precisely if the time phenomenon is so hard to grasp, it remains doubtful whether the interpretation of time that was laid down in the traditional time concept is thoroughly in keeping with the phenomenon of time. And even if it were, still requiring discussion would be the question whether this interpretation of time, although suitable, reaches the phenomenon in its original constitution or whether the common and genuine time concept only expresses a configuring of time that is indeed peculiar to it but does not lay hold of it in its originality.

Only if we impose these reservations on ourselves is there any surety that we can draw something of use for the understanding of the time phenomenon from a critical discussion of the traditional time concept. Now to understand the fundamental-ontological considerations it is indispensable that the time phenomenon should be brought to view in its original structure. Hence it would be altogether pointless if we simply took note of one or more definitions of time in order simply to take the opportunity to offer our own definition. What we need first of all is a many-sided orientation toward the time phenomenon, following the clue of the traditional time concepts. After that it becomes pertinent to inquire in what way the interpretations of time from which these concepts have sprung themselves took sight of the time phenomenon, how far they took into view the original time phenomenon, and how we can achieve the return passage from this time phenomenon first given to the original time.

For the sake of a synoptic view we shall divide §19 into (a) historical

---

2. Simplicius, *In Aristotelis physicorum libros quattuor priores commentaria,* ed. Hermann Diels (Berlin: [G. Reimer], 1882), p. 695, line 17 f.

orientation regarding the traditional concept of time and a delineation of the common understanding of time that lies at the basis of this concept, and (b) the common understanding of time and the return to original time.

a) Historical orientation regarding the traditional concept of time and a delineation of the common understanding of time that lies at the basis of this concept

If we look back historically and survey the various attempts to master time conceptually, it turns out that the ancients had already set forth the essentials that constitute the content of the traditional concept of time. The two ancient interpretations of time which thereafter became standard— Augustine's, which has already been mentioned, and the first great treatise on time by Aristotle—are also by far the most extensive and truly thematic investigations of the time phenomenon itself. Augustine agrees with Aristotle also on a series of essential determinations.

Aristotle's treatise on time is to be found in his *Physics*, 4.10.217^{b}29 – 4.14.224^{a}17. He gives essential supplementary material for his view of time in the early chapters of the *Physics*, book 8. There are also some important passages in *De Anima*, book 3. Among ancient conceptions of time, that of Plotinus also has a certain significance, *Peri aionos kai chronou* (*Enneads* 3.7), "On the Aeon and on Time." Aeon is a peculiar form intermediate between eternity and time. The discussion of the aeon played a great role in the Middle Ages. Plotinus, however, gives us more of a theological speculation about time than an interpretation adhering strictly to the phenomenon itself and forcing the phenomenon into conceptual form. A summary particularly useful for orientation regarding the ancient concept of time is to be found in the appendix that Simplicius provides in his great commentary on Aristotelian physics. At the conclusion of the interpretation of book 4 this commentary provides an independent appendix in which Simplicius deals with time.[3] Among the Scholastics, Thomas Aquinas and Suarez dealt most specifically with the time concept, in close connection with the Aristotelian conception. In modern philosophy the most important investigations of time occur in Leibniz, Kant, and Hegel, and here, too, at bottom, the Aristotelian interpretation of time breaks through everywhere.

From the most recent period we may cite Bergson's investigations of the time phenomenon. They are by far the most independent. He presented the essential results of his inquiries in his *Essai sur les données immédiates de la conscience* (1888). These investigations were extended and set in a wider

---

3. Ibid., pp. 773–800.

context in his major work, *L'évolution créatrice* (1907). As early as his first treatise, Bergson makes the attempt to overcome the Aristotelian interpretation of time and to show its one-sidedness. He tries to get beyond the common concept of time by distinguishing durée, duration, in contrast with time as commonly understood, which he calls temps. In a more recent work, *Durée et simultanéité* (2nd edition, 1923), Bergson provides a critical examination of Einstein's theory of relativity. Bergson's theory of duration itself grew out of a direct critique of the Aristotelian concept of time. The interpretation he gives of time in the common sense rests on a misunderstanding of Aristotle's way of understanding time. Accordingly, his counterconcept to common time, namely duration, is also in this sense untenable. He does not succeed by means of this concept in working his way through to the true phenomenon of time. Nevertheless, Bergson's investigations are valuable because they manifest a philosophical effort to surpass the traditional concept of time.

We have already stressed that the essentials of what can first of all be said about time within the common understanding of it were said in the two ancient interpretations of time by Aristotle and Augustine. Of the two, Aristotle's investigations are conceptually more rigorous and stronger while Augustine sees some dimensions of the time phenomenon more originally. No attempt to get behind the riddle of time can permit itself to dispense with coming to grips with Aristotle. For he expressed in clear conceptual form, for the first time and for a long time after, the common understanding of time, so that his view of time corresponds to the natural concept of time. Aristotle was the last of the great philosophers who had eyes to see and, what is still more decisive, the energy and tenacity to continue to force inquiry back to the phenomena and to the seen and to mistrust from the ground up all wild and windy speculations, no matter how close to the heart of common sense.

We must here deny ourselves a detailed interpretation of Aristotle's treatise as well as Augustine's. We shall select a few characteristic propositions in order to illustrate by them the traditional time concept. In supplementation we shall draw several important thoughts from Leibniz, whose discussions of time, like all of his essential ideas, are scattered about in occasional writings, treatises, and letters.

To the clarification of the Aristotelian time concept we shall preface a short account of the structure of the Aristotelian treatise on time.

α) Outline of Aristotle's treatise on time

The treatise contains five chapters (*Physics*, 4.10 – 14). The *first chapter* (chap. 10), being first, defines the inquiry, which moves in two directions.

The first question is: poteron ton onton estin e ton me onton;[4] does time belong among beings or non-beings? Is it something that exists of itself or does it exist only in such a way that it is co-present in something that exists independently? *How* and *where* is time? The second question runs: tis he phusis autou;[5] what is the nature, the essence, of time? These two questions about time's *mode of being* and its *essential nature* receive proportionately unequal treatment. The first question is discussed in lesser detail; the positive answer is given only in the last chapter $(14.223^a16−224^a17)$. The remaining portions of the treatise are devoted to the investigation and discussion of the second question, What is time? Chapter 10 not only defines both these problems but also discusses provisionally the difficulties implicit in them, and in connection with this it makes reference to previous attempts at a solution. Aristotle's custom is almost without exception to introduce his investigations in this form: historical orientation and discussion of the difficulties, the aporiai. Aporia means: not getting through, being without passage. The problems are at first set in such a way that it appears as though no further passage can be made in these inquiries. The essential content of the problem is provisionally brought closer by this historical orientation and discussion of aporiai.

With reference to the first question, whether time is a being or a me on, a non-being, the latter determination seems to suggest itself as the answer. How should time exist as a whole, an ousia, if the parts that go to make it up are non-existent and are so in different ways? Things past and things future belong to time. The former are *no longer,* the latter are *not yet.* Past and future have the character of a nullity. It is as though time, as Lotze once put it, has two arms which it stretches out in different directions of non-being. Past and future, by their very concepts, are exactly non-existent; at bottom it is only the present, the now, that *is.* But on the other hand, time also is not composed of a manifold of existent nows. For in every now there is only this now, and the others *are* now either not yet or no longer. The now also is never the same and never a single one, but another, a not-the-same and not-one, a manifold. But selfsameness and unity are determinations necessarily belonging to something that exists in itself. If these determinations themselves are lacking to perhaps the only moment of time

---

4. Aristotle, *Physica* (Ross), book 4, 10.217^b31. [W. D. Ross's edition, or editions, of Aristotle's *Physics* can be traced back, at the earliest, to 1936: *Aristotle's Physics,* with introduction and commentary (Oxford: Clarendon, 1936). Heidegger could not have used this text, and the data provided in the *Grundprobleme* text (note 4, page 330) are insufficient to determine which edition is intended. Heidegger could have used the editions by Immanuel Bekker (Berlin, 1843) or Charles Prantl (Leipzig: Teubner, 1879). See note 34 below.]

5. Ibid., 217^b32.

of which it can be said that it *is*, the now, then time seems to belong wholly and completely to not-being and the non-existent (me on). Aristotle provisionally lets the question of the mode of being of time rest with this aporia while he goes on to discuss several traditional views relating to the mode of being as well as the essential nature of time.

One view identifies time with the motion of the universe. He tou holou kinesis,[6] the whole of all beings, which moves, is time itself. In a certain sense this is still conceived mythically. But all mythology has its basis in specific experiences and is anything but pure fiction or invention. It cannot be accidental and arbitrary that in this mythical view time is identified with the motion of the universe. A second view tends in the same direction but is more definite. It says that time is he sphaira aute.[7] Time here is equated with the heavenly sphere which, rotating in a circle, embraces everything and contains everything within itself. To understand this we must bring to mind the ancient picture of the world, according to which the earth is a disk floating in the ocean with the whole of the heavenly sphere surrounding it. In this sphere other spheres are layered one above the other in which the stars are fastened. The outermost heavenly sphere embraces everything that really exists. It and its rotation are identified with time. According to Aristotle the basis for this interpretation is as follows: en te to chrono panta estin kai en te tou holou sphaira;[8] everything that is, is in time; but everything that exists is also inside the revolving vault of heaven, which is the outermost limit of all beings. Time and the outermost heavenly sphere are identical. There is something of experience implicit in this interpretation too: time in connection with the rotation of the sky and time also as that *in* which all beings exist. We say indeed that what is, is *in* time. Even if, says Aristotle, we have to disregard these simple-minded analyses, nevertheless there is a legitimate appearance supporting the view that time is something like motion, kinesis tis. We speak of the flux of time and say that time elapses. For kinesis Aristotle also says metabole. This is the most general concept of motion; literally it means the same as the German Umschlag, a change or turn /sometimes sudden, into its opposite/. But by its nature motion is en auto to kinoumeno, in the moving thing itself or always there exactly where the thing in motion, the kinoumenon or metaballon, itself is. Motion is always in the moving thing; it is not something that floats as it were above the thing in motion; rather, the moving thing itself moves. Motion therefore is always where the moving thing is. But

6. Ibid., 218ª33.
7. Ibid., 218ᵇ1. ["The sphere itself." Trans. R. P. Hardie and R. K. Gaye, in *The Works of Aristotle* (Ross), vol. 2. All further references to the Hardie and Gaye translation of the *Physica* are to this volume in the Ross edition.]
8. Ibid., 218ᵇ6f.

time, says Aristotle, ho de chronos homoios kai pantachou kai para pasin,[9] is, on the contrary, *in a like manner* both *everywhere* and also *beside* everything and close to everything. In this way a distinction is fixed that contrasts time with motion. While motion is always only in the moving thing and is only where the moving thing is, time is everywhere (pantachou), not in one definite place, and it is not in the moving thing itself but para, beside it, in some way close by it. Motion and time differ in how they belong to the moving thing and to that which is in time and which we call the intratemporal /das Innerzeitige/. Thus the first provisional determination that had suggested itself, that time itself might be a motion, collapses. Time itself is not motion, hoti men toinun ouk estin kinesis.[10] On the other hand, however, time also does not exist without motion. Thus the result can now be formulated: time is oute kinesis out' aneu kineseos;[11] it is not itself indeed the motion of the moving thing but still it is *not without* motion. From this it follows that time is connected in some sense with motion; it is not kinesis but kineseos ti, *something at, close to, motion,* something in connection with the motion of the moving thing. The problem of the question about the essential nature of time concentrates on the question: ti tes kineseos estin,[12] *what* connected with motion is time?

In this way the course of the investigation is outlined beforehand. In *chapter 11,* the *second chapter* of the treatise on time, which is the central chapter of the whole treatise, Aristotle reaches the result, the answer to the question what time is. We shall merely record the result here because later we shall want to pursue in more detail the interpretation of the nature of time. He says: touto gar estin ho chronos, arithmos kineseos kata to proteron kai husteron;[13] time is this, namely, something counted which shows itself *in and for* regard to the before and after in motion or, in short, something counted in connection with motion as encountered in the horizon of earlier and later. Aristotle then shows more precisely what is already present in the experience of a motion and how time is encountered there along with it. He makes clear to what extent and in what sense time is arithmos, a number, and how the basic phenomenon of time, to nun, the now, results.

This leads him, in the *third chapter* (chap. 12), to define in greater detail the connection between motion and time and to show that not only is

---

9. Ibid., 218ᵇ13.

10. Ibid., 218ᵇ18.

11. Ibid., 11.219ᵃ1. ["Neither movement nor independent of movement." Trans. Hardie and Gaye.]

12. Ibid., 219ᵃ3. ["What exactly it has to do with movement." Trans. Hardie and Gaye.]

13. Ibid., 219ᵇ1f. ["For time is just this—number of motion in respect of before and after." Trans. Hardie and Gaye.]

motion in time and measured by time but conversely, too, time is measured by motion. Thus there emerges the fundamental question What does it mean to say that something is "in time"? We normally express something's being in time by the German adjective "zeitlich," English "temporal." But for terminological purposes we use the expression "zeitlich" or "temporal" in a different sense and take as the specific designation for the "being in time" of a being the expression *"Innerzeitigkeit,"* "intratemporality." Something is in time, it is intratemporal. Elucidation of the concept of intratemporality clarifies the characterization of time as number. Since rest is itself a limiting case of motion, the relationship between time and rest also becomes clear with the determination of the relationship of time and motion. Likewise, the relation of time to the extratemporal *[Ausserzeitigen]*, usually called the timeless, is cleared up by reference to the concept of intratemporality.

The *fourth chapter* (chap. 13) inquires into the *unity of time in the manifoldness of the sequence of the nows.* Aristotle tries to show here how the now, to nun, constitutes time's real holding-itself-together, its coherence, sunecheia, in Latin continuum, German Stetigkeit, English continuity. The question is how the now holds time together within itself as a whole. All the time-determinations are related to the now. In connection with the explanation of sunecheia Aristotle gives an interpretation of several time-determinations: ede, forthwith, arti, just now, and also palai, before this time or once, and exaiphnes, all of a sudden. Forthwith, just, once, suddenly, later on, formerly are determinations, all of which go back to the nun. Just is seen looking backward from a now; immediately is seen forward, as it were, from a now. Aristotle does not grasp these determinations in their inner connections but merely gives examples of time-determinations without recognizing their systematic order.

The *fifth chapter* (chap. 14) goes back to the determination that was drawn into the definition of time, the proteron and husteron, the *earlier* and *later.* It discusses the *relation* of the earlier and later *to the before and after.* Following these discussions the first problem is taken up again: *Where and how is time?* Aristotle defines this question more closely in book 8 of the *Physics,* in which he brings time into connection with the rotation of the heavens and with the nous. Time is not bound up with a single motion and a definite place. In a certain way it is everywhere. And yet, since by definition it is something counted, it can exist only where a counting exists. But counting is an activity of the soul. Time is in a certain way everywhere and yet it is only in the soul. Here we run up against a difficult problem. What does it mean to say that time is in the soul? This corresponds to the question discussed in connection with the fourth thesis, what it means to say that truth is in the understanding. As long as we do not have an adequate concept of the soul or the understanding—of the Dasein—it remains difficult to say what "time is in the soul" means. Nothing is gained by saying that time is subjective; that would give rise to problems put precisely the wrong way.

The question now arises, How can different entities and different moving things which are in time be in or at the *same* time if they are *different?* How is the *simultaneity* of different things possible? We know that the question about simultaneity or, more precisely, the question of the possibility of an intersubjective establishment of simultaneous events constitutes one of the basic problems of relativity theory. The philosophical treatment of the problem of simultaneity depends on two factors: (1) determination of the concept of intratemporality, the question how *something is in time* at all, and (2) clarification of the question *in what way* and *where time* is or, more precisely, whether time in general *is* and can be said to be.

Since time for Aristotle is something connected with motion and is measured by means of motion, the problem is to find the purest motion, which is the original measure of time. The first and pre-eminent measure of all motion is the rotation (kuklophoria) of the outermost heaven. This motion is a circular motion. Time is thus in a certain sense a circle.

From this brief survey it already appears that Aristotle broached a series of central problems relating to time, and in fact not indiscriminately but in their essential concatenation. Nevertheless, it should be noted that many problems are just touched on by him and also that those with which he deals more circumstantially are by no means without need of further inquiry and new radical formulation as problems. Seen in their entirety, however, all the central problems which were thereafter discussed in the course of the further development of philosophy are already marked out. It can be said that subsequent times did not get essentially beyond the stage of Aristotle's treatment of the problem—apart from a few exceptions in Augustine and Kant, who nevertheless retain in principle the Aristotelian concept of time.

β) Interpretative exposition of Aristotle's concept of time

Following this survey of Aristotle's essay on time we shall try to gain a more thorough understanding of it. In doing so, we shall not keep strictly to the text but, by a free discussion and occasionally by carrying the interpretation somewhat further, we shall try to focus more clearly on the phenomenon as Aristotle sees it. We start here from the definition of time already adduced: touto gar estin ho chronos, arithmos kineseos kata to proteron kai husteron;[14] for time is just this, something counted in con-

---

14. Ibid.

nection with motion that is encountered in the horizon of the earlier and later (motion encountered with regard to the before and after). At first it might be said that this definition of time makes the phenomenon inquired into more opaque than accessible. The first point in the definition implies that time is something we find before us in connection with motion, as pertaining to something that moves as a moving thing, oute kinesis out' aneu kineseos. [15] Let us take a simple example. A vertical rod moves on the blackboard from left to right. We can also let it move in the manner of a rotation with the lower end as pivot. Time is something about the motion, showing itself to us in connection with a moving thing. If we imagine this rod to move or to rotate then we can ask, Where is time here, if it is supposed to pertain to the motion? It is certainly not a property of this rod, not anything corporeal, not heavy, not colored, not hard, not anything that belongs to its extension and continuity (suneches) as such; it is not something, not a piece of the rod's manifold of points, if we think of the rod as a line. Also, however, Aristotle does not in fact say that time is something connected with the moving *thing* as such but rather with its *motion*. But what is the motion of the rod? We say "its change of place, the transition from one place to another—whether in the sense of simple forward motion or continued motion from one point to the other." Time is supposed to be something relating to the motion and not to the moving thing. If we follow the continued movement of the rod, whether in the sense of rotation or the other motion, will we then find time belonging to this continued movement? Does it adhere to the motion as such? If we stop the motion, we say that time continues. Time goes on while the motion ceases. Thus time is not motion, and the rod's motion is not itself time. Aristotle also does not say that time is kinesis, but kineseos ti, something close to, connected with motion. But how? The motion here is the transition of the rod from one place to the other. The moving thing, as moving, is always present at some one place. Is time *at* these places or is it even these places themselves? Obviously not, for if the moving thing has run through the places in its movement, these places are, as such, still existent as definite locations. But the time at which the rod was at this or that place has passed. The place remains, time goes by. Where and how, then, is time *at, with,* the motion? We say that during its motion the moving thing is always *at a place at a time.* The motion is *in* time, *intratemporal.* Is time then something like a container, into which motion is put? And if time is always to be met with in connection with motion, is this container then something that carries motion as such along with it like a snail its shell? But when the rod is resting we again ask where time is. Do we find nothing of time in the thing qua

---

15. Ibid., 219ª1. ["Neither movement nor independent." Trans. Hardie and Gaye.]

resting? Or something? We say "The rod was at rest for a certain length of *time* or *temp*orarily." Nevertheless, although we may look all around the moving thing and the motion itself as change of place, we shall never find time if we hold to what Aristotle says.

We must ourselves retort, naturally we shall not find it. Aristotle does not just remark indefinitely that time is something connected with motion; instead, he says more precisely: arithmos kineseos—a *number* connected with motion or, as he formulates it in one place, ouk ara kinesis ho chronos all' he arithmon echei he kinesis;[16] time is not itself motion but exists so far as motion has a number. Time is a number. This again is astonishing, for numbers are just exactly that of which we say that they are timeless, extra-temporal. How then is time supposed to be a number? But here, as Aristotle expressly stresses, the expression "number" (arithmos) must be understood in the sense of arithmoumenon. Time is number not in the sense of the number that numbers as such but of the number that is *numbered, counted.* Time as number of motion is what is counted in connection with motion. Let us try an experiment. What can I count about the motion of the rod? Obviously, since the motion is a change of place, I can count the individual locations occupied by the rod in transition from one to the other. But, if I add up these locations, the sum of them to all eternity will never give me time but only the whole stretch run through, a piece of space but not time. Now we are able to count and to determine by counting the speed of the rod in its transition from one place to the other. What is speed? If we take the physical concept of speed, s = d/t, then speed is the path traversed divided by the elapsed time. From this formula it can be seen externally that time is involved in speed, because motion requires time. But this does not yet explain what time itself is. We have not come a single step closer to time. What does it mean, then, to say that the rod has a certain speed? Patently, among other things, it means that the rod is moving in time. Its motion runs its course in time. How puzzling it is that all motions *take—use up—time* and yet time doesn't diminish at all. Let us think of 1000 particular motions in the time between ten and eleven o'clock. Think also, as a second instance, of 100,000 motions in the same time. All of them take this same time. In the second instance, when many more of them are taking this time, does the time itself diminish or does it remain quantitatively equal to itself? Is the time that is taken by the motions thereby all used up? If not, then it manifestly does not depend on the motions. Nevertheless, it is supposed to be what is counted in connection with motion. It seems to be pure assertion on Aristotle's part that time is what is counted in connection with motion. Even if we go so far as to mark the rod's change of

---

16. Ibid., 219^{b}3f.

place by numbers, so that we provide each place with a number and thus find something counted or enumerated directly at each place in the transition of the moving thing, we do not uncover time with this device. I take my watch out of my pocket and follow the change of place of the second hand, and I read off one, two, three, four seconds or minutes. This little rod, hurrying on, shows me time, points to time for me, for which reason we call it a pointer, a hand. I read off time from the motion of a rod. Where then is this time? Somewhere inside the works, perhaps, so that if I put the watch into my pocket again I have time in my vest pocket? Naturally not, the answer will be. Yet we ask in return, Where then is time, since it is certainly undeniable that we read it from the watch? The watch, the clock, tells me what time it is, so that I find time in some way present there.

We see that in the end Aristotle is not so wrong when he says that time is what is counted in connection with motion. As evidence we do not need for it something as refined as a modern pocket watch. When a human being in natural, everyday existence follows the course of the sun and says "It is noon," "It is evening," he is telling the time. Time now, suddenly, is in the sun or in the sky and no longer in my vest pocket. But really, then, where is this prodigy at home? How does it happen that we should find time wherever we follow a motion, that we find time somehow attached to the motion and yet do not find it present right at the place where the moving object is? What are we attending to, *toward which horizon are we looking,* when—to keep to a simple example—we say at sunset that evening is coming on and thus determine a *time* of day? Are we looking only toward the particular local horizon, toward the west, or does our encounter with the moving object, the sun here in its apparent motion, look toward a different horizon?

The definition of time given by Aristotle is so ingenious that it also fixes this horizon, within which we are supposed to find, along with what is counted in connection with the motion, none other than time. Aristotle says: arithmos kineseos kata to proteron kai husteron. We translate this as: time is something counted in connection with encountered motion with a view to the before and after, in the horizon of the earlier and later. Time is not only what is counted about the motion, but it is counted there *so far as* that motion stands in the prospect of the before and after when we *follow it as motion.* The horizon sought for is that of the earlier and later. Proteron and husteron are translated as earlier and later, but also as before and after. The first determination, the proteron and husteron taken as earlier and later, seems to be impossible. "Earlier" and "later" are time-determinations. Aristotle says, time is what is counted about the motion we encounter in the horizon of time (of earlier and later). But this simply means that time is something met within the horizon of time. If I say that time is that pertaining to motion which shows itself when I follow it as motion in the horizon of its earlier and later, the definition of time seems to be a trivial tautology: time is the earlier and later, thus *time is time.* Is it worthwhile to busy ourselves with a definition that bears on its brow, as it were, the crudest sort of logical error? Nevertheless, we should not cling to the words. Certainly earlier and later are time phenomena. But the question remains whether what they mean coincides with what is meant in the subject of the definitory statement "time is time." Perhaps the second term "time" means something different and more original than what Aristotle means in the definition itself. Perhaps Aristotle's definition of time is not a tautology but merely betrays the inner coherence of the Aristotelian time phenomenon, that is, of time as commonly understood, with the original time which we are calling temporality. As Aristotle says in his interpretation, time can be interpreted only if it is itself understood again by way of time, that is, by way of *original* time. Therefore, it is not necessary to translate the proteron and husteron in Aristotle's definition of time by the indifferent before and after—even though that has its own specific and proper validity—so that their time character comes out less obviously, in order to avoid the appearance that Aristotle is defining time by going back to time. If the nature of time is in some measure understood, then Aristotle's interpretation and definition of time must be so interpreted, in conformity with its initial approach, that what he takes to be time must be construed by way of time.

Anyone who has once seen these interconnections must plainly demand that *in the definition of time the origin of time in the common sense, of time as we encounter it immediately, should come to light from temporality.* For its origin belongs to its essential nature and thus demands expression in the definition of this nature.

If we permit the earlier and later to remain in the definition of time, this does not yet show how accurate the Aristotelian definition of time is, how far what is counted in connection with motion is time. What is the meaning of "that which is counted in connection with motion encountered in the horizon of the earlier and later"? Time is supposed to be what is encountered in a specifically directed counting of motion. The specific direction of vision in counting is indicated by the kata to proteron kai husteron. What this means will be unveiled for us if we first of all take proteron and husteron as before and after and show by means of our interpretation what Aristotle means by this, so that the translation of proteron and husteron by earlier and later is justified.

Time is supposed to be something counted about motion, and in fact something counted that shows itself to us with respect to the proteron and husteron. We must now clarify what this means and in what way we experience something like time with respect to the before and after. Time is kineseos ti, something we encounter in connection with motion. To motion in general, kinesis or metabole, there belongs kinoumenon kineitai: a moving thing is moving, is in motion. The most general character of motion is metabole, a turn or change or better a transition from something to something.[17] The simplest form of motion, and the one most frequently used by Aristotle in his analysis of motion, of transition, is phora, transition from one place (topos) to another, change of place. This is the motion we are familiar with also as physical motion. In such motion the kinoumenon is the pheromenon, being carried forward from one place to the other. Another form of motion is, for example, alloiosis, becoming different in the sense that one quality changes to another, one particular color to another, and here too there is an advance ek tinos eis ti, *away from something toward something.* But this "away from something toward something" does not have the sense of transition from one place to another. Change of color can occur at the same place. It already becomes clear from this that this remarkable structure of the ek tinos eis ti, "away from something toward something," belongs to motion. The comparison with alloiosis shows that this "away from something toward something" need not necessarily be taken spatially. We shall call this structure of motion its *dimension,* taking the concept of dimension *in a completely formal sense,* in which spatial character is not essential. Dimension expresses a general notion of *stretch;* extension in the sense of spatial dimension then represents a particular modification of stretch. In the case of the determination of ek tinos eis ti we should rid ourselves completely of the spatial idea, something that Aristotle did, too. A completely formal sense of stretching out is intended in "from something to something." It is important to see this, because it was with reference to this determination that the Aristotelian concept of time was misunderstood in the modern period, especially by Bergson; from the outset he took this dimensional character of time in the sense of spatial extension in its reference to motion.

The determination of the suneches, *being-held-together-within-itself,* continuum, *continuity,* also belongs to stretch. Aristotle calls the dimensional character megethos. This determination megethos, extension or magnitude, also *does not have a primarily spatial character,* but that of stretch. There is no break implied in the concept and essential nature of "from something to something;" it is, instead, a stretching out that is closed within itself. When we experience motion in a moving thing, we necessarily experience along

---

17. Cf. *Physica,* 3.1 – 3 and 5. [In book 5, see particularly 224ᵃ21 – 224ᵇ9 and 224ᵇ35ff. The latter begins: "And since every change is *from* something to something—as the word itself (metabole) indicates, implying something 'after' (meta) something else, that is to say something earlier and something later—that which changes must change in one of four ways." Trans. Hardie and Gaye.]

with it suneches, continuity, and in this continuity itself ek tinos eis ti, dimension in the original sense, stretching out (extension). In the case of change of place the extension is locally-spatial. Aristotle expresses this set of circumstances in reverse order when he says that akolouthei to megethei he kinesis,[18] motion follows (comes in the wake of) dimension (extension). This proposition should be understood not ontically but ontologically. It does not mean that a motion proceeds ontically from stretch or continuity, that dimension has motion consequent to it. To say that motion follows continuity or follows dimension means that by the very nature of motion as such dimensionality, and thus continuity, precede it. Extension and continuity are already implicit in motion. They are earlier than motion in the sense of being a priori conditions of motion itself. Where there is motion, there megethos and suneches (sunecheia) are already thought along with it a priori. But this does not signify that motion is identical with extension (space) and continuity, which is clear already from the fact that not every motion is a change of place, a spatial motion, but nevertheless is determined by the ek tinos eis ti. Extension here has a broader sense than specifically spatial dimension. Motion follows continuity, and continuity follows extendedness. Akolouthei expresses the *foundational a priori connection* of *motion* with *continuity* and *extendedness*. Aristotle employs akolouthein in other investigations, too, in this ontological signification. So far as time is kineseos ti, something connected with motion, this means that in thinking time, motion or rest is always thought along with it. In Aristotelian language, time follows, is in succession to, motion. Aristotle says directly: ho chronos akolouthei te kinesei.[19] For change of place the sequence is as follows: place-manifold–(space) extension–continuity–motion–time. Viewed backward from time this means: if time is something connected with motion, then the

---

18. Ibid., 219ª11. ["But what is moved is moved from something to something, and all magnitude is continuous. Therefore the movement goes with the magnitude. Because the magnitude is continuous, the movement too must be continuous, and if the movement, then the time; for the time that has passed is always thought to be in proportion to the movement." Trans. Hardie and Gaye.]

19. Ibid., 219ᵇ23. [A sense of the difficulty of reading this passage may be derived from noting how two translations deal with it. "But the 'now' corresponds to the body that is carried along, as time corresponds to the motion. For it is by means of the body that is carried along that we become aware of the 'before and after' in the motion, and if we regard these as countable we get the 'now.'" Trans. Hardie and Gaye. "And as time follows the analogy of movement, so does the 'now' of time follow the analogy of the moving body, since it is by the moving body that we come to know the before-and-after in movement, and it is in virtue of the countableness of its before-and-afters that the 'now' exists." A note gives an alternative translation of the last two words: "the 'now' is the before and after, *qua* countable." In Aristotle, *The Physics*, trans. Philip H. Wicksteed and Francis M. Cornford, 2 vols. (London: William Heinemann; New York: G. P. Putnam's Sons, 1929), vol. 1, pp. 389–391. All further references to the Wicksteed and Cornford translation of the *Physica* are to this edition, vol. 1.]

genuine connection is thought along with time. And this plainly does not say that time is identical with any of the phenomena thus thought in connection with it.

Unless the ontological sense of akolouthein has been comprehended, the Aristotelian definition of time remains unintelligible. Or else defective interpretations occur, for example that of Bergson, who said that time as Aristotle understands it is space. He was misled into adopting this inadequate interpretation because he took continuity in the narrower sense of the extensional magnitude of space. Aristotle does not reduce time to space nor does he define it merely with the aid of space, as though some spatial determination entered into the definition of time. He only wants to show that and how time is something connected with motion. To this end, however, it becomes necessary to recognize what is already experienced in and with the experience of motion and how time becomes visible in what is thus experienced.

To see more precisely the sense in which time follows upon motion or motion's stretching out, we have to clarify even further for ourselves the experience of motion. The thoughts of motion, continuity, extension—and in the case of change of place, place—are interwoven with the experience of time. When we follow a motion, we encounter time in the process without expressly apprehending it or explicitly intending it. In the concrete experience of motions we keep primarily to the moving thing, the pheromenon; ho ten kinesin gnorizomen;[20] we see the motion in connection with the moving thing. To see motion purely as such is not easy: tode gar ti to pheromenon, he de kinesis ou;[21] the moving thing is always a this-here, a definite entity, while the motion itself does not have a specifically individualized character that would give it its own special stamp. The moving thing is given for us in its individuation and thisness, but motion as such is not given in that way. In experiencing motion we keep to the moving thing, and we thus see the motion *with* the moving thing but do not see it as such.

Corresponding to the way we bring motion closer to ourselves by focusing on the moving thing is the way we experience continuity in the elements constituting a continuum, points in the point manifold of a line. When we experience motion we focus on the moving thing and the particular place from which it makes its transition to another place. In following a motion we experience it in the horizon of a conjointly encountered series of locations on a continuous path. We experience the motion when we see the moving thing in its transition from one place to another. We see how it goes from

---

20. Ibid., 219^{b}17.
21. Ibid., 219^{b}30.

there to here, from a from-there to a to-here. This calls for more precise determination.

It could be said that change of place is a traversing of a continuous series of places, so that I can obtain the motion by taking together all the places traversed, one there and another there, and so on. But if we merely re-count the individual places, reckoning up together all the individual theres and heres, we do not experience any motion. Only when we see the moving thing in its changing over from there to here do we experience motion, transition. We must not take the places as a pure juxtaposition of there and here. Instead we must take this there as "away from there" and this here as "toward here," hence not simply a there and then again another there, but "away from there" and "toward here." We must see the presented contexture of places, the point manifold, in the horizon of an "away from there—toward here." This is primarily what Aristotle's condition kata to proteron kai husteron means. The there is not arbitrary; the from-there is *prior, anteced-ent*. And the to-here or hither is likewise not an arbitrary here, but, as hither, it is *posterior, subsequent*. If we thus see the place manifold in the horizon of the "away from there—toward here" and traverse the individual places in this horizon in seeing the motion, the transition, then we *retain* the first traversed place as the *away-from-there* and *expect* the next place as the *toward-here*. Retaining the prior and expecting the posterior, we see the transition as such. If, thus retentive of the prior and expectant of the pos-terior, we follow the transition as such, the individual places within the whole transition, which can stretch arbitrarily far, we no longer fix the individual places as individual points or as individual theres and heres arbitrarily paired. In order to grasp and formulate the peculiar retention of the prior and expectation of the posterior to come, we say: now here, formerly there, afterward there. Each there in the nexus of "away from there—toward here" is *now*-there, *now*-there, *now*-there. So far as we see the point manifold in the horizon of the proteron and husteron, when following the moving object we say at each time now-here, now-there. Only if we tacitly add this can we read off the time when we look at a watch or clock. We say "now" quite naturally and spontaneously when we look at the timepiece. It is not just a matter of course that we say "now," but in saying it we have already assigned time to the clock. It is not in the clock itself, but in saying "now" we assign it to the clock and the clock gives us the how-many of the nows.[22] What is counted when we count as we follow a tran-sition in the horizon of the ek tinos eis ti, whether aloud or silently, is the

---

22. Assignment [Vorgabe] is at bottom the threefold ecstatically horizonal structure of temporality. Temporality [Zeitlichkeit] assigns the now to itself.

nows. We count a sequence of nows or of thens and at-the-times. The then is the not-yet-now or the now-not-yet; the at-the-time is the now-no-longer or the no-longer-now. The then and the at-the-time both have a now-character, a now-reference. In one place Aristotle says quite concisely, without carrying out the analysis in this detailed way—but without which his whole interpretation of time is unintelligible—to pheromeno akolouthei to nun,[23] the now *follows* the moving thing, the object making the transition from one place to another; that is to say, the now is *seen* concomitantly in experiencing the motion. And to say that it is concomitantly *seen* means for Aristotle, in the broader sense, that it is concomitantly *counted*. What is thus concomitantly counted in following a motion, what is thus said, the nows—this is time. He d' arithmeton to proteron kai husteron, to nun estin.[24] As counted, the nows themselves count—they count the places, so far as these are traversed as places of the motion. Time as arithmos phoras is the counted that counts. Aristotle's interpretation of time matches the phenomenon extremely well when he says that time is something counted connected with motion so far as I see this motion in the horizon ek tinos eis ti, "from something to something."

In one place Aristotle says about proteron and husteron: to de proteron kai husteron en topo proton estin;[25] it is first of all in place, in the change and sequence of places. He is thinking of before and after here as still wholly without any time-determinateness. The Aristotelian definition of time can also be formulated at first in this way: time is what is counted in connection with motion which is experienced with respect to before and after. But what is thus counted is later unveiled as the nows. The nows themselves, however, can be expressed and understood only in the horizon of earlier and later. The "with respect to the before and after" and the "in the horizon of the earlier and later" do not coincide; the second is the interpretation of the first.[26] If we take the proteron and husteron provisionally as before and after, previous and subsequent, the genesis of Aristotle's definition of time becomes clearer. If we take it straight away as earlier and later, then the definition seems absurd at first, but this only indicates that a central problem is still present in it: the question about the origin of the now itself. The first translation gives the literal conception, but the second already includes a large element of interpretation.

We intentionally translated the Aristotelian definition of time as something counted in connection with motion so far as this motion is seen in

---

23. Ibid., 219^{b}22; see also 220^{a}6.
24. Ibid., 219^{b}25.
25. Ibid., 219^{a}14f.
26. Cf. *Sein und Zeit*, pp. 420 ff.

the horizon of earlier and later. We have already taken the proteron-husteron in a narrower sense, which comes out clearly only when the before and after receive further interpretation. Primarily, proteron-husteron means for Aristotle before and after in the sequence of places. It has a non-temporal sense. But the experience of before and after intrinsically presupposes, in a certain way, the experience of time, the earlier and later. Aristotle dealt with the proteron and husteron in detail in book Delta of the *Metaphysics* (11.1018ᵇ9ff). In the treatise on time he wavers in his conception of the proteron-husteron. Most often he takes it directly as earlier and later and not so much in the sense of before and after. He says of them that they have an apostasis pros to nun,²⁷ a distance from the now; in the then a now is concomitantly thought each time as not-yet-now, and similarly in the at-the-time the now concomitantly thought appears as the no-longer-now. The now is the limit for what has gone by and what comes after.

The nows which we count are themselves *in* time: they constitute time. The now has a peculiar double visage, which Aristotle expresses in this way: kai suneches te de ho chronos to nun, kai dieretai kata to nun.²⁸ Time is held together within itself by the now; time's specific continuity is rooted in the now. But conjointly, with respect to the now, time is divided, articulated into the no-longer-now, the earlier, and the not-yet-now, the later. It is only with respect to the now that we can conceive of the then and at-the-time, the later and the earlier. The now that we count in following a motion is *in each instance a different now*. To de nun dia to kineisthai to pheromenon aiei heteron,²⁹ on account of the transition of the moving thing the now is always another, an advance from one place to the other. In each now the now is a different one, but still each different now is, as now, always now. The ever different nows are, *as different,* nevertheless always exactly *the same,* namely, now. Aristotle summarizes the peculiar nature of the now and thus of time—when he interprets time purely by way of the now—in a manner so pregnant that it is possible only in Greek but hardly in German or English: to gar nun to auto ho pot' en, to d' einai auto heteron;³⁰ the

---

27. *Physica,* book 4, 14.223ᵃ5f. [Proteron gar kai husteron legomen kata ten pros to nun apostasin; "for we say 'before' and 'after' with reference to the distance from the 'now.'" Trans. Hardie and Gaye.]

28. *Physica,* book 4, 11.220ᵃ5. ["Time, then, also is both made continuous by the 'now' and divided at it." Trans. Hardie and Gaye.]

29. Ibid., 220ᵃ14.

30. Ibid., 219ᵇ10f. ["But every simultaneous time is self-identical; for the 'now' as a subject is an identity, but it accepts different attributes." The translators note: "E.g., if you come in when I go out, the time of your coming in is in fact the time of my going out, though for it to be the one and to be the other are different things." Trans. Hardie and Gaye. Compare the Wicksteed and Cornford translation: "But at any given moment time is the same

now is the same with respect to what it always already was—that is, in each now it is now; its *essentia,* its what, is always *the same* (tauto)— and nevertheless every now is, by its nature, different in each now, to d' einai auto heteron; nowness, being-now, is always *otherness, being-other* (being-how or howness —*existentia* —heteron). To de nun esti men hos to auto, esti d' hos ou to auto;[31] the now is in a certain way always the same and in a certain way never the same. The now articulates and bounds time with respect to its earlier and later. On the one hand it is indeed always the same, but then it is never the same. So far as it is always at an other and is other (we may think of the sequence of places), it is always something else. This constitutes its always being-now, its otherhood. But what it always already was as that which it is, namely, now—that is the same.

We shall not next enter any further into the problem of the structure of time itself starting from the now-manifold. Instead we ask: What is implied by Aristotle's interpreting time as something counted or as number? What in particular is he trying to make visible in stressing the numerical character of time? What does the characterization of time as number entail for the determination of the essential nature of what we call intratemporality? What does "in time" mean? How can the *being* of time be determined by way of the characterization of time as number?

What is implied by Aristotle's assigning a numerical character to time? What does he see in time? Time is number as that which is counted in following the places traversed by the moving thing, that is, so far as we follow in the motion the transition as such and in doing so say "now."

But also it is not enough that we correlate the nows in juxtaposition to a point-manifold, so as to think of them as being at a standstill in a line. This talk of time as a sequence of nows should not be misunderstood and transferred to the *spatial,* thus leading us to speak of time as a line, a series of points. The now is something counted, but not in the counting of one and the same point. Time is not a manifold of nows thrust together, because at each now every other now already no longer is and because, as we saw earlier, a curious stretching out on both sides into non-being belongs to time. The now is not correlated as a point to a fixed point and it cannot belong to it in that way, because by its essential nature it is both beginning and end. In the now as such there is already present a reference to the no-longer and the not-yet. It has dimension within itself; it stretches out toward a not-yet and a no-longer. The not-yet and no-longer are not patched on to the now as foreign but belong to its very content. Because of this *dimensional*

---

everywhere, for the 'now' itself is identical in its essence, but the relations into which it enters differ in different connexions."]

31. Ibid., 219[b]12f.

content the *now* has within itself the *character of a transition.* The now as such is already in transit. It is not one point alongside another point so that some mediation would be needed for the two. It is intrinsically transition. Because it has this peculiar stretching out within itself, we can conceive of the stretch as being greater or less. The scope of the dimension of a now varies; now in this hour, now in this second. This diversity of scope of dimension is possible only because the now is intrinsically dimensional. Time is not thrust together and summed up out of nows, but the reverse: with reference to the now we can articulate the stretching out of time always only in specific ways. Correlation of the manifold of the nows—where the now is taken as transition—with a point-manifold (line) has only a certain validity, if we take the points of the line themselves as forming beginning and end, as constituting the transition of the continuum, and not as pieces present alongside one another each for itself. A consequence of the impossibility of correlating the nows with isolated point-pieces is that the *now,* on its part, is *a continuum of the flux of time*—not a piece. That is why the nows in the following of motion cannot ever fragment the motion into a collection of immobile parts; instead, what becomes accessible and the object of thought in the now is the transitional in its transition and the resting in its rest. And, conversely, this entails that the now is itself neither in motion nor at rest: it is not "in time."

The *now*—and that means time—is, says Aristotle, *by its essential nature not a limit,* because as transition and dimension it is open on the sides of the not-yet and the no-longer. The now is a limit, in the sense of a closing, of the finished, of the no-further, *only incidentally* with reference to something that ceases *in* a now and *at* a definite point of time. It is not the now that ceases as now; rather, the now as now is, by its essential nature, already the not-yet, already related as dimension to what is to come, whereas it can well be that a motion determined by the said now can cease in this now. With the aid of the now I can mark a limit, but the now as such does not have the character of a limit so far as it is taken within the continuum of time itself. *The now is not limit, but number,* not peras but arithmos. Aristotle explicitly contrasts time as arithmos with peras. The limits of something, he says, are what they are only in one with the being they limit. The limit of something belongs to the mode of being of the limited. This does not hold true for number. Number is not bound to what it numbers. Number can determine something without itself being dependent, for its part, on the intrinsic content and mode of being of what is counted. I can say "ten horses." Here the ten indeed determines the horses, but ten has nothing of the character of horses and their mode of being. Ten is not a limit of horses as horses; for in counting with it I can just as well determine ships, triangles, or trees. What is characteristic about number lies in the fact that it determines—in the Greek sense also de-limits—something in such a way that it itself remains independent of what it delimits. Time as number, as that which was portrayed by us as the counted-counting, does not itself belong to the entity that it counts. When Aristotle says that time is what is *counted* in connection with motion, what he wishes to stress is that, to be sure, we count and determine motion as transition in terms of the now, but that for this reason this counting counted, time, is bound neither to the *intrinsic content* nor the *mode of being* of the moving thing nor to the motion as such. Nevertheless, in our counting as we follow a motion we encounter time as something counted. With this a peculiar character of time is revealed, a character that was interpreted later by Kant in a special sense as form of intuition.

Time is number and not limit, but as number it is at the same time able to measure that with reference to which it is number. Not only is time counted, but as counted it can itself be something that counts in the sense of a measure. Only because time is number in the sense of the counted now can it become a *mensural* number, so that it itself can count in the sense of measuring. This distinction between the now as number in general or what is counted and as the counting counted, along with the delimitation of time as number in contrast with limit, is the essential content of the difficult place in Aristotle's essay on time, into which we shall enter only briefly. Aristotle says: to de nun dia to kineisthai to pheromenon aiei heteron;[32] because the now is what is counted in a transition, it always differs with that which is undergoing the transition. Hosth' ho chronos arithmos ouch hos tes autes stigmes;[33] therefore, time is not number with reference to the same point as a point, that is, the now is not a point-element of continuous time, but as a transition, insofar as it is correlated with a point, with a place in the movement, it is already always beyond the point. As transition it looks backward and forward. It cannot be correlated with an isolated point as selfsame because it is beginning and end: hoti arche kai teleute, all' hos ta eschata tes grammes mallon.[34] Time is number in a manner of speaking—

---

32. Ibid., 220[a]14. [The single passage, 220[a]14 –20, to which notes 32 –35 refer, is reproduced here as a whole. See also the remark and translation added to note 34, below.

"The 'now' on the other hand, since the body carried is moving, is always different.

"Hence time is not number in the sense in which there is 'number' of the same point because it is beginning and end, but rather as the extremities of a line form a number, and not as the parts of the line do so, both for the reason given (for we can use the middle point as two, so that on that analogy time might stand still), and further because obviously the 'now' is no *part* of time nor the section any part of the movement, any more than the points are parts of the line—for it is two *lines* that are *parts* of one line." Trans. Hardie and Gaye.]

33. Ibid., 220[a]14f.

34. Ibid., 220[a]15f. [The *Grundprobleme's* reference to the Ross edition of the *Physica*, which was published in 1936, runs into a specific problem here. The Ross text has the word

it determines as transition the point's extremes outward on both sides of the stretching. This transition belongs to the point and is itself, as now, not a *part* of time, in the sense that this time would be composed of now-parts; instead, each part has transitional character, that is, it is not strictly speaking a part. Therefore Aristotle says directly: ouden morion to nun tou chronou, oud' he diairesis tes kineseos;[35] the now is consequently not a part of time but is always time itself, and, because it is not a part, motion itself—since motion is measured by means of time—also is not cut into parts. Because the now is transition, it is capable of making motion accessible *as motion,* in its unbroken character of transition. That time is a limit in the sense that I say that motion ceases, stands still, in a now—this is a sumbebekos: it is only an attribute of the now, but it does not reach its essential nature.

The now is what it is, he d' arithmei, so far as it counts, hence number. Time as now is not limit but transition, and as transition it is possible number, possible mensural number of motion. It measures a motion or a rest in such a way that a specific motion, a specific change and advance is fixed, for example, the advance *from* one stroke of a second *to* the next, with which then the entire movement is measured. Because the now is transition it always measures a from-to, it measures a how-long, a duration. Time as number fixes the limits of a specific movement. This delimited movement is intended for measuring the whole of the movement to be measured: metrei d' houtos ten kinesin to horisai tina kinesin he katametresei ten holen.[36]

Because time is arithmos, it is metron. The being measured of a moving thing with respect to its motion, this metreisthai, is nothing but to en chrono einai,[37] the motion's "being in time." According to Aristotle, "things are in time" means nothing but that they are measured by time on the basis of their transitional character. The *intratemporality* of things and events must be distinguished from the way the nows, the earlier and later, are in time.

"grammes" in this place, whereas other texts, such as that by Bekker, read "autes." Thus the Ross edition's translation (Hardie and Gaye) refers to the extremities of a *line* (gramme), whereas Heidegger speaks of the *point's* extremes—i.e., the translation Heidegger offers is contrary to the text quoted from Aristotle. But the question arises, further, as to the meaning of "autes" in "ta eschata tes autes." Wicksteed and Cornford (Cornford consulted Bekker, Prantl, and other sources and commentaries; see vol. 1, pp. x–xi) read it as referring to a line, not a point: "but rather as the two extremities of the same line." See also their explanatory note regarding the meaning of the entire passage, p. 392, note *a.* Perhaps Heidegger's expression, "on both sides of the stretching," captures this linear implication.]

35. Ibid., 220[a]19.

36. Ibid., 12.221[a]1f. ["Time is a measure of motion and of being moved, and it measures the motion by determining a motion which will measure exactly the whole motion, as the cubit does the length by determining an amount which will measure out the whole." Trans. Hardie and Gaye.]

37. Ibid., 221[a]4.

Epei d' arithmos ho chronos, to men nun kai to proteron kai hosa toiauta houtos en chrono hos en arithmo monas kai to peritton kai artion (ta men gar tou arithmou ti, ta de tou chronou ti estin) · ta de pragmata hos en arithmo to chrono estin. Ei de touto, periechetai hupo chronou hosper ⟨kai ta en arithmo hup' arithmou ⟩ kai ta en topo hupo topou.[38] The nows are indeed in a certain sense themselves in time, so far as they constitute time. But motion and the moving thing are in time, not in the sense that they belong to time itself, but in the way in which what is counted is in number. The even and odd are in the numbers themselves, but what is counted is also, in a certain way, in the numbers that do the counting. As the counted is in number, so motion is in time. That which is in time, the moving thing, periechetai hup' arithmou,[39] is embraced by the counting number. Time does not itself belong to motion but *embraces* it. The intratemporality of a being means its *being embraced* by time (now) as number (counted). The factor of the periechesthai, being embraced, stresses that time does not itself belong among the beings which are *in* time. So far as we measure a being, either in motion or at rest, by time, we come back from the time that embraces and measures the moving thing to that which is to be measured. If we remain with the image of embrace, time is that which is *further outside,* as compared with movements and with all beings that move or are at rest. It embraces or *holds around* the moving and resting things. We may designate it by an expression whose beauty may be contested: time has the character of a *holdaround,* since it holds beings—moving and resting—around. In a suitable sense we can call time, as this holder-around, a container, provided we do not take "container" in the literal sense of a receptacle like a glass or a box but retain simply the formal element of holding-around.

Given that time embraces beings, it is required that it should somehow be *before* beings, *before* things moving and at rest, encompassing them. Kant calls time the wherein of an order. It is an embracing horizon within which things given can be ordered with respect to their succession.

Due to its transitionary character, says Aristotle, time always measures only the moving thing or else the moving thing in its limiting case, the thing at rest. Metresei d' ho chronos to kinoumenon kai to eremoun, he to

---

38. Ibid., 221ᵃ13–18. [Cf.: "Now taking time as a number scale (a) the 'now' and the 'before' and suchlike exist in time as the monad and the odd and even exist in number (for these latter pertain to number just in the same way in which the former pertain to time); but (b) events have their places in time in a sense analogous to that in which any numbered group of things exist in number (i.e., in such and such a definite number), and such things as these are *embraced* in number (i.e., in time) as things that have locality are embraced in their places." Wicksteed and Cornford, pp. 401–403.]

39. Ibid.

men kinoumenon to de eremoun.[40] Time measures the moving and the resting, so far as the one is in motion and the other at rest. Time measures motion at the thing moving: pose tis,[41] *how great* the transition is, that is, *how many nows* there are in a particular transition from something to something. Time measures the moving thing ouch haplos estai metreton hupo chronou, he poson ti estin, all' he he kinesis autou pose;[42] it measures it not simply as the moving being that it is; if a stone is in motion, time does not measure the stone as such with respect to its specific extension, but the stone insofar as it is moving. Motion is measured, and only motion is measurable, by time, because time, in virtue of its transitionary character, always already means something in transition, changing or resting. So far as motion or rest can be measured by time, and to be measured by time means "to be in time," the moving or resting thing, and only it, is in time. For this reason we say that geometrical relationships and their contents are extratemporal, because they are not in motion and consequently also are not at rest. A triangle is not at rest because it does not move. It is beyond rest and motion, and therefore, in Aristotle's view, it is neither embraced nor embraceable by time.

The interpretation of intratemporality also tells us *what* can be intratemporal as well as, on the other hand, what is extratemporal. Thus it becomes ever more clear how time is something counted in connection with motion. Hama gar kineseos aisthanometha kai chronou;[43] in respect of the moving thing we perceive time together with movement. Where motion is experienced time is unveiled. Kai gar ean e skotos kai meden dia tou somatos paschomen, kinesis de tis en te psuche ene, euthus hama dokei tis gegonenai kai chronos.[44] It is not necessary that we should experience motion in things presently at hand. Even when it is dark, when what is at hand is concealed from us but when we are experiencing our own self, our own mental activities, time is also always already given directly together with the experience, euthus hama. For mental actions also come under the determination of

---

40. Ibid., 221^{b}16–18. ["But time will measure what is moved and what is at rest, the one *qua* moved, the other *qua* at rest." Trans. Hardie and Gaye.]

41. Ibid., 221^{b}19.

42. Ibid., 221^{b}19f. ["Hence what is moved will not be measurable by the time simply in so far as it has quantity, but in so far as its *motion* has quantity." Trans. Hardie and Gaye.]

43. *Physica*, book 4, 11.219^{a}3f. [The entire passage to which notes 43–44 refer is the following: "Now we perceive movement and time together: for even when it is dark and we are not being affected through the body, if any movement takes place in the mind we at once suppose that some time also has elapsed; and not only that but also, when some time is thought to have passed, some movement also along with it seems to have taken place. Hence time is either movement or something that belongs to movement. Since then it is not movement, it must be the other." Trans. Hardie and Gaye.]

44. Ibid., 219^{a}4–6.

motion—motion taken broadly in the Aristotelian sense and not necessarily as local motion. The actions are not intrinsically spatial but they pass over into one another, one changes into the other. In such a mental action we can stop and dwell on something. We may recall the passage in *De inter-pretatione:* histesi he dianoia,[45] thinking stands still with something. The mind, too, has the character of a moving thing. Even if we are not experiencing something moving in the sense of some entity presently at hand, nevertheless motion taken in the broadest sense, hence time, is unveiled for us in experiencing our own self.

However, this gives rise to a difficult problem. Poteron de me ouses psuches eie an ho chronos e ou,[46] whether, if there is no soul, time does or does not exist. Aristotle gives a more specific interpretation to this: Adunatou gar ontos einai tou arithmesontos adunaton kai arithmeton ti einai, hoste delon hoti oud' arithmos. Arithmos gar e to erithmemenon e to arithmeton. Ei de meden allo pephuken arithmein e psuche kai psuches nous, adunaton einai chronon psuches me ouses, all' e touto ho pote on estin ho chronos, hoion ei endechetai kinesin einai aneu psuches. To de proteron kai husteron en kinesei estin · chronos de taut' estin he arithmeta estin.[47] Time is what is counted. If there is no soul then there is no counting, nothing that counts, and if there is nothing that counts then there is nothing countable and nothing counted. If there is no soul then there is no time. Aristotle poses this as a question and at the same time stresses the other possibility, whether time perhaps is in itself in what it is, just as a motion can also exist without a soul. But likewise he emphasizes that the before and after, which is a constitutive determination of time, is *in* motion, and time itself is tauta, the before and after *as counted.* To be counted obviously belongs to the nature of time, so that if there is no counting there is no time, or the converse. Aristotle doesn't pursue this question any further; he merely touches on it, which leads to the question *how* time itself exists.

We see by the interpretation of "being in time" that time, as the embracing, as that in which natural events occur, is, as it were, more objective than all objects. On the other hand, we see also that it exists only *if the soul exists.* It is more objective than all objects and simultaneously it is subjective,

---

45. Aristotle, *De interpretatione,* 16ᵇ20.
46. *Physica,* book 4, 14.223ᵃ21f. [The entire passage to which notes 46–47 refer is the following: "Whether if soul did not exist time would exist or not, is a question that may fairly be asked; for if there cannot be some one to count there cannot be anything that can be counted, so that evidently there cannot be number; for number is either what has been, or what can be, counted. But if nothing but soul, or in soul reason, is qualified to count, there would not be time unless there were soul, but only that of which time is an attribute, i.e., if *movement* can exist without soul, and the before and after are attributes of movement, and time is these *qua* numerable." Trans. Hardie and Gaye.]
47. Ibid., 223ᵃ22–29.

existing only if subjects exist. *What* then is time and *how* does it exist? Is it only subjective, or is it only objective, or is it neither the one nor the other? From our earlier discussions we already know that the concepts "subject" and "object" as they are nowadays employed are ontologically indefinite and hence are inadequate, especially for defining the being that we ourselves are, the being that is meant by soul or subject. We point the question about the being of time in the wrong direction from the beginning if we base it on the alternative as to whether time belongs to the subject or object. An unending dialectic can be developed here without saying the least thing about the matter, just as long as it is not settled *how* the Dasein's being itself is, whether perhaps it is such that the Dasein, inasmuch as it exists, is further outside than any object and at the same time further inside, more inward (more subjective), than any subject or soul (because temporality as transcendence is openness). We indicated earlier that the phenomenon of the world manifests itself to the Dasein. Given that the Dasein exists, is in a world, everything extant that the Dasein encounters is necessarily intraworldly, held-around [con-tained] by the world. We shall see that in fact the *phenomenon of time,* taken in a more original sense, *is interconnected with the concept of the world and thus with the structure of the Dasein itself.* But for the while we must leave untouched the difficulty as Aristotle records it. Time is the before and after insofar as they are counted. As counted it is not antecedently extant in itself. Time does not exist without soul. If time thus becomes dependent on the counting of numbers, it does not follow that it is something mental in the soul. Simultaneously it is en panti, everywhere, en ge, on the earth, en thalatte, in the ocean, en ourano, in the heaven.[48] Time is everywhere and yet nowhere and, still, it is only in the soul.

What is essential for understanding the foregoing interpretation of Aristotle's concept of time lies in correctly understanding the concept of akolouthein, to follow. It means an ontological connection of founding which subsists among time, motion, continuity, and dimension. From this concept of founding, of following in the sense of akolouthein, it cannot be inferred that Aristotle identifies time with space. But it surely does become clear that, in bringing time into immediate connection with motion in the sense of local motion, he approaches the mode of measuring time in just the way it is prescribed in the natural understanding of time and in the natural experience of time itself. Of this Aristotle gives only an explicit interpretation. From the mode of interconnection of the now-sequence with motion we saw that the now itself has transitionary character: as now it is always the not-yet-now and the no-longer-now. Due to this transitionary character,

---

48. Ibid., 223ª17f.

it gets the peculiarity of measuring motion as such, as metabole. Since each now is not a pure point but is intrinsically transition, the now, by its essential nature, is not a limit but a number. The numerical character of the now and of time in general is essential for the fundamental understanding of time because only from this does what we call intratemporality become intelligible. This means that every being is in time. Aristotle interprets "being in time" as being measured by time. Time itself can be measured only because on its part it is something counted and, as this counted thing, it can itself count again, count in the sense of measuring, of the gathering together of a specific so-many.

At the same time the numerical character of time entails that it embraces or contains the beings that are in it, that with reference to objects it is in a certain way more objective than they are themselves. From this there arose the question about the being of time and its connection with the soul. The assignment of time to the soul, which occurs in Aristotle and then in a much more emphatic sense in Augustine, so as always thereafter to make itself conspicuous over and over again in the discussion of the traditional concept of time, led to the problem how far time is objective and how far subjective. We have seen that the question not only cannot be decided but cannot even be put in that way, since both these concepts "object" and "subject" are questionable. We shall see why it can be said neither that time is something objective in the sense that it belongs among objects nor that it is something subjective, existent in the subject. It will turn out that this manner of putting the question is impossible but that both answers—time is objective and time is subjective—get their own right in a certain way from the original concept of temporality. We shall try now to determine this original concept of temporality more particularly by going back to it from time as understood in the common way.

b) The common understanding of time and the return to original time

Our interpretation of Aristotle's concept of time showed that Aristotle characterizes time primarily as a *sequence of nows*, where it should be noted that the nows are not parts from which time is pieced together into a whole. The very way in which we translated Aristotle's definition of time—hence the way we interpreted it—was intended to indicate that, when he defines it with reference to the earlier and later, he is defining it in terms of time as that which is counted in connection with motion. We also stressed that the Aristotelian definition of time does not contain a tautology within itself, but instead Aristotle speaks from the very constraint of the matter itself. Aristotle's definition of time is not in any respect a definition in the academic sense. It characterizes time by defining how what we call time becomes *accessible.* It is an *access definition* or *access characterization.* The type of definiendum is determined by the manner of the sole possible access to it: the counting perception of motion as motion is at the same time the perception of what is counted as time.

What Aristotle presents as time *corresponds to the common prescientific understanding of time. By its own phenomenological content* common time points to an original time, *temporality.* This implies, however, that Aristotle's definition of time is only the *initial approach* to the interpretation of time. The characteristic traits of time as commonly understood must become intelligible by way of original time. If we set this task for ourselves it means that we have to make clear how the *now qua now has transitionary character;* how time as *now, then, and at-the-time embraces beings* and as such an embrace of extant things is still more objective and more extant than everything else (intratemporality); how time is *essentially counted* and how it is pertinent to time that it is *always unveiled.*

The common understanding of time manifests itself explicitly and primarily in the use of the clock, it being a matter of indifference here what perfection the clock has. We saw how we had to convince ourselves in looking at the employment of clocks that we encounter time as we count in following a movement. What this means more specifically, how it is possible, and what it implies for the concept of time—we did not ask about all this. Also, neither Aristotle nor subsequent interpreters of time posed this question. What does it mean to speak of using a clock? We have made clear the Aristotelian interpretation of time in regard to the employment of clocks but without ourselves offering a yet more exact interpretation of that employment. For his part Aristotle does not interpret the use of clocks, doesn't even mention it, but presupposes this natural mode of access to time by way of the clock. The common understanding of time comprehends only the time that reveals itself in counting as a succession of nows. From this understanding of time there arises the concept of time as a sequence of nows, which has been more particularly defined as a unidirectional irreversible sequence of nows one after the other. We shall retain this initial approach to time in terms of clock usage and, by a more precise interpretation of this comportment toward time and of the time thus experienced, advance toward what makes this time itself possible.

α) The mode of being of clock usage. Now, then, and at-the-time as self-expositions of the comportments of enpresenting, expecting, and retaining

What does it mean to read time from a clock? To "look at the clock"? In using a clock, in reading time from it, we do indeed look at the clock but the clock itself is not the object of our regard. We do not occupy ourselves, for example, with our watch as such, as this particular instrument, so as to distinguish it, say, from a coin. But also a clock is not our object as it is for its maker. He doesn't use it as the equipment that it is. In using a clock we do of course perceive the clock, but only and solely in order to allow ourselves to be brought by it to something that the clock itself is not but that it shows as a clock—time. But here too caution is advisable. The point is to grasp the *use of the clock in its original mode of being*. When I use a clock to read the time, I am also *not directed toward time as the proper object* of my vision. I make neither clock nor time the theme of my regard. When I look at my watch I ask, for instance, how much time still remains for me until the scheduled end of the lecture. I am not searching for time as such in order to occupy myself with it; on the contrary, I am occupied in giving a phenomenological exposition. I am concerned to bring it to a close. In noting the time, I am trying to determine what time it is, how much time there is till nine o'clock, so as to finish this or that subject. In ascertaining the time, I am trying to find out how much time there is *till this or that point* so that I may see that I have enough time *in order to* finish the subject. I make inquiry of the clock with the aim of determining how much time I still have *to* do this or that. The time I am trying to determine is always "time to," time *in order to* do this or that, time that I need *for,* time that I can permit myself *in order to* accomplish this or that, time that I must take *for* carrying through this or that. Looking at the clock roots *in* and springs *out* of a "*taking* time." If I am to *take* time then I must have it somewhere or other. In a certain sense we always have time. If often or for the most part we have no time, that is merely a privative mode of our *original having of time*. Time reading in clock usage is founded in a taking-time-for-oneself or, as we also say, taking time into account. The "count" in the accounting here must be understood not in the sense of mere counting but as "reckoning with time," "taking our reckoning in accordance with it," "making allowance for it." Reckoning with time in the form of measuring time arises as a modification from the primary comportment toward time as *guiding oneself according to it*. It is on the basis of this original comportment toward time that we arrive at the measuring of time, that we invent clocks in order to shape our reckoning with time more economically with reference to time. We are always already reckoning with time, taking it into account, before we look at a clock to measure the time. If we observe that in using a clock, in looking at it, there is present already a reckoning with time, then this means that time is already given to us before we use the clock. Somehow it has already been unveiled for us; and it is for this reason alone that we can return to time explicitly with the clock. The position of the clock's hand only determines the how much. But the how much and the so much of time understands time originally as that with which I reckon, as time in order to.... The time that is always already *given* to us so far as we *take* time and take account of time has the character of *"time in order to...."*

When without reflecting we look at a clock in everyday behavior, we always say "now," explicitly or not. But this now is not a naked, pure now but has the character of the *"now it is time to...,"* "now there is still time until...," "now I still have enough time until...." When we look at the clock and say "now" we are not directed toward the now as such but toward that *wherefore* and *whereto* there is still time now; we are directed toward what occupies us, what presses hard upon us, what it is time for, what we want to have time for. When we say "now" we are never directed toward the now as toward a merely extant thing. The Dasein says "now" also when it is not expressly measuring time by the clock. When we simply feel that it is cold here it implies "now it is cold." It should be stressed once again that when we mean and express "now" we are not talking about some extant thing or other. Saying "now" has a different character from saying "this window." In the latter expression I intend thematically that window over there, the object itself. If in saying "now" we are not addressing ourselves to anything extant, then are we addressing ourselves to the being that we ourselves are? But surely I am not the now? Perhaps I am, though, in a certain way. Saying "now" is not a speaking about something as an object, but it is surely a declaration about something. The *Dasein,* which always exists so that it takes time for itself, *expresses itself.* Taking time for itself, it utters itself in such a way that *it is always saying time.* When I say "now" I do not mean the now as such, but in my now-saying I am transient. I am *in motion in* the understanding of now and, in a strict sense, I am really with that *whereto* the time is and *wherefore* I determine the time. However, we say not only "now" but also *"then"* and *"before."* Time is constantly there in such a way that in all our planning and precaution, in all our comportments and all the measures we take, we move in a silent discourse: now, not until, in former times, finally, at the time, before that, and so forth.

We now have to determine more precisely *whence* we actually *take* what we mean by the now without our making it into an object. When I say "then" this means that in this form of discourse I *am expecting* a particular thing which will come or happen on its own or I am expecting something I myself intend to do. I can only say "then" when I am expecting something, only so far as the Dasein as existent is expectant. Such a being-expectant, an *expecting,* expresses itself by means of the then. It utters itself in such a way that it does not expressly mean itself but nevertheless displays its own self in this expression of the then. When I say "at the time" I am able to say it with understanding only if I *retain* something bygone. It is not necessary that I should explicitly recollect it but only that I should somehow retain it as something bygone. The at-the-time is the self-expression of the *retention* of something former, something erstwhile. A specific mode of retention is *forgetting*. This is not nothing; a very definite type of comportment of the self toward the bygone is exhibited in it—a mode in which I close myself off from the bygone, in which it is veiled over for me. And finally, whenever I say "now" I am comporting myself toward something extant or, more precisely, toward something present which is in my present. This comportment toward something present, this having-there of something present, a having which expresses itself in the now, we call the *enprésenting* [*Gegenwärtigen*] of something.

These three determinations, already familiar to Aristotle, the *now* and the modifications of the *at-the-time* as no-longer-now and the *then* as not-yet-now, are the *self-exposition of comportments* which we characterize as expecting, retaining, and enpresenting. Inasmuch as each then is a not-yet-now and each at-the-time a no-longer-now, there is an enpresenting implicit in every expecting and retaining. If I am expecting something, I always see it into a present. Similarly, if I am retaining something, I retain it for a present, so that all expecting and retaining are enpresenting. This shows the *inner coherence* not only of time as expressed but also of these *comportments* in which time expresses itself. If time utters itself with these determinations—now, at-the-time, then—and if further these determinations themselves express an expecting, retaining, and enpresenting, then obviously what is brought out here is *time in a more original sense.* We shall have to ask how what confronts us in the unity of expecting, retaining, and enpresenting can be validly asserted to be original time. This will be the case above all if all the essential moments belonging to the now—its embracing character, its making possible of intratemporality, its transitionary character and that of time's being counted or unveiled—can be made intelligible in their possibility and necessity by way of more original phenomena whose unity we shall come to know as temporality. And temporality in its turn provides the horizon for the understanding of being in general.

Time as Aristotle expounds it and as it is familiar to ordinary consciousness is a sequence of nows from the not-yet-now to the no-longer-now, a sequence of nows which is not arbitrary but whose intrinsic direction is from the future to the past. We also say that time passes, elapses. The sequence of nows is directed uniformly in accordance with this succession from future to past and is not reversible. This sequence of nows is designated as infinite. It is taken to be a universal law that time is infinite.

The common understanding of time first manifests itself explicitly in the use of the clock, in the measurement of time. However, we measure time because we need and use time, because we take time or let it pass, and explicitly regulate and make secure the way we use time by specific time measurement. When we look at a clock, since time itself does not lie in the clock, we assign time to the clock. In looking at the clock we say "now." We have thus given explicit expression to time, which we determine in a merely numerical way from the clock. This saying "now" and the uttering of a then or an at-the-time must have a specific origin. Where do we get the now from when we say "now"? Plainly we do not intend an object, an extant thing; instead, what we call the enpresenting of something, the present, expresses itself in the now. In the at-the-time a retaining pronounces itself, and in the then an expecting. Since each at-the-time is a "no-longer-now" and each then a "not-yet-now," there is always already an enpresenting, a concomitant understanding of the now, incorporated in the uttering of a then that arises from an expecting. Each one of these time-determinations—now, then, at-the-time—is spoken from out of the *unity* of an enpresenting-expecting-retaining (or forgetting). What I expect to come next is spoken of in the *"at once, forthwith."* What I still retain or even have already forgotten is spoken of as the most recent in the *"just now."* The just now stands with its modification in the *horizon of the "earlier,"* which belongs to retaining and forgetting. The forthwith and the then stand in the *horizon of the "later-on,"* which belongs to expecting. All nows stand in the *horizon of the "today,"* the "present," that is the horizon of enpresenting. The time intended by means of the now, then, and at-the-time is the time with which the Dasein that takes time reckons. But where does it get the time it reckons with and which it expresses in the now, then, and at-the-time? We shall still defer answering this question. But it is already clear that this answer is nothing but the elucidation by way of original time of the origin of the now, then (not-yet-now), and at-the-time (no-longer-now), of time as sequence of nows (succession).

β) The structural moments of expressed time: significance, datability, spannedness, publicness

The question is, How must we define more precisely this enpresenting, expecting, and retaining which express themselves in the now, then, and at-the-time? We can do this only if we are certain that we already see in its full structure what the Aristotelian interpretation of time knows as the now-sequence. However, this is not the case in the way Aristotle and the whole of the subsequent tradition characterize time. It is first of all necessary, then, to delineate more precisely the structure of expressed time, the now, then, and at-the-time.

We have already touched on one essential moment of the time read from the clock that we generally take or leave for ourselves, but without assigning it to the now as a structure. All time we read from the clock is time to..., "time to do this or that," *appropriate* or *inappropriate* time. The time we read from the clock always has as its opposite the wrong time, as when we say that someone comes at the wrong time or is on time. We have already had this peculiar character of time in view in another context when we characterized the concept of the world and saw that in it there is intended a whole of relations having the character of the in-order-to. We designated by the term "significance" this totality of relations of the in-order-to, for-the-sake-of, for-that-purpose, to-that-end. Time as right and wrong time has the *character of significance,* the character that characterizes the world as world in general. It is for this reason that we call the time with which we reckon, which we leave for ourselves, *world-time.* This does not mean that the time we read from the clock is something extant like intraworldly things. We know, of course, that the world is not an extant entity, not nature, but that which first makes possible the uncoveredness of nature. It is therefore also inappropriate, as frequently happens, to call this time nature-time or natural time. There is no nature-time, since all time belongs essentially to the Dasein. But there is indeed a world-time. We give time the name of world-time because it has the character of *significance,* which is overlooked in the Aristotelian definition of time and everywhere in the traditional determination of time.

A second factor along with the significance of time is its *datability.* Each now is expressed in an enpresenting of something in unity with an expecting and retaining. When I say "now" I am always tacitly adding *"now, when such and such."* When I say "then" I always mean *"then, when."* When I say "at the time" I mean *"at the time when."* To every now there belongs a "when"— now, when such and such. By the term "datability" we denote this relational structure of the now as now-when, of the at-the-time as at-the-time-when, and of the then as then-when. Every now dates itself as "now, when such and such is occurring, happening, or in existence." Even if I can no longer determine exactly and unequivocally the when of an at-the-time-when, the at-the-time has this relation. Only because the relation of dating belongs essentially to the at-the-time, now, and then, can the date be indefinite, hazy, and uncertain. The date itself does not need to be calendrical in the narrower sense. The calendar date is only one particular mode of everyday dating. The indefiniteness of the date does not imply a shortcoming in datability as essential structure of the now, at-the-time, and then. These must belong to it in order for it to be able to be indefinite as a date. We say, for example, "at the time when the French were in Germany," and we speak of the "French time." The dating can be calendrically indeterminate but it is nevertheless determined by a particular historical happening or some other event. No matter how broad, certain, and unequivocal the dating may be of a "now when," an "at-the-time when," and a "then when," the structural moment of datability belongs to the essential constitution of the now, at-the-time, and then. The "now when," "at-the-time when," and "then when" are related essentially to an entity that gives a date to the datable. The time that is commonly conceived as a sequence of nows must be taken as this dating relation. This relation should not be overlooked and suppressed. Nevertheless, the common conception of time as a sequence of nows is just as little aware of the moment of pre-calendrical datability as of that of significance. The common conception thinks of the nows as free-floating, relationless, intrinsically patched on to one another and intrinsically successive. In contrast to this we have to see that every now, every at-the-time, and every then is datable by its very structure, always already related to something, and in its expression is more or less definitely dated from something. The fact that the essential dating relation of the now, the no-longer-now, and the not-yet-now was overlooked in the traditional theories of time is further evidence of how far precisely what is taken for granted as self-evident lies from the concept. For what is more a matter of course than that by the now we mean "now, when this or that exists or is happening"? Why could time-structures as elemental as those of significance and datability remain hidden from the traditional time concept? Why did it overlook them and why did it have to overlook them? We shall learn how to understand this from the structure of temporality itself.

In expecting, the Dasein says "then," in enpresenting "now," in retaining "at-the-time." Each "then" is uttered as a not-yet in the understanding of a now, in an enpresenting. In the expectant expression of the then a *"till then"* is always understood from the standpoint of a now. In each then the understanding of a now-till-then is tacitly but conjointly involved. The stretch from now till then is articulated by means of the then itself. The relation "from now till then" is not first established as supplementary between a now and a then but is already present in the expectant enpresenting expressed in the then. It lies just as much in the now as in the not-yet and then, which is related to a now. When I say "then" as starting from a "now," I always already mean a definite *meanwhile* until then. What we call *duration,* the *during,* the *enduring* of time, lies in this meanwhile. Once again the structure of datability that has just been exhibited belongs to this determination as to a time character: "meanwhile," that is, "while this or that is happening." This meanwhile can itself be more exactly determined and divided again by particular "from then to thens" which articulate the meanwhile. Lasting or enduring is especially accessible in the articulated meanwhile or during. What becomes accessible is that what is meant by the "from now till then," time, stretches out. We call what is thus articulated in these characters of the meanwhile, the during, and the till-then, the *spannedness* of time. By the meanwhile and the during we mean a span of time. This is the feature that Aristotle rightly assigns to the now when he says that it has a certain transitionary character. Time is intrinsically spanned and stretched. Every now, then, and at-the-time not only has a date but is spanned and stretched within itself: "now, during the lecture," "now, during the recess." No now and no time-moment can be punctualized. Every time-moment is spanned intrinsically, the span's breadth being variable. It varies, among other things, with what in each case dates the now.

But significance, datability, and spannedness (stretchedness) do not comprise the full structure of the now, at-the-time, and then. The final character of time in the sense of calculated and expressed time we call the *publicness* of time. Whether publicly announced or not, the now is expressed. When we say "now" we mean "now, when this thing or event is happening." The dated now has a certain stretchedness. As we express the dated and spanned now *in our being with one another* each one of us understands the others. When any one of us says "now," we all understand this now, even though each of us perhaps dates this now by starting from a different thing or event: "now, when the professor is speaking," "now, when the students are writing," or "now, in the morning," "now, toward the end of the semester." To understand the expressed now as a now we do not at all have to agree in our dating of it. The expressed now is intelligible to everyone in our being with one another. Although each one of us utters his own now, it is nevertheless the now for everyone. The accessibility of the now for everyone, without prejudice to the diverse datings, characterizes time as public. The now is accessible to everyone and thus belongs to no one. On account of this character of time a peculiar objectivity is assigned to it. The now belongs neither to me nor to anyone else, but it is somehow there. There is time, time is given, it is extant, without our being able to say how and where it is.

We also lose time, just as immediately as we constantly take time for ourselves. We leave time for ourselves with something, and in fact in such a way that while we do so the time is not there. As we lose time, we give it away. But losing time is a particularly carefree leaving time for oneself, one way in which we have time in the oblivious passing of our lives.

We have pointed to a series of characters of the time that Aristotle has in view when he defines it as counted. The time that we take for ourselves and that we express in the now, then, and at-the-time has the structural moments of significance, datability, stretchedness, and publicness. The time with which we reckon, in the broader sense of reckoning, is datable, spanned, public, and has the character of significance, belonging to the world itself. But how do these structural moments belong essentially to time? How are these structures themselves possible?

γ) Expressed time and its derivation from existential
temporality. The ecstatic and horizonal character of temporality

It is only if we keep in view the full structure of the now-sequence in
these aspects that we can inquire concretely: Where does that time originate
which we know *first of all* and which we know *solely?* Can these structural
moments of time, and thus time itself just as it expresses itself, be understood by means of *what* is expressed in the now, then, and at-the-time, by
means of enpresenting, expecting, and retaining? When we are expecting
any particular happening, we comport our Dasein always in some particular
way toward our own most peculiar ability to be. Even if what we are
expecting may be some event, some occurrence, still our own Dasein is
always conjointly expected in the expecting of the occurrence itself. The
Dasein understands itself by way of its own most peculiar capacity to be,
of which it is expectant. In thus comporting toward its own most peculiar
capacity to be, *it is ahead of itself.* Expecting a possibility, I come from this
possibility toward that which I myself am. The Dasein, expecting its ability
to be, *comes toward itself.* In this coming-toward-itself, expectant of a possibility, the Dasein is *futural* in an original sense. This coming-toward-
oneself from one's most peculiar possibility, a coming-toward which is
implicit in the Dasein's existence and of which all expecting is a specific
mode, is the *primary concept of the future.* This existential concept of the
future is the presupposition for the common concept of the future in the
sense of the not-yet-now.

Retaining or forgetting something, the Dasein always comports itself
somehow toward what it itself already has been. It is only—as it always
factically is—in such a way that it *has in each instance already been* the being
that it is. In comporting ourselves toward an entity as bygone, we retain it
in a certain way or we forget it. In retaining and forgetting, the Dasein is
itself concomitantly retained. It concomitantly retains its own self in *what
it already has been.* That which the Dasein has already been in each instance,
its *[past as]* *having-been-ness [Gewesenheit]*, belongs concomitantly to its
future. This having-been-ness, understood primarily, precisely does *not*
mean that the Dasein no longer in fact is; just the contrary, the Dasein *is*
precisely in fact what it *was.* That which we *are* as having been has not
gone by, passed away, in the sense in which we say that we could shuffle off
our past like a garment. The Dasein can as little get rid of its *[past as]*
bygoneness as escape its death. In every sense and in every case everything
we have been is an essential determination of our existence. Even if in some
way, by some manipulations, I may be able to keep my bygoneness far from
myself, nevertheless, forgetting, repressing, suppressing are modes in which

I myself am my own having-been-ness. The Dasein, in being, necessarily always has been. It can *be* as having been only as long as it exists. And it is precisely when the Dasein no longer is, that it also no longer has been. It has *been* only so long as it is. This entails that /pastness in the sense of/ having-been-ness belongs to the Dasein's existence. From the viewpoint of the moment of the future, as previously characterized, this means that since the Dasein always comports itself more or less explicitly toward a specific capacity-to-be of its own self, since the Dasein always comes-toward-itself from out of a possibility of itself, it therewith also always *comes-back-to* what it has been. Having-been-ness, the past in the existential sense, belongs with equal originality to the future in the original (existential) sense. In one with the future and the present, /the past as/ having-been-ness first makes existence possible.

The present in the existential sense is not the same as presence or as extantness. The Dasein, in existing, is always dwelling with extant beings, beings that are at hand. It has such beings in its present. Only as enpresenting is the Dasein futural and past /as having-been/ in the particular sense. As expecting a possibility the Dasein is always in such a way that it comports itself enpresentingly toward something at hand and keeps this extant entity as something present in its, the Dasein's, own present. Attendant upon this is the fact that we are most frequently lost in this present and it appears as though future and past as bygoneness or, more precisely, the past as having-been-ness, were blacked out, as though the Dasein were at every moment always leaping into the present. This is an illusion that in its turn has its own causes and requires an explanation which, however, we shall forgo in this context. What alone is important here is to see more or less that we are talking about future, past /having-been-ness/ and present in a more original (existential) sense and are employing these three determinations in a signification that *lies in advance of common time.* The original unity of the future, past, and present which we have portrayed is the phenomenon of original time, which we call *temporality.* Temporality *temporalizes itself* in the ever current unity of future, past /having-been-ness/, and present. What we denominate in this way must be distinguished from then, at-the-time, and now. The latter time-determinations are what they are only by originating in temporality, as temporality expresses itself. Expecting, the future, retaining, the past, and enpresenting, the present—all of these express themselves by means of the now, then, and at-the-time. In expressing itself, temporality temporalizes the only time that the common understanding of time is aware of.

The essence of the future lies in *coming-toward-oneself;* that of the past /having-been-ness/ lies in *going-back-to;* and that of the present in *staying-with, dwelling-with,* that is, being-with. These characters of the *toward, back-*

to, with reveal the basic constitution of temporality. As determined by this toward, back-to, and with, temporality is *outside itself.* Time is carried away within itself as future, past, and present. As future, the Dasein *is carried away to* its past /has-been/ capacity-to-be; as past /having-been/, it *is carried away to* its having-been-ness; and as enpresenting, it *is carried away to* some other being or beings. Temporality as unity of future, past, and present does not carry the Dasein away just at times and occasionally; instead, as *temporality*, it is itself *the original outside-itself*, the ekstatikon. We call this character of carrying-away the *ecstatic character* of time. Time is not carried away merely on occasion in a supplementary and accidental way; rather, future is carried away intrinsically as toward—it is ecstatic. The same holds for past and present. We therefore call future, past, and present the three *ecstases* of temporality; they belong together intrinsically with co-equal originality.

It is important to see this ecstatic character of time in more precise detail. This interconnection can be brought to view in the concrete conscious realization of all sorts of phenomena, but only if the guiding clue is available. The term "ecstatic" has nothing to do with ecstatic states of mind and the like. The common Greek expression ekstatikon means stepping-outside-self. It is affiliated with the term "existence." It is with this ecstatic character that we interpret existence, which, viewed ontologically, is the original unity of being-outside-self that comes-toward-self, comes-back-to-self, and en-presents. In its ecstatic character, temporality is the condition of the constitution of the Dasein's being.

Within itself, original time is outside itself; that is the nature of its temporalizing. It is this outside-itself itself. That is to say, it is not something that might first be extant as a thing and thereafter outside itself, so that it would be leaving itself behind itself. Instead, within its own self, intrinsically, it is nothing but the outside-itself pure and simple. As this ecstatic character is distinctive of temporality, each ecstasis, which temporalizes only in temporalizing unity with the others, contains within its own nature a *carrying-away toward something* in a formal sense. Every such remotion is intrinsically *open.* A peculiar *openness,* which is given with the outside-itself, belongs to ecstasis. That toward which each ecstasis is intrinsically open in a specific way we call the *horizon of the ecstasis.* The horizon is the *open expanse* toward which remotion as such is outside itself. *The carrying-off opens up this horizon and keeps it open.* As ecstatic unity of future, past, and present, temporality has a horizon determined by the ecstases. Temporality, as the original unity of future, past, and present, is *ecstatically-horizonal* intrinsically. "Horizonal" means "characterized by a horizon given with the ecstasis itself." Ecstatic-horizonal temporality makes possible not only the constitution of the Dasein's being, but also the temporalizing of the only time of which the common understanding of time is aware and which we designate generally as the irreversible sequence of nows.

We shall not now enter into further detail regarding the connection between the phenomenon of *intentionality* and that of ecstatic-horizonal temporality. Intentionality—being directed toward something and the intimate connection of intentio and intentum present in it—which is commonly spoken of in phenomenology as the ultimate primal phenomenon, has the condition of its possibility in temporality and temporality's ecstatic-horizonal character. The Dasein is intentional only because it is determined essentially by temporality. The Dasein's essential determination by which it intrinsically *transcends* is likewise connected with the ecstatic-horizonal character. How these two characters, intentionality and transcendence, are interconnected with temporality will become apparent to us. At the same time we shall understand how ontology, by making being its theme, is a transcendental science. But first, since we did not expressly interpret temporality by way of the Dasein, we must make the phenomenon more familiar to ourselves.

δ) The derivation of the structural moments of now-time from ecstatic-horizonal temporality. The mode of being of falling as the reason for the covering up of original time

The conception of time as a now-sequence is not aware of the derivation of this time from original time and overlooks all the essential features belonging to the now-sequence as such. As commonly understood, time is intrinsically a free-floating sequence of nows. It is simply there; its givenness must be acknowledged. Now that we have characterized temporality in a rough way, the question arises whether we can let the now-sequence arise out of original temporality, with explicit reference to the essential structures—significance, datability, spannedness, and publicness. If time temporalizes itself as a now-sequence from out of the original temporality, then *these structures must become intelligible by way of the ecstatic-horizonal constitution of temporality.* What is more, if the temporality in which time temporalizes itself as time-sequence constitutes the Dasein's ontological constitution, and if the factical Dasein experiences and knows time first and primarily only as it is commonly understood, then we should also be able to explain by recourse to the Dasein's temporality *why* factical Dasein knows time primarily only as now-sequence and, further, *why* the common understanding of time either overlooks or does not suitably understand time's essential structural moments of significance, datability, spannedness, and publicness. If it is possible—if indeed it is even necessary—to show that what is commonly known as time springs from what we have characterized as temporality, then this justifies calling that from which common time derives by the name of original time. For the question could then be asked why we still designate the unity of future, past, and present in this original sense as time. Is it not something different? This question is answered in the negative as soon as it is seen that the now, the then, and the at-the-time are nothing but temporality expressing itself. It is only for this reason that the now is a *time* character and that the then and the at-the-time are *temp*oral.

The question now is, How does time in the common sense root in temporality itself—how does time in the common sense derive from temporality or, more precisely, how does temporality itself temporalize the only time that the common understanding knows? Every now is by its nature a now-when. Because of this relation of datability, it is related to some being by reference to which it has its date. This character of being a now-when-this-or-that, the relation of datability, is possible only because the now is ecstatically open as a time-determination, having its source in temporality. The now belongs to a particular ecstasis, the present in the sense of the enpresenting *of* something. In the enpresenting of a being the enpresenting, intrinsically, is related ecstatically to something. In expressing itself as ecstatically related, saying "now" in this self-expression and meaning by the now the present, this ecstatic-horizonal—and thus intrinsically ecstatic— now is *related to...;* each now, qua now, is "now when this or that." The enpresenting of a being lets that being be encountered in such a way that when, expressing itself, the enpresenting says "now," this now, because of the ecstatic character of enpresenting, must have the present-character "now, when this or that." Correspondingly, every at-the-time is an at-the-time-when and every then is a then-when. If I say "now" and express it in an enpresenting and as this enpresenting, then, because of the enpresenting of something, I encounter some being as that by reference to which the expressed now dates itself. Because we enunciate the now in each case in and from an enpresenting of some being, the now that is thus voiced is itself structurally enpresenting. It has the relation of datability, the factual dating always differing in point of content. The now and every other time-determination has its dating relation from the ecstatic character of temporality itself. The fact that the now is always a "now when this or that," every at-the-time an "at-the-time when," and every then a "then when" merely shows that time as temporality—as enpresenting, retaining, and expecting—already lets beings be encountered as uncovered. In other words, time in the common sense, the now as seen via this dating relation, is only the index of original temporality.

Every now and every time-determination is *spanned* within itself, has a range that varies and does not first grow by means of a summation of individual nows as dimensionless points. The now does not acquire a breadth and range by my collecting together a number of nows, but just the reverse: each now already has this spannedness within itself in a primary way. Even if I were to reduce the now to a millionth of a second it would still have a breadth, because it already has it by its very nature and neither gains it by a summation nor loses it by a diminution. The now and every time-determination has a spannedness intrinsically. And this, too, has its basis in the fact that the now is nothing but the "expression," the "speaking out," of original temporality itself in its ecstatic character. Spannedness is spoken concomitantly in every spoken now, because by means of the now and the other time-determinations an enpresenting expresses itself which temporalizes in ecstatic unity with expecting and retaining. A stretchedness which enters into expressed time is already originally present in the ecstatic character of temporality. Since every expecting has the character of coming-toward-self and every retaining the character of back-to, even if in the mode of forgetting, and every coming-toward-self is intrinsically a back-to, temporality qua ecstatic is *stretched out within its own self*. As the primary outside-self, temporality is stretch itself. Stretch does not first result from the fact that I shove the moments of time together but just the reverse: the character of the continuity and spannedness of time in the common sense has its origin in the original stretch of temporality itself as ecstatic.

The now and every other expressed time-determination is *publicly accessible* to the understanding of each Dasein in the Daseins' being-with-one-another. This factor of the publicness of time is also rooted in the ecstatic-horizonal character of temporality. Because temporality is intrinsically the outside-itself, it is as such already intrinsically disclosed and open for itself along the directions of the three ecstases. Therefore each uttered, each expressed, now is immediately known as such to everyone. The now is not the sort of thing that only one or another of us could somehow find out; it is not something about which one of us might perhaps know but another might not; rather, in the Daseins' being-with-one-another itself, in their communal being-in-the-world, there is already present the unity of temporality itself as open for itself.

Because of its character of significance, we called the time of everyday time-understanding *world-time*. We had already indicated earlier that the Dasein's basic constitution is being-in-the-world and in fact being there in such a way that the existent Dasein is occupied in its existence with this being, which means at the same time that it is occupied with its ability to be in the world. The Dasein is occupied with its own most peculiar ability to be or, as we also say, the Dasein in each instance uses itself primarily for its own self. If it expresses itself as enpresenting in the now, expecting in the then, and retaining in the at-the-time—if temporality expresses *itself* in these time-determinations, then expressed time here is simultaneously that *for* which the Dasein uses itself, *for the sake of which* the Dasein itself is. In temporality's self-expression the expressed time is to be understood in the character of the for-the-sake-of and the in-order-to. Expressed time has *in itself the character of world*—which can also be confirmed by means of still other, more difficult connections into which we shall not at present enter. If the Dasein uses itself for itself, and the Dasein's temporality expresses itself in the now, then expressed time is always something with which the Dasein is itself occupied. Time is always time as the right time or the wrong time.

We can see from the elucidation of the structural moments of significance, datability, spannedness, and publicness that and how the basic determinations of time in the common sense arise from the ecstatic-horizonal unity of expecting, retaining, and enpresenting. What we are commonly familiar with as time originates with respect to its time character from ecstatic-horizonal temporality; therefore, that from which the derivative time stems must be called time in a primary sense: the time that temporalizes itself and, as such, temporalizes world-time. If original time qua temporality makes possible the Dasein's ontological constitution, and this being, the Dasein, *is* in such a way that it temporalizes itself, then this being with the mode of being of existent Dasein must be called originally and fitly the *temporal entity simply as such*. It now becomes clear why we do not call a stone temporal, even though it moves or is at rest in time. Its being is not determined by temporality. The Dasein, however, is not merely and not primarily intratemporal, occurring and extant in a world, but is intrinsically temporal in an original, fundamental way. Nevertheless, the Dasein is also in a certain way *in* time, for we can view it in a certain respect as an extant entity.

Now that we have derived the characters of common time from original temporality and have thus demonstrated why we designate the origin as time with a greater legitimacy than that which originates from it, we must ask the following questions. How does it happen that the common understanding of time knows time only as an irreversible sequence of nows; that the essential characters of that sequence—significance and datability—remain concealed from it; and that the structural moments of spannedness and publicness remain ultimately unintelligible to it; so that it conceives of time as a manifold of naked nows which have no further structure but are always merely nows, one following the other from future into past in an infinite succession? The covering up of the specific structural moments of world-time, the covering up of their origination in temporality, and the covering up of temporality itself—all have their ground in that mode of being of the Dasein which we call *falling*. Without going into further detail regarding this phenomenon, we may portray it in terms of what we have already touched on several times. We have seen that the Dasein is always primarily oriented toward beings as extant things, so that it also determines its own being by means of the mode of being of the extant. It also calls the ego, the subject, a res, a substantia, a subjectum. What appears here in a theoretical field of developed ontology is a general determination of the Dasein itself, namely, that it has the tendency to understand itself primarily by way of things and to derive the concept of being from the extant. For common experience what happens is that beings are encountered in time. Aristotle says that time is kineseos ti, something *connected with* motion. But this means that time *is* in a certain way. If the common understanding of time is aware of being only in the sense of extant being, being at hand, then time, being publicly accessible *along with* motion, must necessarily be something extant. As the Dasein encounters time, time gets interpreted also as something somehow extant, particularly if it reveals itself as being in a certain connection precisely with extant nature. In some way or other time is *concomitantly extant,* whether in the objects or in the subjects or everywhere. The time that is known as the now and as a manifold and succession of nows is an *extant sequence.* The nows appear to be intratemporal. They come and go like beings; like extant entities they perish, becoming no longer extant. The common experience of beings has at its disposal no other horizon for understanding being than that of extantness, being at hand. Matters like significance and datability remain a closed book for this way of understanding being. Time becomes the intrinsically free-floating runoff of a sequence of nows. For the common conception of time this process is extant, just as space is. Starting from this view, it arrives at the opinion that time is infinite, endless, whereas by its very nature temporality is finite. Since the common vision of time is directed solely toward the extant and the non-extant in the sense of the not-yet-extant and the no-longer-extant, the nows in their succession remain the sole thing that is relevant for it. Implicit in the Dasein's own mode of being is that it knows the sequence of nows only in this naked form of the nows of sequential juxtaposition. Only on this presupposition, too, is Aristotle's manner of inquiry possible when he asks whether time is something that is or whether it is a non-existent and discusses this question with reference to past and future in the common sense of being-no-longer and being-not-yet. In this question about the being of time, Aristotle understands being in the sense of extantness. If you take being in this sense, then you have to say that the now which is no longer extant in the sense of the bygone now and the now which is not yet extant in the sense of the now yet to come, are not—that is, are not extant. Seen in this way, what *is* in time is only the now that is extant in each now. Aristotle's aporia with reference to the being of time—which is still the principal difficulty today—derives from the concept of being as equal to being extant.

It is from the same direction of thought in the common understanding of time that the universally familiar thesis that time is infinite originates.

Each now has a transitionary character; each now is by its essential nature not-yet and no-longer. In whatever now I may wish to stop, I stand in a not-yet or a no-longer. Each now at which I wished to posit an end, purely in thought, would be misunderstood as now if I wished to cut it off either on the side of the past or on that of the future, because it points beyond itself. If the nature of time is understood in this way, it follows that time must then be conceived as an endless sequence of nows. This endlessness is inferred purely deductively from the isolated concept of the now. And also, the inference to the endlessness of time, which has a legitimate sense within certain limits, is possible only if the now is taken in the sense of the clipped sequence of nows. It can be made clear—as was shown in *Being and Time*—that the endlessness of common time can enter the Dasein's mind only because temporality itself, intrinsically, forgets its own essential finitude. Only because temporality in the authentic sense is finite is inauthentic time in the sense of common time infinite. The infinity of time is not a positive feature of time but a privation which characterizes a negative character of temporality. It is not possible to go into further detail here on the finitude of time, because it is connected with the difficult problem of death, and this is not the place to analyze death in that connection.

We have stressed that the common understanding of time is not expressly aware of the characters of the now, significance, datability, spannedness, and publicness. We must however qualify this statement at least to some degree, since the Aristotelian interpretation of time already shows that, even if time is taken merely as the time we reckon with, certain characters of time come to view. But they cannot be made an explicit problem as long as the common conception of time represents the sole guide to the interpretation of time. Aristotle assigns transitionary character to the now; he defines the time in which we encounter beings as a number that embraces (holds-around) beings; time as counted is referred to a reckoning with it, in which it is unveiled. The determinations of transition, holding-around, and unveiledness are the nearest characters in which time manifests itself as a sequence of nows. Looked at more closely, they point back to the moments we have come to know in a different connection.

The transitionary character belongs to each now because temporality, as ecstatic unity, is stretched out within itself. The ecstatic connection of coming-toward (expecting), in which the Dasein at the same time comes back to itself (retains itself), for the first time provides, in unity with an enpresenting, the condition of the possibility that expressed time, the now, is dimensionally future and past, that each now stretches itself out as such, within itself, with respect to the not-yet and the no-longer. The transitionary character of each now is nothing but what we described as the spannedness of time.

That time should hold-around beings, con-tain them, in such a way that we recognize what it holds as intratemporal, is possible and necessary because of the character of time as world-time. Due to its ecstatic character temporality is, as it were, further outside than any possible object which the Dasein can encounter as temporal. Because of this, any being that the Dasein encounters is already embraced by time from the very outset.

Similarly, the essential countedness of time is rooted in the ecstatic-horizonal constitution of temporality. Time's character as container and as world-time, as well as its essential unveiledness, will emerge still more clearly in what follows.

It should suffice that we now have an approximate view of time as sequence of nows with respect to its derivation from temporality; we can thus recognize that the essential structure of temporality is the self-enclosed ecstatic-horizonal unity of future, past, and present in the sense explained. *Temporality [Zeitlichkeit] is the condition of the possibility of the constitution of the Dasein's being. However, to this constitution there belongs understanding of being,* for the Dasein, as existent, comports itself toward beings which are not Daseins and beings which are. Accordingly, *temporality must also be the condition of possibility of the understanding of being that belongs to the Dasein.* How does temporality make such understanding of being possible? How is time as temporality the horizon for the explicit understanding of being as such, if being is supposed to be the theme of the science of ontology, or scientific philosophy? In its role as condition of possibility of the understanding of being, both pre-ontological and ontological, we shall call temporality *Temporality [Temporalität].*

§20. Temporality [Zeitlichkeit] and Temporality [Temporalität]

What has to be shown is this: temporality is the condition of the possibility of all understanding of being; *being is understood and conceptually comprehended by means of time.* When temporality functions as such a condition we call it Temporality. The understanding of being, the development of this understanding in ontology, and scientific philosophy are to be exhibited in their Temporal possibility. What exactly is the meaning of this *"understanding of being"* into whose Temporal possibility we are inquiring? By the discussion of the four theses we have shown in different ways that and how something like an understanding of being belongs to the existent Dasein. We now stand before or, better, in the fact that we understand being but nevertheless do not conceptually comprehend it.

a) Understanding as a basic determination of being-in-the-world

What is the difference between understanding and conceptual comprehension? What do "to understand" and "understanding" mean at all /as act and as achievement/? It might be said that understanding /as achievement, Verständnis/ is a type of cognition and, correspondingly, understanding /as act, Verstehen/ is a specific type of cognitive comportment. Following Dilthey's precedent, the tendency today is to contrast understanding as a specific kind of knowing with a different kind of knowing, namely, explaining. We shall not enter into this discussion of the relationship between explanation and understanding, avoiding it above all because these discussions suffer from a fundamental defect that makes them unfruitful. The defect is that there is lacking an adequate interpretation of what we understand in general by cognition, of which explanation and understanding are supposed to be "kinds." A whole typology of kinds of cognition can be enumerated and ordinary common sense can be impressed by this, but philosophically it is meaningless as long as it remains unclear what sort of knowing this understanding is supposed to be in distinction from the type of cognition represented by explanation. In whatever way we conceive of knowing, it is, qua that which embraces knowing and understanding in the ordinary conception of it, a *comportment toward beings*—if for the while we can disregard philosophical cognition as a relationship to being. But all practical-technical commerce with beings is also a comportment toward beings. And an understanding of being is also present in practical-technical comportment toward beings so far as we have at all to do with beings as beings. In all comportment toward beings—whether it is specifically cognitive, which is most frequently called theoretical, or whether it is practical-technical—an understanding of being is already involved. For a being can be encountered by us *as* a being only in the light of the understanding of being. If, however, an understanding of being always already lies at the basis of all comportment of the Dasein toward beings, whether nature or history, whether theoretical or practical, then plainly I cannot adequately define the concept of understanding if, in trying to make the definition, I look solely to specific types of cognitive comportment toward beings. Thus what is required is to find a sufficiently original concept of understanding from which alone not only all modes of cognition but every type of comportment that relates to beings by inspection and circumspection can be conceived in a fundamental way.

If there is present an /act of/ *understanding* in the /achieved/ *understanding* of being and this understanding of being is constitutive for the ontological constitution of the Dasein, it follows that the /act of/ *understanding* is an original *determination of the Dasein's existence*, regardless of whether the

Dasein pursues science in the manner of explanation or of understanding. And what is more, in the end understanding is not at all primarily a condition but—since existence is indeed more than mere cognition in the usual spectator sense of knowledge and such knowledge presupposes existence—a basic determination of existence itself. This, in fact, is how we have to take the concept of understanding.

Let us try to delineate this concept without as yet making explicit reference to the understanding involved in the understanding of being. How does understanding belong to the Dasein's existence, apart from whether the Dasein does or does not practise psychology or history as understanding? To exist is essentially, even if not only, to understand. We made some remarks earlier about the essential structure of existence. To the Dasein's existence there belongs being-in-the-world, and in fact in such a way that this being-in-the-world is occupied *with* this being itself. It is *occupied with* this being; this entity, the Dasein, has its own being under control, as it comports itself in this or that way toward its capacity to be, as it has already decided for or against it. "The Dasein is occupied with its own being" means more precisely: it is occupied with its own *ability to be.* As existent, the Dasein is free for specific possibilities of its own self. It is its own most peculiar able-to-be. These possibilities of itself are not empty logical possibilities lying outside itself, in which it can engage or from which it could keep aloof; instead they are, as such, determinations of existence. If the Dasein is free for definite possibilities of itself, for its ability to be, then the Dasein *is* in this *being-free-for;* it *is* these possibilities themselves. They *are* only as possibilities of the existent Dasein in whatever way the Dasein may comport toward them. The possibility is in every instance that of one's own most peculiar being. It is the possibility it is only if the Dasein becomes existent in it. To be one's own most peculiar ability to be, to take it over and keep oneself in the possibility, to understand oneself in one's own factual freedom, that is, *to understand oneself in the being of one's own most peculiar ability-to-be, is the original existential concept of understanding.* In German we say that someone can vorstehen something—literally, stand in front of or ahead of it, that is, stand at its head, administer, manage, preside over it. This is equivalent to saying that he versteht sich darauf, understands in the sense of being skilled or expert at it, has the know-how of it. The meaning of the term "understanding" [Verstehen] as defined above is intended to go back to this usage in ordinary language. If understanding is a basic determination of existence, it is as such the condition of possibility for all of the Dasein's particular possible manners of comportment. It is the condition of possibility for all kinds of comportment, not only practical but also cognitive. The explanatory and understanding sciences—if this classification is admitted as being at all legitimate—are possible only because the Dasein, as existent, is itself an intrinsically understanding entity.

We shall now attempt to clarify the structure of the understanding that is constitutive of existence. To understand means, more precisely, *to project oneself upon a possibility,* in this *projection* to keep oneself at all times in a possibility. A can-be, a possibility *as* possibility, *is there* only in projection, in projecting oneself upon that can-be. If in contrast I merely reflect on some empty possibility into which I could enter and, as it were, just gab about it, then this possibility *is not there,* precisely as possibility; instead for me it is, as we might say, actual. The character of possibility *becomes* manifest and *is* manifest only in projection, so long as the possibility is held fast in the projection. Projection contains two things. First, that *upon which* the Dasein projects itself is a can-be of its own self. The can-be is unveiled primarily in and through the projection, but in such a way that the possibility upon which the Dasein projects itself is not itself apprehended objectively. Secondly, this projection *upon* something is always a projecting *of....* If the Dasein projects itself upon a possibility, it is projecting itself in the sense that it is unveiling itself as this can-be, in this specific being. If the Dasein projects itself upon a possibility and understands itself in that possibility, this understanding, this becoming manifest of the self, is not a self-contemplation in the sense that the ego would become the object of some cognition or other; rather, the projection is the way in which I *am* the possibility; it is the way in which I exist freely. The essential core of understanding as projection is the Dasein's understanding itself existentielly in it.* Since projection unveils without making what is unveiled as such into an object of contemplation, there is present in all understanding an *insight* of the Dasein into itself. However, this insight is not a free-floating knowledge about itself. The knowledge of insight has genuine truth-character, adequately unveiling the existence of the Dasein which is supposed to be unveiled by it, only if it has the primary character of self-understanding. Understanding as the Dasein's self-projection is the Dasein's fundamental mode of *happening.* As we may also say, it is the authentic meaning of action. It is by understanding that the Dasein's happening is characterized—

---

*The term "existentiell"—the standard translation in *Being and Time* for existenziell—is defined by Heidegger in the following way: "Dasein always understands itself in terms of its existence—in terms of a possibility of itself: to be itself or not itself. Dasein has either chosen these possibilities itself, or got itself into them, or grown up in them already. Only the particular Dasein decides its existence, whether it does so by taking hold or by neglecting. The question of existence never gets straightened out except through existing itself. The understanding of oneself which leads along this way we call 'existentiell.'" Trans. Macquarrie and Robinson, *Being and Time,* "The Ontical Priority of the Question of Being," p. 33 (*Sein und Zeit,* p. 12).

its *historicality*. Understanding is not a mode of cognition but the basic determination of existing. We also call it existentiell understanding because in it existence, as the Dasein's happening in its history, temporalizes itself. The Dasein becomes what it is in and through this understanding; and it is always only that which it has chosen itself to be, that which it understands itself to be in the projection of its own most peculiar ability-to-be.

This must suffice as a sketch of the concept of understanding in its constitutive character for the Dasein's existence. The following task now arises: (1) *by starting from temporality, to elucidate this understanding, in its possibility,* so far as it constitutes existence, and at the same time (2) to set it off from the understanding which we describe in the narrower sense as the understanding-of-being in general. The Dasein projects upon its possibilities the understanding belonging to existence. Because the Dasein is essentially being-in-the-world, projection unveils in every instance a possibility of being-in-the-world. In its function of unveiling, understanding is not related to an isolated punctual ego but to factically existent being-able-to-be-in-the-world. This entails that along with understanding there is always already projected a *particular possible being with the others* and a *particular possible being toward intraworldly beings.* Because being-in-the-world belongs to the basic constitution of the Dasein, the existent Dasein is essentially *being-with* others *as being-among* intraworldly beings. As being-in-the-world it is never first merely being among things extant within the world, then subsequently to uncover other human beings as also being among them. Instead, as being-in-the-world it is being with others, apart from whether and how others are factically there with it themselves. On the other hand, however, the Dasein is also not first merely being-with others, only then later to run up against intraworldly things in its being-with-others; instead, being-with-others means being-with other being-in-the-world—being-with-in-the-world. It is wrong to oppose to objects an isolated ego-subject, without seeing in the Dasein the basic constitution of being-in-the-world; but it is equally wrong to suppose that the problem is seen in principle and progress made toward answering it if the solipsism of the isolated ego is replaced by a solipsism en deux in the I-thou relationship. As a relationship between Dasein and Dasein this has its possibility only on the basis of being-in-the-world. Put otherwise, being-in-the-world is with equal originality both being-with and being-among. Quite different from this is the problem as to how the correlative Dasein of the thou is relevant for each of the individual, factically ontical-existentiell possibilities of the individual Dasein. But these are questions of concrete anthropology.[1]

---

1. As to what the a priori of this presupposition is, cf. *Sein und Zeit*, div. 1, chap. 4. ["Being-in-the-world as being-with and being-one's-self. The 'They.'"]

In self-understanding there is understood the being-in-the-world with which specific possibilities of being-with others and of dealing with intra-worldly beings are traced out. In self-understanding as being-able-to-be-in-the-world, *world* is understood with equal originality. Because by its concept understanding is free self-understanding by way of an apprehended possibility of one's own factical being-in-the-world, it has the intrinsic possibility of shifting in various directions. This means that the factical Dasein can understand itself primarily via intraworldly beings which it encounters. It can let its existence be determined primarily not by itself but by things and circumstances and by the others. It is the understanding that we call *inauthentic understanding*, which we described earlier and which now becomes clarified by the fundamental concept of understanding. "Inauthentic" does not mean here that it is not an actual understanding; it denotes an understanding in which the existent Dasein does not understand itself primarily by that apprehended possibility of itself which is most peculiarly its own. Or again, projection can be accomplished primarily from the freedom of our own most peculiar Dasein and back into it, as authentic understanding. These free possibilities involved in understanding itself are not to be pursued here any further.

b) Existentiell understanding, understanding of being, projection of being

We may keep in mind, then, that understanding, as the projection which has been protrayed, is a basic determination of the Dasein's existence. It relates to the Dasein itself, hence to a being, and is therefore an ontical understanding. Because it is related to existence, we call it existentiell understanding. But since in this existentiell understanding the Dasein, as a being, is projected upon its ability-to-be, being in the sense of existence is understood in it. An understanding of the being of existence in general is enclosed in every existentiell understanding. Now the Dasein is being-in-the-world and, in equal originality with its facticity, a *world is disclosed and other Daseins are disclosed with it and intraworldly beings are encountered;* consequently, *the Dasein understands, in equal originality with its understanding of existence, the existence of other Daseins* and *the being of intraworldly beings.* At first, however, the understanding of the being of the Dasein and of things extant is not divided and articulated into specific modes of being and it is not comprehended as such. *Existence, being extant or at hand, being handy, being the fellow-Dasein of others*—these are not conceptually comprehended each in its own sense of being, but instead they are understood *indifferently in an understanding of being* that makes possible and guides both the experience of nature and the self-apprehension of the history of being-with-one-another. In existentiell understanding, in which factical being-in-the-world becomes visible and transparent, there is always already present an understanding of being which relates not only to the Dasein itself but also to all beings which are unveiled fundamentally with being-in-the-world. *In it there is present an understanding* which, *as projection,* not only understands beings by way of being but, since being itself is understood, *has also in some way projected being as such.*

In our analysis of the structure of ontical understanding we came across a stratification of projections present in it itself and making it possible. The projections are, as it were, inserted in front of one another. "Stratification" is admittedly a tricky image. We shall see that there can be no talk of unilinear interlacing stratification of projections in which one determines the others. In *existentiell understanding* one's own Dasein is first experienced as something that is, a being, and in that process being is understood. If we say that being is understood in the existentiell understanding of the Dasein and if we note that understanding is a projecting, then in the *understanding of being* there is present a further projection: being is understood only as, on its own part, it is *projected upon something.* What it is projected upon remains at first obscure. It can then be said that this projection, the understanding of being in experiencing beings, is on its own part, as understanding, projected upon something which at first is still in question. We understand a being only as we project it upon being. In the process, being itself must be understood in a certain way; being must in its turn be projected upon something. We shall not now touch on the question that arises here, whether this recursion from one projection to the next does not open up a progressus in infinitum. At present we are in search only of the *connection between* the *experiencing of a being,* the *understanding of being,* and the *projection upon…* *which in its turn is present in the understanding of being.* It is enough that we see the distinction between the existentiell understanding of Dasein as a being and the understanding of being, which qua understanding of being must itself, in conformity with its character as projection, project being upon something. At first we can understand only indirectly that upon which being, if and when it is understood, must be disclosed. But we may not flinch from it, so long as we take seriously the facticity of our own existence and our being-with other Dasein and see that and how we understand world, the intraworldly, existence, and co-existent Dasein in its being. If Dasein harbors the understanding of being within itself, and if temporality makes possible the Dasein in its ontological constitution, then *temporality* must also be the *condition of the possibility* of the *understanding of being* and hence of the *projection of being upon time.* The question is whether time is indeed that upon which being is itself projected—whether time is that by way of which we understand the like of being.

In order to ward off a fatal misunderstanding, we need a brief digression. Our aim is to give a fundamental clarification of the possibility of the understanding of being in general. With regard to the Dasein's comportment toward beings, our interpretation of the understanding of being in general has presented only a necessary but not a sufficient condition. For I can comport toward beings only if those beings can themselves be encountered in the brightness of the understanding of being. This is the necessary condition. In terms of fundamental ontology it can also be expressed by saying that all understanding is essentially related to an affective self-finding which belongs to understanding itself.[2] To be affectively self-finding is the formal structure of what we call mood, passion, affect, and the like, which are constitutive for all comportment toward beings, although they do not by themselves alone make such comportment possible but always only in one with understanding, which gives its light to each mood, each passion, each affect. Being itself, if indeed we understand it, must somehow or other be projected upon something. This does not mean that in this projection being must be objectively apprehended or interpreted and defined, conceptually comprehended, as something objectively apprehended. Being is projected upon something from which it becomes understandable, but in an *unobjective* way. It is understood as yet pre-conceptually, without a logos; we therefore call it *the pre-ontological understanding of being*. Pre-ontological understanding of being is a kind of understanding of being. It coincides so little with the ontical experience of beings that ontical experience necessarily presupposes a pre-ontological understanding of being as an essential condition. The experience of beings does not have any explicit ontology as a constituent, but, on the other hand, the understanding of being in general in the pre-conceptual sense is certainly the condition of possibility that being should be objectified, thematized at all. It is in the objectification of being as such that the basic act constitutive of ontology as a science is performed. The essential feature in every science, philosophy included, is that it constitutes itself in the objectification of something already in some way unveiled, antecedently given. What is given can be a being that lies present before us, but it can also be being itself in the pre-ontological understanding of being. The way in which being is given is fundamentally different from the way beings are given, but both can certainly become objects. They can become objects, however, only if they are unveiled in some way *before* the objectification and *for* it. On the other hand, if something becomes an object, and in fact just as it offers itself in its own self, this objectification does not signify a subjective apprehension and re-interpretation of what is laid hold of as object. The basic act of objectification, whether of being or

---

2. Cf. *Sein und Zeit,* §29 ff.

of beings—and regardless of the fundamental diversity in the two cases—has the function of *explicitly* projecting what is antecedently given upon that on which it has *already* been projected in pre-scientific experience or understanding. If being is to become objectified—if the understanding of being is to be possible as a science in the sense of ontology—if there is to be philosophy at all, then that upon which the understanding of being, qua understanding, has already pre-conceptually projected being must become unveiled in an explicit projection.

We confront the task not only of going forth and back from a being to its being but, if we are inquiring into the condition of possibility of the understanding of being as such, *of inquiring even beyond being as to that upon which being itself, as being, is projected.* This seems to be a curious enterprise, to inquire beyond being; perhaps it has arisen from the fatal embarrassment that the problems have emanated from philosophy; it is apparently merely the despairing attempt of philosophy to assert itself as over against the so-called facts.

At the beginning of this course we stressed that the more fundamentally the simplest problems of philosophy are posed, without any of the vanities of the allegedly more advanced moderns and without the host of secondary questions arbitrarily snatched up by the mania for criticism, the more immediately will we stand by ourselves in direct communication with actual philosophizing. We have seen from various angles that the question about being in general is indeed no longer explicitly raised but that it everywhere demands to be raised. If we pose the question again, then we understand at the same time that philosophy has not made any further progress with its cardinal question than it had already in Plato and that in the end its innermost longing is not so much to get on further with it, which would be to move further away from itself, as rather *to come to itself.* In Hegel, philosophy—that is, ancient philosophy—is in a certain sense thought through to its end. He was completely in the right when he himself expressed this consciousness. But there exists just as much the legitimate demand to start anew, to understand the finiteness of the Hegelian system and to see that Hegel himself has come to an end with philosophy because he moves in the circle of philosophical problems. This circling in the circle forbids him to move back to the center of the circle and to revise it from the ground up. It is not necessary to seek another circle beyond the circle. Hegel saw everything that is possible. But the question is whether he saw it from the radical center of philosophy, whether he exhausted all the possibilities of the beginning so as to say that he is at the end. No extensive demonstration is needed to make clear how immediately, in our attempt to get beyond being to the light from which and in which it itself comes into the brightness of an understanding, we are moving within one of Plato's fundamental problems. There is no occasion here to delineate the Platonic order of inquiry in further detail. But a rough reference to it is necessary so that the view may be progressively dispelled that our fundamental-ontological problem, the question about the possibility of the understanding of being in general, is simply an accidental, eccentric, and trivial rumination.

At the end of the sixth book of the *Republic,* in a context that cannot occupy us in further detail here, Plato gives a division of the different realms of beings, with particular regard to the possible modes of access to them. He distinguishes the two realms of the horaton and the noeton, things visible to the eyes and things thinkable. The visible is that which is unveiled by sense, the thinkable that which understanding or reason perceives. For seeing with the eyes there is required not only eyes and not only the being that is seen but a third, phos, light, or, more precisely, the sun, helios. The eye can unveil only in the light. All unveiling requires an antecedent illu-mining. The eye must be helioeides. Goethe translates this by "sonnenhaft" /like, of the type of, the sun/. The eye sees only in the light of something. Correspondingly, all non-sensible cognition—all the sciences and in partic-ular all philosophical knowledge—can unveil being only if it has being's *specific illumination*—if the noeisthai also gains its own specific phos, its light. What sunlight is for sensuous vision the idea tou agathou, the idea of the good, is for scientific thinking, and in particular for philosophical knowledge. At first this sounds obscure and unintelligible; how should the idea of the good have a function for knowledge corresponding to that which the light of the sun has for sense perception? As sensible cognition is helioeides, so correspondingly all gignoskein, all cognition, is agathoeides, determined by the idea of the agathon. We have no expression for "deter-mined by the idea of the good" which would correspond to the expression "sunlike." But the correspondence goes even further: Ton helion tois ho-romenois ou monon oimai ten tou horasthai dunamin parechein pheseis, alla kai ten genesin kai auxen kai trophen, ou genesin auton onta.[3] "You will, I believe, also say, the sun furnishes to the seen not only the possibility of being seen, but gives to the seen, as beings, also becoming, growth, and nurture, without itself [the sun] being a becoming." This extended deter-mination is correspondingly applied to knowledge. Plato says: Kai tois gignoskomenois toinun me monon to gignoskesthai phanai hupo tou agathou pareinai, alla kai to einai te kai ten ousian hup' ekeinou autois proseinai, ouk ousias ontos tou agathou, all' eti epekeina tes ousias presbeia kai dunamei huperechontos.[4] "So then you must also say that the known

---

3. Plato (Burnet), *Republic,* 6.509^b2-^b4. [*Politeia,* in *Platonis opera,* ed. John Burnet, vol. 4 (Oxford: Clarendon Press, 1899).]

4. Ibid., 509^b6-^b10.

not only receives its being known from a good, but also it has from thence *that* it is and *what* it is, in such a way indeed that the good is not itself the being-how and being-what, but even outstrips being in dignity and power." That which illuminates the knowledge of beings (positive science) and the knowledge of being (philosophical knowledge) as unveiling lies even beyond being. Only if we stand in this light do we cognize beings and understand being. The understanding of being is rooted in the projection of an epekeina tes ousias. Plato thus comes upon something that he describes as outstripping being, going beyond being. This has the function of light, of illumination, for all unveiling of beings or, in this case, illumination for the understanding of being itself.

The basic condition for the knowledge of beings as well as for the understanding of being is: standing in an illuminating light. Or, to express it without an image: something upon which, in understanding, we have projected that which is to be understood. Understanding must itself *somehow see, as unveiled, that upon which it projects.* The basic facts of the antecedent illumination for all unveiling are so fundamental that it is always only with the possibility of being able to see into the light, to see in the light, that the corresponding possibility of knowing something as actual is assured. We must not only understand actuality in order to be able to experience something actual, but the understanding of actuality must on its side already have its illuminating beforehand. The understanding of being already moves in a *horizon* that is everywhere *illuminated, giving luminous brightness.* It is not an accident that Plato, or Socrates in the dialogue, explains the context to Glaucon by a simile. The fact that Plato reaches for a simile when he comes to the extreme boundary of philosophical inquiry, the beginning and end of philosophy, is no accident. And the content of the simile, especially, is not accidental. It is the simile of the cave, which Plato interprets at the beginning of the seventh book of the *Republic*. Man's existence, living on the disk of earth arched over by the sky, is like a life in the cave. All vision needs light, although the light is not itself seen. The Dasein's coming into the light means its attainment of the understanding of truth in general. The understanding of truth is the condition of possibility for scope and access to the actual. We must here relinquish the idea of interpreting in all its dimensions this inexhaustible simile.

Plato describes a cave in which humans have their hands, feet, and heads fettered, with their eyes turned to the cave's wall. Behind them there is a small exit from the cave, through which light falls into the cave in back of its inhabitants, so that their own shadows necessarily fall on the wall lying opposite them. Fettered and bound firmly so that they can only look ahead of them, they see only their own shadows on the wall. Behind them, between them and the light, there is a path with a partition, like the partitions puppeteers have. On this path other humans, behind the prisoners, carry past all sorts of implements such as are used in everyday life. These objects throw their own shadows and are visible as moving objects on the opposite wall. The prisoners discuss among themselves what they see on the wall. What they see there is for them the world, actual beings. Suppose one of the prisoners is released, so that he can turn around and look into the light, and even move out of the cave and walk toward the light itself; he will first be dazzled and will only slowly become accustomed to the light and see the things that stand outside the cave in the light. Let us now assume that, with the sun in his eyes, he returns to the cave and converses once again with those who are sitting in the cave. The cave dwellers will take him to be mad; they would like to kill him because he wants to persuade them that the objects they see and have deemed to be real throughout their lives are only shadows. Plato wants to show by this that the condition for the possibility of recognizing something as a shadow in distinction from the real does not consist in my seeing an enormous quantity of given things. If the cave dwellers were to see more clearly for all eternity only what they now see on the wall, they would never gain the insight that it is only shadows. The basic condition for the possibility of understanding the actual *as* actual is to look into the sun, so that the eye of knowledge should become sunlike. Ordinary common sense, in the cave of its know-it-all, wiseacre pretensions, is narrow-minded; it has to be extricated from this cave. For it, what it is released to is, as Hegel says, die verkehrte Welt—the inverted, topsy-turvy world. We, too, with this apparently quite abstract question about the conditions of the possibility of the understanding of being, want to do nothing but bring ourselves out of the cave into the light, but in all sobriety and in the complete disenchantment of purely objective inquiry.

What we are in search of is the epekeina tes ousias. For Plato this epekeina is the condition of possibility for all knowledge. Plato says, first, that the agathon or the idea agathou is en to gnosto teleutaia he tou agathou idea kai mogis horasthai;[5] in knowledge or in the knowable and intelligible, and in general in the whole sphere of that which is in any way accessible to us, the idea of the good is that which lies at the end, toward which all cognition runs back or, conversely, from which it begins. The agathon is mogis horasthai, hardly to be seen. Secondly, Plato says of the agathon: en te noeto aute kuria aletheian kai noun paraschomene.[6] It is that which has dominion in the knowable and renders knowledge and truth possible. It thus becomes clear how the epekeina tes ousias is that which has to be inquired after, if indeed being is to be the object for knowledge. How the epekeina must be

---

5. Ibid., 7.517^{b}8 f.
6. Ibid., 517^{c}3 f.

defined, what the "beyond" means, what the idea of the good signifies in Plato and in what way the idea of the good is that which is supposed to render knowledge and truth possible—all this is in many respects obscure. We shall not enter here into the difficulties of Platonic interpretation nor into the demonstration of the connection of the idea of the good with what we discussed earlier regarding the ancient understanding of being, its derivation from production. It appears as though our thesis that ancient philosophy interprets being in the horizon of production in the broadest sense would have no connection at all with what Plato notes as condition of possibility of the understanding of being. Our interpretation of ancient ontology and its guiding clue seems to be arbitrary. What could the idea of the good have to do with production? Without entering further into this matter, we offer only the hint that the idea agathou is nothing but the demiourgos, the producer pure and simple. This lets us see already how the idea agathou is connected with poiein, praxis, techne in the broadest sense.

c) The temporal interpretation of existentiell understanding, both authentic and inauthentic

The question about the possibility of the understanding of being runs into something that transcends being, a *beyond*. As to what makes understanding of being possible, we shall find it without an image only if we first ask: *What makes understanding possible as such?* One essential moment of understanding is projection: understanding itself belongs to the basic constitution of the Dasein. We shall inquire further into this phenomenon and its possibility, and to this end we may also recall something noted earlier. Understanding belongs to the basic constitution of the Dasein; but the Dasein is rooted in temporality. How is temporality the condition of possibility for understanding in general? How is *projection grounded in temporality?* In what way is temporality the condition of possibility for the understanding of being? Do we in fact understand the being of beings by means of time? We shall attempt, first of all, a temporal interpretation of understanding, taking understanding as ontical, existentiell understanding and not yet as understanding of being. We shall then inquire further how our existent comportment toward beings, toward the extant in the wider sense, is grounded as understanding in temporality, and how, further back beyond that, the understanding of being that belongs to this existent comportment toward beings is conditioned on its part by time. Is the possibility and structure of the distinction between being and beings grounded in temporality? Must the ontological difference be interpreted Temporally?

How is existentiell understanding determined by temporality? We heard earlier that temporality is the equally original ecstatic-horizonal unity of future, past, and present. Understanding is a basic determination of existence. And *resoluteness* is our name for authentic existence, the existence of the Dasein in which the Dasein is itself in and from its own most peculiar possibility, a possibility that has been seized on and chosen by the Dasein itself. Resoluteness has its own peculiar temporality. Let us try to demonstrate it briefly now, though only in a specific respect, which however is certainly very essential. If authentic existence, resoluteness, is grounded in a specific mode of temporality, then a specific present belongs to resoluteness. Present, an ecstatic-horizonal phenomenon, implies enpresenting of.... In resoluteness the Dasein understands itself from its own most peculiar can-be. Understanding is primarily futural, for it comes toward itself from its chosen possibility of itself. In coming-toward-itself the Dasein has also already taken itself over as the being that it in each case already has been. In resoluteness, that is, in self-understanding via its own most peculiar can-be—in this coming-toward-itself from its own most peculiar possibility, the Dasein comes back to that which it is and takes itself over as the being that it is. In coming back to itself, it *brings* itself with everything that it is *back again* into its own most peculiar chosen can-be. The temporal mode in which it is as and what it *was* we call /bringing-back-again, that is,/ *repetition*. Repetition is a peculiar mode in which the Dasein *was, has been*. Resoluteness temporalizes itself as repetitive coming-back-toward-itself from a chosen possibility to which the Dasein, coming-toward-itself, *has run out in front of itself* /preceded itself/. In the ecstatic unity of *repetitive self-precedence*, in this past and future, there lies a specific present. Whereas the enpresenting of something for the most part and chiefly dwells with things, gets entangled in its own self, lets itself be drawn along by things so as to be merged with what it is enpresenting—whereas enpresenting for the most part runs away from itself, loses itself within itself, so that the past becomes a forgetting and the future an expecting of what is just coming on—the present that belongs to resoluteness is *held* in the specific future (self-precedence) and past (repetition). The present that is held in resoluteness and springs from it we call the *instant*. Since we intend by this name a mode of the present—the phenomenon indicated by it has ecstatic-horizonal character—this means that the instant is *an enpresenting* of something present which, as belonging to projection, discloses the situation upon which resoluteness has resolved. In the instant as an ecstasis the existent Dasein is carried away, as resolved, into the current factically determined possibilities, circumstances, contingencies of the situation of its action. The instant /the Augenblick, the twinkling of an eye/ is that which, arising from resoluteness, has an eye first of all and solely for what constitutes the situation of action. It is the mode of resolute existence in which the Dasein, as being-in-the-world, holds and keeps its world in view. But because the Dasein, as being-in-the-world, is at the same time being-with other Daseins, authentically existent being-with-one-another must also determine itself primarily by way of the individual's resoluteness. Only from and in its resolute individuation is the Dasein authentically free and open for the thou. Being-with-one-another is not a tenacious intrusion of the I upon the thou, derived from their common concealed helplessness; instead, existence as together and with one another is founded on the genuine individuation of the individual, determined by enpresenting in the sense of the instant. Individuation does not mean clinging obstinately to one's own private wishes but being free for the factical possibilities of current existence.

From what has been said one thing should become clear, that the instant belongs to the Dasein's original and authentic temporality and represents the primary and authentic mode of the present as enpresenting. We heard earlier that enpresenting expresses itself in the now, that the now as time in which beings are encountered arises from original temporality. Since the now always arises from the present, this means that the now originates from, comes from, the instant. It is for this reason that the phenomenon of the instant cannot be understood from the now, as Kierkegaard tries to do. To be sure, he understands the instant quite well in its real contents, but he does not succeed in expounding the specific temporality of the instant. Instead, he identifies the instant with the now of time in the common sense. Starting from here he constructs the paradoxical relationships of the now to eternity. But the phenomenon of the instant cannot be understood from the now even if we take the now in its full structure. The only thing that can be shown is that the now most expeditiously manifests its full structure precisely where the Dasein as resolute enpresenting expresses itself by means of the now. The instant is an original phenomenon of original temporality, whereas the now is merely a phenomenon of derivative time. Aristotle saw the phenomenon of the instant, the kairos, and he defined it in the sixth book of his *Nichomachean Ethics;* but, again, he did it in such a way that he failed to bring the specific time character of the kairos into connection with what he otherwise knows as time (nun).

The present pertinent to the Dasein's temporality does not constantly have the character of the instant. The Dasein does not constantly exist as resolute but is usually irresolute, closed off to itself in its own most peculiar ability to be, and not determined primarily from its most peculiar ability to be in the way it projects its possibilities. The Dasein's temporality does not constantly temporalize itself from that temporality's authentic future. Nevertheless, this inconstancy of existence, its being generally irresolute, does not mean that in its existence the irresolute Dasein at times lacks a future. It only means that temporality itself, with respect to its different ecstases, especially the future, is changeable. Irresolute existence is so little a non-existence that it is precisely this irresoluteness which characterizes the everyday actuality of the Dasein.

Because we are trying to expound existent comportment in the everyday sense toward the beings most proximately given, we must turn our view upon everyday, inauthentic, irresolute existence and ask what the character is of the *temporality of inauthentic self-understanding,* of the Dasein's irresolute projection of itself upon possibilities. We know that the Dasein is being-in-the-world; factically existing as such, it is being-among intraworldly beings and being-with-other Daseins. The Dasein understands itself at first and usually from things. The others, the fellow humans, are also there with the Dasein even when they are not to be found there in immediately tangible proximity. In the way they are there with the Dasein they are also jointly understood with it via things. Let us recall Rilke's description in which he shows how the inhabitants of the demolished house, those fellow humans, are encountered with its wall. The fellow humans with whom we have to do daily are also there, even without any explicit existentiell relation of one Dasein to others. Keeping all of this in mind, we may now turn our exploratory regard solely to *understanding comportment toward things handy and things extant.*

We understand ourselves by way of things, in the sense of the self-understanding of everyday Dasein. To understand ourselves from the things with which we are occupied means to project our own ability to be upon such features of the business of our everyday occupation as the feasible, urgent, indispensable, expedient. The Dasein understands itself from the ability to be that is determined by the success and failure, the feasibility and unfeasibility, of its commerce with things. The Dasein thus comes toward itself from out of the things. It expects its own can-be as the can-be of a being which relies on what things give or what they refuse. It is as though the Dasein's can-be were projected by the things, by the Dasein's commerce with them, and not primarily by the Dasein itself from its own most peculiar self, which nevertheless exists, just as it is, always as dealing with things. This inauthentic self-understanding by way of things has, indeed, the character of coming-toward-itself, of the future, but this is *inauthentic future;* we characterize it as *expecting [Gewärtigen].* Only because the Dasein is expectant of its can-be in the sense described, as coming from the things it attends to and cares for—only because of this expecting can it anticipate, *await* something fom the things or wait for the way they run off. Expecting must *already beforehand have unveiled a sphere* from which something can be awaited. Expecting is thus not a subspecies of waiting for or anticipating but just the reverse: waiting for, anticipating, is grounded in an expecting, a looking-forward-to. When in our commerce with things we lose ourselves in and with them, we are expectant of our can-be in the way it is determined via the feasibility and unfeasibility of the things with which we are concerned. We do not expressly come back to ourselves in an authentic projection upon our own most peculiar can-be. This implies at the same time that we do not repeat the being we have been, we do not take ourselves over in our facticity. What we are—and what we have been is always contained in this—lies in some way behind us, *forgotten*. Expecting our own can-be to come from things, we have forgotten the factical Dasein in its having-been. This forgetting is not the absence and failure to appear of a recollection, so that in the place of a recollection there would be nothing. It is, rather, a peculiar positively ecstatic mode of temporality. The ecstasis of forgetting something has the character of disengagement from one's most peculiar having-been-ness, and indeed in such a way that the disengaging-from closes off that from which it disengages. Forgetting, in closing off the past—and this is the peculiar feature of that ecstasis—closes itself off for itself. The characteristic of forgetting is that it forgets itself. It is implicit in the ecstatic nature of forgetting that it not only forgets the forgotten but forgets the forgetting itself. This is why to the common pre-phenomenological understanding it appears as though forgetting is nothing at all. Forgottenness is an elementary mode of temporality in which we *are* primarily and for the most part our own having-been. But this shows that the past, in the sense of having-been-ness, must not be defined in terms of the common concept of the bygone. The bygone is that of which we say that it no longer is. Having-been-ness, however, is a mode of being, the determination of the way in which the Dasein is as existent. A thing that is not temporal, whose being is not determined by means of temporality, but merely occurs within time, can never have-been, because it does not exist. Only what is intrinsically futural can have-been; things, at best, are over and done with. Understanding oneself by way of feasible and directly encountered things involves a *self*-forgetting. The possibility of retaining something which one was just now expecting rests only on the basis of the original forgottenness that belongs to the factical Dasein. To this *retaining* related to things there corresponds again a non-retaining, a *forgetting in the derivative sense*. It becomes clear from this that *recollection* is possible only on the basis of and because of the original forgottenness that belongs to the Dasein and not conversely. Because the Dasein is expectant of itself by way of the feasible, that with which it is dealing at the moment is in its present. Self-understanding, in equal originality with future and past, is an *enpresenting*. The enpresenting of the inauthentic understanding that predominates in the Dasein will occupy us more particularly in the sequel. Negatively, it must be said that the present of inauthentic understanding does not have the character of the instant, because the temporalizing of this mode of the present is determined by way of the inauthentic future. Accordingly, inauthentic understanding has the character of *forgetful-enpresenting-expectance.*

d) The temporality of the understanding of functionality and its totality (world)

This temporal characterization of inauthentic understanding has clarified only one possibility of the Dasein's existentiell (ontical) understanding as the existent being. We require, however, a clarification of the understanding of being which is always already implicit in the existentiell understanding of beings. But we do not wish to explain the understanding of being in regard to existentiell understanding, whether authentic or inauthentic, but rather with a view to the Dasein's existent comportment toward the things it encounters in its immediate neighborhood. We shall try to *clarify the understanding of being* which relates to *beings which are not of the nature of Dasein.* It is the understanding of the being of those beings we encounter nearest to us with which we deal irresolutely, beings which are also there when we are not occupied with them. We are taking this direction of interpretation not because it is easier but because we shall thus gain an original understanding of the problems we discussed earlier, all of which are oriented toward beings as extant.

Let us once more take note of the whole context of the problem and the direction of our inquiry. What we are seeking is the *condition of the possibility of that understanding-of-being which understands beings of the type of the handy and the at-hand.* Beings of these kinds are encountered as we deal with them in our everyday concerns. This commerce with the beings we most immediately encounter is, as existent comportment of the Dasein toward beings, founded in the basic constitution of existence, in being-in-the-world. The beings with which we are occupied are therefore encountered as intra-worldly beings. Since the Dasein is being-in-the-world and the basic constitution of the Dasein lies in temporality, *commerce with intraworldly beings is grounded in a specific temporality of being-in-the-world.* The structure of being-in-the-world is unitary but it is also organized. Our object here must be to understand via temporality the organized totality of this structure, which means, however, that we must interpret the phenomenon of being-in as such and the phenomenon of the world in their temporal constitution. This will lead us to the connection between temporality and transcendence, since being-in-the-world is the phenomenon in which it becomes originally manifest how the Dasein by its very nature is "beyond itself." Starting from this transcendence, we comprehend the possibility of the understanding of being that is implicit in and illuminates our commerce with intraworldly

beings. This then leads to the question of the interrelations of the understanding of being, transcendence, and temporality. And from that point we
shall attempt to portray temporality as horizon of the understanding of
being. That is, we shall attempt the definition of the concept of Temporality.

In returning now to inquire about the condition of the possibility of
understanding being—an understanding that belongs to our commerce
with the beings we encounter—we shall ask first about the *condition of
possibility of being-in-the-world in general,* which is based on *temporality.* It is
only from the temporality of being-in-the-world that we shall understand
how being-in-the-world is already, as such, understanding of being. The
being most nearly encountered, that with which we have to do, has the
ontological constitution of *equipment.* This entity is not merely extant but,
in conformity with its equipmental character, belongs to an equipmental
contexture within which it has its specific equipmental function, which primarily constitutes its being. Equipment, taken in this ontological sense, is
not only equipment for writing or sewing; it includes everything we make
use of domestically or in public life. In this broad ontological sense bridges,
streets, street lamps are also items of equipment. We call the whole of all
these beings the *handy [*das *Zuhandene].* What is essential in this connection
is not whether or not the handy is in nearest proximity, whether it is closer
by than purely extant, at-hand things, but only that it is handy in and for
daily use or that, looked at conversely, in its factical being-in-the-world the
Dasein is well practised in a specific way in handling this being, in such a
way that it understands this being as something of its own making. In the
use of equipment the Dasein is also always already being-with others, and
here it is completely indifferent whether another Dasein is or is not factually
present.

Equipment is encountered always within an equipmental contexture.
Each single piece of equipment carries this contexture along with it, and it
is *this* equipment only with regard to that contexture. The specific *thisness*
of a piece of equipment, its *individuation,* if we take the word in a completely
formal sense, is not determined primarily by space and time in the sense
that it appears in a determinate space- and time-position. Instead, what
determines a piece of equipment as an individual is its equipmental character
and equipmental contexture. What then is it that constitutes the specific
equipmental character of a piece of equipment? Equipmental character is
constituted by what we call *Bewandtnis, functionality.* The being of something
we use, for instance, a hammer or a door, is characterized by a specific way
of being put to use, of functioning. This entity is "in order to hammer," "in
order to make leaving, entering, and closing possible." Equipment is "in
order to." This proposition has an ontological and not merely an ontical
meaning; a being is not what and how it is, for example, a hammer, and

then in addition something "with which to hammer." Rather, what and how it is as this entity, its *whatness* and *howness,* is constituted by this in-order-to as such, by its functionality. A being of the nature of equipment is thus encountered as the being that it *is in itself* if and when we understand beforehand the following: functionality, functionality relations, functionality totality. In dealing with equipment we can use it as equipment only if we have already beforehand *projected this entity upon functionality relation.* This antecedent understanding of functionality, this projecting of equipment onto its functionality character, we call *letting-function.* This expression, too, has its ontological sense suited to the present context of discourse. *In* hammering we let the hammer function *with* something. The *wherein* of our letting-function is that *for which* the equipment is destined as such; the for-which characterizes this specific equipment as what and how it is. We are *expectant of the for-which* in using the equipment. "To let function in something" means expectance of a for-which. Letting-function, as letting-function-*in,* is always at the same time a "letting-function *with* something." That with which there is functionality is in each case determined via the for-which. *Expecting* the for-which, we *retain* the *with-which* in our view; keeping it in view, we first understand the equipment as equipment in its specific functionality relation. Letting-function, that is, the understanding of the functionality which makes possible an equipmental use at all, is a retentive expectance, in which the equipment is *enpresented* as this specific equipment. In expectant-retentive enpresenting, the equipment comes into play, becomes present, enters into a present *[Gegen-wart].* The expecting of the for-which is not a contemplation of an end and much less the awaiting of a result. Expectance does not at all have the character of an ontical apprehension; nor is retention of the wherewith a contemplative dwelling with something. This becomes clear if we bring to conscious realization unconstructively an immediate employment of equipment. When I am completely engrossed in dealing with something and make use of some equipment in this activity, I am just not directed toward the equipment as such, say, toward the tool. And I am just as little directed toward the work itself. Instead, in my occupation I move *in* the functionality relations as such. In understanding them I dwell with the equipmental contexture that is handy. I stand neither with the one nor with the other but move in the in-order-to. It is for this reason that we proceed *in order* in dealing with things—we do not merely approach them as they lie before us but have ordered *com*merce with them as they exhibit themselves as equipment in an equipmental contexture. Letting-function, as understanding of functionality, is that projection which first of all gives to the Dasein the light in whose luminosity things of the nature of equipment are encountered.

Letting-function, as *understanding of functionality,* has a *temporal consti-*

tution. But it itself *points back to a still more original temporality.* Only when we have apprehended the more original temporalizing are we able to survey in what way the *understanding of the being* of beings—here either of the equipmental character and *handiness* of handy equipment or of the thing-hood of extant things and the *at-handness* of the at-hand—is *made possible by time* and thus becomes transparent.

We shall not yet presently pursue this temporality but instead ask more precisely what the basic condition is for our apprehending an equipmental contexture as equipmental *contexture.* First of all, we have seen only in general what the presupposition is for an instrumental usage: understanding of functionality. But all equipment is as equipment within an equipmental contexture. This contexture is not a supplementary product of some extant equipment; rather, an individual piece of equipment, as individual, is handy and extant only within an equipmental contexture. The understanding of equipmental contexture as contexture precedes every individual use of equipment. With the analysis of the understanding of an equipmental con-texture in the *totality* of its functionality, we come across the analysis of the phenomenon that we pointed to earlier, the concept and phenomenon of the *world.* Since the world is a structural moment of being-in-the-world and being-in-the-world is the ontological constitution of the Dasein, the analysis of the world brings us at the same time to an understanding of being-in-the-world and of its possibility by way of time. Interpretation of the possibility of being-in-the-world on the basis of temporality is already in-trinsically interpretation of the possibility of an understanding of being in which, with equal originality, we understand the being of the Dasein, the being of fellow-Daseins or of the others, and the being of the extant and handy entities always encountered in a disclosed world. This kind of un-derstanding of being is, nevertheless, indifferent, unarticulated at first. It is for the most part—for reasons lying in the Dasein itself—oriented toward those beings in which the Dasein has first and for the most part lost itself, extant beings, for which reason also the ontological interpretation of being at the beginning of philosophy, in antiquity, develops in orientation toward the extant. This interpretation of being becomes philosophically inadequate as soon as it widens out universally and attempts to understand existence also along the lines of this concept of being, whereas the procedure should be exactly the reverse.

e) Being-in-the-world, transcendence, and temporality. The horizonal schemata of ecstatic temporality

We must now formulate in a more fundamental way what we described in reference to existentiell understanding, authentic as well as inauthentic.

We must focus more closely on the concept of *the Dasein's transcendence* in order to see the connection of the Dasein's transcendence with the understanding of being, from which alone we can then carry our inquiry back to the temporality of the understanding of being as such.

Functionality is understood in commerce with the beings we encounter in closest proximity—equipment. Everything for which and in which there is a letting-function with something, is what it is within an in-order-to. The relations of the in-order-to, but also those of the purpose-free and purposeless, root either ultimately or initially in the *for-the-sake-of-which*. They are understood only if the Dasein understands something of the nature of the for-the-sake-of-itself. As existent, the Dasein understands something of the nature of a "for-the-sake-of-itself," because its own being is determined by this: that, as existent, the Dasein is occupied in its own being with its ability to be. Only so far as the for-the-sake-of a can-be is understood can something like an in-order-to (a relation of functionality) be unveiled. That all functional relations are grounded ontologically in a for-the-sake-of in no way decides whether, ontically, all beings are for the sake of the human Dasein. The ontological rooting of the ontological structures of beings and of their possible intelligibility in the for-the-sake-of-which is still extraneous to the ontical assertion that nature was created or exists for the purpose of the human Dasein. The ontical assertion about the purposiveness of the actual world is not posited in the ontological rooting just mentioned. In fact, the latter is presented primarily precisely in order to make evident how the understanding of the being of an entity which is and can be in itself, even without the Dasein existing, is possible only on the basis of the ontological rooting of functionality relations in the for-the-sake-of-which. Only on the basis of the clarified ontological interconnections of the possible ways of understanding being, and thus also of functionality relations, with the for-the-sake-of is it at all decidable whether the question of an ontical teleology of the universe of beings has a legitimate philosophical sense or whether it doesn't rather represent an invasion by common sense into the problems of philosophy. That the ontological structure of in-order-to relations is grounded in a for-the-sake-of implies nothing about whether the ontical relations between beings, between nature and the Dasein, exhibit a purposive contexture.

Since the Dasein exists as a being which is occupied in its being with its can-be, it has already understood the like of the "for the sake of itself." Only on the basis of this understanding is existence possible. The Dasein must give its own can-be to itself to be understood. It gives itself the task of signifying how things stand with its can-be. The whole of these relations, everything that belongs to the structure of the totality with which the Dasein can give itself something to be understood, to signify to itself its ability to be, we call *significance [Bedeutsamkeit]*. This is the structure of what we call *world in the strictly ontological sense.*

We saw earlier that the Dasein understands itself first and for the most part via things; in unity with that, the co-existence of other Daseins is understood. Understanding of the can-be of the Dasein as being-with others is already implicit in functionality relations. The Dasein is, as such, essentially open for the co-existence of other Daseins. Factical Dasein is, explicitly or not, for-the-sake-of-being-able-to-be-with-one-another. This is possible, however, only because the Dasein is determined from the very outset by being-with others. When we say that the Dasein exists for the sake of itself, this is an ontological determination of existence. This existential proposition doesn't as yet prejudge anything about existentiell possibilities. The proposition "The Dasein exists essentially for the sake of itself" does not assert ontically that the factual purpose of the factical Dasein is to care exclusively and primarily for itself and to use others as instruments toward this end. Such a factual-ontical interpretation is possible only on the basis of the ontological constitution of the Dasein, that it is in general for-the-sake-of its own self. Only because it is this can it be with other Daseins and only on the same condition can another Dasein, which in turn is occupied with its own being, enter into an essential existential relation to one that is other than itself.

The basic constitution of the Dasein is being-in-the-world. This now means more precisely that in its existence the Dasein is occupied *with, about,* being-able-to-be-in-the-world. It has in every instance already projected itself upon that. Thus in the Dasein's existence there is implicit something like an *antecedent understanding of world, significance.* Earlier we gave a provisional definition of the concept of world and showed there that the world is not the sum of all extant beings, not the universe of natural things—that the world is not at all anything extant or handy. The concept of world is not a determination of the intraworldly being as a being which is extant in itself. World is a determination of the Dasein's being. This is expressed from the outset when we say that Dasein exists as being-in-the-world. The world belongs to the Dasein's existential constitution. World is not extant but world exists. Only so long as Dasein is, is existent, is world given. Since in *understanding world* the relations of the in-order-to, of functionality and being-for-the-sake-of are understood, it is essentially *self-understanding,* and self-understanding is Dasein-understanding. Contained in this, again, there is the understanding of being-with-others and the understanding of being able to be-among and dwell-among extant entities. The Dasein is not at first merely a being-with others so as thereupon to emerge from this being-with-one-another into an objective world, to come out to things. This approach would be just as unsuccessful as subjective idealism, which starts first with a subject, which then in some manner creates an object for itself. To start with an I-thou relationship as a relationship of two subjects would entail that at first there are two subjects, taken simply as two, which then create a relation to others. Rather, just as the Dasein is originally being with others, so it is originally being with the handy and the extant. Similarly, the Dasein is just as little at first merely a dwelling among things so as then occasionally to discover among these things beings with its own kind of being; instead, as the being which is occupied with itself, the Dasein is with equal originality being-with others *and* being-among intraworldly beings. The world, within which these latter beings are encountered, is—because every Dasein is of its own self existent being-with others—always already world which the one shares with the others. Only because the Dasein is antecedently constituted as being-in-the-world can one Dasein existentially communicate something factically to another; but this factical existential communication does not first constitute the possibility that one Dasein has a single world with another Dasein. The different modes of factical being-with-one-another constitute in each case only the factical possibilities of the range and genuineness of disclosure of the world and the different factical possibilities of intersubjective confirmation of what is uncovered and of intersubjective foundation of the unanimity of world-understanding and the factical possibilities of the provision and guidance of existentiell possibilities of the individual. But it is again not an accident that we elucidate for ourselves what world means in an ontological sense chiefly in terms of intraworldly beings, to which there belong not only the handy and the extant but also, for a naive understanding, the Dasein of others. Fellow humans are certainly also extant; they join in constituting the world. For this common concept of the world it is sufficient to point to the concept of the cosmos, for instance, in Paul. Cosmos here means not only the whole of plants, animals, and earth, but primarily the Dasein of the human being in the sense of God-forsaken man in his association with earth, stars, animals, and plants.

World exists—that is, it is—only if Dasein exists, only if there is Dasein. Only if world is there, if Dasein exists as being-in-the-world, is there understanding of being, and only if this understanding exists are intraworldly beings unveiled as extant and handy. World-understanding as Dasein-understanding is self-understanding. Self and world belong together in the single entity, the Dasein. Self and world are not two beings, like subject and object, or like I and thou, but self and world are the basic determination of the Dasein itself in the unity of the structure of being-in-the-world. Only because the "subject" is determined by being-in-the-world can it become, as this self, a thou for another. Only because I am an existent self am I a possible thou for another as self. The basic condition for the possibility of the self's being a possible thou in being-with others is based on the circumstance that the Dasein as the self that it is, is such that it exists as being-in-the-world. For "thou" means "you who are with me in a world." If the I-thou relationship represents a distinctive existence relationship, this cannot be recognized existentially, hence philosophically, as long as it is not asked what existence in general means. But being-in-the-world belongs to existence. That the being which exists in this way is occupied in its being with its ability to be—this selfhood is the ontological presupposition for the selflessness in which every Dasein comports itself toward the other in the existent I-thou relationship. Self and world belong together in the unity of the basic constitution of the Dasein, the unity of being-in-the-world. This is the condition of possibility for understanding the other Dasein and intraworldly beings in particular. The possibility of understanding the being of intraworldly beings, as well as the possibility of understanding the Dasein itself, is possible only on the basis of being-in-the-world.

We now ask, How is *the whole of this structure,* of being-in-the-world, *founded in temporality?* Being-in-the-*world* belongs to the basic constitution of the being that is in each case mine, that at each time I *myself* am. Self and world belong together; they belong to the unity of the constitution of the Dasein and, with equal originality, they determine the "subject." In other words, the being that we ourselves in each case are, the Dasein, is the *transcendent.*

What has so far been said will become clearer by means of the exposition of the concept of *transcendence.* Transcendere signifies literally to step over, pass over, go through, and occasionally also to surpass. We define the philosophical concept of transcendence following the pattern of the original meaning and not so much with regard to traditional philosophical usage, which besides is quite ambiguous and indefinite. It is from the ontological concept of transcendence properly understood that an understanding can first of all be gained of what Kant was seeking, at bottom, when transcendence moved for him into the center of philosophical inquiry, so much so that he called his philosophy transcendental philosophy. In delineating the transcendence concept, we have to keep in view the basic structures already exhibited of the constitution of the Dasein's being. In order to avoid making the first fundamental considerations too heavy, we have purposely disregarded the full development of the basic structure of care. Consequently, the following exposition of the transcendence concept is not adequate, but it suffices for what we chiefly need here.

In the popular philosophical sense of the word, the transcendent is the being that lies beyond, the otherworldly being. Frequently the term is used to designate God. In theory of knowledge the transcendent is understood as what lies beyond the subject's sphere, things in themselves, objects. In this sense the transcendent is that which lies outside the subject. It is, then, that which steps beyond or has already stepped beyond the boundaries of the subject—as if it had ever been inside them—as if the Dasein steps beyond itself only when it comports itself toward a thing. The thing doesn't at all transcend and is not at all the transcendent in the sense of that which has stepped beyond. Even less is it the transcendent in the genuine sense of the word. The overstepping as such, or that whose mode of being must be defined precisely by this overstepping, properly understood, is the Dasein. We have more than once seen that in its experience of beings and particularly in dealing with handy equipment the Dasein always already understands functionality—that the Dasein returns to beings of that sort only from its antecedent understanding of functionality contexture, significance, world. Beings must stand in the light of understood functionality if we are to encounter handy equipment. Equipment and the handy confront us in the horizon of an understood world; they are encountered always as intraworldly beings. World is understood beforehand when objects encounter us. It was for this reason we said that the world is in a certain sense further outside than all objects, that it is more objective than all objects but, nevertheless, does not have the mode of being of objects. The mode of being of the world is not the extantness of objects; instead, the world exists. The world—still in the orientation of the common transcendence concept—is the truly transcendent, that which is still further beyond than objects, and at the same time this beyond is, as an existent, a basic determination of being-in-the-world, of the Dasein. If the world is the transcendent, then what is *truly transcendent* is the *Dasein*. With this we first arrive at the *genuine ontological sense of transcendence,* which also ties in with the basic sense of the term from the common standpoint. Transcendere means to step over; the transcendens, the transcendent, is *that which oversteps as such* and not that toward which I step over. The world is transcendent because, belonging to the structure of being-in-the-world, it constitutes stepping-over-to... as such. The Dasein itself oversteps in its being and thus is exactly *not the immanent.* The transcending beings are not the objects—things can never transcend or be transcendent; rather, it is the "subjects"—in the rightly understood sense of the Dasein—which transcend, step through and step over themselves. Only a being with the mode of being of the Dasein transcends, in such a way in fact that transcendence is precisely what essentially characterizes its being. Exactly that which is called immanence in theory of knowledge in a complete inversion of the phenomenological facts, the sphere of the subject, is intrinsically and primarily and alone the transcendent. Because the Dasein is constituted by being-in-the-world, it is a being which in its being is out *beyond* itself. The epekeina belongs to the Dasein's own most peculiar structure of being. This transcending does not only and not primarily mean a self-relating of a subject to an object; rather, transcendence means *to understand oneself from a world.* The Dasein is as such out beyond itself. Only a being to whose ontological constitution transcendence belongs has the possibility of being anything like a self. Transcendence is even the presupposition for the Dasein's having the character of a self. The *selfhood* of the Dasein is *founded on its transcendence,* and the Dasein is not first an ego-self which then oversteps something or other. The "toward-itself" and the "out-from-itself" are implicit in the concept of selfhood. What exists as a self can do so only as a transcendent being. This selfhood, founded on transcendence, the possible toward-itself and out-from-itself, is the presupposition for the way the Dasein factically has various possibilities of being its own and of losing itself. But it is also the presupposition for the Dasein's being-with others in the sense of the I-self with the thou-self. The Dasein does not exist at first in some mysterious way so as then to accomplish the step beyond itself to others or to extant things. Existence, instead, always already means to step beyond or, better, having stepped beyond.

The Dasein is the transcendent being. Objects and things are never transcendent. *The original nature of transcendence makes itself manifest in the basic constitution of being-in-the-world.* The transcendence, the over-and-out-beyond of the Dasein makes it possible for the Dasein to comport itself to beings, whether to extant things, to others, or to itself, as beings. Transcendence is unveiled to the Dasein itself, even if not qua transcendence. It makes possible coming back to beings, so that the antecedent understanding of being is founded on transcendence. The being we call the Dasein is as such open for.... Openness belongs to its being. The Dasein is its Da, its here-there, in which it is here for itself and in which others are there with it; and it is at this Da that the handy and the extant are met with.

Leibniz called mental-psychical substances monads, or, more precisely, he interpreted all substances in general as monads (unities). With reference to the monads he pronounced the well-known proposition that the monads have no windows, do not look outside themselves, do not look out from inside their own capsules. The monads have no windows because they need none. They need none, have no need to look outside the interior of the capsule, because that which they have within themselves as their possession suffices for them. Each monad is representational, as such, in diverse degrees of wakefulness. In each monad, in conformity with its possibility, there is represented the universe of all the other monads, the totality of all beings. Each monad already represents in its interior the whole of the world. The individual monads differ according to the level of their wakefulness in regard to the clarity in which the whole of the world, the universe of the remaining monads, is accessible to it for its own self. Each monad, each substance, is intrinsically representation: it represents to itself the universe of all beings.

What the Leibnizian proposition about the monads being without windows basically means can truly be made clear only by way of the basic constitution of the Dasein which we have developed—being-in-the-world, or transcendence. As a monad, the Dasein needs no window in order first of all to look out toward something outside itself, not because, as Leibniz thinks, all beings are already accessible within its capsule, so that the monad can quite well be closed off and encapsulated within itself, but because the monad, the Dasein, in its own being (transcendence) is already outside, among other beings, and this implies always with its own self. The Dasein *is* not at all in a capsule. Due to the original transcendence, a window would be superfluous for the Dasein. In his monadological interpretation of substance, Leibniz doubtless had a genuine phenomenon in view in the windowlessness of the monads. It was only his orientation to the traditional concept of substance that prevented him from conceiving of the original ground of the windowlessness and thus from truly interpreting the phenomenon he saw. He was not able to see that the monad, because it is essentially representational, mirroring a world, is transcendence and not a substantival extant entity, a windowless capsule. Transcendence is not instituted by an object coming together with a subject, or a thou with an I, but the Dasein itself, as "being-a-subject," transcends. The Dasein as such is being-toward-itself, being-with others, and being-among entities handy and extant. In the structural moments of *toward-itself, with-others,* and *among-the-extant* there is implicit throughout the *character of overstepping,* of transcendence. We call the unity of these relations the Dasein's being-in, with the sense that the Dasein possesses an original familiarity with itself, with others, and with entities handy and extant. This familiarity is as such *familiarity in a world.*

Being-in is essentially being-in-the-world. This becomes clear from what has already been said. As selfhood, the Dasein is *for the sake of itself.* This is the original mode in which it is toward-itself. However, it is itself, the Dasein, only as being among handy entities, entities which it understands by way of an in-order-to contexture. The in-order-to relations are rooted in the for-the-sake-of. The unity of this whole of relations belonging to the Dasein's being-in is the world. Being-in is being-in-the-world.

How is this being-in-the-world itself possible as a whole? More precisely, why does transcendence ground the primary structure of being-in-the-world as such? In what is the Dasein's transcendence itself grounded? We shall give the answer with regard to the two structural moments which have just been considered separately but intrinsically belong together, "being-in" and "world." *Being-in* as *toward-itself,* as for-the-sake-of itself, is possible only on the basis of the *future,* because this structural moment of time is intrinsically ecstatic. The *ecstatic character of time makes possible the Dasein's specific overstepping character, transcendence,* and thus also the world. Then—and with this we come to the most central determination of the world and of temporality—the ecstases of temporality (future, past, and present) are not simply removals to..., not removals as it were to the nothing. Rather, as removals to... and thus because of the ecstatic character of each of them, they each have a *horizon* which is prescribed by the mode of the removal, the carrying-away, the mode of the future, past, and present, and *which belongs to the ecstasis itself.* Each ecstasis, as removal to..., has at the same time within itself and belonging to it a pre-delineation of the formal structure of the *whereto of the removal.* We call this *whither of the ecstasis* the horizon or, more precisely, the *horizonal schema of the ecstasis.* Each ecstasis has within itself a completely determinate schema which modifies itself in coordination with the manner in which temporality temporalizes itself, the manner in which the ecstases modify themselves. Just as the ecstases intrinsically constitute the unity of temporality, so in each case there corresponds to the ecstatic unity of temporality such a unity of its horizonal schemata. The *transcendence of being-in-the-world is founded* in its specific wholeness *on the original ecstatic-horizonal unity of temporality.* If transcendence makes possible the understanding of being and if transcendence is founded on the ecstatic-horizonal constitution of temporality, then temporality is the condition of the possibility of the understanding of being.

§21. *Temporality* [*Temporalität*] *and being*

The task now is to comprehend how, on the basis of the *temporality that grounds the Dasein's transcendence,* the Dasein's *Temporality makes possible the understanding of being.* The most original temporalizing of temporality as such is Temporality. In connection with it we have always already oriented our considerations toward the question of the possibility of a specific understanding of being, namely, the *understanding of being in the sense of extantness in its broadest signification.* We have shown further how commerce with beings is grounded, as commerce, in temporality. But from this we have only partly inferred that this commerce is also understanding of being and is possible, precisely as such, on the basis of temporality. It must now be shown explicitly *how* the *understanding of the handiness* of handy equipment is as such a *world-understanding,* and how this *world-understanding, as the Dasein's transcendence, is rooted in the ecstatic-horizonal constitution of the Dasein's temporality.* Understanding of the handiness of the handy *has already projected such being upon time.* Roughly speaking, use of time is made in the understanding of being, without pre-philosophical and non-philosophical Dasein knowing about it explicitly. Nevertheless, this interconnection between being and time is not totally hidden from the Dasein but is familiar to it in an interpretation which, to be sure, is very much misunderstood and very misleading. In a certain way, the Dasein understands that the interpretation of being is connected in some form or other with time. Pre-philosophical as well as philosophical knowledge customarily distinguishes beings in respect of their mode of being with regard to time. Ancient philosophy defines as the being that *is* in the most primary and truest sense, the aei on, the *ever*-being, and distinguishes it from the changeable, which only sometimes is, sometimes is not. In ordinary discourse, a being of this latter kind is called a temporal being. "Temporal" means here "running its course in time." From this delineation of the everlasting and the temporal, the characterization then goes on to define the timeless and the supratemporal. Timeless beings are beings of the type of numbers, pure space determinations, whereas the supratemporal is the eternal in the sense of aeternitas as distinguished from sempiternitas. In these distinctions of the various types of being with regard to time, time is taken in the common sense as intratemporality. It cannot be an accident that, when they characterize being, both pre-philosophical and philosophical understanding are already oriented toward time. On the other hand, we saw that when Kant tries to conceive being as such and defines it as position, he manifestly makes no use of time in the common sense. But it does not follow from this that he made no use of temporality in the original sense of Temporality, without an understanding of being, without himself being in the clear about the condition of possibility of his ontological propositions.

We shall attempt a *Temporal interpretation of the being of those extant entities in our nearest neighborhood, handiness;* and we shall show in an exemplary way with regard to transcendence how the understanding of being is possible Temporally. By this means it is proved that the function of time is to make possible the understanding of being. In connection with this we shall return to the first *thesis,* that of *Kant,* and will try to establish on the basis of our results so far the degree to which our critique of Kant was valid and in what way it must be fundamentally supplemented in its positive part.

a) The Temporal interpretation of being as being handy. Praesens as horizonal schema of the ecstasis of enpresenting

Let us recall the temporality of our dealings with equipment which was described earlier. This commerce as such makes an equipmental contexture primarily and suitably accessible. A trivial example. If we observe a shoe-maker's shop, we can indeed identify all sorts of extant things on hand. But which entities are there and how these entities are handy, in line with their inherent character, is unveiled for us only in dealing appropriately with equipment such as tools, leather, and shoes. Only one who understands is able to uncover by himself this environing world of the shoemaker's. We can of course receive instruction about the use of the equipment and the procedures involved; and on the basis of the understanding thus gained we are put in a position, as we say, to reproduce in thought the factical commerce with these things. But it is only in the tiniest spheres of the beings with which we are acquainted that we are so well versed as to have at our command the specific way of dealing with equipment which uncovers this equipment as such. The entire range of intraworldly beings accessible to us at any time is not suitably accessible to us in an equally original way. There are many things we merely know something about but do not know how to manage with them. They confront us as beings, to be sure, but as unfamiliar beings. Many beings, including even those already uncovered, have the character of unfamiliarity. This character is positively distinctive of beings as they first confront us. We cannot go into this in more detail, especially since this privative mode of uncoveredness of the extant can be comprehended ontologically only from the structure of primary familiarity. Basically, therefore, we must keep in mind the point that the usual approach in theory of knowledge, according to which a manifold of arbitrarily occurring things or objects is supposed to be homogeneously given to us, does not do justice to the primary facts and consequently makes the investigative approach of theory of knowledge artificial from the very start. Original familiarity with beings lies in *dealing with them* appropriately. This commerce constitutes itself with respect to its temporality in a *retentive-expectant enpresenting of the equipmental contexture* as such. It is first of all letting-function, as the antecedent understanding of functionality, which lets a being be understood as the being that it is, so that it is understood by looking to its being. To the being of this being there belong its inherent content, the specific whatness, and a way of being. The *whatness* of the beings confronting us every day is defined by their equipmental character. The *way* a being with this essential character, equipment, is, we call *being-handy* or handiness, which we distinguish from being extant, at hand. If a particular piece of equipment is not handy in the immediately environing world, not near enough to be handled, then this "not-handy" is in no way equivalent to not-being. Perhaps the equipment in question has been carried off or mislaid; we say that we cannot lay our hands on it, it is unavailable. The *unavailable* is only a mode of the handy. When we say that something has become unavailable, we do not normally mean that it has simply been annihilated. Of course, something can be unavailable in such a way that it no longer is at all, that it has been annihilated. But the question then arises as to what this annihilation means, whether it can be equated with not-being and nothing. In any event, we see again that even in a rough analysis a multiplicity of intrinsically founded levels of being are manifested within the being of things and of equipment alone. How the understanding of equipment traces back to the understanding of functionality, significance, and world, and hence to the ecstatic-horizonal constitution of the Dasein, has already been roughly shown. We are now interested solely in the mode of being of equipment, its *handiness, with regard to its Temporal possibility,* that is, with regard to how we understand handiness as such in temporal terms.

From the reference to the possible modification of the being of the handy in becoming unavailable, we can infer that *handiness* and *unavailability* are specific *variations of a single basic phenomenon,* which we may characterize formally as *presence* and *absence* and in general as *praesens.* If handiness or the being of this being has a *praesensial meaning,* then this would signify that this mode of being is understood Temporally, that is to say, understood from the temporalizing of temporality in the sense of the ecstatic-horizonal unity described earlier. Here, in the dimension of the interpretation of being via time, we are purposely making use of Latinate expressions for all the determinations of time, in order to keep them distinct in the terminology itself from the time-determinations in the previously described sense. *What does praesens mean with regard to time and temporality in general?* If we were to answer that it is the moment of the present, that would be saying very little. The question remains why we do not say "the present" instead of "praesens." If nevertheless we employ this term, this new usage must correspond to a new meaning. If the difference in names is to be justified the two phenomena, the present and praesens, should not mean the same thing. But is praesens perhaps identical with the phenomenon of the present which we came to know as the now, the nun, toward which the common interpretation of time is oriented when it says that time is an irreversible sequence of nows? But praesens and now, too, are not identical. For the now is a character of intratemporality, of the handy and the extant, whereas praesens is supposed to constitute the condition of possibility of understanding handiness as such. Everything handy is, to be sure, "in time," intratemporal; we can say of it that the handy "is now," "was at the time," or "will then be" available. When we describe the handy as being intratemporal, we are already presupposing that we understand the handy *as* handy, understanding this being in the mode of being of handiness. This antecedent understanding of the handiness of the handy should become possible precisely through praesens. The now as a determination of time qua intratemporality cannot therefore take over the Temporal interpretation of the being of beings, here of handiness. In all now-determination, in all common time-determination of the handy, if indeed the handy is already understood, time is employed in a more original sense. This means that the common characterization of the being of beings in regard to time—temporal, timeless, supratemporal—is untenable for us. It is not an ontological but an ontical interpretation, in which time itself is taken as a being.

Praesens is a more original phenomenon than the now. The instant is more original than the now for the reason that the instant is a mode of the pre-sent, of the enpresenting of something, which can express itself with the saying of "now." We thus come back again to the present and the question arises anew, Is praesens after all identical with present? In no way. We distinguished the *present,* the *enpresenting of...,* as one of the *ecstases of temporality.* The name *"praesens"* itself already indicates that we do *not* mean by it *an ecstatic phenomenon* as we do with present and future, at any rate not the ecstatic phenomenon of temporality with regard to its ecstatic structure. Nevertheless, there exists a *connection between present and praesens* which is not accidental. We have pointed to the fact that the ecstases of temporality are not simply removals to..., in which the direction of the removal goes as it were to the nothing or is as yet indeterminate. Instead, each ecstasis as such has a horizon that is determined by it and that first of all completes that ecstasis' own structure. *Enpresenting,* whether authentic in the sense of the instant or inauthentic, *projects that which it enpresents,* that which can possibly confront us in and for a present, *upon* something like *praesens.* The ecstasis of the present is as such the condition of possibility of a specific "beyond itself," of transcendence, the projection upon praesens. As the condition of possibility of the "beyond itself," the ecstasis of the present has within itself *a schematic pre-designation* of the *where out there* this "beyond itself" is. That which lies beyond the ecstasis as such, due to the character of the ecstasis and as determined by that character, or, more precisely, that which determines the *whither of the "beyond itself"* as such in general, is *praesens as horizon.* The present projects itself within itself ecstatically upon praesens. Praesens is not identical with present, but, as *basic determination of the horizonal schema of this ecstasis,* it joins in constituting the complete time-structure of the present. Corresponding remarks apply to the other two ecstases, future and past (repetition, forgetting, retaining).

In order not to confuse unduly our vision of the phenomena of temporality, which moreover are themselves so hard to grasp, we shall restrict ourselves to the explication of the present and its ecstatic horizon, praesens. Enpresenting is the ecstasis in the temporalizing of temporality which understands itself as such upon praesens. As removal to..., the present is a being-open for *entities confronting us,* which are thus *understood antecedently*

upon praesens. Everything that is encountered in the enpresenting is understood as a presencing entity /Anwesendes/—that is, it is understood upon
presence—on the basis of the horizon, praesens, already removed in the
ecstasis. If handiness and unavailability signify something like presence and
absence—praesens modified and modifiable thus and so—the being of the
beings encountered within the world is projected praesensially, which
means, fundamentally, Temporally. *Accordingly, we understand being from
the original horizonal schema of the ecstases of temporality.* The schemata of
the ecstases cannot be structurally detached from them, but the orientation
of understanding can certainly be turned primarily toward the schema as
such. The temporality which is thus primarily carried away to the horizonal
schemata of temporality as conditions of the possibility of the understanding
of being, constitutes the content of the general concept of Temporality.
[T]emporality is *temporality with regard to the unity of the horizonal schemata
belonging to it,* in our case the present with regard to praesens. In each
instance the inner Temporal interconnections of the horizonal schemata of
time vary also according to the mode of temporalizing of temporality, which
always temporalizes itself in the unity of its ecstases in such a way that the
precedence of one ecstasis always modifies the others along with it.

In its ecstatic-horizonal unity temporality is the basic condition of the
possibility of the epekeina, the transcendence constitutive of the Dasein
itself. Temporality is itself the basic condition of the possibility of all understanding that is founded on transcendence and whose essential structure
lies in projection. Looking backward, we can say that temporality is, intrinsically, original self-projection simply as such, so that wherever and whenever
understanding exists—we are here disregarding the other moments of the
Dasein—this understanding is possible only in temporality's self-projection.
Temporality exists—ist da—as unveiled, because it makes possible the "Da"
and its unveiledness in general.

If temporality is self-projection simply as such, as the condition of the
possibility of all projecting, then this implies that temporality is in some
sense already concomitantly unveiled in all factual projection—that somewhere and somehow time breaks through, even if only in the common
understanding or misunderstanding of it. Wherever a Da, a here-there, is
intrinsically unveiled, temporality manifests itself. However hidden temporality may be, and above all with regard to its Temporality, and however
little the Dasein explicitly knows about it, however distant it has hitherto
lain from all thematic apprehension, its temporalizing holds sway throughout the Dasein in a way even more elemental than the light of day as the
basic condition of everyday circumspective seeing with our eyes, toward
which we do not turn when engaged in everyday commerce with things.
Because the ecstatic-horizonal unity of temporality is intrinsically self-

projection pure and simple, because as ecstatic it makes possible all projecting upon... and represents, together with the horizon belonging to the
ecstasis, the condition of possibility of an upon-which, an out-toward-which
in general, it can no longer be asked upon what the schemata can on their
part be projected, and so on in infinitum. The series, mentioned earlier, of
projections as it were inserted one before the other—understanding of
beings, projection upon being, understanding of being, projection upon
time—has its end at the horizon of the ecstatic unity of temporality. We
cannot establish this here in a more primordial way; to do that we would
have to go into the problem of the finiteness of time. At this horizon each
ecstasis of time, hence temporality itself, has its end. But this end is nothing
but the beginning and starting point for the possibility of all projecting. If
anyone wished to protest that the description of that to which the ecstasis
as such is carried away, the description of this as horizon, is after all only
an interpretation once more of the whither in general to which an ecstasis
points, then the answer would be as follows. The concept "horizon" in the
common sense presupposes exactly what we are calling the ecstatic horizon.
There would be nothing like a horizon for us if there were not ecstatic
openness for... and a schematic determination of that openness, say, in the
sense of praesens. The same holds for the concept of the schema.

Fundamentally it must be noted that if we define temporality as the
original constitution of the Dasein and thus as the origin of the possibility
of the understanding of being, then Temporality as origin is necessarily
richer and more pregnant than anything that may arise from it. This makes
manifest a peculiar circumstance, which is relevant throughout the whole
of philosophy, namely, that within the ontological sphere the possible is
higher than everything actual. All origination and all genesis in the field of
the ontological is not growth and unfolding but degeneration, since everything arising *arises*, that is, in a certain way runs *away*, removes itself from
the superior force of the source. A being can be uncovered as a being of the
ontological type of the handy, it can be encountered in our commerce with
it as the being *which* it is and *how* it is in itself, only if and when this
uncovering and commerce with it are illuminated by a praesens somehow
understood. This praesens is the horizonal schema of the ecstasis which
determines primarily the temporalizing of the temporality of all dealings
with the handy. We did indeed show that the temporality of dealing with
equipment is a retentive-expectant enpresenting. The ecstasis of the present
is the controlling ecstasis in the temporality of commerce with the handy.
It is for this reason that the being of the handy—namely, handiness—is
understood primarily by way of praesens.

The result of our considerations thus far, which were intended to serve
to exhibit the Temporality of being, can be summarized in a single sentence.

The handiness of the handy, the being of this kind of beings, is understood as praesens, a praesens which, as non-conceptually understandable, is already unveiled in the self-projection of temporality, by means of whose temporalizing anything like existent commerce with entities handy and extant [at hand] becomes possible.

Handiness formally implies praesens, presence [Anwesenheit], but a praesens of a peculiar sort. The primarily praesensial schema belonging to handiness as to a specific mode of being requires a more particular determination with regard to its praesensial content. Since, without complete mastery of the phenomenological method and above all without security of procedure in this problem area, the understanding of the Temporal interpretation continually runs into difficulties, let us try to procure indirectly at least an idea of how a wealth of complex structures is implicit in the content of the praesens belonging to handiness.

Everything positive becomes particularly clear when seen from the side of the privative. We cannot now pursue the reasons why that is so. Incidentally speaking, they lie equally in the nature of temporality and in that of the negation rooted in it. If the positive becomes particularly clarified by way of the privative, then for our problem this means that the Temporal interpretation of handiness in its sense of being must be more clearly attainable in orientation toward non-handiness. To understand this characterization of handiness from the direction of non-handiness, we must take note that the beings we encounter in everyday commerce have in a preeminent way the character of *unobtrusiveness.* We do not always and continually have explicit perception of the things surrounding us in a familiar environment, certainly not in such a way that we would be aware of them expressly as handy. It is precisely because an explicit awareness and assurance of their being at hand does not occur that we have them around us in a peculiar way, just as they are in themselves. In the indifferent imperturbability of our customary commerce with them, they become accessible precisely with regard to their unobtrusive presence. The presupposition for the possible equanimity of our dealing with things is, among others, the *uninterrupted quality* of that commerce. It must not be held up in its progress. At the basis of this undisturbed imperturbability of our commerce with things, there lies a peculiar temporality which makes it possible to take a handy equipmental contexture in such a way that we lose ourselves in it. The temporality of dealing with equipment is primarily an enpresenting. But, according to what was previously said, there belongs to it a specific praesensial constitution of the horizon of the present, on the basis of which the specific presence of the handy, in distinction, say, from what is merely at hand, extant, becomes antecedently intelligible. The undisturbed character of imperturbable commerce with the handy becomes visible as such if we contrast it with the disturbed quality of the commerce, and indeed a disturbance that proceeds from the being itself with which we are dealing.

Equipmental contexture has the characteristic that the individual kinds and pieces of equipment are correlated among themselves with each other, not only with reference to their inherent character but also in such a way that each piece of equipment has the place belonging to it. *The place of a piece of equipment* within an equipmental contexture is always determined with regard to the handy quality of the handy thing prescribed and required by the functionality totality. If a habitual procedure gets interrupted by that with which it is occupied, then the activity halts, and in fact in such a way that the procedure does not simply break off but, as held up, merely dwells explicitly upon that with which it has to do. The most severe case in which a habitual occupation of any sort can be interrupted and brought to a halt occurs when some equipment pertinent to the equipmental contexture is missing. Being missing means the unavailability of something otherwise handy, its un-handiness. The question is, How can something missing fall upon our attention? How can we become aware of something unavailable? How is the uncovering of a missing thing possible? Is there any sort of access to the unavailable and non-handy? Is there a mode of exhibition of what is not handy? Obviously, for we also say "I see some that are not here." What is the mode of access to the unavailable? The peculiar way in which the unavailable is uncovered is *missing it.* How is this kind of comportment ontologically possible? What is the temporality of missing something? Taken formally, missing is the counter-comportment to *finding.* The finding of something, however, is a species of enpresenting something, and consequently not-finding is a not-enpresenting. Is missing then a not-enpresenting, a not-letting something be encountered, an absence and omission of an enpresenting? Is that how the matter really stands? Can missing be a *not-*letting-encounter, although we have already said that it is the *access to* the unavailable as such? Missing is so little a not-enpresenting that its nature lies precisely in a specific mode of enpresenting. Missing is not a not-finding of something. If we do not meet with something, this not-meeting doesn't always have to be a missing it. This is expressed by the circumstance that in such cases we can subsequently say "The thing not met with— I can also miss it." Missing is the not-finding of something we have been expecting as needed. In reference to our dealing with equipment this is the same as saying: what we need in use of the equipment itself. Only in a circumspective letting-function, in which we understand the encountered entity by way of its functionality, its in-order-to relations—in which we expect a for-what and enpresent what is useful in bringing it about—only there can we find that something is missing. Missing is a not-enpresenting, not in the sense of a remaining away of the present, but rather an *un-enpresenting* as a specific mode of the present in unity with an expecting and retaining of something available. Consequently, to missing, as a specific enpresenting, there corresponds not no horizon at all, but a *specially modified horizon of the present, of praesens*. To the ecstasis of the unenpresenting that makes missing possible there belongs the horizonal schema of *absens*. This modification of praesens to absens, in which praesens preserves itself as modified, cannot be interpreted more precisely without entering upon a characterization of this modification in general, that is, upon modification of praesens as not, as negative, and clarifying it in its interconnectedness with time. If circumspective letting-function were not from the very outset an expectance, and if this expectance did not temporalize itself, as an ecstasis, in ecstatic unity with an enpresenting, hence if a pertinent horizonal schema were not antecedently unveiled in this ecstatic unity, if the Dasein were not a temporal Dasein in the original sense of time, then the Dasein could never find that something is missing. In other words, there would be lacking the possibility of an essential factor of commerce with and orientation within the intraworldly.

Conversely, the possibility of being surprised by a newly emerging thing which does not appear beforehand in the customary context is grounded in this, that the expectant enpresenting of the handy is unexpectant of something else which stands in a possible functionality connection with what is at first handy. Missing, however, is also not just the uncovering of the non-handy but an explicit enpresenting of what is precisely already and at least still handy. The absensial modification, precisely, of the praesens belonging to the enpresenting of commerce /with the handy/, the praesens being given with the missing, is what makes the handy become conspicuous. With this a fundamental but difficult problem lays claim to our attention. When we formally call the ab-sensial a negation of the praesensial, may it not be, exactly, that a negative moment is constituting itself in the structure of the being of the handy, that is, primarily in handiness? In fundamental terms, to what extent is a negative, a not, involved in Temporality in general and, conjointly, in temporality? We may even inquire to what extent time itself is the condition of possibility of nullity in general. Because the modification of praesens into absens, of presence into absence—a modification belonging to temporality (to the ecstasis of the present as well as to the other ecstases)—has the character of negativity, of the not, of not-presencing, the question arises as to where in general the root of this not lies. Closer consideration shows that the not and also the essential nature of the not, nullity, likewise can be interpreted only by way of the nature of time and that it is only by starting from this that the possibility of modification—for example, the modification of presence into absence—can be explained. In the end, Hegel is on the track of a fundamental truth when he says that being and nothing are identical, that is, belong together. Of course, the more radical question is, What makes such an original belonging-together at all possible?

We are not well enough prepared to penetrate into this obscure region. It will suffice if it becomes clear how only by going back to temporality as Temporality, to the horizon of the ecstases, can light be shed on the interpretation of being—and in the first place the specific mode of being, handiness and extantness.

We may summarize by unfolding backward the foregoing exposition of Temporality. The handiness of the handy is determined by way of a praesens. Praesens belongs as horizonal schema to a present, which temporalizes itself as an ecstasis in the unity of a temporality which, in the case before us, makes possible commerce with the handy. To this comportment toward beings there belongs an understanding of being, because the temporalizing of the ecstases—here that of the present—has intrinsically projected itself upon their */the ecstases'/* horizon (praesens). The possibility of the understanding of being lies in the circumstance that in making commerce with beings possible *as* the present, *as* ecstasis, the present has the horizon of praesens. Temporality in general is ecstatic-horizonal self-projection simply as such, on the basis of which the Dasein's transcendence is possible. Rooted in this transcendence is the Dasein's basic constitution, being-in-the-world, or care, which in turn makes intentionality possible.

The Dasein, however—as we have said over and over—is the being to whose existence the understanding of being belongs. A sufficiently original interpretation of the Dasein's basic constitution in general, the exposition of temporality as such, must furnish the basis for clearing up by means of temporality—or more precisely by means of the horizonal schema of temporality, Temporality—the possibility of understanding being. If, then, philosophical investigation from the beginning of antiquity—we may think, for example, of Parmenides: to gar auto noein estin te kai einai, being and thinking are the same; or of Heraclitus: being is the logos—oriented itself toward reason, soul, mind, spirit, consciousness, self-consciousness, subjectivity, this is not an accident and has so little to do with world-view that, instead, the admittedly still hidden basic content of the problems of ontology as such pressed and directed scientific inquiry. The trend toward the "subject"—not always uniformly unequivocal and clear—is based on the fact that philosophical inquiry somehow understood that the basis for every substantial philosophical problem could and had to be procured from an adequate elucidation of the "subject." For our part we have seen positively that an adequate elucidation of the Dasein, achieved by going back to temporality, can alone prepare the ground for meaningfully putting the question about the possible understanding of being in general. Consequently, in the first part of our critical discussion of the basic ontological problems we pointed positively to the way the trend of inquiry is toward the "subject," how it unconsciously demands a preparatory ontological interpretation of the Dasein.

b) The Kantian interpretation of being and the problematic of Temporality [Temporalität]

Following this exposition of the being of the extant in general in the broadest sense with regard to praesens, we may now return to the *Kantian thesis* and our critique of it, so as to give this critique a more original foundation by the results achieved in the meantime. There will thus emerge an explicit confrontation between the *Kantian interpretation of being* and the *Temporal problematic* which has been developed. Kant's thesis asserts something negative and something positive. Negatively, being is not a real predicate; positively, being equals position, existence (extantness) equals absolute position. Our criticism had to do with the positive content of the thesis. We did not criticize it by opposing to it a so-called different standpoint from which then to play off objections to it. Our aim was rather to go along with his thesis and his attempt at the interpretation of being and to inquire, in this attendant examination, what further clarification its content itself requires if the thesis is to remain tenable as substantiated by the phenomenon itself. Being is position; extantness or, as Kant says, existence [Dasein] is absolute position or perception. We first ran into a characteristic ambiguity in the expression "perception," according to which it means perceiving, perceived, and perceivedness. This ambiguity is not accidental but gives expression to a phenomenal fact. What we call perception has an intrinsic structure that is so multiform-uniform that it makes possible this ambiguity of designation in different respects. What is designated by perception is a phenomenon whose structure is determined by intentionality. Intentionality, self-relation to something, seemed at first sight to be something trivial. However, the phenomenon proved to be puzzling as soon as we recognized clearly that a correct understanding of this structure has to be on its guard against two common errors which are not yet overcome even in phenomenology (erroneous objectivizing, erroneous subjectivizing). Intentionality is not an extant relation between an 'extant subject and an extant object but is constitutive for the relational character of the subject's comportment as such. As the structure of subject-comportment, it is not something immanent to the subject which would then need supplementation by a transcendence; instead, transcendence, and hence intentionality, belongs to the nature of the entity that comports itself intentionally. Intentionality is neither something objective nor something subjective in the traditional sense.

In addition, we gained further essential insight regarding a factor belonging essentially to intentionality. Not only do intentio and intentum belong to it but also each intentio has a directional sense, which must be interpreted with reference to perception as follows. Extantness must be antecedently understood if an extant entity is to be uncoverable as such; in the perceivedness of the perceived there is already present an understanding of the extantness of the extant.

And with regard to perceivedness, too, there was the puzzle which recurred in the fourth thesis: perceivedness is a mode of uncoveredness and unveiledness, hence of truth. The perceivedness of the perceived is a determination of the perceived extant entity and yet it has the mode of being not of that entity but rather of the percipient Dasein. Perceivedness is in a certain way objective, in a certain way subjective, and yet neither of the two. In our first consideration of intentionality we stressed that the question how directive sense, the understanding of being, belongs to intentio, and how intentio itself is possible as this necessary reference, is not only unanswered in phenomenology but not even asked. This question will occupy us later.

We have thus found the answers for the positive completion of our earlier critique. When Kant says that being equals perception, then in view of the ambiguity of perception this cannot mean that being equals perceiving; nor can it mean that being equals the perceived, the entity itself. But also it cannot mean that being equals perceivedness, equals positedness. For perceivedness already presupposes an understanding of the *being* of the perceived entities.

We can now say that *the unveiledness of an entity presupposes* an illumination, *an understanding of the being of the entity.* The unveiledness of something is intrinsically related to what is unveiled; in the perceivedness of the perceived entity its being is already concomitantly understood. The being of a being cannot be identified with the perceivedness of the perceived. We saw with reference to the perceivedness of the perceived that on the one hand it is a determination of the perceived entity but on the other hand it belongs to the perceiving—it is in a certain way objective and in a certain way subjective. But the separation of subject and object is inadequate; it does not make possible any access to the unity of the phenomenon.

We know, however, that this self-direction toward something, *intentionality,* is possible only if the Dasein as such is intrinsically *transcendent.* It can be transcendent only if the Dasein's basic constitution is grounded originally in *ecstatic-horizonal temporality.* The whole of perception's intentional structure of perceiving, perceived, and perceivedness—and that of every other mode of intentionality—is grounded in the ecstatic-horizonal constitution of temporality. In perceiving, the Dasein, in accordance with its own comportmental sense, lets that toward which it is directed, the [intended] entity, be encountered in such a way that it understands this entity in its incarnate character as an in-itself. This understanding is also present when perception takes the form of illusion. In hallucination, too, the hallucinated [object] is understood in conformity with the directional sense of the hallucination as an illusory *perception*, as something incarnately present. Perception, as intentional comportment having the directional sense mentioned, is a distinctive mode of the enpresenting of something. *The ecstasis of the present is the foundation for the specifically intentional transcendence of the perception of extant entities.* To an ecstasis as such, to the carrying away, there belongs a horizonal schema—as, for instance, praesens is the horizonal schema for the present. An understanding of being can already be present in intentional perception because the temporalizing of the ecstasis as such, enpresenting as such, understands in its own horizon, thus by way of praesens, that which it enpresents, understanding it as something present [Anwesendes]. Put otherwise, a directional sense can be present in the intentionality of perception only if perception's direction understands itself by way of the horizon of the temporal mode that makes possible perceiving as such: the horizon of praesens. When Kant says, therefore, that existence—that is, for us, extantness, being on or at hand— is perception, this thesis is extremely rough and misleading; all the same it points to the correct direction of the problem. On our interpretation, "being is perception" now means: being is an intentional comportment of a peculiar sort, namely, enpresenting; it is an ecstasis in the unity of temporality with a schema of its own, praesens. "Being equals perception," when interpreted in original phenomenological terms, means: being equals presence, praesens. At the same time, it thus turns out that Kant interprets being and being-existent exactly as ancient philosophy does, for which that which *is* is the hupokeimenon, which has the character of ousia. In Aristotle's time ousia in its everyday, pre-philosophical sense is still equivalent to property, estate, but as a philosophical term it signifies presence. Of course, like Kant, the Greeks had hardly the least knowledge that they were interpreting being in the sense of the extant in its extantness, its mere being at hand, by way of time, or from what original context they had drawn this interpretation of being. Instead, they followed the immediate propensity of the existent Dasein, which, in its everyday mode of being, understands beings first of all in the sense of the extant and understands the being of beings in an inchoate Temporal manner. Reference to the fact that the Greeks understood being by way of the present, by means of praesens, is a confirmation not to be overestimated for our interpretation of the possibility of understanding being by time; but it nevertheless does not establish it basically. Still, it is testimony that in our own interpretation of being we are attempting nothing other than the repetition of the problems of ancient philosophy in order to radicalize them in this repetition by their own selves.

We can continue to clarify *the Temporal content of Kant's thesis* that being equals perception by a brief explication of its negative content, according to which being is not a real predicate, does not belong to the res or real thing-content of the being. Being, existence, is for Kant, rather, a *logical* predicate. He says once in a posthumously published manuscript on metaphysics: "Accordingly, all concepts are predicates; however, they signify either things or their position: the former is a real predicate, the latter merely a logical predicate."[1] In Temporal language, this means that a being can no doubt be found as extant in an enpresenting, but this enpresenting itself does not let the *being* of the extant entity be encountered as such. And yet, what is meant by "the being of that which an enpresenting lets be encountered" becomes intelligible, precisely, only in one with the enpresenting of something extant and is already antecedently intelligible in that enpresenting. What Kant calls a "logical predicate" can only be understood in an enpresenting if praesens belongs to the enpresenting's ecstatic projection; and only from this as its source can that predicate be drawn for a predication. Kant says: "Anyone who denies existence [the extantness of a being] removes the thing with all its predicates. Existence [extantness] can indeed be a logical predicate but never a real predicate of a thing."[2] To deny the existence, extantness, of a being, to assert non-existence, means to say "A is not extant." Kant calls this denial of extantness removing the being with all its predicates. Conversely then—it could be said in supplementation—the assertion "A exists" is not a removing, not a removere but an admovere. Admovere, however, means "to draw near," "to bring or place near," "to let encounter," an enpresenting of a being as such. The addition "as such" means: the entity taken in its own self, not with regard to any relation to another and not with regard to relations subsisting within its essential content, but the entity in itself, not relatively but absolutely in its own self. Kant therefore defines existence as absolute position. Position is to be interpreted here again as we interpreted perception: not the positing and not the posited and also not positedness; instead, being is that which is already understood in positing as the letting-stand of something on its own self; it is what is already understood in positing as a specific intentional

---

1. Academy edition, vol. 17 (vol. 4 of div. 3), No. 4017, p. 387. [Immanuel Kant, *Gesammelte Schriften* (Berlin and New York: W. de Gruyter, 1902).]
2. Ibid.

comportment according to its directional sense: the thing's being-stood-upon-its-own-self with all its predicates, the self-determined presence of a thing. Only through Temporal interpretation does Kant's assertion that being equals position, so striking at first, acquire a realizable sense, which the Neo-Kantians have fundamentally misunderstood. Kant obviously did not intend his proposition that being equals position to mean that the subject would first create the thing and bring it into being out of its own self; instead, he surely understood the equivalence of being and position in the way we have interpreted him, without having the possibility of bringing this understanding into explicit conceptual form, because he lacked the means for an original interpretation. Being as a so-called logical predicate already lies latently at the basis of everything real. It is precisely because Kant bases the problem of being on the proposition, in a genuinely Greek way (logos), that he must of necessity fail to recognize the essential differences and therefore /the essential/ interrelations. Real and logical predication differ not only by the content of the predicates but primarily by the understanding that receives expression through the corresponding assertion as the interpretation of what is understood. In Kant the phenomenologically decisive thing remains obscure, namely, that in asserting existence, extantness, some being is indeed always intended, but the understanding does not look to that entity as such in order to derive being from it as an existent predicate. The glance of understanding in the assertion of being looks toward something else, which, however, is already understood precisely in commerce with beings and in access to them. Expressed in Temporal language, the enpresenting of something has, as such, a reference to beings; but this means that as ecstasis it lets that for which it is open be encountered in the light of its own—the enpresenting's—horizon, which thus is itself assertible in the enpresenting of something. If we stay within the assertion of the being of an existent entity, "A is," but existence /in the sense of extantness/ is not a real determination of the existent, there remains to us the possibility of turning back from the real reference to the subject. However, this is not the case, because being means praesens and praesens constitutes precisely the ecstatic horizon which the Dasein, as temporal already understands, and in fact understands in the ecstasis, in the removal, and therefore not at all in reflection on the subject. In reference to the Kantian interpretation of being as logical predicate, it therefore becomes doubtful whether the term "logical" is valid here. But the reason why Kant calls being a logical predicate is connected with his ontological, that is, transcendental, mode of inquiry, and it leads us to a fundamental confrontation with this type of inquiry, which we shall discuss in the context of the *Critique of Pure Reason* next semester. With reference to the Temporal interpretation of the being of the extant by means of praesens, in comparison with the Kantian interpretation of being as position, it should have become clear how only a phenomenological interpretation affords the possibility of opening up a positive understanding of the Kantian problems and his solutions of them, which means putting the Kantian problem on a phenomenological basis.

We have not yet discussed the question of how far our investigations hitherto have been *phenomenological* and what "phenomenological" means here. This will be dealt with in connection with the expositions of the following paragraph.

§22. Being and beings.
The ontological difference

a) Temporality /Zeitlichkeit/, Temporality /Temporalität/, and ontological difference

As ecstatic-horizonal unity of temporalizing, temporality is the condition of possibility of transcendence and thus also the condition of possibility of the intentionality that is founded in transcendence. Because of its ecstatic character, temporality makes possible the being of a being which as a self deals existently with others and, as thus existent, deals with beings as handy or as extant. Temporality makes possible the Dasein's comportment as a comportment toward beings, whether toward itself, toward others, or toward the handy or the extant. Because of the unity of the horizonal schemata that belongs to its ecstatic unity, temporality makes possible the understanding of being, so that it is only in the light of this understanding of being that the Dasein can comport itself toward its own self, toward others as beings, and toward the extant as beings. Because temporality constitutes the basic constitution of the being we call the Dasein, to which entity the understanding of being belongs as determination of its existence, and because time constitutes the original self-projection pure and simple, being is already always unveiled—hence beings are either disclosed or un-covered—in every factical Dasein, since it exists. The pertinent horizonal schemata are projected with and in the temporalizing of the ecstases—this is intrinsically involved in the nature of removal to...—and in such a way, in fact, that the ecstatically, hence intentionally, structured comportments toward something always understand this something *as* a being, hence in its being. But it is not necessary that comportment toward a being, even though it understands the being of that being, must explicitly distinguish this understood being of the being from the being toward which it comports itself, and it is still less necessary that this distinction between being and a being should be comprehended conceptually at all. On the contrary, being

itself is even treated at first like a being and explained by means of determinations of beings, as at the beginning of ancient philosophy. When Thales
answers the question What is that which is? by saying "Water," he is here
explaining beings by means of a being, something that is, although at
bottom he is seeking to determine what that which is, is *as* a being. In the
question he therefore understands something like being, but in the answer
he interprets being as a being. This type of interpretation of being then
remains customary in ancient philosophy for a long time afterward, even
after the essential advances made by Plato and Aristotle in formulating the
problems, and at bottom this interpretation has remained the usual one in
philosophy right down to the present day.

In the question as to what that which is, is *as* something that is—what
a being is *as* a being—being is treated like a being. Nevertheless, although
unsuitably interpreted, it is still made a problem. Somehow the Dasein
knows about something like being. Since it exists, the Dasein understands
being and comports itself toward beings. The distinction between being
and beings *is there [ist da]*, latent in the Dasein and its existence, even if not
in explicit awareness. The distinction *is there, ist da* [i.e. exists]; that is to
say, it has the mode of being of the Dasein: it belongs to existence. Existence
means, as it were, "to be in the performance of this distinction." Only a
soul that can make this distinction has the aptitude, going beyond the
animal's soul, to become the soul of a human being. The *distinction between
being and beings is temporalized in the temporalizing of temporality.* Only
because this distinction is always already temporalizing itself on the basis
of temporality and conjointly with temporality and is thus somehow projected, and thus unveiled, can it be known expressly and explicitly and, as
known, be interrogated and, as interrogated, investigated and, as investigated, conceptually comprehended. The distinction between being and
beings exists *pre-ontologically,* without an explicit concept of being, *latent in
the Dasein's existence.* As such it can become *an explicitly understood difference.*
On the basis of temporality there belongs to the Dasein's existence the
immediate unity of the understanding of being and comportment toward
beings. Only because this distinction belongs to existence can the distinction
become explicit in different ways. Because when this distinction between
being and beings becomes explicit the terms distinguished contrast with
each other, being thereby becomes a possible theme for conceptual comprehension (logos). For this reason we call the distinction between being
and beings, when it is carried out explicitly, the *ontological difference* [die
ontologische Differenz]. This explicit accomplishment and the development
of the ontological difference is therefore also, since it is founded on the
Dasein's existence, not arbitrary and incidental but a basic comportment of
the Dasein in which ontology, that is, philosophy, constitutes itself as a

science. To comprehend the possibility and character of this constituting of philosophy as science in the Dasein's existence, a few prefatory remarks are necessary about the concept of science in general. In connection with this we shall try to show that philosophy as a science is no arbitrary whim of the Dasein's but that its free possibility, its existentiell necessity, is founded on the Dasein's essential nature.

b) Temporality *[Zeitlichkeit]* and the objectification of beings (positive science) and of being (philosophy)

The *concept of philosophy,* as well as that of the *non-philosophical sciences,* can be expounded only by way of a properly understood concept of the Dasein. It is only by this exposition that a clear foundation can be given for what we asserted dogmatically at the beginning of these lectures when we differentiated philosophy as a science from the formation of a world-view on the one hand and from the positive sciences on the other. Science is a kind of cognition. Cognition has the basic character of unveiling. We characterized the unveiledness of something as truth. Science is a kind of cognizing for the sake of unveiledness as such. Truth is a determination (a warranty or responsibility) of the Dasein, that is, a free and freely seized possibility of its existence. Science, as a specific type of cognition for the sake of unveiledness, is a possibility of existing in the sense of a task that can be freely taken up and freely worked out. Science is cognizing for the sake of unveiledness as such. What is to be unveiled should become manifest, solely in view of its own self, in whatever its pure essential character and specific mode of being may be. What is to be unveiled is the sole court of appeal of its determinability, of the concepts that are suitable for interpreting it. As a specific type of cognition thus described, science establishes itself essentially on the basis of what is already in some way given. What is already unveiled pre-scientifically can become an *object* of scientific investigation. A *scientific investigation constitutes itself* in the *objectification of what has somehow already been unveiled.*

What does this mean? The objectification will differ depending on *what* and *how* something is given. Now we see that with the factical existence of the Dasein *beings* are always already unveiled or given; and in the understanding of being that goes with them, *being* is also already unveiled or given. Beings and being are unveiled, though still without differentiation, nevertheless with equal originality. Moreover, with the factical existence of the Dasein two essential fundamental possibilities of objectification are posited, both of which—since being is always the being of a being, and a being *as* a being always is—are manifestly related to each other regardless of their fundamental diversity. Because the carrying out of the distinction between being and beings is always already proceeding in the Dasein's temporality, *temporality* is *the root* and the *ground for* both *the possibility* and, properly understood, the *factical necessity of the objectification of the given beings and the given being.* The given beings are to be met with directly in the factical Dasein in the direction in which its existentiell comportment tends. Beings are given in the distinctive sense that it is exactly they which lie in view in a primary way for the Dasein and its existence. Beings are just simply present there; that which is is the positum /what is laid down there/, and indeed it is present not only as nature in the broadest sense but also as Dasein itself. The positive sciences constitute themselves in the objectification of beings where the objectification holds itself in the direction of the tendency of everyday direct apprehension.

Being is indeed also already unveiled in the understanding of being; nevertheless, the Dasein as existent does not comport itself toward being as such directly, not even to its own being as such in the sense that it might perhaps understand its being ontologically; but since the Dasein is occupied with its own ability-to-be, this can-be is understood primarily as the can-be of the being that in each case I myself am. Being is, to be sure, also familiar and consequently in some manner given, but it is not to be met with in the direction of tendency of everyday-factical existence as comportment toward beings. The objectification of that which is, in which the positive sciences variously constitute themselves in conformity with the intrinsic content and mode of being of the specific region of being, has its center in the projection, in each case, of the ontological constitution of the beings which are to become objects. This projection of the ontological constitution of a region of beings, which is the essential nature of the objectification that is foundational for the positive sciences, is nevertheless not an ontological investigation of the being of the beings in question, but still has the character of pre-ontological awareness, into which, to be sure, an already available knowledge of ontological determinations of the relevant beings can enter and factually always does enter. It was thus that modern natural science constituted itself in the objectification of nature by way of a mathematical projection of nature. In this projection the basic determinations were exhibited which belong to nature in general, although their ontological character was not realized. Galileo, who accomplished this primary step, developed this projection from and in a knowledge about basic ontological concepts of nature like motion, space, time, matter, which he took over from ancient philosophy or from Scholasticism, without *merely* taking them over in this specific form. We cannot here enter further into the problems of the objectification that is constitutive for the positive sciences in the sense of the projection of the constitution of being. We need only keep in mind that the *positive sciences of beings,* too, precisely in what first of all gives them their validity, *relate* necessarily if only *pre-ontologically to the being of beings.* This, however, does not mean that they already explicitly encroach upon the domain of ontology.

Our question aims at the objectification of being as such, at the second essential possibility of objectification, in which philosophy is supposed to constitute itself as science.

Being is familiar in the Dasein's factical existence—whether scientific or pre-scientific—but the factical Dasein is disoriented with reference to it. Beings are not only familiar but present, right on hand. The Dasein comports itself directly only to beings, for which the understanding of being is controlling. Fundamentally the objectification of being is always possible, since being is in some way unveiled. But the direction of the possible projection of being as such is too doubtful, indefinite, and insecure to gather it as an object expressly from this projection. After our earlier discussions, no further allusions are needed to make clear that at first and for a long time original temporality, not to say Temporality, and hence that upon which we have projected being in order to make being the object of Temporal interpretation, remains hidden. But it is not only temporality that is concealed; even more well-known phenomena, like that of transcendence, the phenomena of world and being-in-the-world, are covered over. Nevertheless, they are not completely hidden, for the Dasein knows about something like ego and other. The concealment of transcendence is not a total unawareness but, what is much more fateful, a misunderstanding, a faulty interpretation. Faulty interpretations, misunderstandings, put much more stubborn obstacles in the way of authentic cognition than a total ignorance. However, these faulty interpretations of transcendence, of the basic relationship of the Dasein to beings and to itself, are no mere defects of thought or acumen. They have their reason and their necessity in the Dasein's own historical existence. In the end, these faulty interpretations *must* be made, so that the Dasein may reach the path to the true phenomena by correcting them. Without our knowing where the faulty interpretation lies, we can be quietly persuaded that there is also a faulty interpretation concealed within the Temporal interpretation of being as such, and again no arbitrary one. It would run counter to the sense of philosophizing and of science if we were not willing to understand that a fundamental untruth can dwell with what is actually seen and genuinely interpreted. The history of philosophy bears witness how, with regard to the horizon essentially necessary for them and to the assurance of that horizon, all ontological interpretations are more like a groping about than an inquiry clear in its method. Even the basic act of the constitution of ontology, of philosophy, the objectification of being, *the projection of being upon the horizon of its understandability,* and precisely this basic act, is delivered up to uncertainty and stands continually in danger of being reversed, because this objectification of being must necessarily move in a projective direction that runs counter to everyday comportment toward beings. For this reason the projection of being itself necessarily becomes an ontical projection, or else it takes the direction toward thought, comprehension, soul, mind, spirit, subject, without understanding the necessity of an originally preparatory ontological disposition of these areas, in other words, the necessity of being serious about its work. For it is said that subject and consciousness must not be reified, must not be treated as a purely extant thing; this has been heard for a long time at every philosophical street-corner; but now even this is no longer heard.

Our account of the ontological interpretation of the handy in its handiness showed that we project being upon praesens, hence upon Temporality. Because Temporal projection makes possible an objectification of being and assures conceptualizability, and thereby constitutes ontology in general as a science, we call this science in distinction from the positive sciences the *Temporal science*. All of its interpretations are developed by following the guidance of an adequately presented temporality in the sense of Temporality. All the propositions of ontology are Temporal propositions. Their truths unveil structures and possibilities of being in the light of Temporality. All ontological propositions have the character of *Temporal truth, veritas temporalis*.

By our analysis of being-in-the-world, we showed that transcendence belongs to the Dasein's ontological constitution. The Dasein is itself the transcendent. It oversteps itself—it surpasses itself in transcendence. Transcendence first of all makes possible existence in the sense of comporting oneself to oneself as a being, to others as beings, and to beings in the sense of either the handy or the extant. Thus transcendence as such, in the sense of our interpretation, is the first condition of possibility of the understanding of being, the first and nearest upon which an ontology has to project being. The objectification of being can first be accomplished in regard to transcendence. The science of being thus constituted we call the science that inquires and interprets in the light of transcendence properly understood: *transcendental science*. To be sure, this concept of transcendental science does not coincide directly with the Kantian; but we are certainly in a position to explicate by means of the *more original concept of transcendence* the Kantian idea of the transcendental and of philosophy as transcendental philosophy in their basic tendencies.

We showed, however, that transcendence, on its part, is rooted in temporality and thus in Temporality. Hence *time is the primary horizon of transcendental science, of ontology*, or, in short, it is the *transcendental horizon*. It is for this reason that the title of the first part of the investigation of *Being and Time* reads "The interpretation of Dasein in terms of temporality and the explication of time as the transcendental horizon for the question about being." Ontology is at bottom Temporal science; therefore philosophy, understood in the proper sense and not taken straightway in a Kantian sense, is transcendental philosophy—but not conversely.

c) Temporality /Temporalität/ and a priori of being. The phenomenological method of ontology

Because they are assertions about being in the light of time properly understood, all ontological propositions are Temporal propositions. It is only because ontological propositions are Temporal propositions that they can and must be *a priori propositions*. It is only because ontology is a Temporal science that something like the a priori appears in it. A priori means "from the earlier" or "the earlier." *"Earlier"* is patently a *time-determination*. If we have been observant, it must have occurred to us that in our explications we employed no word more frequently than the expression "already." It "already antecedently" lies at the ground; "it must always already be understood beforehand"; where beings are encountered, being has "already beforehand" been projected. In using all of these temporal, really Temporal, terms we have in mind something that the tradition since Plato calls the a priori, even if it may not use the very term itself. In the preface to his *Metaphysische Anfangsgründe der Naturwissenschaft* /Metaphysical principles of natural science/, Kant says: "Now to cognize something a priori means to cognize it from its mere possibility."[1] Consequently, a priori means that which makes beings as beings possible in *what* and *how* they are. But why is this possibility or, more precisely, this determinant of possibility labeled by the term "earlier"? Obviously not because we recognize it earlier than beings. For what we experience first and foremost is beings, that which is; we recognize being only later or maybe even not at all. This time-determination "earlier" cannot refer to the temporal order given by the common concept of time in the sense of intratemporality. On the other hand, it cannot be denied that a time-determination is present in the concept of the a priori, the earlier. But, because it is not seen how the interpretation of being necessarily occurs in the horizon of time, the effort has to be made to explain away the time-determination by means of the a priori. Some go so far as to say that the a priori—the essentialities, the determination of beings in their being—is extratemporal, supratemporal, timeless. The enabling a priori and the possibilities it enables are characterized by a time-

---

1. Kant, *Werke* (Cassirer), vol. 4, p. 372.

determination, the earlier, because in this a priori nothing of time is supposed to be present, hence lucus a non lucendo? Believe it if you wish.

On the other hand, it is also characteristic of the state of philosophical inquiry today and has been for a long time that, while there has been extensive controversy about whether or not the a priori can be known, it has never occurred to the protagonists to ask first what could really have been meant by the fact that a time-determination turns up here and why it must turn up at all. As long as we orient ourselves toward the common concept of time we are at an impasse, and negatively it is no less than consistent to deny dogmatically that the a priori has anything to do with time. However, time in the sense commonly understood, which is our topic here, is indeed only one derivative, even if legitimate, of the original time, on which the Dasein's ontological constitution is based. *It is only by means of the Temporality of the understanding of being that it can be explained why the ontological determinations of being have the character of apriority.* We shall attempt to sketch this briefly, so far as it permits of being done along general lines.

We have seen that all comportment toward beings already understands being, and not just incidentally: being must necessarily be understood precursorily (pre-cedently). The possibility of comportment toward beings demands a precursory understanding of being, and the possibility of the understanding of being demands in its turn a precursory projection upon time. But where is the final stage of this demand for ever further precursory conditions? It is temporality itself as the basic constitution of the Dasein. Temporality, due to its horizonal-ecstatic nature, makes possible *at once* the understanding of being and comportment toward beings; therefore, that which does the enabling as well as the enablings themselves, that is, the possibilities in the Kantian sense, are "temporal," that is to say, Temporal, in their specific interconnection. Because the original determinant of possibility, the origin of possibility itself, is time, time temporalizes itself as the absolutely earliest. *Time is earlier than any possible earlier* of whatever sort, because it is the basic condition for an earlier as such. And because time as the source of all enablings (possibilities) is the earliest, all possibilities as such in their possibility-making function have the character of the earlier. That is to say, they are a priori. But, from the fact that time is the earliest in the sense of being the possibility of every earlier and of every a priori foundational ordering, it does not follow that time is ontically the first being; nor does it follow that time is forever and eternal, quite apart from the impropriety of calling time a being at all.

We have heard that the Dasein dwells daily and first and for the most part solely with beings, even though it must already have understood being in that very process and in order to accomplish it. However, because the

Dasein spends itself on and loses itself in that which is, in beings, both in itself, the Dasein, and in the sort of beings that it itself is not, the Dasein knows nothing about its having already understood being. Factically the existent Dasein has forgotten this prius. Accordingly, if being, which has already always been understood "earlier," is to become an express *object,* then the objectification of this prius, which was forgotten, must have the character of a coming back to what was already once and already earlier understood. Plato, the discoverer of the a priori, also saw this character of the objectification of being when he characterized it as anamnesis, recollection. We shall furnish only some brief evidence for this from one of the main dialogues for these contexts, the *Phaedrus.*

Ou gar he ge mepote idousa ten aletheian eis tode hexei to schema. Dei gar anthropon sunienai kat' eidos legomenon, ek pollon ion aistheseon eis hen logismo sunairoumenon · touto d'estin anamnesis ekeinon ha pot' eiden hemon he psuche sumporeutheisa theo kai huperidousa ha nun einai phamen, kai anakupsasa eis to on ontos. Dio de dikaios mone pteroutai he tou philosophou dianoia · pros gar ekeinois aei estin mneme kata dunamin, pros hoisper theos on theios estin.[2]

For a soul which has never seen the truth, which does not understand the truth in general as such, can never take on the human form; for man, in conformity with his mode of being, must understand by addressing that which *is* in regard to its essence, its being, in such a way that starting from the multiplicity of perceived [beings] he draws it back to a single concept. This conceptual cognition of beings in their being is a recollection of what our soul saw previously, that is, precursorily—what it saw when following God and thus taking no notice of what we now, in everyday existence, call that which is, and in this disregard raising up its head above beings toward the true being, toward being itself. Therefore, it is just that the thinking of the philosopher alone is truly fitted with wings, for this thinking, as far as possible, always stays with the things in which God, abiding, is for that very reason divine. Plato points above all to the *Phaedo* for the corresponding interpretation of learning and knowing in general and the foundation of learning in recollection: hoti hemin he mathesis ouk allo ti e anamnesis tugchanei ousa;[3] learning itself is nothing but recollection. The ascent of the soul to being from the depths of beings, by means of conceptual thought of the essence, has the character of the recollection of something already previously seen. Expressed without the myth of the soul, this means that being has the character of the prius which the human being, who is familiar first and foremost merely with beings, has forgotten. The liberation of the

---

2. Plato (Burnet), *Phaedrus,* 249ᵇ5-ᶜ6. [In *Platonis opera,* ed. John Burnet, vol. 2.]

3. Plato (Burnet), *Phaedo,* 72ᵉ5 f. [In *Platonis opera,* ed. John Burnet, vol. 1.]

fettered cave dwellers from the cave and their turning around to the light is nothing but a drawing oneself back from this oblivion to the recollection of the prius, in which there lies enclosed the possibility of understanding being itself.

By means of this reference we have made known *the connection of apriority with Temporality* merely in its basic features. All a priori Temporal—all philosophical—concept formation is fundamentally opposed to that of the positive sciences. To recognize this adequately, further investigation is required into the mystery of apriority and the method of knowledge of the a priori. The center of development of ontological inquiry in general lies in the exposition of the Dasein's temporality, specifically in regard to its Temporal function. Here we must in all sobriety understand clearly that temporality is in no way something that is to be beheld in some superabundant and enigmatic intuition; it discloses itself only in conceptual labor of a specific sort. But also it is not merely hypothetically supposed at the beginning without our having some vision of it itself. We can follow it quite well in the basic features of its constitution, the possibilities of its temporalization and its modifications, but only in going back from the factually concrete nature of the Dasein's existence, and this means in and from orientation to that being /Seienden/ which is unveiled along with the Dasein itself and is encountered for the Dasein.

Surveying the whole we note that in the Dasein's existence there is an essentially twofold possibility of objectification of the given. Factually, the possibility of two basic types of science is initially established with the Dasein's existence: objectification of beings as positive science; objectification of being as Temporal or transcendental science, ontology, philosophy. There exists no comportment to beings that would not understand being. No understanding of being is possible that would not root in a comportment toward beings. Understanding of being and comportment to beings do not come together only afterward and by chance; always already latently present in the Dasein's existence, they unfold as summoned from the ecstatic-horizonal constitution of temporality and as made possible by it in their belonging together. As long as this belonging together of comportment toward beings and understanding of being is not conceived by means of temporality, philosophical inquiry remains exposed to a double danger, to which it has succumbed over and over again in its history until now. Either everything ontical is dissolved into the ontological (Hegel), without insight into the ground of possibility of ontology itself; or else the ontological is denied altogether and explained away ontically, without an understanding of the ontological presuppositions which every ontical explanation already harbors as such within itself. This double uncertainty pervading the whole of the philosophical tradition until the present time, on the side of the ontological as well as that of the ontical, this lack of a radically founded understanding of the problem, also has over and over again either impeded the assurance and development of the method of ontology, of scientific philosophy, or prematurely distorted any genuine approaches that were actually achieved.

As a method however, the *method of ontology* is nothing but the sequence of the steps involved in the approach to being as such and the elaboration of its structures. We call this method of ontology *phenomenology*. In more precise language, phenomenological investigation is explicit effort applied to the method of ontology. However, such endeavors, their success or failure, depend primarily on how far phenomenology has assured for itself the object of philosophy—how far, in correspondence with its own principle, it is unbiased enough in the face of what the things themselves demand. We cannot now enter any further into the essential and fundamental constituent parts of this method. In fact, we have applied it constantly. What we would have to do would be merely to go over the course already pursued, but now with explicit reflection on it. But what is most essential is first of all to have traversed the whole path once, so as, for one thing, to learn to wonder scientifically about the mystery of things and, for another, to banish all illusions, which settle down and nest with particular stubbornness precisely in philosophy.

There is no such thing as *the one* phenomenology, and if there could be such a thing it would never become anything like a philosophical technique. For implicit in the essential nature of all genuine method as a path toward the disclosure of objects is the tendency to order itself always toward that which it itself discloses. When a method is genuine and provides access to the objects, it is precisely then that the progress made by following it and the growing originality of the disclosure will cause the very method that was used to become necessarily obsolete. The only thing that is truly new in science and in philosophy is the genuine questioning and struggle with things which is at the service of this questioning.

In this struggle, however, and even without useless polemics, the conflict is carried on with what today more than ever before threatens philosophy from all the precincts of intellectual life: the formation of world-views, magic, and the positive sciences that have forgotten their own limits. In Kant's time the forces mentioned first—the formation of world-views, magic, myth—were called philosophy of feeling, Gefühlsphilosophie. What Kant, the first and last scientific philosopher in the grand style since Plato and Aristotle, had to say anent the philosophy of feeling may well close these lectures. If our course itself never attained it, Kant's example may nevertheless summon us to sobriety and real work. We quote from the short essay "Von einem neuerdings erhobenen vornehmen Ton in der Philosophie" /On a genteel tone recently sounded in philosophy/ (1796). Kant here comes to speak of Plato and distinguishes between Plato the academic and Plato—as he says—the "letter-writer." "Plato the academic, therefore, though not of his own fault (for he employed his intellectual intuitions only backward for the purpose of *elucidating* the possibility of a synthetic cognition a priori, not forward in order to *expand* it by those Ideas which were legible in the divine understanding), became the father of all enthusiasm in philosophy. But I would not wish to confuse Plato the letter-writer (recently translated into German) with the academic."[4] Kant quotes one passage from Plato's seventh epistle, which he adduces as evidence for Plato himself as an enthusiast.

Who does not see here the mystagoge, who gushes not merely for himself but is at the same time a clubbist and in speaking to his adepts in contrast with the people (meaning all the uninitiated) really puts on airs! May I be permitted to cite a few modern examples of this elegance. In modern mystical-Platonic language we read, "All human philosophy can only depict the dawn; of the sun we can only have a presentiment." But really, no one can have a presentiment of a sun if he hasn't already seen one; for it could very well be that on our globe day regularly followed night (as in the Mosaic story of creation) without anyone ever being able to see a sun, because of the constantly overcast sky, and all our usual business could still follow its proper course according to this alternation (of days and seasons). Nevertheless, in such circumstances a true philosopher would indeed not have a presentiment of, not *surmise,* a sun (for that's not his thing), but perhaps he could still *deliberate* about whether this phenomenon might not be explained by assuming an hypothesis of such an astronomical body, and he might thus by good luck hit on the right answer. To gaze into the sun (the suprasensible) without becoming blind may not be possible, but to see it adequately in reflection (in the reason that illuminates the soul morally) and even in a practical respect, as the older Plato did, is quite feasible: in contrast with which the Neoplatonists "certainly give us merely a stage sun," because they wish to deceive us by feeling (pre-sentiments, surmises), that is, merely by the subjective, which gives no concept at all of the object, so as to put us off with the illusion of a knowledge of the objective, which borders on rapturous gush. The platonizing philosopher of feeling is inexhaustible in such figurative expressions, which are supposed to make this surmising intelligible: for example, "to approach so closely to the goddess Wisdom that the rustle of her robe can be heard"; but also in com-mending the art of this sham-Plato, "although he cannot lift the veil of Isis, nevertheless to make it so thin that one can surmise the Goddess behind it."

---

4. Kant, Academy edition [*Gesammelte Schriften*], vol. 8, p. 398.

How thin we are not told; presumably, however, not so thick that you can make anything you like out of the apparition: for otherwise it would be a seeing which indeed should be avoided.[5]

Kant concludes the essay: "For the rest, 'if,' without taking this proposal as a comparison, as Fontenelle said on another occasion, 'Mr. N. still insists on believing in the oracle, no one can prevent him.' "[6]

---

5. Ibid., pp. 398–399.
6. Ibid., p. 406.

EDITOR'S EPILOGUE

This book reproduces the text of the course of lectures given under the same title during the summer semester of 1927 at the University of Marburg/Lahn.

Mr. Fritz Heidegger provided the handwritten prototype. The typewritten copy and the manuscript were collated by the editor. The passages not yet deciphered by Mr. Fritz Heidegger—above all, the insertions and marginal notes on the right side of the manuscript pages—had to be carried over so as to fill out the text. The completed copy was then additionally compared with a transcription of the lectures by Simon Moser (Karlsruhe), a student of Heidegger's at that time. In doing so it became evident that we were dealing here with a set of shorthand notes whose accuracy was very good, which the notetaker had transcribed by typewriter. After its completion Heidegger read over this transcription several times and furnished it here and there with marginalia.

The text printed here was composed under Heidegger's direction by putting together the manuscript and the transcript following the guidelines given by him. The handwritten manuscript contains the text of the lectures, worked out, occasionally also consisting of captionlike references, and divided into parts, chapters, and paragraphs. Nevertheless, during the actual lecturing Heidegger departed from the manuscript to the extent of often giving to the thought a revised formulation or expounding more broadly and with greater differentiation a thought that had been recorded in an abbreviated form. Similarly, while and after making the written copy, he inscribed on the pages of the manuscript insertions specified on the right side and marginalia that had been formulated more fully in the oral lecture. Transformations, deviations, and expansions that arose in the course of the delivery of the lectures were recorded in the stenographic transcript and could be worked into the manuscript for publication.

Among the materials taken over from the transcript there are also the recapitulations at the beginning of each two-hour lecture. Where they were not concerned with mere repetitions but with summaries in a modified formulation and with supplementary observations, they were fitted into the lecture's course of thought.

All items taken over from the transcript were investigated for authenticity by testing their style. Occasional errors of hearing could be corrected by comparison with the handwritten copy.

Still, the relationship of the transcript to the manuscript would be inadequately characterized if it were not mentioned that numerous remarks contained in the manuscript were omitted during the oral delivery, so that in this regard the transcript must yield to the manuscript.

In preparing the manuscript for publication, the editor endeavored to intertwine transcript and manuscript so that no thought either set down in writing or conceived during the lectures has been lost.

The text of the lectures was reviewed for publication. Expletives and repetitions peculiar to oral style were removed. Nevertheless, the aim remained to retain the lecture style. An ampler division of the often quite lengthy paragraphs seemed useful, so as to make possible a differentiated survey of the contents.

Explanations by Heidegger inside quotations and their translations are set in square brackets.

The course of lectures puts into practice the central theme of the third division of part 1 of *Being and Time:* the answer to the fundamental-ontological question governing the analytic of Dasein, namely, the question of the meaning of being in general, by reference to "time" as the horizon of all understanding of being. As the structure of the course shows, the "Temporality of being" is laid bare not by resuming immediately where the second division of *Being and Time* concluded, but by a new, historically oriented approach (Part One of the lectures). This lets us see *that* and *how* the treatment of the question of being and of the analytic of Dasein pertaining to it arises from a more original appropriation of the Western tradition, of the orientation of its metaphysical-ontological inquiry, and not actually from motives germane to existential philosophy or the phenomenology of consciousness. Although of the three parts originally conceived in the "Outline of the Course" the limited number of lecture hours permitted only a development of Part One and the first chapter of Part Two, the many anticipations of the later chapters provide an insight into those parts that were not developed. Anyhow, for the discussion of the theme of "Time and Being," chapter 1 of Part Two is decisive. The text here published also does not facilitate in its unfinished form an understanding of the systematic ground-plan of the question of being as it showed itself for Heidegger from the standpoint of his path of thought at that time. At the same time, the course contains the first public communication of the "ontological difference."

I owe cordial thanks to Mr. Wilhelm von Herrmann, Lic. theol., for his aid in the laborious task of collation as well as for his helpful dictation of the manuscript for publication and his aid in reading the proofs. My thanks go further to Mr. Murray Miles, Cand. Phil., and Mr. Hartmut Tietjen, Cand. Phil., for their careful and conscientious help with the proofs.

Friedrich-Wilhelm von Herrmann

Translator's Appendix
A Note on the Da and the Dasein

The three most common German words for existence are: das Dasein, das Vorhandensein (die Vorhandenheit), and die Existenz. Most writers use them more or less interchangeably although there are semantic differences among them. As Heidegger explains in §7, Kant uses either Dasein or Existenz whether he is talking about the existence of God, of human beings, or of non-human things of nature. The Scholastics used existentia for similar purposes. Heidegger believes that there is a difference of fundamental significance between the mode of being of human beings and that of natural things qua natural—leaving aside questions of theology. He therefore co-opts both Dasein and Existenz for human beings and leaves Vorhandensein (and Vorhandenheit, its equivalent) for non-human beings.

In §7 it is too early to explain the difference between human and non-human being: the course itself has to make clear the distinction and the reasons for it. The thinking behind the distinction had already been set forth in *Being and Time*. Two paragraphs from that work are presented in this Appendix.

As indicated in §7, Dasein is to be the name for the being, das Seiende, which each human being is. It falls on the "beings" side of the ontological difference. Existenz (existence, in translation) is then to designate the mode or way of being, the Seinsart or Seinsweise, of this entity; hence this term falls on the "being" side, the Sein-side, of the ontological difference. Existenz is the way or mode of being of the Dasein; the Dasein *is* by existing. For the most part Heidegger uses the entire form "das Dasein" rather than the shortened quasi-generalized (and at the same time namelike) form "Dasein," and in the translation this usage is followed, so that we speak for the most part not, as in the original translation of *Being and Time,* of Dasein, but of *the* Dasein. This usage helps to keep in mind the point that the Dasein is not a Sein but a Seiendes, not a sort of being but a being, though of course it has its own specific mode or way of being, its own Sein, which is named Existenz.

At the same time, the German word "Dasein" connotes, sometimes more vividly and explicitly than at other times, the being, Sein, which belongs to this being, Seienden. Its being—that is, its Existenz—is, among other things, precisely Da-sein, literally, to-be-da. And this "da" of the Dasein is extremely important for Heidegger's thinking. For it registers a fundamental ontological role of the human being as the Dasein.

The human being is, as it were, the mediator between being and beings, the one who holds open the difference between them. Of all the beings we know, Heidegger believed, the human being alone has the required *Seins-verständnis,* understanding-of-being. The understanding-of-being is a pre-condition for any human comportment toward beings, and all our comportment toward beings is carried out in the light of (in the clearing opened up by) our understanding of their being. Because we have under-standing-of-being prior to the encountering of beings (not to say prior to any conceptualized science of being, or ontology), we are able to project being as horizon upon which beings are understood as the beings they are. (What this being-horizon is itself projected upon becomes a further question in fun-damental ontology.) We are therefore able to project world; for world is the context of significance that belongs to the special mode of being labeled func-tionality. And within the world there can be not only functional entities—entities that are handy, having the mode of being called handiness, Zuhand-enheit—but also beings that are released from all functionality-connections and are understood as merely there as such, extant, at-hand entities, whose mode of being is Vorhandenheit, Vorhandensein: extantness, at-handness, presence-at-hand.

Now the essential precondition for being able to project world at all, and therefore to let beings of the ontological character of the handy and the extant be and be encountered as such, is the capacity to open-up, let-be-uncovered, -disclosed, -unveiled. This is the obverse side of what, in tradi-tional phenomenology, has gone under the name of consciousness. Unless there is an openness, a clearing in which the distinction between being and beings can appear, so that beings can come forth and be encountered in their being and their being can function as horizon for them as these beings, there can be no such phenomena at all as beings, being, and their mutual belonging together.

Heidegger does not deny the "independent being" of nature and of natural things. He is speaking about world and our being-in-the-world and what is and can be unveiled in the context of being-in-the-world. He is talking phenomenology.

The ability to open-up, let-be-unveiled as uncovered or disclosed is the ability to exist as the Da. In German, the adverb "da" can mean several things—here, there, where, when, then, at the time—in addition to special functions it has a participial form, component of compounds, and conjunc-tion. In the constitution of the verb "dasein" and the correlative noun "Dasein" the da suggests, first of all, the here or the there, the somewhere

as a definite location; dasein is to be here or to be there; Dasein is being-here
or being-there. There are also overtones of being at some more or less
definite time: being-then, being-when, being-at-the-time. These temporal
connotations fit into Heidegger's usage, but the aspect first stressed in *Being
and Time* is the spatial one. Later, when the role of time and temporality,
especially Temporality, is comprehended as constitutive for the Dasein's
being, the notion of the Da takes on a temporal sense which does not appear
so clearly at the beginning. (See, for instance, the connection between ecstasis and openness, p. 267.)

In this Appendix we are concentrating solely on the beginning. When
time and temporality become thematic—as in the latter part of *Being and
Time* and of *Basic Problems*—the temporal overtones sound more distinctly
and vividly for the reader.

As Heidegger explains in the passages to be cited from *Being and Time,*
here and there are possible only in an essential disclosedness which lets
spatiality be. Spatiality is itself disclosed as the being of the Da. Only given
such disclosed spatiality can a world and its contents be "there" for the
human being (though the world is not there in the same way as any entity
within the world), and only so can the human being be "here" as this "I-
here" in its being-toward the beings that are "there." And the decisive point
is that this Da or essential disclosedness—by which spatiality, a spatial
world, and spatial interrelationships of entities within the world and of
being-in-the-world (Dasein) toward such entities are all possible—is an
essential aspect of the ontological constitution of the being which each
human being is, and which is *therefore* called the Dasein.

The ontological role of the human being qua Dasein, then, is just that:
to be the Da, to be its Da, namely, to be the essential disclosedness by
which the here and the there first become possible, or by which the spatiality
of the world becomes possible within which beings can be distinguished
from their being and understood by way of their being and so encountered
as the beings they are, so that human comportment toward them as beings
becomes possible.

The German for to be the Da is Da-sein. The entity, the being whose
role it is to be the (its) Da can therefore be called the Dasein. Here Heidegger
uses a Sein-word, a being-word, to denominate a Seienden, to name certain
beings, those whose role it is to sustain this mode of being. The Dasein's
role is to sustain Da-sein, and that is why it has this special ontological
name.

No English equivalent is quite possible, not being-here, nor being-there,
nor being-here-there. The reason is that the Da is not just a here or a there
or a here-there, but rather is the essential disclosure by which here, there,

and here-there become possible. It is their source. In the translation I have occasionally used "here-there," but it could obviously be misleading and the reading should be corrected by this note.

Because of the uniqueness of the signification to be attached to the term "Dasein," I have followed the precedent of the original translators of *Being and Time* and retained it in German. It has, anyway, already become a technical term in the philosophical language that now belongs to the Anglo-American community.

Here are the passages from *Being and Time.* They are from chapter 5, which is devoted to a thematic analysis of being-in as such. (See our Lexicon: being, -in.) A large part of the exposition treats of the existential constitution of the Da.

(1) The being which is essentially constituted by being-in-the-world *is* itself in every case its "Da." In its familiar meaning the "Da" points to "here" and "there." The "here" of an "I-here" is always understood *via* a handy "there" in the sense of a being-toward this "there"—a being-toward which is deseverant-directional-concernful. The Dasein's existential spatiality, which determines for it its "location" in such a form, is itself grounded on being-in-the-world. The there is a determination of something encountered within the *world.* "Here" and "there" are possible only in a "Da," that is to say, only if there is a being which has disclosed spatiality as the being of the "Da." This entity bears in its own most peculiar being the character of not being closed-up /Unverschlossenheit/. The expression "Da" means this essential disclosedness /Erschlossenheit/. By this disclosedness this entity (the Dasein) is "da" for itself in one with the being-da of world.

When we talk in an ontically figurative way of the *lumen naturale* in man, we mean nothing but the existential-ontological structure of this entity, that it *is* in such a way as to be its Da. To say that it is "illuminated" means that it is cleared in and of its own self *as* being-in-the-world, not by any other entity but instead in such a way that it itself *is* the clearing. It is only to an entity which is existentially cleared in this way that the extant becomes accessible in the light, hidden in the dark. The Dasein brings its Da with it from the very beginning; lacking the Da it is not only factually not the entity with this essential nature but is not this entity at all. *The Dasein is its disclosedness.* [1]

(2) The leading question of this chapter has been about the being of the Da. Its theme was the ontological constitution of the disclosedness belonging essentially to the Dasein. The being of this disclosedness is constituted in affective self-finding /Befindlichkeit, "state-of-mind" in the Macquarrie and Robinson translation; see our Lexicon: affective self-finding/, understanding,

---

1. Martin Heidegger, *Sein und Zeit,* 8th ed. (Tübingen: Max Niemeyer, 1957), pp. 132—133; trans. John Macquarrie and Edward Robinson, *Being and Time* (New York: Harper and Row, 1962), p. 171.

and discourse. The everyday mode of being of disclosedness is characterized by chatter, curiosity, and ambiguity. These in turn exhibit the movement of falling, whose essential characteristics are temptation, tranquilizing, estrangement, and entanglement.

But with this analysis the whole of the existential constitution of the Dasein has been laid bare in its chief features and the phenomenal basis has been gained for a "comprehensive" interpretation of the Dasein's being as care.[2]

---

2. *Sein und Zeit*, p. 180; *Being and Time*, p. 224.

Lexicon

ability-to-be (Seinkönnen; see alternative translations: capacity-to-be; can-be), 270, 276, 278, 279, 289, 295

absence (Abwesenheit), 305, 307, 310, 311

absens: modification of praesens, in missing something, 311. *See* Latinate

absolute, 103

absolutism, 222

abstractum, 187

access, 49, 109–110, 317; a. to the available, 309–310

accidens, 91

accident, 85, 130, 143, 149

action, 101, 127, 141–142; a. and feeling of respect, 137–138; understanding as "the authentic meaning of action," 277; the instant and the situation of a., 287

actual, actuality, actualization (wirklich, Wirklichkeit, Verwirklichung), actualitas, 28, 29, 33, 34, 37, 38, 40, 43, 46ff., 50, 55, 67–68, 71ff., 78, 79, 82, 84, 85, 87–88, 88–89, 91ff., 94, 95, 97ff., 101ff., 107–108, 110, 111, 112, 117ff., 120, 122, 123, 125, 128, 152, 179, 189, 277, 284–285; being-actual, 109; actuality as ontological constitution of the actual, compared with humanity and the human, equity and the equitable, 138–139; actuality of the actual, 108, 123; actualization, 97–98, 104–105, 107; actuality understood with reference to actualization and being enacted (ancient, medieval), 102ff.; understood as action inward upon subject and action of forces (modern), 104–105; traditional concept, 105

actus, actum, agere, agens, 102–103

additio existentiae, 90; a. entis, 91

addition, 33ff., 39, 40–41, 45, 46–47, 97. *See* theses: 1st thesis, Kantian

admovere, 316

Aegidius Romanus (Giles of Rome, Egidio Colonna), 93, 103

aeon, in Plotinus and medieval thought, 231

aesthetic beholding, 110

aeternitas, 303

affection, 144, 149

affective self-finding, as formal structure of mood, passion, affect: its relation to understanding as necessary condition for the Dasein's comportments, 281. *See in Being and Time:* state of mind, Befindlichkeit, sich befinden

agreement, between ideas and things, 206–207

akolouthein, to follow, 243; its ontological meaning and Aristotle's use of it, 243–244; essential for understanding Aristotle's concept of time, its meaning, 255

aletheia, aletheuein: aletheuein as function of logos according to Aristotle (to make manifest or reveal), 215. *See* truth

Alexander of Aphrodisias, 182

261−262, 263−264, 272, 273, 288, 315, 319, 328; his view of the being of the copula, 180ff.; on the meaning of "is," 182; ambiguity of his truth thesis, 214ff.; critique of his truth thesis, 216−217; proper understanding of his truth thesis, 217; on time, 328ff.; interpretation of his concept of time, 237ff.; the primary meaning of his kata to proteron kai husteron, 245; his interpretation of time matches the phenomenon, 246; genesis of his definition of time, 246; implication of his numerical interpretation of time, 248ff., summary interpretation of his theory of time, 256−257; evaluation of his implicit concept of time, as presentation of common understanding of time, 257; his interpretation of time overlooked significance and datability, 261ff.; his interpretation of time, as under the influence of falling, 271−272. See time, Aristotle's definition discussed

arithmetic, 54

articulation, 208, 210; spoken a. and the logos, 207

articulation of being, 18, 78, 119; general problem, connected with thesis 2, of the articulation of each being into a being *that* it is and the *how* of its being, 120; connection between basic a. and ontological difference, 120; a. into essentia and existentia, 120; "The articulation of being varies each time with the way of being of a being," 120

aseity, 82

assensus, assent, 195

assertion (Aussage; *see* proposition), 33−34, 126, 177, 180, 183ff., 187ff., 200, 202ff., 205ff., 207ff., 210ff., 213ff., 217ff.; a. as sequence of words (Hobbes), 185; truth of a., 189, 213ff.; accidental, real a., 195, 202; verbal a., 195, 202ff.; incorrectly taken first as verbal sequence, 206, 212; its foundation in being-in-the-world, 208; its structure, 209ff.; taken as predication, 209; its cognitive function as secondary, 210, 211; a. and copula, 210ff.; a. as communicatively determinant exhibition, 210ff., 219; a. signifies a being in its unveiledness and presupposes that unveiledness, 213; a. as dispartively determinant display, 209ff.; its being-true as unveiling, 215ff., 217, 218; its truth as related to predicative exhibition of a being: unveiling letting-be-encountered, 215; appropriation of a being in true a. about it, 219; its apophantic, exhibitive nature: "Assertion is exhibitive letting-be-seen of beings," 219; a. of being, 317

assertoric, 37

assigning time to the clock, 245, 261

at-hand, at-handness (vorhanden, Vorhandenheit, Vorhandensein; also being-at-hand; *see* alternative translations: extant, extantness; present-at-hand), 101, 104, 108−109, 111, 114, 119ff., 123, 203, 253−254, 266, 279, 292, 294, 304 (distinguished from being-handy, Zuhandensein, handiness; *see* handy)

at once, 261

at-the-time, 246−247, 269−270; why the a. is temporal, 269; derived from the ecstatic character of temporality, 269

Augustine, 82, 237; his well-known remark about time, 229; on time, 231−232

Augustinian Order, 93

Aussage, 180

authentic (eigentlich), 170ff., 175, 286ff., 306; a. and inauthentic self-understanding, 160−161, 279; a. temporality as finite versus inauthentic time as infinite, 273; a. and inauthentic understanding, 279, 286ff.; a. existence, defined, 287; "Authenticity is only a modification but not a total obliteration of inauthenticity," 171

autotelic, 147

stand being from the original horizonal schema of the ecstases of temporality," 307; WAY of
being (Seinsweise), 15, 18, 23, 24, 122ff., *see* way of being; mode of being; b.-WITH, 161,
168; b.-with the handy and the extant (the at-hand), 297; b.-with-one-another, 270,
279–280, 288, 296; b.-with-others, 278, 292, 301; b.-WITHIN-THE-WORLD (Innerwelt-
lichkeit), 165ff., *see* intraworldly; b.-WITHIN-TIME (Innerzeitigkeit), *see* intratemporal; b.
as WHONESS-EXISTENCE versus essentia-existentia, 120

being-in-the-world (In-der-Welt-sein), 161, 162, 164, 166, 168ff., 170ff., 174, 175, 207, 208,
216, 217, 270, 276, 278–279, 279–280, 288, 289, 292, 294ff., 312, 322, 323; b. and
DASEIN: b. belongs to the Dasein's existence, 166, 298; it is the basic determination of
existence, 174; a basic structure of the Dasein, 175; a determination of the Dasein, 175;
the basic constitution of the Dasein, 208, 296; belongs to the basic constitution of the
Dasein, 278; how the Dasein is as b., 278; interrelations of self, world, and understanding
in unity of structure of the Dasein as b., 297–298; b. as FOUNDATION OF INTENTIONALITY,
161ff.; presupposition for apprehension of anything at all, 164; its MEANING, 296; is
OCCUPIED WITH ITS OWN BEING, 276; b. and TEMPORALITY: ground of temporality of
commerce with intrawordly beings, 291; "It is only from the temporality of being-in-the-
world that we shall understand how being-in-the-world is already, as such, understanding
of being," 292; how it is founded on temporality, 298; b. and TRUTH, 216; b. and
UNDERSTANDING OF BEING, 292; condition of possibility for all UNDERSTANDING OF
BEINGS, 298

beings, a being, that which is, what is, entities, an entity (Seiendes, das Seiende, as contrasted
with das Sein, being, *q.v.: see* ontological difference), 10–11, 13, 16, 21–22, 24, 35, 47,
50, 52, 53, 66, 70, 72, 74, 77ff., 81ff., 84ff., 87, 88, 91–92, 98–99, 100, 105, 106ff., 112ff.,
118–119, 119ff., 128, 139, 141, 148ff., 154, 166, 168ff., 177, 182–183, 197, 202, 207ff.,
210ff., 216, 217, 218ff., 227, 265ff., 272, 291ff., 294ff., 300, 304–305, 318ff., 320ff.; the
b. that is pure ACTUALITY versus affected with possibility, 82; ADDITION to a b., 91; BEING
of beings, handiness of the handy, at-handness of the at-hand, thingness of things, being
of the Dasein, of fellow-Daseins, 294; COMPORTMENT TOWARD beings, 274, 275; objective
concept of beings, 83–84; beings as CREATED, uncreated, 82, 88–89, 91ff., 93–94, 94ff.,
98–99, 100, 104; the DASEIN: *see* Dasein (the), as the being that we ourselves are; beings
as DISPLAYED in assertion, 209ff.; the b. that exists by reason of its ESSENCE versus by
participation in a b. that exists on its own, 82; the properly ESSENTIAL b., 90; the FALSE
and apparent as beings, 207–208; FINITE beings, 79, 81ff., 93, 148; FREE beings, 148; the
b. that is FROM ITSELF, from another, 82; how beings are GIVEN for the Dasein, 320–321;
HANDY beings, 308–309; beings dealt with as handy or as extant, 318; HISTORICAL beings,
169–170; INFINITE beings, 79, 81; how a b. is encountered "IN ITSELF" via antecedent
understanding of functionality, etc., 293; every b. is IN TIME, 256; INTRAWORLDLY beings,
280, *see* intraworldly; LIVING beings, 10; beings as thought in the LOGOS, 206; the b. that
is in each case MINE, that in each case I myself am, 298; *see* Dasein (the), as the being that
we ourselves are; NON-beings, 95; OBJECTIFICATION of beings, constitutive for the positive
sciences, 320ff.; ONTOLOGICAL CONSTITUTION of beings, 78; PROJECTION of ontological
constitution of a region of beings, 321; RATIONAL beings, 138; "SELF and world are not
two beings," 297; the b. that is meant by SOUL or SUBJECT, 255; to be as it is, a b. does
not need TRUTH, unveiledness, 220–221; UNDERSTANDING of the being of beings made
possible by time, 294; UNIVERSE of beings, 82; UNVEILEDNESS of beings in their being,
210

belonging-together, 83, 209, 312; b. of self and world, 297

Bergson, Henri, 231–232, criticism of his view of the dimensional character of time, 244

between: truth lies in the middle, "between" things and the Dasein, 214. *See* middle; truth

Bewandtnis (functionality, *q.v.*), 164; "Equipmental character is constituted by what we call *Bewandtnis, functionality*," 292

beyond (*cf.* Greek expressions, epekeina), 284, 285; beyond, that transcends being, 286; the Dasein, as transcendent, is beyond itself, 291, 299–300; "beyond itself," 306

Bezeichnung (designation, Husserl), 185

biology and philosophy, 191

birth certificate, 100, 116

Bismarck, Otto von, 5

body, 143, 146, 203

Bonaventura, 30

Brentano, Franz, 58

bygone (vergangen, Vergangenheit), expression for the past, distinguished from the past as having-been-ness, 290. *See* has been; past

calendar date, 262

can-be (Seinkönnen; *see alternate translations:* ability-to-be; capacity-to-be), 277, 289–290, 295

capacity-to-be (can-be, ability-to-be), 170, 267, 276

Capreolus, Joannes, 93, 103–104

care, 312; purposely disregarded, 298

carry away (entrücken; alternative translations, carry off, remove [*q.v.*]; ecstasis), 267, 287, 307; a carrying-away belongs to each of the ecstases of time, 267

Cassirer, Ernst, 27

categorical: c. assertion, proposition, judgment, 200; c. imperative, ontological significance of Kant's formulation, 139

category, 36–37, 45, 75, 89, 124, 129, 143ff., 146; Kant's table of categories, 36–37; formal-apophantic categories, 126–127; Kant's categories as basic ontological concepts, 143; as fundamental concepts of nature, 145

Catholic, 80; C. phenomenology, 20; theology, 118

cause, causation, causality, 87, 92, 148–149, 187; causa prima, 119; causality of nature and freedom (Kant), 148; copula as index of c. of assignment of different names to the same thing (Hobbes), 186–187, 188, 192

cave: Plato's cave simile interpreted, 284ff.

ceasing-to-be, 93

centaur, 204

certitudo, 86

change, 107; c. of place (phora), 238ff., 243 (and sequence of the a priori connections); qualitative c. (alloiosis), 242

changeable, 303

choice, 138; purposeful c. of self, 170; the Dasein's self-choice through understanding, 278; self-choice in resoluteness, authentic existence, 287

Christian, 103; C. theology, 118; C. world-view, 118

Christology, 80

circle, 224, 237

circumspection, circum-sight (Umsicht, Um-sicht, um-sichtig), 109, 163, 311

clock, 229, 240, 245, 257ff.; reading time from a clock, 258; clock-usage: its mode of being, 258; source of invention of clocks: economical reckoning with time, 258; time measurement, as explicit manifestation of common understanding of time, 260–261

co-Dasein, fellow-Dasein, 279

cogito, cogitatio, 126

cognition, cognitive faculty, 46–47, 50, 99, 101, 104, 149–150, 283–284; essence of the cognitive faculty, 66; "Only the creator is capable of a true and proper cognition of being," (paraphrase of Kant), 150; our inadequate interpretation of c., 275; philosophical c. as a relationship to being, distinguished from other cognitive comportments toward beings, 275; c. and understanding, 276, 277–278; c. and science, 320. See unveil; uncover; disclose

combination, 36, 127, 129, 144, 195, 199, 202, 203, 204, 205, 206; c. of S and P in a proposition, expressed by "is," 182; c. as present in idea of being, 212

coming-back-to, 300. See past

coming-to-be, 107

coming-toward: coming-toward-itself, 265, 287; coming-toward-itself from things, 289; coming-toward-oneself, 265. See future, existential concept

commerce (Umgang, umgehen): c. with BEINGS, 118, 169, 317; c. with immediately encountered beings, as founded in existence, 291–292, and grounded on a specific temporality, 292, 302; its specific temporality as retentive-expectant enpresenting of equipmental contexture, 304; c. with EQUIPMENT, 295, 303–304; c. with HANDY AND EXTANT ENTITIES, as dependent on temporality, praesens, 309; c. with the INTRAWORLDLY, 311; its uninterrupted quality, 309; c. with THINGS, 168, 289–290, 293

commercium: c. of free beings, 148–149 (Kant)

common sense: sound common sense, the so-called healthy human understanding (Hegel), 14

communication, 211–212; meaning of c., 210; its relationship to being-in-the-world and world as shared by Daseins, 297ff.

complementum possibilitatis, 33

comportment (Verhalten, Verhaltung; see alternative translation: behavior), 16, 47, 50, 56ff., 60, 61, 64, 65, 71, 75, 108, 109, 110–111, 122, 265; c. toward BEINGS, 16; not limited to cognitive, theoretical c., 275; grounded as understanding in temporality, 286; mutual entry into same c. in COMMUNICATION, 210; the DASEIN'S c. toward beings: toward itself, other Daseins, the handy, the extant, 318; the Dasein's c. toward its own most peculiar ability to be, 265; c. and EGO OR SUBJECT, 61; ego as ground of its unity in the multiplicity of its comportments (Kant), 127; ENPRESENTING c. to the at-hand, extant entity, 266; comporting EXISTINGLY toward the extant, 65; EVERYDAY c., 289; c. toward the HANDY, 312; INTENTIONAL CHARACTER of comportments, 58ff., 61, 155; intentional c., 64, 69, 158ff.; intentional c. to beings, including the self, and the indifferent understanding of their being, 175–176; intentional c. of assertion, 208; c. and INTENTIONALITY, 61, 64; intentionality "belongs to the essential nature of comportments, so that to speak of intentional comportment is already a pleonasm," 61; a basic c. by which the Dasein develops ONTOLOGY as a science, 319–320; PERCEPTUAL c., 71; PRODUCTIVE, productive-intuitive c., 105, 106ff., 109–110, 112ff., 115ff., 118; that to which each c. RELATES, 122; natural comportmental RELATIONSHIP to things, 162, 173; TEMPORAL c., 265ff.; enpresenting, expecting, retaining as comportments in which TIME expresses itself, 257ff., 260; original, primary c. toward time: guiding oneself according to time, 258; UNDERSTANDING c. in communication, 210; and toward things handy and things extant, described, 289ff.; c. toward beings belongs together with UNDERSTANDING OF BEING, 327; UNVEILING as c. of the ego, 216

compositio, 78, 88−89, 91, 92; c. realis, 92

comprehension, conceptual (Begreifen, begreifen; *cf.* concept = Begriff), 14, 279, 319, 323; c. versus understanding, 274−275

conceal, concealment, concealedness (verbergen, Verbergung, Verborgenheit, Verborgensein), 215; c. of temporality, Temporality, transcendence, world, being-in-the-world, but not complete, 322

concept (Begriff), 30ff., 38ff., 41, 83−84, 94, 100, 129, 153, 317; c. of BEING as emptiest and simplest, 16, 84; Kant's c. of being or existence, 42, 43ff.; (*see* being; existence; perception; position); c. of being as positedness of combination in judgment, 179−180; CONCEPTUS, 83ff.; COPULA as combinatory c., 199; c. of the COSMOS as in Paul, 297; c. of DIMENSION, 242; c. of EIDOS, 106, 151; c. of LIFE: its philosophical content, formulated with the aid of the c. of existence, is being-in-the-world, 173; metabole, Umschlag, as the most general c. of MOTION, 234; basic ontological concepts of NATURE (Galileo), 321; c. of OBJECTIVITY OF OBJECTS in Neo-Kantianism, 202; ORIGIN of c. of: existence, 100, 102ff.; essence, 100; c. of OUSIA in Greek ontology, 151; concepts and PHENOMENA, 159−160; c. of PHILOSOPHY and the non-philosophical sciences, depends on c. of the Dasein, 320; c. of REALITY, 34ff., 37, 43; c. of SUBJECT, 167−168; Kant's c. of SUBJECT-OBJECT, 155; c. of TEMPORALITY, to be defined, 292; common c. of TIME, 228, 324−325; concepts of time: traditional, 230, 231; natural, 232; c. of TRANSCENDENCE, philosophical, explained, 298ff.; "more original concept of transcendence," 323; c. of TRUTH, 214; UNANALYZABLE c., 44; c. of UNDERSTANDING: how it must be taken, 276; delineation of it, 276ff.; c. of WORLD, 164−165, 165 (phenomenological versus pre-philosophical), 174, 294, 296ff.; common c. of the world, 297

concept formation, in philosophy: why opposed to that of the positive sciences, 327

conceptualizability, 323. *See* comprehension, conceptual

concreation, 104

concretum, 187

concioushood (Bewusstheit, technical term introduced by Natorp), 156

consciousness, 21, 73, 156, 158−159, 223, 323; being as c. (Husserl), 124−125; c. of productive project, 151; c. and truth, 214

consignification, 181

conspicuous: what makes the handy become c., 311

constancy, 11

constitution, 56, 59, 64, 65 (This term appears in many contexts; *see,* for instance, Dasein (the), constitution, or intentionality, constitution.)

construction, phenomenological, 22. *See* phenomenological

container: time as c., 252, 255. *See* embrace; hold-around

contemplation, 293

content, 85, 92, 102, 215; c. of judgment, 202; possible eternal subsistence of c. of true proposition, independently of the latter's truth, 221; phenomenological c. of common time, 257; real (sachliche) content, 304, 316 (*see* Sache; thing; essence. The Lexicon does not atempt to list the occurrences of the adjective "sachlich," which appears frequently, most often translated by inherent, intrinsic, more rarely by thing as in thing-content.)

contexture, 163ff., 208−209; c. of things, 175; c. of phenomena belonging to the logos, 207. *See* equipmental, contexture; function; significance; world

continuity (Stetigkeit; sunecheia), 236, 238, 242ff.; experience of c. in elements of a continuum, 244

continuum, 236, 242; the now as c. of flux of time, 249

contradiction, 39, 54, 74

copula, 15, 24, 39, 40, 75, 177, 179; AMBIGUITY in c. (Mill), 194ff.; BEING of the c.: in the horizon of whatness (essentia) (Hobbes), 183ff.; according to Aristotle, 180ff.; in the horizon of essence and existence (Mill), 192ff., summary account, 201ff.; function of c. as COMBINING AND SEPARATING: sunthesis and diairesis, 199; EXAMPLES for interpretation by the different theories of the being of the c., 203−204; its INDIFFERENCE, 210ff.; being of the c. and theory of double JUDGMENT (Lotze), 198ff.; NEGATIVE c., denied by Lotze, 199; c. as sign of PREDICATION (Mill), 193−194; PROBLEM of the c., 179−180; functional SENSE assigned to the c. by Hobbes, 186; characteristic TREATMENTS of the c., 179; c. defined as TRUTH by Hobbes, 188. *See* "is"

cosmology, 80; cosmologia rationalis, 80

cosmos, 115, 165

count, counting, counted, 237, 239ff., 254, 255; the nows as counted, 245−246; countedness of time, rooted in ecstatic-horizonal constitution of temporality, 274. *See* time, Aristotle's definition discussed

Counter-Reformation, 79

cover up, covering up (verdecken, Verdeckung; *cf.* conceal = verbergen): covering-up of original time, due to falling, 271ff.; covering-up of structural moments of world-time, grounded in falling, 271

creation, 93, 98−99, 101, 104, 118

creator, 104, 150, 151

creatura, creatures, 81, 82, 91

critical: philosophy as the critical science, 17

culture, 169−170

Da (here, there, here-there). *See* Translator's Appendix, "A Note on the Da and the Dasein" 333ff.; the Da, the here-there, as the Dasein's openness, 300; the Da as where the handy and the extant are encountered, 300; the Da, toward-itself as for-the-sake-of, 301; "Temporality exists—ist da—as unveiled, because it makes possible the 'Da' and its unveiledness in general," 307

Dasein (the), 6ff., 9ff., 18ff., 22, 24, 28, 43, 55, 56, 58, 59, 64ff., 69ff., 73ff., 87, 101−102, 105, 108, 110−111, 113ff., 118, 119ff., 122−123, 141, 144, 147, 154−155, 157, 158ff., 161−162, 164ff., 170−171, 174ff., 183, 207ff., 211, 214ff., 217−218, 219ff., 222ff., 227−228, 237, 255, 259, 265ff., 268, 270ff., 275ff., 279ff., 284, 286ff., 291, 293−294, 295ff., 302−303, 307−308, 311ff., 313ff., 317, 318ff., 320ff., 325ff.; the D. is occupied with its ABILITY-TO-BE, 295; ontological ANALYTIC of the D., 16, 19; the D. as a whole, condition for ascertaining the structure of ASSERTION, 209; the D.'s understanding of modes of being is presupposed in assertion, 211−212; the BEING of the D., 153, 169−170;

the D. as the being to whose being (existence) an understanding of beings belongs, 312, and to the interpretation of which all the problems of ontology return, 154; the D. and the question of the being of being, 222−223; how the D. is in its being-free-for its own possibilities, 276, 277; the D. latently or pre-ontologically distinguishes being and beings, 319; the D.'s relation to beings and to being, 320ff., 325−326; COMMON CONCEPTION of the D., 110; the D.'s COMPORTMENTS, 57ff., 110−111, 122, 158, as intentional, 161; toward beings, 318, the necessary conditions: understanding and affective self-finding, 281; a basic CONSTITUTION of the D., 64; existential constitution of the D.'s being, ontological constitution of the D., 74−75, 117, 119, 122, 154ff., 162, 171, 174, 268, 274, 294, 312; CONTRAST between the D. and extant beings, 64, 164; existential DETERMI-NATION of the D., 214; the D. as the being to whose mode of being DISCLOSURE belongs essentially, 18 (see Da); disclosure of the D. for itself, 111, 158ff.; the D.'s ECSTATIC-HORIZONAL constitution, 302, 305; the D.'s EXISTENCE as being-in-the-world, 164; FAC-TICAL D. as for-the-sake-of-being-able-to-be-with-one-another, 296; the D.'s FORGETTING of its prior understanding of being, 326; the D.'s distinctive FUNCTION for making possible an adequately founded ontological inquiry in general, 16−17, 22, 56, 122; the D. as theme of FUNDAMENTAL ONTOLOGY, 223−224; the D. as FUTURAL, 265; the D.'s relation to the HANDY, 292; MEANING of the term "Dasein" for us and in Kant and Scholasticism, 28; MODE OF BEING of the D., 64, 161, 174; ONTOLOGICAL PRIORITY of the D., 223−224; ONTOLOGY of the D., 55, 56, 75 ("the ontology of the Dasein represents the latent goal and constant and more or less evident demand of the whole development of Western philosophy"), 117, 167; the D.'s primary ORIENTATION toward beings as extant things, which influences the D.'s understanding of being and of itself, 271−272; the D. as PAST in the existential sense of having-been-ness: "The Dasein can as little get rid of its /past as/ bygoneness as escape its death. In every sense and in every case everything we have been is an essential determination of our existence. . . . The Dasein, in being, necessarily always has been. . . . This entails that /pastness in the sense of/ having-been-ness belongs to the Dasein's existence," 265−266; need for PREPARATORY ONTOLOGICAL INVESTIGA-TION of the D., 224; exposition of the D.'s basic constitution as preparatory, presupposed from Being and Time, 228; preparatory ontological interpretation of the D., 313; the D.'s enpresenting and its PRESENT, 266; the D. as "free and open for the thou" only in RESOLUTE INDIVIDUATION, 288; "SELF and world belong together in the single entity, the Dasein," 297; the D.'s SELF-GIVENNESS, its (pre-reflexive) givenness to itself (but see reflection): "The self is there for the Dasein itself without reflection and without inner perception, before all reflection," 159; SELF-PURPOSIVENESS and the ontological constitution of the D., 141, 295−296; meaning of "The Dasein exists for-the-sake-of-itself" as ontological, not ontical, 296; the D.'s ontological constitution as for-the-sake-of-itself, 296; the D.'s SELF-UNDERSTANDING, 110; via its capacity-to-be, 265; existential, ontological STRUCTURE of the D., 64, 166, 170; the D.'s ontological constitution as rooting in TEMPORALITY, 228; the D.'s temporal comportment and self-expression, 259; the D.'s three basic temporal comportments, as expressible by the then, at-the-time, and now, 259−260; why the D. must be called the temporal entity as such, contrasted with other entities, 271; how the D. is led to cover up original temporality and interpret time as extant, 271−272; tem-porality as condition of possibility of the D.'s being, 274; temporality and the D.'s un-derstanding of being, 280; the D.'s basic constitution lies in temporality, 291; the D. as

embrace (umgreifen), 252, 254, 274; "Time does not itself belong to motion but *embraces* it," 252; time as embracing beings, 252, 274; "Due to its ecstatic character temporality is, as it were, further outside than any possible object which the Dasein can encounter as temporal. Because of this, any being that the Dasein encounters is already embraced by time from the very outset," 274

empiricism, British, 195

encounter (begegnen, Begegnung), 70, 118, 169, 171, 219, 273–274, 290, 294–295, 297, 307, 310, 317; A BEING "can be encountered by us *as* a being only in the light of the understanding of being," 275; e. with HANDY AND AT-HAND BEINGS, 291; MOTION encountered with regard to the before and after, 238; how TIME is encountered, 235; in connection with encountered motion, 237–238; immediately, 241; in connection with motion, 244; as something counted, 250

end, ends, 138, 141–142, 147, 148; man, and every rational being, as an end in himself (Kant), 138; realm of ends: its ontical sense as the commercium or being-with-one-another of persons as such, the realm of freedom (Kant), 139, 141; end-in-itself, 147

endure, enduring, 263

enpresent, enpresenting (gegenwärtigen, Gegenwärtigen), 257, 260–261, 261ff., 265ff., 269ff., 287–288, 290–291, 310–311, 315, 316; enpresenting of A BEING, 269; enpresenting DEFINED, 260, 306–307; e. of EQUIPMENT: "In expectant-retentive enpresenting, the equipment comes into play, becomes present, enters into a present /Gegen-wart/," 293; e. in dealing with equipment, 309; e. implicit in EXPECTING AND RETAINING, 260; how incorporated in each expecting and retaining, 260; e. of the INAUTHENTIC UNDERSTANDING, 291; e. in MISSING AND FINDING SOMETHING, 310–311; e. and "NOW", 260–261; e. of something, the PRESENT, expresses itself in the now, 261; e. "for the most part" contrasted with e. in RESOLUTENESS, 287; e. of something, expressed TEMPORALLY, 317. See temporal, comportments

ens, 35, 81–82, 83ff., 90–91, 92, 99, 183, 194; ens a se, ab alio, 82, 88–89; actus purus, ens potentiale, 82, 88; conceptus formalis entis, conceptus objectivus entis, 83–84; ens creatum, increatum, 82, 89, 91, 92, 98, 118–119, 152; "ens" as participle, as noun, 84–85; esse, ens, beingness as producedness, 152; ens finitum, infinitum, 79, 81–82, 89, 148, 151; ens necessarium, contingens, 82; ens per essentiam, per participationem, 82; ens perfectissimum, 79; ens rationis, 81, 183; ens reale, 183; ens realissimum (allerrealstes Wesen, the most real of all beings), 37, 148. *See* esse

entitas, 89, 194

entity, entities (Seiendes, das Seiende; *see alternative translation*: beings), 165, 168, 169, 212–213, 218–219; historical e., 169–170; how the extant e. can be true, 218–219; presencing e., 307

environing world (Umwelt), 171

environment (Umgebung), 168

epistemological, epistemology, 59, 128; epistemological realism, 62

equipment (Zeug), 162ff., 171, 258, 292ff., 295, 299, 303ff., 308ff.; DESIGNATION: "The *nearest things* that surround us we call *equipment*," 163; EMPLOYMENT of e., described, 293; ENPRESENTING of e., 293; relation of e. to its EQUIPMENTAL CONTEXTURE, 292, 294; e.-FOR, 163–164; conditions for encountering HANDY e., 299; e. is IN-ORDER-TO in an ontological sense: its whatness and howness are constituted by functionality, 292–293;

examples of e., taken in broad ONTOLOGICAL SENSE, 292; how e. is UNVEILED as such, 483; e. is USABLE as such only if already projected upon a functional relation, 293

equipmental (adjective translating the noun-form Zeug when it functions as initial component of a compound word such as Zeugcharakter, Zeugzusammenhang): e. CHARACTER, 292, 304; constituted by functionality (Bewandtnis, q.v.), 292; e. CONTEXTURE, 162ff., 171, 292ff., 303–304, 309–310; condition for its apprehension as contexture, 294; understanding of it precedes use of equipment, 294; e. FUNCTION, 292; primarily constitutes the being of equipment, 292; e. USE, made possible by letting-function (understanding of functionality), 292–293; e. WHOLE, 163

error, 37; its possibility, 216

esse, 83ff., 87, 88, 92, 109, 112, 152, 203–204; the est for Hobbes, 198. See ens

essence, 15, 30ff., 77ff., 79, 82–83, 85ff., 88ff., 91ff., 93, 94ff., 99, 100, 138–139, 203; essential proposition (Mill), 195ff., 203; superessential e., 90; interpretation of e. in ancient and in modern ontology, 106ff.; e. of time, 233ff.

essentia, 15, 18, 24, 31, 77ff., 83ff., 88ff., 91ff., 93–94, 94ff., 99ff., 106ff., 112ff., 119ff., 138, 187, 194, 198, 202, 203–204, 218; e. DEI, 79; DISTINCTION between e. and existentia, 88ff.; e. of MAN and of things, 141; e. as translation of OUSIA, 108–109; PROBLEMATIC as universally valid concept, 119, 120; e. REALIS, 85, 86

eternity, 115, 303

everlasting, 303

evil, 37–38

exemplary entity, 123; nature as e., 123

exhibition (Aufzeigung), 209–210, 210ff., 215, 218; e. as basic structure of ASSERTION, 209: "The primary moment of the structure of assertion is fixed by exhibition," 210; exhibitive DISCOURSE, 180; e. as intentionally UNVEILING COMPORTMENT, 218; "Exhibition has the character of *unveiling*, and it can be determination and communication only because it unveils. This unveiling, which is the *basic function of assertion*, constitutes the character traditionally designated as *being-true*," 215. See apophansis; display

exist, existence, existentiality (This entry covers occurrences in the sense of Existenz, but also includes some in the sense of Dasein, Vorhandenheit, Vorhandensein. For certain special occurrences, see Existenz.) 9ff., 15, 18–19, 20, 24, 27ff., 30ff., 36ff., 39ff., 43ff., 47ff., 49–50, 54ff., 64ff., 71ff., 74–75, 77ff., 83ff., 86ff., 88ff., 91ff., 93–94, 94ff., 99–100, 100ff., 108, 109, 111, 112, 117, 120–121, 137ff., 141, 145, 147, 153, 154, 157, 158ff., 161, 164ff., 168ff., 170ff., 174, 175, 176, 187–188, 191, 194ff., 201ff., 208–209, 211, 216–217, 217–218, 219ff., 222–223, 227ff., 233–234, 259, 270, 274, 275ff., 279–280, 295ff., 297–298, 309, 317, 318ff., 322, 328: ASSERTING existence, 317; AUTHENTIC AND INAUTHENTIC existence, 170–171, 175; everyday, inauthentic irresolute existence, 289; authentic existence, defined, 170, as resolute, 287–288; AUTOTELIC existence, 141, 170; "The Dasein exists; that is to say, it is for the sake of its own capacity-to-be-in-the-world," 170; existence of BEING AND TRUTH, 223; constitution of the Dasein's existence as BEING-IN-THE-WORLD, 174; basic CONSTITUTION of existence, 291; existence, interpreted by the ECSTATIC CHARACTER OF TIME: it is "the original unity of being-outside-self that comes-toward-self, comes-back-to-self, and enpresents. In its ecstatic character, temporality is the condition of the constitution of the Dasein's being," 267; EVERYDAY existence, 170, 171; natural everyday existence, 240; question of MEANING AND MOVEMENTS of existence,

154; existence MEANS: to be in the carrying through of the distinction between being and beings, 319; "To exist . . . means, among other things, to be as comporting with beings. It belongs to the nature of the Dasein to exist in such a way that it is always already with other beings," 157; "To exist means to be in a world. Being-in-the-world is an essential structure of the Dasein's being. . . . The structure of being-in-the-world makes manifest the essential peculiarity of the Dasein, that it projects a world for itself, and it does this not subsequently and occasionally but, rather, the projecting of the world belongs to the Dasein's being. In this projection the Dasein has always already *stepped out beyond itself, ex-sistere; it is in* a world. . . . The reason why we reserve the concept 'existence' for the Dasein's being lies in the fact that being-in-the-world belongs to this its being," 169–170; NATURAL CONCEPTION of existence, 102; existence as absolute POSITION, 32, 39ff., 42–43, 43ff., 48–49; as absolute position, interpreted Temporally, 316ff.; POSSIBLE existence, 78; existence always already means to STEP BEYOND or, better, having stepped beyond, 300, *see* transcendence; existence of TIME, 233–234, 236–237; existential concept of time: future, past, present, 265ff.; existence is made possible by TRANSCENDENCE, 323; ". . . TRUTH belongs to the Dasein; truth exists," 219; existence and UNDERSTANDING, 277–278; "An understanding of the being of existence in general is enclosed in every existentiell understanding," 279; existence as the Dasein's WAY OF BEING, 28, mode of being, 64; existence WORDS, for us and in the tradition, 28; ". . . the WORLD is not extant but rather it exists, it has the Dasein's mode of being," 166

existent (n.), 95

existentia, 15, 24, 28, 77ff., 83ff., 86ff., 91ff., 93–94, 94ff., 99–100, 100ff., 106ff., 112ff., 117ff., 120, 202ff., 218

existential analytic, 227; its outcome from *Being and Time:* the constitution of the being of the Dasein is grounded in temporality, 228

existentiell, 277–278, 291, 294, 296, 297; "related to existence," 279; e. understanding, 277ff., 286ff.; in e. understanding the Dasein is projected upon its ability to be, 279–280

Existenz, 28, 43, 120, 141, 154

existere, 92, 109, 112, 115, 119. *See* esse

expect, expecting, expectance (gewärtig sein, Gewärtigen), 259–260, 261, 265, 266, 270, 271, 289ff., 310–311; expecting a FOR-WHAT, 310; expecting the FOR-WHICH in using equipment, 293; the Dasein always expects ITSELF in expecting any particular happening, 265; expecting as a LOOKING-FORWARD-TO, 289; expecting the POSTERIOR, 245; the PROJECTIVE, active character of expectance in production, 293; RETENTIVE expectance, 293; expecting and "THEN," 259; an expecting expresses itself in the then, 261; expecting as ground of WAITING-FOR, 289. *See* temporal, comportments; transition, experience of; motion, experience of

experience, 22, 37, 41, 48, 56, 61–62, 129, 229, 234; e. of BEFORE AND AFTER, 247; ontical e. of BEINGS presupposes pre-ontological understanding of being, 281; e. of EARLIER AND LATER (time), 247; e. of MOTION, 242–243, 244ff.; NATURAL e., 229; time as given with e. of the SELF, of mental actions qua motions (Aristotle), 253–254; common e. of THINGS, 205; e. of TIME, 244, 268

explanatory and understanding sciences, 276–277

expression, 259, 270; how assertion expresses ANTECEDENTLY UNDERSTOOD BEING, 211; e. of TEMPORAL COMPORTMENTS: now, then, at-the-time as self-expressions of the temporal

preparatory ontological analytic of the Dasein, 19–20, 24, 224; the need to repeat it at a higher level, 224; fundamental-ontological problem of the possibility of the understanding of being in general, 281–282. Note that the title given to Part Two, p. 321, refers to the "fundamental-ontological" question as that of the meaning of being in general

further outside, further inside, 299. *See* inside; outside

futural, 265; the Dasein as f.: coming toward itself from its most peculiar possibility, 265

future, 233, 265, 266–267, 272–273, 306; the f. as basis of possibility of BEING-IN, 302; COMMON CONCEPT of the f., the not-yet-now, 233–234, 260–261, 265; the f. in the COMMON SENSE by way of things, inauthentic, 289ff.; the f. as ECSTATIC, 266–267; ESSENCE of the f., 266; original EXISTENTIAL CONCEPT of the f., as presupposition for common concept, 265, and defined as the "coming-toward-oneself from one's most peculiar possibility," 265

Galileo Galilei, 321

Gattung (genus), 107

Gefühlsphilosophie (philosophy of feeling = philosophizing by feeling), 328

Gegenstand (object), 200

Genesis, 118

genesis, 308. *See* degeneration

genuine and ungenuine: not synonymous with authentic and inauthentic, 160–161

genus, 107

geometry, 53–54, 55, 70

Germany, 192, 262

Gestalt, 106

given (from: es gibt, it gives, i.e., there is), 10, 190–191; the givenness of beings and of being, 10–11, 281

Glaucon, 284

God, 27ff., 29ff., (*see* ontological argument), 38ff., 43, 79ff., 88, 90–91, 97–98, 100, 103, 124, 138, 146, 151, 176, 297, 298; G. as ENS INCREATUM and causa prima of beings, 118–119; ONTOLOGY of G., 81–82; G. as PRODUCER of things, 105; G. as PROTOTYPE of all being, 148

Godhead, 90

Goethe, Johann Wolfgang von, 4, 283

good: IDEA of the good in Plato, with hint that "the idea agathou is nothing but the demiourgos pure and simple," 285–286; Plato on the good as OUTSTRIPPING BEING, 284

grammar, 126

Greek, Greeks, 73, 85ff., 106ff., 115–116, 117, 183, 207, 215–216, 315, 317

Greek expressions: aei on, 115, 303; agathon, 283, 285; aisthesis, 110; akolouthein, 243–244, 255; aletheuein, 73, 188, 215, 217; alloiosis, 242; anamnesis, 326; apophansis, 209; aporia, 162, 233; arithmos, 235, 239, 249, 251; bios, 121; deloun, 215, 217; diairesis, 182, 199, 209, 212; dianoia: en dianoia, on en dianoia, 182–183, 188, 214, 216; dioxis, 136; dunamei on, 88; eidolon, 189; eidos, 86, 106ff., 109, 151; einai, 109, 115; ekstatikon, 267; ek tinos eis ti, 242, 245; energeia, 87, 104; entelecheia, 87; epekeina, 284, 285, 299, 307; gene ton onton, 107; genos, 106, 107; gignoskein, 283; helios, 283; horaton, 283; horismos, 86, 106, 108; horos, 106; hule, 107, 116; hupokeimenon (*cf.* subjectum), 38, 108, 127, 130,

148, 153, 187, 315; idea, 53, 106, 109; idein, 74; kairos, 288; kat' exochen, 126; kineseos ti, 238, 242, 272; kinesis, 234–235, 238, 242; kinoumenon, 234, 242; kuklophoria, 237; logos, 22, 73, 110, 121, 130, 177, 180, 183–184, 205–206, 209, 212, 215, 223, 312, 317; logos apophantikos, 180; logos ousias, 84; logos psuches, 73; megethos, 242; metaballon, 234; metabole, 234, 242, 256; methexis, 82; metron, 251; morphe, 83, 86, 106ff., 108, 116; noein, noeton, 109, 117–118, 283; nous, 73, 110, 121, 223, 236; nun, 236, 288, 305; omma tes psuches, 109; on: me on, 208, 233, ouk on, 208, to on, 53, 194; orexis, 136; ousia, 86, 106, 108–109, 110, 115, 119, 148, 194, 233, 315; peras, 249; periechesthai, 252; phainesthai, 209; phantasia, 107; pheromenon, 242, 244; phora, 242; phos, 283; phuge, 136; phusis, 86, 106, 107, 138; poiein, 286; pragma: en pragmasin, 182–183, 188, 214; praxis, 286; prossemainei, 181; prote philosophia, 79; proteron kai husteron, 236, 241ff., 245ff.; psuche, 73, 110, 121, 223; semantikos, 180; sumbebekos, 251; sumbolon, 185; sunecheia, suneches, 236, 238, 242–243; sunthesis, 181, 199, 209, 212; techne, 53, 286; teleion, 108; theorein, 110, 117; ti esti, ti estin, 34, 85; topos, 242; to ti en einai, 85, 106, 107; zoe, 121

ground, 72, 92, 271; EGO as g. of its determinations, 127; ego as g. of possibility of all being (Kant), 128; ontological grounding of all FUNCTIONALITY RELATIONS in the for-the-sake-of-which, 295; all INTENTIONAL COMPORTMENT is grounded on the basic constitution of being-in-the-world, 175; g. of the ONTOLOGICAL DIFFERENCE, 228; g. of coupling of names in the PROPOSITION (Hobbes), 186–187; grounding of RESOLUTENESS in its own more original and authentic temporality, 287–288; TEMPORALITY as g. of the Dasein's ontological constitution, 227–228

growth, 308

hallucination, 60, 315

hammering, 293

hand (as in vorhanden, at hand, present at hand = extant), 101, 104, 114

handy, being-handy, handiness (zuhanden, Zuhandensein, Zuhandenheit), 279, 289, 292–293, 296, 299ff., 303ff., 307, 309ff., 323; negative moment in structure of handiness: ABSENS, 311; the handy, DEFINED as the whole of all beings having the ontological constitution of equipment, 292; being-handy DISTINGUISHED FROM EXTANTNESS, 304; handiness and PRAESENS: why h. is understood primarily via praesens, 308; how h. is understood as praesens, 309; h. implies a peculiar sense of praesens, 309, a specific praesensial constitution of the horizon of the present, 309; h. determined by praesens, 312

happen, happening (geschehen, Geschehen, cf. history): "Understanding as the Dasein's self-projection is the Dasein's fundamental mode of happening," 277–278

harmonia praestabilita, 148

Hartmann, Nicolai, 62

has been, having-been-ness (gewesen, Gewesenheit), 265–266, 287, 290; what we have been is always contained in what we are, 290; a non-temporal (merely intratemporal) entity cannot have-been, 290. See past

heavens, 236; outermost heavenly sphere, 234, 237

Hegel, Georg Wilhelm Friedrich, 3, 5, 11, 13, 14, 22, 29, 74, 80, 81, 83, 91, 112, 118, 125 (subject-object distinction), 127, 148, 152–153, 159, 177, 178, 199, 231, 327; revival of H., 100–101; on overcoming and appropriating H., 178; H. on identity of being and

treatment of LOGIC, 177; K. "does not get beyond the ONTOLOGY OF THE EXTANT," 148; he follows ancient and medieval ontology in his basic ontological orientation, 152; he did not advance to the specific ontological constitution of the Dasein, 153; his PHILOSOPHY as "transcendental philosophy," 298; his PROOF of the impossibility of ontology of the subject: insufficiency of the argument, 145ff.; REVIVAL of K., 100–101; K.'s THESIS: being is not a real predicate, being is position, existence is absolute position or perception: 15, 27ff., 39ff., 43ff., 55ff., 67ff., 72ff., 77–78; see theses, 1st thesis, Kantian; review of the Kantian thesis and author's criticism of it, and answers which complete the criticism, 313ff.; K. on TIME, 252; K.'s idea of the TRANSCENDENTAL and of philosophy, 323. See the numerous references to Kant under interpretation

Kierkegaard, Søren: criticism of his doctrine of the instant /called either the Instant or the Moment in Kierkegaard translations/, 288

knowledge, 200–201, 208, 220, 283ff.; APRIORITY of k., 20, 24; pre-philosophical and philosophical k. regarding BEING AND TIME, 303; k. of FACT, 202; k. as JUDGMENT (Neo-Kantianism), 202; k. of a PRODUCT, 149ff.; SUBJECT'S k. of its predicates, as self-consciousness, 152; THEORY of k., 298ff., 304

language, 190–191, 208; linguistic usage, 195, as historical, 208–209. See speech

Lask, Emil, 178

lasting, 263

Latinate: author's use of Latinate expressions in his German text, for all time-determinations; the reason why, 305

laying-asunder (diairesis), 212

leaping into the present, 266

Leibniz, Gottfried Wilhelm, 11, 34–35, 74, 88, 92, 119, 127, 174, 231, 300–301; his proposition about monads clarified and criticized via the Dasein's transcendence, 301

let, letting: let something stand of its own self, 117; let something be encountered, 118; let be in and with, 293

let-function, letting-function (bewendenlassen, Bewendenlassen), 293–294, 304, 310; defined: "This antecedent understanding of functionality, this projecting of equipment onto its functionality character, we call letting-function /Bewendenlassen/," in an ontological sense, 293; meaning of "to let function in something," 293; "Letting-function, as understanding of functionality, is that projection which first of all gives to the Dasein the light in whose luminosity things of the nature of equipment are encountered," 293; letting-function points back to a more original temporality, 294

lie-before, lie present there (vorliegen), 108, 148, 152, 281, 293

lie-between, 218. See middle

life, living being, 9, 10, 51–52, 54, 121, 129, 131, 173 (see concept, life), 190–191

light, illumination, 283ff.

limit, 249; the now is not a l., 249ff., 256

literature, creative (Dichtung), 171ff.

Locke, John, 192

logic, 15, 24, 33–34, 40, 55, 74, 126, 183, 187, 194, 198ff., 207, 317; sense in which ancient ontology is a logic of BEING, 73; HISTORY of l., 179ff.; l. became separate (philosophical) discipline, 177; treatment of l. by Kant, 177, Hegel, 177, nineteenth century (Mill, Lotze,

of motion and telling time, 245; the n. follows the moving thing, 246; the n. as counted concomitantly in following a motion, 246; ORIGIN of the n., 261; the n. originates from the instant, it is derivative, 288; the n. distinguished from PRAESENS, 305; n.-REFERENCE of the then and at-the-time, 247; n.-SEQUENCE, 268; common time as infinite irreversible sequence of nows, 260; now-sequence, in common conception of time, 263; nows, understood by the falling Dasein as infinite succession, 272; "clipped sequence of nows," 273; n. as SPANNED, 269−270; n. and TEMPORALITY: n. as derived from ecstatic character of temporality, 269; now-time, its structural moments derived from ecstatic-horizonal temporality, 268ff.; "the now is nothing but the 'expression,' the 'speaking out,' of original temporality itself in its ecstatic character," 270; derivation of time, as now-sequence, from temporality, 274; n. and TIME: nows as in time, constitutive of time, 247; n. as not in time, 249; n. as time itself, not a part of time, 251; why the n. is a time-character, 269; n., then, at-the-time /time determinations/, 246; now-determination, 306; n. and TRANSITION: the nows as counted in following a transition, 245−246; n. as having dimension within itself, stretching out toward a not-yet and a no-longer: intrinsically transition, 248, 250−251; "Because the now is transition, it is capable of making motion accessible *as motion,* in its unbroken character of transition," 251; n. as transitionary, always the not-yet-now and no-longer-now, 255, 273

now-here, 245

now-there, 245

now-till-then, 263. *See* span

number, 249ff.; the now as n., not limit, 256

numerical character of the now and time: basis for understanding intratemporality, 256; entails that time embraces the beings in it (Aristotle), 256

object, objective (Gegenstand, Objekt), 37, 38, 41, 45ff., 59ff., 63, 64, 65ff., 68−69, 123, 125, 126, 128, 130−131, 138, 140, 166, 200−201, 202, 204, 215, 255, 256, 274, 297, 299−300, 313−314, 320ff.; beings and being as objects, 281−282; time "is more objective than all objects and simultaneously it is subjective," 254

object-ego, 130, 131, 142; empirical object-ego, 132

objectification (Vergegenständlichung): the TWO ESSENTIAL POSSIBILITIES: o. of being (philosophy) and o. of beings (positive sciences), 320ff., 322ff., 327; o. of BEING: 281; "It is in the objectification of being as such that the basic act constitutive of ontology as a science is performed," 281; projection of being upon the horizon of its understandability, 322; begins with projection of being upon transcendence, 323; as a coming back to what has been forgotten, 326

objectivizing (Objektivierung): erroneous o. of intentionality, 59ff., 65, 313

occasionalism, 148

occupy, be occupied with (The idiom is "es geht um." In *Being and Time* this was rendered by the phrase "is an issue for," in order to avoid the ambiguous conflict with the term "concern," which was used with reference to extant things. The translations "occupy," "be occupied with," give a closer rendering and still avoid the conflict with concern of *Being and Time,* although if we were starting fresh the term "concern" would surely be better.), the Dasein's occupation with its own being, its own ability-to-be, 276, 295

Ockham, William of, 183

ontical, 11, 19–20, 54, 100, 121, 137, 145, 155, 219, 227, 279, 281, 291, 295, 296, 327–328;
   o. foundation of ontology, 20 (*see* fundamental ontology; Translator's Introduction, xxiff.,
   xxviff.); o. propositions, knowledge, 144; o. understanding, 279–280; stratification of
   projections in o. understanding, 280; o. versus ontological interpretation, 306; o. projection, 323
ontological, ontology, 11ff., 15ff., 19ff., 23–24, 27, 29ff., 54, 55ff., 74ff., 77ff., 88, 90, 100,
   113, 117ff., 119ff., 128, 145, 195, 198, 199, 220–221, 222ff., 225, 227ff., 271, 281–282,
   295–296, 308, 313, 322ff., 328; ANCIENT o. (Greek), 29, 66, 73 ("a logic of being"),
   86–87, 90, 101–102, 105, 106ff., 110ff., 115ff., 117ff., 121, 147–148, 150–151, 177;
   origin of ancient o. from the productive and intuitive comportments toward beings, 115ff.,
   118; why the A PRIORI appears in o., 324; o. analytic, 16; preparatory o. analytic of the
   Dasein's existential constitution, 227; o. CATEGORIES, 117; basic o. CONCEPTS, 100, 116;
   ancient basic concepts of o., 118–119; CONDITIONS of coming-to-be and perishing,
   169–170; o. CONSTITUTION, 52, 54, 55, 65, 78; of being, 15, 52, 77, 78; of the being that
   we ourselves are, 140, 298; of the Dasein, 74–75, 119, 122, 154, 171, 174, 294; of man,
   138; of the person, 137ff.; of producing, 109; CORRELATION of ontologies with kinds of
   beings (Kant), 139; o. and the DASEIN, 110–111; "all ontology, even the most primitive,
   necessarily looks back to the Dasein," 122; it depends on laying open the ontological
   constitution of the Dasein, 154; it constitutes itself a science in the Dasein's explicit
   carrying out of the ontological difference, 319–320; *see* fundamental ontology; Translator's Introduction, xxiff., xxviff.; o. DESCRIBED as "determination of the meaning of being
   by way of time," 17; basic o. DETERMINATIONS of a being, 105; o. DIFFERENCE, *see*
   ontological difference; o. of the EXTANT, 148; traditional o. of extantness, 147; FUNDA-
   MENTAL o., *see* fundamental ontology; FUNDAMENTAL QUESTION of o., 223; FUNDAMEN-
   TAL SUBJECT OF RESEARCH in o., Temporality, 17; GENERAL o. and o. of nature, mind,
   God, 80; o. of HISTORY, 170; o. of HUMAN EXISTENCE, 137; o. concept of HUMANITY, 138;
   o. INQUIRY, 111, 200; relation of an o. theory to theories of the "IS," 198–222ff.; continuity
   of KANTIAN o. with ancient and medieval, 117ff.; MEDIEVAL o., 24, 29, 73, 74, 77ff., 101,
   102, 105, 117, 147, 152; METHOD of o., 19ff.; four tasks of inquiry into o. method (ontical
   foundation and fundamental analytic of the Dasein; the a priori; the three components
   of method; phenomenology as procedure), 19ff., 24; the three basic components of ontological method: reduction, construction, destruction, 21ff.; MODERN o., 15, 24, 104,
   105, 122ff.; NAIVE AND REFLECTIVE o., 110–111; OBJECTIFICATION OF BEING as basic
   constitutive ontological act, 281; ONTICAL FOUNDATION of o., 19 (*see* fundamental ontology); o. of PERSON, 137ff.; o. meaning of person, most manifest in respect, 138;
   PHENOMENOLOGICAL METHOD of o., 20, 324ff.; phenomenological o., 24; o. and PHILOS-
   OPHY, 11ff., 24; o. PROBLEMS, *see* ontological problems; o. in its first naive orientation:
   PRODUCTIVE OR PERCEPTUAL-INTUITIVE, 117; o. PROPOSITIONS are all Temporal, 324;
   why they are Temporal and a priori, 324; o. PROTOTYPE: God as o. prototype throughout
   the history of philosophy, 148; RADICAL o., 224; o. constitutes itself a SCIENCE in the
   Dasein's explicit carrying out of the ontological difference, 319–320; o. as TEMPORAL
   SCIENCE, 324; "Because Temporal projection makes possible an objectification of being
   and assures conceptualizability, and thereby constitutes ontology in general as a science,
   we call this science in distinction from the positive sciences the TEMPORAL SCIENCE.
   . . . All the propositions of ontology are Temporal propositions," 323; o. THEMATIZATION

of being, 227; TRADITIONAL o., 37, 102, 124, 147, 165; how o. is a TRANSCENDENTAL
SCIENCE, 268, 323; basis for UNIVERSAL SIGNIFICANCE assignable to the fundamental
concepts of ancient o., 116. *See* phenomenology; philosophy

ontological argument, 30ff., 42, 43; Thomas Aquinas' criticism, 31−32; Kant's criticism,
32ff.

ontological difference, 17, 52, 72, 75, 78, 120, 225, 318ff., 332; the o.d. defined as the
difference between a being (or beings) and being, 120; it becomes "more complicated,"
120; it is "the distinction between being and beings, when it is carried out explicitly," 319;
must it be interpreted Temporally? 286; it is *"temporalized in the temporalizing of temporality,"* 319 (*cf.* temporalize). Among the four basic problems of ontology-philosophy-
phenomenology, that of the o.d. is the first and is the only one given detailed discussion
in the present lecture course. *See* ontological problems

ontological problems, 17ff., 77−78. "If philosophy is the science of being, then the FIRST
AND LAST AND BASIC PROBLEM OF PHILOSOPHY must be, What does being signify? Whence
can something like being in general be understood? How is understanding of being at all
possible?" 15, 16, 23; FOUR BASIC PROBLEMS of the science of being, 17ff.: (1) ontological
difference, 17−18, 24, 72, 120, 225, 227ff., 318ff.; (2) articulation of being, 18, 24, 78,
120; (3) modifications of being and unity of concept of being, 18, 24, 121, 154ff., 173ff.;
(4) truth-character of being, 18−19, 24, 179, 183, 201, 205, 214, 218ff., 222ff., 225

open, 270, 306; openness belonging to ecstasis, 267; "Openness belongs to /the Dasein's/
being. The Dasein is its Da, its here-there, in which it is here for itself and in which others
are there with it," 300. *See* Da

orientation, 163, 230−231, 307; o. regarding the BASIC PROBLEM OF ONTOLOGY, 224; all
elucidation of being is oriented to the DASEIN, 223; o. toward EXTANT BEINGS, 294; o.
within the INTRAWORLDLY, 311; o. toward NON-HANDINESS, 309; o. of PHILOSOPHICAL
PROBLEMS in the tradition, Descartes, and Kant, 122−123, 312; o. toward the TIME-
PHENOMENON, 230

origin, 86; o. of concepts of ESSENCE AND EXISTENCE, 100ff.; (common) o. of concepts of
ESSENTIA AND EXISTENTIA, 105, 110, 119; o. of concept of ESSENTIA in reference to
production, 105, 106ff.; o. of concept of EXISTENTIA or existence as actualization and
actuality, 101ff., 104−105; o. of concepts of MATTER AND MATERIAL, 115−116; temporality as o. of TIME (in the common sense), 241; o. of common time in original temporality,
268ff.

original, 162, 265ff., 279, 304, 306; o. mode of being of CLOCK USAGE, 258; o. constitution
of the DASEIN'S BEING, 228; o. EXISTENTIAL SENSE of: the future (Zukunft), 265, past
(Gewesenheit, having-been-ness), 265−266, and present (Gegenwart), 266; TEMPORAL-
ITY as o. time, 241; TIME in its originality, 230; return to o. time, 230; o. comportment
toward time, 258; o. having of time, 258; unity of future, past, and present—original
time—temporality, 266

other, others, 322−323

otherness, 73

ousia: its various senses, 151. *See* Greek expressions

outer sense, 143

outside, 66, 149; the DASEIN as further o. than any object and further inside than any
subject, 255; o.-ITSELF and time as ecstatic, 267; temporality as the primary outside-itself,

phenomenon, phenomena, 113, 161, 165, 305, 306, 322; p. of BEING-IN AND WORLD, 291; the INSTANT AND THE NOW compared as p., 287−288; p. of INTENTIONALITY, 268; p. of PERCEPTION, 313; p. of the PRESENT AND PRAESENS, 305, 306; p. of TEMPORALITY, 268−306; p. of TIME, 230, 237; p. of the WORLD, 165, 167−168, 294

philosophy, 1, 3−4, 4ff., 11ff., 17ff., 19ff., 23−24, 29, 51ff., 56, 57−58, 73ff., 77, 82, 111−112, 121, 165ff., 177, 191, 194, 227, 281ff., 294, 295, 298, 322−323; ACADEMIC AND COSMIC conceptions of p. (Kant), 7ff.; ANCIENT p., 73, 77ff., 83ff., 96, 98, 116, 117ff., 123−124, 155, 165, 207, 209, 286, 315−316, 319, 321; its orientation toward reason, mind, the subject, 312; BEING AS BASIC PROBLEM: 11ff., esp. 16; "the question about the meaning and ground of being," 223; BEING, IN EARLY p.: early p. interprets being in orientation toward the extant, 294; CONTEMPORARY "anxiety in the face of philosophy", 167; contemporary p., 90, 167, 325; philosophical CONVERSATION, 210; CURRENT PRE-DICAMENT of p., 281ff.; p. and the DASEIN: throughout its history, p. is oriented to the Dasein, 367f.; as a science, it is founded on the Dasein's existence, 319−320; HISTORY of p., 22, 29, 124, 224; MEDIEVAL p., 77, 79, 83ff., 102, see Middle Ages; Scholastics; MODERN p., 61, 73, 80, 90, 119, 148; modern p.'s primary orientation toward the subject, 123ff., 142; POST-KANTIAN p., 29; PRE-KANTIAN p., 29, 98; PRE-PHILOSOPHICAL, 114, 165−166; pre-philosophical knowledge, 111, 121; PROBLEMATIC of p., 152; PROBLEMS of p., 155, 295; allegedly central philosophical problem, 62; see problem, problems; PROTE PHILO-SOPHIA, 79; p. as SCIENCE OF BEING, 11ff., 52ff., 320ff.; SCIENTIFIC p., 3−4, 7, 23, 322; "All philosophy . . . returns to the SOUL, mind, consciousness, subject, ego in clarifying the basic ontological phenomena," 73; "Philosophy must perhaps start from the 'SUBJECT' and return to the 'subject' in its ultimate questions, and yet for all that it may not pose its questions in a one-sidedly subjectivistic manner," 155; a philosophical TASK: p. must comprehend conceptually the belonging-together of comportment to beings and under-standing of being, 327; THEME of p.: "what is taken for granted as being self-evident is the true and sole theme of philosophy," 58; p. as TRANSCENDENTAL, 128, 324 ("in the proper sense"); WESTERN p., 3, 75, 112; p. and WORLD: p. has not yet recognized the concept or phenomenon of world, 165; p. and WORLD-VIEW, 4ff.

phone, 206

place: relation of time to place, 238; p. of equipment within an equipmental contexture, 310

plants, 165, 297

Plato, 22, 52ff., 73, 82, 107, 109, 111, 124, 183, 194, 199, 208, 209, 282ff., 319, 328−329; P. on truth-function of logos, 354; P.'s doctrine of knowledge and simile of the cave, 283ff.; P. as discoverer of the a priori: anamnesis, recollection, in the Phaedrus and Phaedo, 326−327

pleasure: faculty of p. and unpleasure, 132−133

Plotinus, 81

poetry (Dichtung), 171; "Poetry, creative literature, is nothing but the elementary emergence into words, the becoming-uncovered, of existence as being-in-the-world. For the others who before it were blind, the world first becomes visible by what is thus spoken," 171−172. See Rilke

point: the now and the p., 248−249

pope, 80−81

Porphyry, 182

present (adj.), be present, something present, presence (These terms translate two German words: (1) the adjective "vorhanden" and its modifications, otherwise rendered in the present volume as extant, at-hand, present-at-hand; (2) the verb "anwesen," its participial adjective "anwesend," and corresponding noun forms. In some passages Heidegger brings the two together and thus establishes an important link between extantness and presence as we have these terms in English. In addition, he explicitly associates a noun form, "Anwesen," in one of its normal German senses—as meaning real property in the form of present premises—with the Greek ousia, which has a similar sense; and this adds a new dimension to the linkage between being in the sense of Vorhandensein—extantness, at-handness—and being in the sense of Anwesenheit—presentness, presence.) 94, 108–109, 260, 305, 309, 311, 315; presence and absence as "praesens modified and modifiable thus and so," 307. *See* absence; absens; Anwesen

present (noun: Gegenwart; corresponding adjective = gegenwärtig), 101, 233, 260, 266, 269, 287, 305, 311, 312; the p. as ECSTATIC, 266ff.; ESSENCE of the p., 266; the p. EXPLICATED, 306ff.; the p. as related to the EXTANT, 315; what the p. is, 306; the p. as relating to the HANDY, 312; ecstasis of the p. as primary in commerce with the handy, 308; the p. as temporalized in resoluteness is the INSTANT, contrasted with the present of ordinary comportment, the now, 287ff. (*see* instant); the p. not constantly the instant, 288; why the inauthentic p. is not an instant, 290–291; the p. expresses itself in the NOW, 261; the p. in the ORIGINAL, EXISTENTIAL SENSE of the Dasein's enpresenting, dwelling with, 266; the p. as having the horizon of PRAESENS, 312

present-at-hand (vorhanden; *see alternative translations:* at-hand, extant), 109

presuppose, presupposition, 12, 52ff., 71, 294; EXISTENTIAL CONCEPTS OF FUTURE, PAST, PRESENT as presuppositions of common concepts of future, past, present, 265ff.; PHILOSOPHY "deals with what every positing of beings . . . must already *presuppose* essentially," 12; ontological presuppositions of POSITIVE SCIENCES, 52ff.; presupposing TRUTH: must timeless truth be presupposed?, 220; "Truth is the presupposition for our being able to presuppose anything at all. . . . Presupposition everywhere presupposes truth," 221

pretense, 216

primus: p. et principium ens, p. significatum, p. analogatum, p. divisio entis, 81

prior, 245; how being and existence are understood prior to beings, 74

privative, 304; p. and positive, 309

problem, problems, 11, 15ff., 24, 29, 140, 167, 223–224, 309, 312–313. (A) THE BASIC PROBLEM OF PHILOSOPHY OR ONTOLOGY: THE MEANING OF BEING IN GENERAL, 16, 222ff., 225ff., 313. (B) THE FOUR BASIC PROBLEMS OF PHENOMENOLOGY (ontology, philosophy), each of which underlies one of the four theses; LISTED, 19, 24, 225; THEIR SYSTEMATIC UNITY, 19, 76. (B1) THE FIRST PROBLEM, THE PROBLEM OF THE ONTOLOGICAL DIFFERENCE, the distinction (made explicit) between being and beings, 17–18, 19, 55, 72, 78, 120, 225, 227ff. (B2) THE SECOND PROBLEM, THE BASIC ARTICULATION OF BEING, the essential content of a being and its mode of being, 18, 19, 121ff.; how the Scholastics handled the problem, 79ff., 88ff.; history of the problem, 81; three interpretative views regarding the problem in Scholasticism: Thomas, Scotus, Suarez, 89–90; its treatment in medieval mysticism (Eckhart), 90–91; its treatment by Thomas Aquinas and his followers, Aegidius Romanus and Joannes Capreolus, 91ff., by Scotus, 93–94, and by Suarez, 94–95, 96ff.; access to the problem, 95–96; orientation of the question toward

production, 98–99, 101–102, 105, 106ff.; in Greek ontology, 110ff., 118–119; phenomenological clarification of the problem, 99ff.; treatment of the distinction between essentia
and existentia, 99–100, 101, 102ff.; inadequate foundation of traditional treatment of the
problem, 112ff., 119; inner connection between traditional and Kantian treatment of the
problem, 117ff. (B3) THE THIRD PROBLEM, THE POSSIBLE MODIFICATIONS OF BEING AND
THE UNITY OF THE CONCEPT OF BEING, 18, 19, 121, 123, 124–125, 154, 173ff., 225;
diversities of being versus unity of concept of being, 125; ontological distinction of subject-
object, 122, 124, 125; Kant on the distinction, 125; Descartes' distinction between res
cogitans and res extensa, 125ff.; detailed discussion of Kant on personality and its three
senses—transcendental, psychological, moral, 125ff.; person versus thing, 137ff.; critique
of Kantian solution of the problem of "the being of the being which we humans each
ourselves are," 140ff.; summary view of Kant's interpretation of subjectivity, 146–147;
the horizon of production, 147ff., 150ff.; fundamental problem of the multiplicity of ways
of being and unity of the concept of being in general, 154ff.; problem of the distinction
of the being of the Dasein from other being, 154, 158ff., 161ff., 168ff. (the being of nature,
of historical, cultural entities, the world, the Dasein); the fundamental problem summarized, 173ff. (B4) THE FOURTH PROBLEM, THE TRUTH-CHARACTER OF BEING, 18–19,
177ff., 179ff., 180ff., 183–184, 192, 200–201, 201–202, 204–205, 205ff., 222ff., 225;
the central problem here, discussed in the limited horizon of the "is," the being of the
copula, 177; "forced aside into logic," 177; connection of copula with basic ontological
problems, 179; characteristic treatments of the problem of the copula: Aristotle, Hobbes,
Mill, Lotze, 201ff.; being in the sense of the copula is, for Aristotle, synthesis in the logos,
183; Hobbes' nominalistic formulation of the problem, 183; copula as index of cause on
which coupling of names is grounded, 186; connection with truth, 188ff.; critique of
Hobbes' nominalism, 191–192; Mill's change from nominalism to dominantly non-
nominalist view, 192–193; copula as sign of predication, 193–194; and of existence, 194;
Mill's distinctions regarding propositions and functions of copula, 195; the "is" as "it
means," 197; critique of Mill's distinctions, 197–198; ambiguity of copula, 197–198;
Mill's emphasis on "is" in sense of "exists," 198; Lotze's view, 198; impossibility of negative
copula, 199; doctrine of principal and subordinate thoughts, 199–200; the "is" as signifying combination and truth, 200; consequences of Lotze's approach for nineteenth- and
twentieth-century thought, 200–201; survey of interpretations of the "is" and characteristic determinations for the copula, 201ff; summary review of characteristic treatments
of the problem of the copula, 202; examples of propositions to test understanding of this
contexture, 203–204; brief outline of all the different interpretations of the copula, and
what the being of the copula signifies, 204; implied senses of being, 204–205; query
regarding validity of this approach to the question of the meaning of being, 205; inadequacy of dealing with assertion in terms of the being of the copula, 205ff.; the decisive
question: what belongs to assertion beyond the verbal sequence, 206, how grasp the
relational whole here? 205ff.; detailed discussion of assertion from phenomenological
viewpoint: structures, 207ff., apophantic character, 209–210, assertion as communicatively determinant exhibition, and its relation to the "is" of the copula, 210ff.; problem
of relation of assertional truth to being of the entity asserted about, 213ff., assertional
truth: uncovering and disclosing as ways of unveiling, 215ff.; existential mode of being
of truth, and how it "lies between" subject and object, connected with the Dasein's

transcendence, 217−218; how truth exists, and its relationship to the existence of the Dasein, 219ff.; existential mode of being of truth and the basic ontological question of the meaning of being in general, 222ff.; special question of the meaning of the "is" in ontological propositions, e.g., "being *is* this or that," "being *is*," 222; the basic question of ontology, ontological priority of the Dasein, and the need for a preparatory ontological analytic of the Dasein as fundamental ontology (*q.v.*), 223−224

problems, specific (In the course of the lectures the author formulated many specific problems which were dealt with as the discussion proceeded. Among them, in addition to the particular problems raised within the framework of the four basic problems above, are questions relating particularly to the Dasein and to time. The question regarding the Dasein has to do with the nature of the being (Sein) of the being (Seiendes) which each human being itself is; the human being is a certain entity which has a certain mode of being, and the question has to do with this mode of being. *See* Dasein (the), as the being that we ourselves are, and 140. The Dasein, as ontical (a being), has an ontological priority (a priority with respect to being and the understanding of being), which leads to the problems of a fundamental ontology, 223−224; *see* fundamental ontology. Pursuit of the question of the condition of possibility of the understanding of being in the Dasein leads to the entire problematic of time and temporality, through which time can be seen as the horizon of all understanding of being. The problems here fall into THREE MAIN DIVISIONS. (A) What is the nature of time as commonly understood and as specifically articulated in Aristotle's treatise on time (which gives explicit formulation to the common view of time)? (B) How is time as commonly understood derivative from original time, the original temporality of expecting, retaining, and enpresenting? (C) How can time, and especially original time, original temporality, be conceptually comprehended as the condition of possibility of all understanding of being and hence of ontology as the science of being? The following is a representative listing of appearance of these three parts of the overall problematic.) (A) TIME AS COMMONLY UNDERSTOOD AND AS ARTICULATED BY ARISTOTLE: Aristotle's two chief problems concerning time, 232ff.; problem of the origin of the now, 246; if there is no soul does time exist? Aristotle's specific interpretation of this problem, 254; "*What* then is time and *how* does it exist? Is it only subjective, or is it only objective, or is it neither the one nor the other?" 255, and forecast of the answer, 256. (B) HOW IS TIME AS COMMONLY UNDERSTOOD DERIVATIVE FROM ORIGINAL TIME? 256; problem of clock-usage, 257; to what do we address ourselves in saying "now," "then," "before [at-the-time]"? 259; whence do we take the now without making it an object? 259; "We shall have to ask how what confronts us in the unity of expecting, retaining, and enpresenting can be validly asserted to be original time," 260; where do we get the now from? from enpresenting, 261; whence does the Dasein get the time it reckons with and expresses in the now, then, and at-the-time? 261; answer to be given by showing its origin in original time, temporality, 261, 265; what makes common time possible? 257, 259, and how does it derive from original time? 269; why did the traditional time concept have to overlook significance and datability? answer will derive from the structure of temporality, 263; why does the common understanding of time ignore the structural moments and conceive of time merely as a manifold of unstructured nows? 271ff. (C) TIME, AND ESPECIALLY ORIGINAL TIME, ORIGINAL TEMPORALITY, AS CONDITION OF POSSIBILITY OF ALL UNDERSTANDING OF BEING AND HENCE OF THAT PARTICULAR UNDERSTANDING OF BEING WHICH

METHOD, 22; p. upon PRAESENS, 306; praesensial p., Temporal p., 307; series of projections: understanding of beings, projection upon being, understanding of being, projection upon time; the end of the series (horizon of ecstatic unity of temporality), 308; TIME is "the original self-projection pure and simple," 308; the p. upon something involved in the UNDERSTANDING OF BEING, 280; "We understand a being only as we project it upon being. In the process, being itself must be understood in a certain way; being must in its turn be projected upon something," 280; "Understanding must itself *somehow see, as unveiled, that upon which it projects,*" 284; p. as an essential moment of understanding, 286; p. of WORLD, 168, 170

property (ousia), 108

proposition, propositio, 75, 180, 182, 183ff., 188ff., 193ff., 200, 201, 202ff., 206, 218; Hobbes' definition of the p., 184–185; Mill's account of the p., 193ff.; Mill's classification of propositions as essential-verbal-analytic versus accidental-real-synthetic, 195, 204; criticized, 197–198; structure of the p., 312ff.; defect in starting from the uttered p., 212; Temporal propositions (*see* ontology; philosophy), 324. *See* assertion; logos

proteron and husteron: question whether to be translated as earlier and later or before and after, 240–241, 245ff., 247; non-temporal sense in Aristotle, before and after in sequence of places, 246; temporal sense in Aristotle, earlier and later, 246–247

psychical, 58, 206

psychology, 49ff, 54, 58, 65, 80, 130, 131; psychologia rationalis, 80; psychology as ontical science versus philosophy as ontological, 52, 142; psychological ego, 130

publicness: p. as a structural element of expressed time, 261, 264; p. of time, derived from ecstatic character of temporality, 270

purpose: purposiveness, its structure and ontological possibility, 170; purpose-free, purposeless, 295

quality, 36, 89, 143

quantity, 143

question: q. of what, who, 120; quid est res, what is the thing? 120. *See* problem

quidditas, 31, 38, 85, 86, 88, 89, 94, 102, 119, 186–187; man's quidditas, 138; quod quid erat esse, 85, 105. *See* what; essence

ratio, 31, 95–96; r. abstractissima et simplicissima, 84; r. entis, 84; ratio, intentio intellecta, 84

rational, rationality, 131–132; r. beings, 138

reach, of perception, 67

real, realis, reality, realness, Realität, 28–29, 31, 33ff., 37–38, 42, 43, 45–46, 68, 75–76, 77–78, 85ff., 88, 89, 91ff., 95ff., 98–99, 101–102, 107–108, 119, 125, 148, 149, 187, 189, 195, 197, 198, 203–204; real predicate, 33ff., 43, 316–317; real propositions, 195ff.; three categories or fields of the real as recognized by J. S. Mill, 198; objective reality, 37–38; realitas objectiva, 38; realitas actualis, 38. *See* res, Sache, thing

realism, 167, 175

reason, 92, 94ff., 121, 141, 223; law of sufficient r., 92

receptivity, 144, 149, 151

reciprocity, 148–149

in this role as such a condition of possibility. For this purpose the Latinate equivalent of the German was used. But in English we already employ the Latinate expression for normal reference to the temporal. What then can we do? We might try an equivalent from the other classical language, Greek, as for instance, chronal and chronality. This was experimented with and found not completely satisfactory. The sense of identity with the concept of the temporal is not strong enough, the idiom is a little too strange, and unwanted associations enter, like that of the chronometer, which measures clock-time rather than Temporalität, and that of the chronic, as in chronic diseases and chronic habits. Another possibility is to find an English equivalent, like timelike, timely, timeish. However, beside being awkward, none of these gives the true intended meaning. It was decided, therefore, to employ a special device, capitalization, for the purpose. This gives us Temporal to correlate with German temporal and Temporality with Temporalität. Capitalization introduces typographical difficulties with the beginnings of printed sentences and in speaking one has to add the expression "capital-t" to refer to the terms. Another experiment was earlier made with the forms c-temporal and c-temporality, where the letter c stands for "condition of possibility," to remind us that here we are speaking of the temporal and temporality understood as condition of possibility. But this mode of expression is unnatural and awkward and experiments with readers were sufficient to establish their dislike for it. Consequently it was decided to accept the relatively minor infelicity of capitalization, where the capital letter functions as a *recollective index*, informing the reader about the transcendental role of temporality when that is under consideration. Indeed, the capital t could be taken as representative of the notion of the transcendental and the term Temporality may then be read as meaning temporality understood as transcendental horizon for the understanding of being and condition of possibility for all understanding of being and hence for the solution of the basic problem of ontology, namely, the problem of the meaning of being in general.), 17, 228, 274, 302, 305, 312, 313, 318, 322ff., 324ff.; T. DEFINED by the ontological problematic related to temporality: "It means temporality insofar as temporality itself is made into a theme as the condition of the possibility of the understanding of being and of ontology as such. The term 'Temporality' is intended to indicate that temporality, in existential analytic, represents the horizon from which we understand being," 228; T. defined as temporality in its role as condition of possibility of the understanding of being, both pre-ontological and ontological, 274; concept of T. to be defined, 292; Temporal interpretation of the BEING OF BEINGS, 306; T. interpretation of the BEING OF THE EXTANT by means of praesens, 317–318; CENTRAL ROLE of T. in ontological inquiry, 327; "The fundamental subject of research in ontology . . . is *Temporality*," 17; content of its general CONCEPT , "*[T]*emporality is *temporality with regard to the unity of the horizonal schemata belonging to it*," 307; T. interpretation of HANDINESS, 305, 309; T. content of KANT'S THESIS, 316; T. PROJECTION, 323; T. PROPOSITIONS, 323; T. SCIENCE (ontology), 323; T. TRUTH (veritas temporalis), 323, backward SUMMARY of exposition of T., 312

temporal, temporality (zeitlich, Zeitlichkeit; *cf.* the previous entry for the German temporal, Temporalität, translated as Temporal, Temporality), 16, 20, 228–229, 229ff., 236, 273–274, 278, 286ff., 294ff., 298, 302–303, 303ff., 306ff., 309ff., 318ff., 320ff.; AUTHENTIC t., 273; how BEING-IN-THE-WORLD is founded on t., 298ff.; temporal COMPORTMENTS: expecting and "then," retaining and "at the time," enpresenting and "now," 259ff.; their

toward things, 173, *see* orientation; ONTOLOGICAL CHARACTER of things, 174; things are not genuinely TRANSCENDENT, 299; things as TRUE, 189; thing of USE, 108. *See* Ding; res; Sache

thinking, thought, 50, 57, 62, 65, 83, 97, 126ff., 130–131, 144–145, 163, 183, 185, 206–207, 216, 323; ANCIENT thought, 101, 106, 115, *see:* ontology, ancient; philosophy, ancient; ARTICULATED thinking, the proposition, 188; COMBINATORY thinking, 180; thinking as FREE COMPORTMENT of the Dasein, 216–217; HISTORY of thought, 124; MODERN thought, problems of, 127; MYTHICAL, MAGICAL thinking, 121; PRINCIPAL AND SUBSIDIARY thought in judgment (Lotze), 199, 202, 204, 218; TRADITIONAL thought, 112, 183, 189, *see* ontology, traditional

Thomas Aquinas, 12, 20, 30ff., 42, 58, 79–80, 83ff., 87, 88ff., 91ff., 124, 182, 189, 231; T. A. on the ontological proof, 30ff.

Thomistic doctrine and disciples, 79, 89ff., 91ff., 93. *See* Aegidius Romanus; Capreolus, Joannes

thou, 278; the t., its meaning and condition of possibility, 297–298. *See* I-thou

time, 20, 69, 71, 145, 181, 229ff., 231–232, 232ff., 237ff., 256ff., 274ff., 302ff., 305, 318ff.; t. as origin of possibility, is absolutely earliest and ultimate ground of the A PRIORI, 325; t. as A PRIORI OF THE EGO, 145; is ARISTOTLE'S DEFINITION of time a tautology? 240–241; for Aristotle and ordinary consciousness, t. is an infinite irreversible sequence of nows, 256, 260, 268, 271ff.; t. is not A BEING, 325; reading t. from the CLOCK, 245, 257ff.; assigning t. to the clock, 245; t. as shown by a clock, 258; determination of time to (in order to, for) as purpose of clock usage, 258–259; COMMON CONCEPT of t., 228; common concept of t. (intratemporality), 324–325; t. in its common sense springs from temporality, 228; COMMON UNDERSTANDING of t., 229ff., 257ff., 260, 268ff.; how t. is constantly present in all COMPORTMENTS, 260; t. as CONTAINER, 273 (*see* embrace; hold-around); t. as what is COUNTED IN CONNECTION WITH MOTION, 237ff., 240; t. as the counted that counts, 246; "Time itself can be measured only because . . . it is something counted and, as this counted thing, it can itself count again," (interpretation of Aristotle), 256; why original t. is COVERED UP: the mode of being of falling, 271ff.; expressed t. as DATABLE, 262; DETERMINATIONS of t.: forthwith, just now, once, all of a sudden, 236, earlier and later, 240; the three time-determinations as determinations of expressed t.—now, then, at-the-time—are spoken from out of the unity of an enpresenting-expecting-retaining (or forgetting), 261, 263–264, 269ff., 306; DIRECTION of t., 260; ECSTATIC CHARACTER of t. defined in terms of carrying away, ecstasis, 267; ecstatic character of original t. described, 267; why ECSTATIC-HORIZONAL TEMPORALITY must be called time in a primary sense: the t. that temporalizes itself and, as such, temporalizes world-time, 271; t. as EMBRACING motion, 252, and beings, 252 (*see* container; embrace; hold-around); ESSENTIAL NATURE of t., 233, 235, 255–256, 273ff.; t. EXISTS only if the soul exists, 254; EXPRESSED t. AND EXPRESSION of t.: t. utters itself with the determinations of now, at-the-time, then, 261; the structural moments of expressed time are significance, datability, spanneddess, and publicness, 261ff. and 261, 262, 263, 264 (order of their definition); t. as intrinsically spanned and stretched, 264; expressed t., the now, at-the-time, and then, 265; publicness of expressed t., 264; expressed t. derived from existential temporality, 265ff., 271; expressed t. as that for which the Dasein uses itself, for the sake of which the Dasein is, 270; t. as right or wrong t., 261–262, 271 (*see* significance); t. is not an EXTANT THING,

uncover, uncovering, uncoveredness (entdecken, Entdeckung, Entdecktheit), 48–49, 50, 69ff., 73, 133, 163, 168–169, 171–173 (an unusual use), 174, 208, 213ff., 216, 219, 220–221, 297, 304, 314, 318; uncoveredness of BEINGS, 67ff., 72; uncovering DEFINED: "We shall call the unveiling of an extant being—for example, nature in the broadest sense—*uncovering*," 215; uncoveredness and DISCLOSEDNESS, 72, 215; uncovering as ONE WAY OF UNVEILING, 215ff. *See* disclose; truth; unveil; and *cf.* p. 318

understand, understanding (verstehen, Verstand = faculty of understanding, Verstehen = act of understanding), 33, 46, 57, 70ff., 72, 94, 105, 111, 114, 147, 163, 165–166, 171, 208, 214, 216, 218, 229ff., 236–237, 260–261, 270, 284ff., 293–294, 302–303, 309, 315; u. as ACHIEVEMENT, Verständnis, and as ACT, Verstehen, 275; u. the ACTUAL as actual, 285; BEING of the u., 214; u. of BEING-IN-THE-WORLD, 294; u. as a basic determination of being-in-the-world, 275ff.; how u. unveils possibilities of being-in-the-world; being-with, being-toward, being-among, 278; u. as possible only on the basis of being-in-the-world, 298; u. the BEING OF BEINGS, 116; only a BEING THAT EXISTS, that is in the manner of being-in-the-world, understands that which is, beings, 208; u. of a being as present, 306–307; u. of beings extant before and for production, 116; u. of BEING-WITH-OTHERS, implicit in functionality relations, 296; u. of being-with-others, etc., contained in self- and world-understanding, 296–297; COMMON meaning and u., 197; common u. of ancient basic concepts, 119; ordinary, common u., 166–167; common, philistine u., 220; common u. of time, 231ff., 266, not entirely unaware of the various characters of expressed time, as in Aristotle's view, 273; u. as condition of possibility for both cognitive and practical COMPORTMENT, 276; u. comportment toward things, 289; CONCEPT of u. cannot be defined adequately in terms of cognitive comportment toward beings, neglecting practical-technical comportment, 275; the original existential concept of u., "*to understand oneself in the being of one's own most peculiar ability-to-be*," 276, *and contrast*, "The Dasein understands itself first by way of /intraworldly/ beings: it is at first unveiled to itself in its inauthentic selfhood," 171; u. and basic CONSTITUTION OF THE DASEIN, 286; u. /as act, verstehen/ an original determination of the DASEIN'S EXISTENCE, 275; u. as a basic determination of existence, 276, 278, 279, 286; how u. belongs to the Dasein's existence: sketch of concept of u. as constitutive of the Dasein's existence, 276ff.; DIFFERENCE between pre-conceptual u. and conceptual comprehension (Begreifen), 281–282; u. of EQUIPMENT as equipment, 292ff., 305; EVERYDAY u. of beings, 176; u. as EXISTENTIELL, 279; temporal interpretation of u. as existentiell, 286ff.; existentiell u., authentic or inauthentic, 294; "Understanding is not a mode of cognition but the basic determination of EXISTING," 278; u. of EXTANTNESS, 70–71, 119; u. of FUNCTIONALITY, 293–294, 305; u. via functionality, 310; u. as primarily FUTURAL, 287; the GLANCE of understanding in the assertion of being, 317; u. of HANDINESS in temporal terms, 305; u. the handy as handy, 305; INAUTHENTIC u., an u. in which the Dasein understands itself primarily via encountered intraworldly beings rather than via its own most peculiar possibility, 279, 290–291; NON-CONCEPTUAL u., 309; u. as ONTICAL, 280; u. ORIENTED TO PRODUCTION, 116; PRE-PHENOMENOLOGICAL u., 290; u. of PRESENT, PAST, AND FUTURE in original, existential sense, 266ff.; u. peculiar to PRODUCTIVE INTENTIONALITY, 114; to understand means to PROJECT oneself upon a possibility, 277; essential core of u. as PROJECTION, existentiell self-understanding, 277; u. as projection, 279; u. and SELF-understanding, 279; u. of TRUTH, 216ff., 284; u. as UNVEILING EXHIBITION OF SOMETHING (*cf.* apophansis),

unveil, unveiling, unveiledness (enthüllen, Enthüllen, Enthülltheit), 67, 72, 165, 169, 171, 174, 176, 190, 205, 208, 210, 211ff., 213ff., 217–218, 218ff., 230, 241, 253, 277, 278, 280, 300, 304, 307, 309, 311, 314, 322; ASSERTIONAL EXHIBITION as unveiling, 215, and its variations correlative with the entity asserted about, 215; unveiledness as determination of the BEING OF A BEING, 217–218; unveiledness of BEINGS in their being, as ontological presupposition for the "is" of assertion, 212; unveiledness of beings and of being, 281; definition of unveiling as BEING-TRUE defended, 216; unveiling, COGNITION, and science, 319–320; unveiling and unveiledness, grounded in the DASEIN'S TRANSCENDENCE: "they exist only so far as the Dasein itself exists," 222; the Dasein's self-unveiling in understanding, 277; relation of unveiledness to the EXTANT, 218; INTENTIONAL STRUCTURE of unveiling, 217–218; unveiledness of an entity PRESUPPOSES understanding of the being of the entity, 314; unveiledness of that upon which understanding projects, 284; unveiledness of the SELF to itself, 159ff.; TIME as already unveiled, 258; unveiledness of time, 274; unveiledness of WHATNESS in assertion, 218ff. See disclose; uncover; truth

Ursache (cause), 87–88

Urteil (judgment), 180

use, 68, 114, 116, 117, 304, 310

utility, utilitarian, 68

utterance, 210, 218; u. of ASSERTIONS, 211ff.; "in every uttered assertion the being-true of the assertion is itself co-intended," 213; u. which expresses EXHIBITION, 218

validity, 119, 201, 202

veiled over, 260

verb (Zeitwort, time-word), 181

verbal (phone, word), 184, 192, 206; v. ARTICULATION, 208; v. PROPOSITIONS, 195ff., 202ff.; v. SEQUENCE, 192, 205ff.; v. SOUND, 206–207

veritas, 188

verkehrte Welt, die (Hegel's expression for the world of philosophical thinking; cf. his *Phenomenology of Spirit*, "Force and the Understanding: Appearance and the Supersensible World"; the author cites this expression from a still earlier work). See inverted world

visual awareness, 122

vitality, 10

voluntas, 58

vorfinden, 109

vorhanden, Vorhandenes, Vorhandenheit, Vorhandensein (extant, at hand, present at hand, that which is extant, etc., extantness, etc., being-extant, etc.), 39, 43, 101, 104, 108–109, 139

vorliegen (lie-before there), 108

vorstehen: v. and the meaning of Verstehen, understanding, 276

waiting-for: grounded in expecting, 289

was, 287

watch. See clock

way of being (Seinsweise, Weise-zu-sein; cf. mode of being), 18, 23, 24, 28, 70, 74, 78, 85, 154, 216; w. of ACTION, 142; BASIC ways of being, 225; the DASEIN'S w., 28, 167; w. of the

DATE DUE

AUG 2 5 1995		
AUG 2 1 1997		
OCT 1 2 2000		
FEB 1 4 2001		
MAR 1 6 2001		
MAR 3 0 2001		
MAY 0 2 2001		
JUN 1 9 2001		
AUG 1 7 2001		
OCT 0 1 2001		
DEC 1 4 2001		
JAN 3 0 2002		
APR MAR 1 9 2003 2002		
MAR 1 9 2003		
AUG 1 2 2005		

DEMCO 38-297